Prentice Hall Guide to Basic Writing

SECOND EDITION

Emil Roy

University of South Carolina

Sandra Roy

Dalton College

Prentice Hall, *Englewood Cliffs, New Jersey 07632*

Editorial/production supervision and
   interior design: Patricia V. Amoroso
Cover design: Ben Santora
Acquisitions editor: Carol Wada
Prepress buyer: Herb Klein
Manufacturing buyer: Bob Anderson
Editorial assistant: Joan Polk
Copyeditor: Virginia Rubens

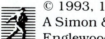 © 1993, 1989 by Prentice-Hall, Inc.
A Simon & Schuster Company
Englewood Cliffs, New Jersey 07632

Printed in the United States of America

10 9 8 7 6 5 4 3 2 1

ISBN 0-13-720707-7

PRENTICE-HALL INTERNATIONAL (UK) LIMITED, *London*
PRENTICE-HALL OF AUSTRALIA PTY. LIMITED, *Sydney*
PRENTICE-HALL CANADA INC., *Toronto*
PRENTICE-HALL HISPANOAMERICANA, S.A., *Mexico*
PRENTICE-HALL OF INDIA PRIVATE LIMITED, *New Delhi*
PRENTICE-HALL OF JAPAN, INC., *Tokyo*
SIMON & SCHUSTER ASIA PTE. LTD., *Singapore*
EDITORA PRENTICE-HALL DO BRASIL, LTDA., *Rio de Janeiro*

Contents

Preface

The *Prentice Hall Guide to Basic Writing* is designed for students who need a broad range of helping devices to improve their writing skills. We have based it closely on our teaching experiences at the University of South Carolina–Aiken and Dalton College (Georgia). By using writing examples created by both professional writers and our students, we guide users of the book through the process of composing. In addition, the many detailed, useful exercises appeal directly to the students' interests.

The book begins with the process of generating ideas, designing a paragraph, and giving paragraphs unity and coherence. The second section takes up all the paragraph types usually required in college writing classes, from the simplest (examples) to the more complex (comparison and contrast, persuasion). The third section deals with elements of style such as consistency, variety, and word choice. The fourth section explores the elements of the expository essay and timed writings. The fifth section takes up basic grammar. The sixth section deals with mechanics, comma use, minor punctuation rules, and spelling.

Chapter 1, "Generating Ideas," links six prewriting devices to the process of writing paragraphs and essays. The subsequent chapters on paragraph and essay writing all use one or more of these devices to help students get started.

Chapter 2, "Designing Paragraphs," takes students through the seven-step process of putting together a typical paragraph. As in all the writing chapters, interspersed exercises help students solve problems encountered at each stage of the process.

Chapter 3, "Unifying Paragraphs," adds new material. Its exercises emphasize the ordering and linking of words and ideas.

All nine chapters in the second section focus on writing various types of paragraphs. We have added new chapters on examples, defining, and dividing and classifying. Each of these chapters takes a process approach. Their emphases on generating ideas, revising, and proofreading appear in few other basic textbooks. These chapters include samples of both professional and student writing for illustration and analysis. By closely studying the writing of others, students become better readers as well as more competent writers. We have also added many new exercises to lead users through each step of the writing process.

The third section gives added importance to matters of sentence consistency, variety, and effective word choice. These chapters immediately follow the paragraph chapters to reinforce their concepts of revision. The rewritten and additional exercises ask users to identify problems and solve them in writing.

The fourth section, Chapter 16, "Designing the Essay," explores the process of writing an expository essay. It applies and extends ideas from the earlier chapters on writing paragraphs. Chapter 17 helps students deal with timed examinations. The fourth section also includes a new chapter on exit examinations. Many schools use these exams to test the writing proficiency of their students before they leave the freshman writing sequence or graduate. A wealth of new exercises takes students through these processes simply and thoroughly.

The fifth section helps instructors deal intensively with grammatical problems. To help both basic writing students and those who speak English as a second language, the many new exercises treat grammar simply and methodically. If instructors wish, they may select exercises to treat grammatical problems as they emerge from writing assignments. Or they may assign particular problems for work out of class.

The sixth and final section takes up mechanics and punctuation, with heavy stress on comma use. It also deals with minor punctuation marks and spelling problems. In this section, as in the preceding one, we have kept the interests of both basic writing and ESL students in mind.

ACKNOWLEDGMENTS

We wish to thank the reviewers of this book for their valuable assistance: Professor Sally Geil, Brevard Community College; Dr. Christine Briggs, Henry Ford Community College; Professor Rita Bova, Columbus State Community College; Professor Mary Carol Doyle, St. Louis Community College; and Professor Robert Scattergood, Belmont Technical College.

Suggestions to Instructors Using This Book

The students who take this course, usually unwillingly, reflect a wide spectrum of ages, backgrounds, races, and national origins. One thing they have in common, though, is that much of their writing contains serious grammatical and mechanical errors. They also have difficulty focusing on topics, keeping their writing flowing, or supporting ideas with details. Their previous experiences with writing were often negative, raising barriers to be overcome and rules to be unlearned. For such students writing is less a process than a jumble of half-remembered, often contradictory rules to be either followed without question or circumvented.

To become more accessible to these students, we like classrooms with portable desks, or at least space between them, allowing us to walk around the class easily. We like to confer briefly with individual students. We use comments to help break writing blocks, and we encourage them with praise and approval.

THE COURSE BEGINNINGS

Because this book stresses working together, we use the first day for mini-interviewing sessions. We pair the students and ask each to interview his or her partner before introducing the partner to the rest of the class. This opening exercise asks them to get to know another person well, ask probing questions, and pay close attention to answers. We remind them to learn to pronounce another person's name perfectly. This opener also sets a friendly, interdependent tone for the course while breaking the ice and lessening the stiff formality with which courses often begin. As instructors know, a student can learn from many sources, including fellow students.

Although this book does not stress computer use, we spend the first two or three class periods teaching the students to use a word processing program. Some schools possess adequate computer labs that include word processing and other software. We also ask the bookstore to stock an inexpensive word processing program. This time is well spent, we have found, since it pays dividends later. The thesaurus and spell-check utilities heighten the students' sense of word mastery and spelling competence. We also show them how to apply a style checker such as RightWriter to their work. These useful programs spot many punctuation problems, passive verbs, usage problems, and other aspects of style.

By the beginning of the second week, we begin classes with journal writing. We give students suggested topics, though they may choose their own; we urge them to freewrite without stopping to cross out, correct, or look up. Once they have completed an entry, we suggest that they give it a title and index it by writing topic notes in the margins. We reward them at the end of the course by assigning 10 percent of their final grades to their journals, giving an "A" for forty pages, a "B" for thirty-five pages, and so on. We don't pay much attention to quality for this assignment, but assign the grades strictly on the basis of quantity. Popular general topics include "My Life So Far" or "The History of My Family." Such topics encourage self-development. They also serve as a departure from the usual "Today I went to class . . ." type of entries, which students often find tedious.

Once the students have written several entries, we ask them to exchange journals, read them, and respond. We place error-hunting off bounds for the journals as well as for their first drafts. Rather, we suggest that they ask themselves these questions: "What ideas, phrases, or images has the writer used well? Where does the reader need more information?" Students find this sort of feedback helpful and stimulating, and the momentum often carries over into their study times outside of class. As we move around the class, we observe when particular students are experiencing difficulties with grammatical or mechanical problems. Many will write fragments and run-ons, though some learn to solve these problems faster than others. The better writers in the class often enjoy being assigned to help others solve these problems.

Prentice Hall provides adopters of this text with a computer program called **Blue Pencil** (for IBM computers and clones) to help students solve grammatical and mechanical problems. Blue Pencil deals with ten different categories of skills, including commas, usage, and subject-verb agreement. For instructors whose classes include ESL students, Prentice Hall has created a **Reading Strategy Series** (also for IBM and clones), which contains many cloze and contextual reading exercises. It is designed to help ESL students increase their reading speed, use grammar and vocabulary as clues to reading comprehension, and make assumptions about the context of a reading passage.

Users of this book will note that the initial chapter's emphasis on prewriting carries over to all the writing chapters in the first half of the text. We initially try to familiarize the students with techniques ranging from freewriting to clustering to the reporter's questions. By breaking down the problem-solving process into a series of steps, we transfer pressure to write error-free papers until the very end of the process. Learning the steps in the writing process helps to teach students that while everyone composes a little differently, each step follows its own rules. They need not rush the process of paper-writing.

Prewriting also lends itself to collaborative writing. We usually introduce an approach like clustering by writing a topic on the board, circling it, and then inviting students to contribute ideas. Students usually pick up this device quickly and use it spontaneously, but often stop too soon, leaving it incomplete. They need encouragement to flesh out their prewriting with concrete, specific examples.

The first paragraph assignment utilizes a process from one of the early chapters: description, narrative, or supporting with examples. These paragraphs lend themselves to the students' personal experiences and follow familiar patterns. When the students hand in their assignments we grade them rigorously, noting their strong points as well as their errors. However, we give the students the opportunity to revise their paragraphs and resubmit them within a strict time limit, usually a week. We then regrade them, replacing the earlier grade with the later one.

This practice does not increase the instructor's paper load. For one thing, we limit the number of paragraph types assigned. In addition, because the rewrites are usually significantly improved, they require less instructor time to read them. The initial assignment will also alert an instructor to problems experienced by the class as a whole, as well as to those giving particular trouble to individual students. By learning that writing is a process made up of steps, students will discover that they can limit their range of choices, depending on the stage they have reached with their writing. It is worth noting that the **Prentice Hall Grade Manager** is a useful piece of computer software for keeping student records and calculating their grades.

CLASS AND PEER REVIEW OF THE STUDENTS' WORK

Near the end of each writing chapter, we analyze a sample of student writing in depth, using questions to guide the revision process. Many instructors will use examples of paragraphs written by their own students. They can project them, place them on transparencies, or—at times—reproduce enough copies for all the class members. The questions we include stress the high points of the composing process, not just the vague impressions gained by students regarding vividness or emotion. The process also leaves proofreading to the very end of paragraph writing, though students can be encouraged to make a habit of spell-checking and style-checking their paragraphs.

WRITING ASSIGNMENTS

Each of the writing chapters provides students with a few topics for their paragraphs, suggests other choices with examples of professional writing, and includes still more topics at the ends of chapters. As Josephine Miles long ago pointed out, no topic is too abstract or difficult if students know how to predicate. While instructors may start a writing assignment with a topic like "My Summer Vacation," they enhance it with intelligent questions to lay out the directions for the paragraph. The student learns to turn a topic into a statement, such as "My summer vacation was most pleasurable (or frightening, or dismal) when I . . . ." We like to write with the students, usually on a chalkboard, often describing our thought processes aloud as we move along. We know that our students are certainly not professional writers, perhaps never will be. However, the steps in the composing process are similar for all writers.

PREPARING FOR THE EXIT EXAM

Many colleges and systems require students to demonstrate their writing proficiency by passing an exit exam. These exams give students a limited choice among topics; usually they must be completed within a rigid time limit of an hour or less. The kinds of essays produced for this exam are rather artificial and do not exist outside the academy. Nevertheless, these exams are widely used, with significant consequences for both students and basic writing instructors. We have applied the process approach to this task in Chapter 18, building in lessons that students will later make use of, especially when writing under the pressure of time deadlines. As in our other writing chapters, students will learn to plan ahead, allocate their time, and organize and support their ideas.

PEER REVIEW OF WRITTEN PRODUCTS

Our text encourages students to work together almost from the beginning of each writing assignment. In order to work well, the writing process makes the correcting of errors the last step although, in reality, students will become aware of mistakes in both their own work and in the works of others. However, the questions we supply focus on helpful, encouraging input from peers rather than correcting spelling or mechanical mistakes. Students like exchanging their work, seeking advice and approval from their peers. If given encouragement, they pick up on this spontaneously, often discussing their projects with one another with little prompting from the instructor. The questions we supply emphasize formal aspects of student writing, helping them use other papers as mirrors for their own work.

GRADING PAPERS

Inside the back cover of our book, we have keyed writing problems to their treatments in the text. However, we also developed for our own use a grading sheet that helps us point out both strengths and weaknesses to students. As a matter of principle, we use black or blue ink rather than red. Though we attempt to find every error (and strength) in students' papers from the beginning, our own preference for walking among the students' desks, speaking to students individually, and providing a strong incentive for revision takes most of the sting out of initially low grades.

We have also found that while many skills carry over from paper to paper, occasionally some do not. Cause and effect papers require longer, more complex sentences than narratives and process papers. Since writing requires answering a multitude of questions, students often forget imperfectly learned lessons; the revising process, when properly rewarded, works far better, we have found, than simply leaving error-fraught early drafts in students' hands with no possibility of redemption. In the last analysis, however, this book can only supplement the one-on-one interaction between instructor and student so vital to writing improvement.

Generating Ideas

Section One: Steps in the Writing Process

The process of writing moves through the following steps:

- Discovering a topic
- Prewriting
- Shaping the topic
- Writing the first draft
- Revising
- Editing and proofreading

As this list indicates, writing is more than a *product*. It is a *process* that moves through several steps. Although writers work in different ways, the process approach involves at least two stages. First, you must discover what you think about a topic. Then you develop your writing through several steps, often swinging back and forth between steps. To get started, you need a topic, a situation, or a question. Sometimes you are assigned a topic; at other times, you create a list of topics and narrow it down. Some writers then begin writing—quickly or slowly—to break a writer's block, or to pull ideas from their minds. Others use devices like those in this chapter to generate ideas. They may list or brainstorm thoughts and phrases. It is not a lockstep series, so you must learn what works best for you.

Looking over these jottings, called *prewriting*, you then *shape* your approach by writing a topic sentence (for a paragraph) or a thesis (for an essay). As you sum up in advance, you explain how you feel about your subject or how it affects others. To focus your ideas, you need to visualize an audience for your writing. Before beginning your paper, then, you have chosen a topic, considered how to order and support your ideas, and pondered your audience's reactions to your writing.

You then base a *first draft* on these early steps. While some writers rewrite and correct as they draft, beginning writers should probably develop a first draft as quickly and fully as possible. You will do your best writing when you *rewrite* your draft—adding, deleting, rearranging, and substituting. We encourage you to ask a friend or classmate to read your drafts and make suggestions. What is already well done? Where does the reader need more information, stated more clearly? Let a revised draft cool for a time, if possible, and then return to it. If you can't spell a word, guess at the spelling, but check it for later attention. If you draft your paper on a computer, you can make changes easily without recopying. In the last editing and proofreading stage, a computer's spell- and style-checking capabilities will save time and effort.

This chapter will take up several methods for getting a paragraph started:

- Freewriting
- Brainstorming
- Clustering
- The reporter's questions
- Keeping a journal

Section Two: Freewriting

When you freewrite, you put down your thoughts quickly without much deliberation or reflection. You don't cross out words or rewrite. Freewriting works well for developing an idea with examples, for describing a place or person, or for narrating an incident.

The warm sun hit my back as I walked down the dirt road with my dog.....

If you want to use a word you can't spell, guess at its meaning and put a check next to it. Keeping your thoughts flowing is more important than complete accuracy. If you get stalled, fill in with, "I can't think of anything to write." Or repeat the previous sentence until a new idea comes to you. One student freewrote this entry:

Have you ever noticed that if you look into darkness long enough, you see things? For example, when you close your eyes, you can see dots and lines, sometimes colors—purples and flashing pinks. You can imagine that you see something or somebody moving. Maybe somebody is perching quietly on your desk chair, watching you intently as you pretend to sleep. The darkness is a good place for your imagination. At night I wake up because of a noise and imagine I see something. It takes me forever to go back to sleep because I think someone is under my bed, in my closet, or in my bathroom. Usually I check in my bathroom when I come home from a date or a night class, but there is never anyone there.

EXERCISE 1.1

Freewrite at random without any particular topic in mind.

- Gather your materials and find a comfortable place to work. Avoid being distracted by friends, a television, or a telephone. Write freely for fifteen or twenty minutes.
- At the end of your freewrite, sum up your approach in a concluding sentence. Our writer said, "In the darkness, I often imagine exciting and scary things."
- Then think of a title, and write it at the top of your paper. The writer of the example above labeled her entry "Dark Imaginings."

EXERCISE 1.2

Focus your freewriting. Write several paragraphs, basing each of them on one of the following topics:

- The way a town or city looks from a nearby hilltop
- Circus animals
- Someone who enjoys messiness
- Sorting through your closet or bureau, deciding what to keep and what to discard

Sum up your ideas in a final sentence; underline it. Then give your freewrite a title; write it at the top.

Section Three: Brainstorming

Use a sheet of paper or a blackboard. Put your topic at the top. List all the ideas related to your topic. Don't reject *any* idea, no matter how farfetched or unconventional it may seem. After you have run out of ideas, look over the list. Cross off dull or obvious ones that don't fit. Brainstorming will help you generate examples and supporting details, especially to describe a person or place, define a term, or even compare and contrast. One student brainstormed on the idea, "the most relaxing place on earth":

The beach, because of the ocean

Can't sit in Grand Canyon in bathing suit

Sun beaming—bronze body

Miles and miles of beautiful, roaring waters

Slowly moving ship or sailboats

Calm sensation thinking about it

Children playing in the sand, making sand castles

Sand between your toes

Couple of different radio stations in the background

Beers in cooler

People jogging

No traffic jams, hustling commuters

As this student brainstormed, she simply listed illustrations: ways in which the beach is restful. As she jotted down the details and examples, she narrowed her topic: *The restful beach is better than everyday commuting.* With this focus in mind, she could generate more facts about the noise and confusion of commuting. She could then contrast her everyday life with the quiet of the beach.

EXERCISE 1.3

Brainstorm on one of the following ideas or on another one that you find interesting. Write it at the top of a piece of paper, and list all the details and examples you can think of.

- Buying a used car
- Making a new start in life
- Having fun at a party
- Coping with a loss

After you have filled the page, write a sentence that sums up your main impression or conclusion.

Section Four: Informal Outlining

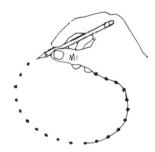

Prewriting also includes informal or scratch outlines. It's sometimes a good way to get started. Outlining will help you handle descriptions of a process, dividing and classifying, linking causes to effects, and persuading readers. Special types of outlines will also help you compare and contrast. If you've already made some notes, it helps you sort out your ideas. Scratch outlines also help you handle timed writings. By outlining, you get words down on paper quickly and begin thinking about ordering your paragraph or paper. The rules are simple:

1. Pick a topic, or use the one assigned.
2. Decide how to organize it. You may use one of these approaches:
   - Its history
   - How it looks
   - What cause(s) things to happen
   - How it works
3. Line up each main point on the left margin.

4. Fill in below it with details, indenting each one. Don't use Roman numerals or capital letters; they'll get in your way. You will probably think of some very specific details to include in your outline. Indent them farther from the left margin than the points that precede them.

5. Sum up in a sentence.

6. Restate your main idea narrowly and specifically. Use more than one sentence if necessary.

Lynne has used an informal outline to help her think about growing up.

Topic: Being a daughter

Organization: Time from childhood to the present

Summary: How Dad wanted a boy, what I did, how I rebelled, and how Dad got his son.

Scratch Outline

What Dad did before I was born
  Gave me a boy's name
  Filled baby's room with "boy toys"
    baseball hats and bats
    footballs and basketballs
    cars
    guns
What I did
  Was pushed into competing
    Won every race in 50-yard dash from third to sixth grade
    Hated competition—does strange things to me to this day
    Was Bill Potter's daughter—felt I *had* to win
  Told Dad after sixth grade—would do things for me, not for him
  Became outgoing and popular
    Involved in Student Council
    On school paper
    Became cheerleader
What Dad did
  Parents adopted "missing son"
    Big blue eyes
    Blond curling hair
    Nose cute as button
  Billy grew up
    Tall
    Intelligent
    Athletic (Thank God!)
    Took pressures off me—we became good friends

Summary: Dad tried to make me into the athletic son he never had, but I couldn't take it.

Restatement: Dad pushed me into athletics. I won for a while, but I rebelled. Then I became my own person. Dad adopted the son he wanted. My brother and I became good friends.

EXERCISE 1.4

Invent a topic or use one of these:

- How to meet men or women
- The corner of Whiskey Road and Easy Street
- A night club or discothèque crowd
- The most important values of your generation

Then fill out your outline on a sheet of paper, using these prompts:

Topic: _____

Organization: _____

Outline:

Summary: _____
_____

Restatement: _____
_____

Section Five: Clustering

Clustering not only helps you think of new ideas but also helps you link them to specific examples and tie them together. Use clustering to develop examples, describe a place or person, or define a term. To begin clustering, place your topic—a word or phrase—in the center of the page. Draw a circle or square around it. Then

- Think of other words suggested by the central term.
- Write them in around the central word.
- Circle each one and connect it to the word in the center with lines or arrows.
- Carry the process as far as you can.

Let your thoughts flow freely. Don't stop too soon. Fill up your page with specific details, facts, or illustrations. Then look at the cluster as a whole. Can you use more lines or arrows to link things that belong together? Take a minute to briefly sum up your main idea. It might serve as a topic sentence for a paragraph. Our sample cluster works out the topic "dreams of luxury."

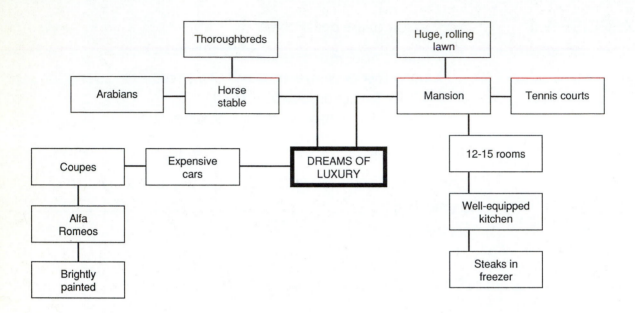

Summary: My dreams of luxury include a twelve- to fifteen-room mansion, expensive cars and, most importantly, my own stable of race horses.

EXERCISE 1.5

Choose a general concept or process from this list, or make up one of your own:

- Creating your own TV show
- Going on a blind date
- Finding total happiness
- A model physical fitness plan

Your topic: _____

Place it in the middle of a blank page. Then add details around the central topic. Connect them with lines or arrows as you go, adding as many details or examples as you can.

Once you have completed your cluster, sum up your main idea in a sentence. Then exchange your paper with a classmate for review.

Section Six: The Reporter's Questions

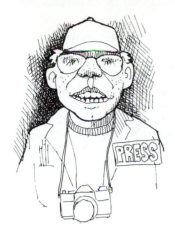

The "reporter's questions" help us probe a topic. We ask **"Who? What? Where? When? Why? How?"** These questions help us turn up parts of an idea we might otherwise overlook. The reporter's questions work well with every possible approach to a topic, from simply describing a person or place to the more demanding task of persuading the reader. Remember: fitting each detail into *exactly* the right slot matters very little. Instead, try to list a lot of specific examples, facts, and illustrations.

Crystal used the reporter's questions to probe her topic, "An Older Person Who Influenced My Life":

Who?	Harvey B. Shealy, 89-year-old former owner of Shealy's Barber Shop.
What?	Barbered for sixty-five years, once mayor of town, very knowledgeable, excellent memory, tells stories about yesteryear, gay 20's, and depression years; full head of thick gray hair—has worn flattop since 1919.
Where?	In Saluda, S.C., owner of Shealy's Barber Shop.
When?	Born in 1898, had many women friends, did not marry until middle thirties, has five children, sold shop to oldest son (my boss), Harvey E. Shealy (50); still cuts hair; always worked; never took vacation.
Why?	Worked with him 2 ½ years at barber shop; he was responsible for helping several residents overcome tough periods in their lives.
How?	Overcame cancer (twice); speaks with talking machine (larynx machine); favorite president: Franklin D. Roosevelt; likes dirty funny jokes, but won't tell them to women; likes to play practical jokes; friendly but stubborn; always walked out on street to talk to the men; laughs a lot.

This student has listed a wealth of details to describe a character vividly and realistically. In a paragraph, she could choose between Shealy's history, his everyday habits, or his interactions with friends.

INVENTING YOUR OWN QUESTIONS

If the reporter's questions seem to limit you, make them fit your topic. Extend them as you keep your main idea in mind. Inventing your own questions works especially well to divide and classify, to link causes and effects, to compare and contrast, and to persuade readers. One student wrote these questions to explore her topic, "Making a Move":

Why did I want to move? In 1988, my fiancé was killed in a car accident. My daughter was only two. I realized how precious and fleeting life could be.

How did I feel at the time? I needed a new environment, a change in my life. I couldn't stand it in the same place at the time.

What kind of new place did I need? I wanted to be close to my grand-mother. In an emergency, I might need her to care for my little girl. Greenville was near my home; it is also surrounded by foothills, with the Cherokee Mountains not far off.

How did I find a new job? I subscribed to the Greenville newspaper to get the classified ads in every Sunday paper. Then I sent out three résumés and got three interviews. One interview went very well.

Why did I take my present job? I could work with a pediatrician in a clinic along with two family practitioners. The doctor had just gotten her medical license. This was the first time she had ever worked as a doctor. The job would begin in one month. So this gave me plenty of time to find an apartment and get settled.

How did I find a place to stay? I stayed with my cousin in Greenville for two days while I looked around.

Why did I choose the place I did? I found a condo only two blocks from my job. It was actually cheaper than the apartments listed there. I was also able to get my daughter Emily enrolled in a daycare just down the road.

The student summed up the idea she had explored: "Why I like working in a doctor's office."

EXERCISE 1.6

Choose one of the following topics, or invent your own:

- A dream come true
- Seeking identity
- An unexplained act
- How parents should prepare their children for school

Your topic: _____

Answer the following questions by making some notes:

Who? _____

_____

What? _____

_____

Where? _____

_____

When? _____

_____

Why? _____

_____

How? _____

_____

Sum up your main idea: _____

_____

How could you use these notes to write a vignette (a very brief short story) about your topic?

_____

_____

EXERCISE 1.7

Invent four or five of your own questions regarding one of the ideas in the exercise above. Consider your approach, point of view, and audience.

Section Seven: Keeping a Journal

To write in a journal, you should:

- Keep your journal in a three-ring or spiral notebook or on a bound set of 5″ × 8″ cards. Carry around a glue stick or tube, a scissors, even cellophane tape.

- Clip and collect various items—a cartoon such as *Hagar* or *Peanuts*, a quotation or news article, an especially appealing ad, or an address to write to.
- Leave space to make notes or comments, or to draw lines and arrows. Don't try to be neat.
- Write fifteen to twenty minutes a day. If you write at the same time and place each day it will become a habit.
- Leave space for titles. Consider including a date and time of day, notes in the margin, summaries of what you've said.

EXERCISE 1.8

Your journal is more than a daily diary. It is a personal record of your feelings and experiences. It will help you learn more about yourself. And you will generate some ideas for classroom writings. Here are some topics to explore in your journal:

1. What makes you an exceptional person?
2. Write some animal fables followed by a moral.
3. Write a letter to the editor dealing with a current issue.
4. Describe your ideal job—or the worst job you ever had.
5. What is happening to your career goals?

Designing Paragraphs

This chapter will guide you through the steps to observe in writing a paragraph. You won't follow these steps in lockstep order, of course. In practice, you will move back and forth between them. But this list will help you keep track of important writing tasks.

A **paragraph** is a group of linked sentences that usually develop a single thought. Paragraphs range in length from as short as three or four sentences to as long as twelve to fifteen sentences. Your paragraphs will usually include between five and ten sentences apiece.

Section One: Choosing a Topic

In order to begin writing a paragraph, you will need to choose a topic. If you can, pick something that you are interested in. You should also decide how you feel about the topic. Most of your writing will be **persuasive**—that is, you will appeal to your readers' values and feelings. You will try to get them to see your topic sympathetically, from your point of view. You will also inform your readers. They should learn something new and interesting from your writing.

To get started on a topic, fill in one of the following incomplete sentences:

The best way to deal with my parents (or children) is _____

_____ .

The most unusual person I ever met is _____

_____ .

I have fun at a party by _____

_____ .

The most peaceful place I know is _____

_____ .

Once you have chosen your topic, explain your attitude, opinion, or point of view. Add a sentence that answers this question:

I care about (name your topic) _____ because

_____ .

To develop your topic, you need a **purpose** and a sense of **audience.** Focus on these aspects by checking one or more of the following options:

What *purpose* might you have for writing about your topic?

- _____ To inform

- _____ To persuade

- _____ To tell how to do something

What *audience* would be interested in reading about your topic?

- _____ Someone like you

- _____ A friend or relative

- _____ A group like members of this class

- _____ A highly educated professional

Section Two: Generating Ideas

Once you have chosen your topic, you need to generate illustrations: specific details, examples, and impressions. This is called *prewriting.* In the first chapter, we introduced several prewriting approaches: brainstorming, free-writing, clustering, questions, and journal-keeping. Try all of them to see which approach works best for you.

BRAINSTORMING

Use brainstorming to develop supporting illustrations. These include facts, details, incidents, reasons, or examples.

1. A *fact* is something real or actual. One writer uses facts to show that female wrestling is popular in Japan:

- A Sunday match draws a 12 percent viewer rating;

- 3,000 schoolgirls apply for the ten or so wrestling openings each year;
- Last year thousands of girls signed up for a spot with the All-Japan Women's Pro Wrestling Promotion.

2. A *detail* is an individual part of a larger whole. For example, a writer uses *details* to show the beginning of a match between women wrestlers in Japan:

   - The women spring onto the mat and glare at the spectators;
   - The crowd gives an ear-splitting cheer;
   - Spotlights focus on the ring as other lights dim;
   - The women grab microphones;
   - A hush falls.

3. *Incidents* include actual events which have occurred. A writer uses them to describe a Japanese match between female wrestlers:

   - Fans shower the ring with paper streamers;
   - Party crackers pop;
   - Balloons glide through the air;
   - Confetti rains down;
   - Members of fan clubs hang banners from balconies.

4. *Reasons* explain *why* you support a particular point. A writer includes typical responses to the question of why Japanese girls want to become wrestlers:

   - "They're just so good," say Tomoko Takahashi, a 17-year-old. "I'm crazy about them."
   - "They're so strong," said another teenager, with a sigh.
   - "They're such nice girls," gushes 42-year-old Ginko Takasaki.
   - "They're so pretty and charming, just like a picture."

5. *Examples* present or describe members of a group that are typical of the larger group. Examples are used to describe "Dump" Matsumoto, the "220-pound wrestler Japan loves to hate":

   - She has a human skull painted on her cheek;
   - She uses bruise-purple makeup;
   - She dyes her hair orange;
   - She carries a big stick.

You will often use more than one kind of support to develop your paragraphs. While a descriptive paragraph may use mostly facts and examples, a persuasive one will rely heavily on reasons. You may combine your types of support depending on your topic, your purpose, and your audience.

EXERCISE 2.1

*Use **facts, details, incidents, examples,** or **reasons** to develop one of the following topic sentences. List five or six instances for the topic sentence you choose.*

1. Registration for college at the beginning of this semester was especially frustrating.

2. The most unpredictable day I ever spent was _____.

3. I can resist anything but temptation.

4. Keeping up my car is very expensive.

5. Students should be graded more (or less) in terms of ability than performance.

_____ _____

_____ _____

_____ _____

CLUSTERING

Clustering is simple and easy to use. First, place your topic in the center of a blank page. Circle it. Write in other related words around your topic. Then circle them, and connect them to your main topic with lines or arrows. Leave space around these new ideas. Then write in specific examples, facts, or sense impressions around your subtopics. Circle them and draw lines connecting them to your subtopics. Charlotte used a cluster to deal with her topic, "Tempting Foods." She moved from general to specific, like this:

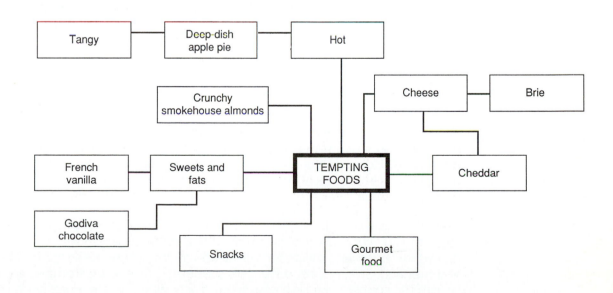

QUESTIONS

Tom asked questions that expanded the "reporter's queries." They helped him open up new insights into his topic. Tom applied these questions to his topic: "My past twenty years."

What is it like? Describe it. This is my twentieth birthday, my real birthday, the date that I was born twenty years ago in Phnom Penh, Cambodia; my father changed my birthday to July 16, as soon as I was born, for reasons still unclear to me.

Where did it come from? (What causes it?) Born in 1966, legally, I am still 19 years old; spent first nine years of life in Phnom Penh, leading the life of a son of a rich, famous, and loving father.

Can you relate an incident about it? Mother, brother, and I escaped war just eleven days before the Communists took total control of Cambodia; managed to escape to Paris, only to find out week later that war was over; recently found meaning in celebration of Chinese New Year with family: small feast for all close ones that have passed away.

What are your most outstanding memories about it? Childhood like that of prince: lived in large mansion provided with servants and chauffeurs left and right; life and goals set: to become doctor like father and manage estate he would someday leave me.

What are its parts? I spent most of early life in luxury and emotional security; loss of father in war and escape, first to Paris, then to U.S.; uncertain and lonely future as college student in American South.

Are there any instructions for making or doing it? Must make new beginning; must make own career (as electrical engineer) in college; find American girl friend (maybe wife); become good American without forgetting Cambodia or losing love for it; soon move out on my own.

How do you feel about it? Feel, and felt, lost, devastated, lucky, guilty (to have survived when father didn't), cheated of inheritance, angry.

Why is it valuable? Gives me determination to make own way, helps me find and appreciate friends (girl friend Roxanne comforted me after accident in my car).

What can you compare it to? Seems like terrible illness or loss of limb.

Can you argue for or against it? Running away was extremely traumatic and upsetting, but it forced me to plan own life without relying on father and inheritance.

FREEWRITING

To freewrite, just begin writing. Get as many words as possible down on paper. As you write, it may help to read over what you have put down to get more ideas. However, don't cross out words or rewrite yet. If you get stalled, fill in with "I can't think of anything to write," or repeat the previous sentence until a new idea comes to you. One student freewrote this entry:

One night he walked in and caught them together. The angry look on Bob's face showed every ounce of rage that he felt. His face swelled with anger, and his eyes gleamed with the sweet satisfaction of discovering his suspicions were well founded. Sweat popped from his sunburned face as he stomped angrily toward the couple locked in a passionate clinch. When he screamed her name, the girl jumped and twisted her face toward him. The anger on Bob's contorted face faded quickly, turning to sheepishness. Mistaken identity!

EXERCISE 2.2

Write your topic and your feelings about it below. Then generate ideas by clustering, brainstorming, questions, or freewriting.

Topic: _____

Your feelings about it: _____

Your choice of prewriting device: _____

Do your prewriting here:

Section Three: Planning and Organizing the Paragraph

IDENTIFYING THE TOPIC SENTENCE

A paragraph usually includes a **topic sentence.** This word group tells the reader

- The most important idea in the paragraph, and
- How the paragraph is held together, unifying it.

Readers expect to find topic sentences at or near the beginnings of paragraphs. If a writer sums up the main idea in two sentences, this summary is called a *topic statement.*

The **body** of the paragraph fills out ideas with related ones. The sentences that follow the topic sentence are usually more specific and detailed. They give the reader illustrations or facts. Professional writers don't always begin their own paragraphs with topic sentences. However, you should begin your paragraphs with topic sentences to help you organize your thoughts.

EXERCISE 2.3

The following essay includes several paragraphs. Mark each topic sentence by putting a capital T in the blank before it. We have done the first three for you. Remember: Professional writers often do not place the topic sentences at the beginning of each paragraph.

_____ As I compose these words, I am spending the night in an institution.

19

_____ In the rooms around me are former drug addicts and pushers, ex-convicts and prostitutes.

_____ Yet I feel as safe as I ever have.

Sums up the Foundation's unique quality. __T__ I am visiting the Delancey Street Foundation, a place that can safely claim to be like no other in the world.

_____ The building I am to sleep in is a mansion on the Pacific Heights that once housed the Soviet consulate.

_____ It is one of two Delancey Street residences in San Francisco, five nationwide.

_____ It looks out on a view that sweeps from the Golden Gate Bridge down the bay past Alcatraz.

Begins a new paragraph. _____ Normally, only a handful of the very wealthy could afford to live in such splendor.

Tells how it is unusual: who started it and how. __T__ But this house was bought and paid for by the people who live in it and run it.

_____ They are onetime drug abusers and felons.

_____ Today, they run businesses that make millions of dollars.

_____ They take not a penny of government money.

_____ They serve as deputy sheriffs and police officers, lawyers and business leaders.

_____ Nobody, including themselves, ever believed that they would be anything but worthless.

Begins a new paragraph. _____ "I was in prison most of my life before I came to Delancey Street," says Abe, an assistant to the foundation's president.

_____ "I was in San Quentin for armed robbery."

_____ Abe is a tall man, well dressed.

_____ "I was in a prison gang," he recalls. "I was using drugs.

_____ I had to turn my life around."

These two sentences make up the paragraph's topic statement. __Ta__ Abe left San Quentin more than a decade ago.

__Tb__ Today, he spends his life helping others to turn their lives around.

Prepares the reader for a list that defines the center's functions. __T__ "Delancey Street does several opposite things at the same time," says its president, Mimi Silbert.

_____ "It is a treatment place.

_____ It is a vocational school.

_____ It is like a college in some senses.

_____ Because we make our own money by ourselves, it really functions as a business."

Provides a crucial fact. __T__ Delancey Street was started 16 years ago by a group of former drug addicts.

_____ They borrowed $1,000 from a loan shark for their working capital.

_____ From their own experience, they knew that the usual government-funded programs were failing most drug abusers.

20

_____ Silbert signed on to help and suggested a name for the group.

_____ Delancey Street was a place on New York's Lower East Side where immigrants congregated at the turn of the century.

This sentence begins a new paragraph.

_____ "When people first come in here," she says, "we call it 'immigration'."

_____ They are a group of people who don't know how to make their way in American society.

This concluding sentence could also function as a topic sentence, as it sums up.

__T__ Like immigrants, they have to band together, to get strength from supporting each other.

Sums up, preparing for supporting details.

__T__ "The first thing we do in immigration is change your image.

_____ We break the street and prison image.

_____ Everybody gets his or her hair cut short.

_____ Women remove all their makeup and the fake jewels that adorn them."

This sentence begins a new paragraph.

_____ At "The Club," a converted hotel where most immigrants reside, dinner is served at cloth-covered, candlelit tables.

Sums up a general rule.

__T__ Residents come home from work, then dress before eating.

_____ Many are learning the proper use of utensils for the first time.

_____ John arrived at Delancey Street on drugs, and drunk as well.

_____ He was made to sit on a bench in the lobby of The Club until he sobered up.

Sums up the main idea negatively, preparing for details which explain.

__T__ "We don't have a formal detoxification program," Silbert says.

_____ "We have a living room couch.

_____ You can detox from heroin on the couch.

_____ It's like having a bad flu.

_____ We cook a lot of homemade chicken soup and provide a lot of concern."

Begins a new paragraph.

_____ Like everyone who comes to Delancey Street, John promised to stay at least two years.

_____ He must take part in what is less a drug-treatment program than a life-treatment program.

This sentence and the next one sum up a generalization, of which the John anecdote is an illustration.

__T__ Explains Silbert, "We hardly ever talk about drugs.

_____ We teach them how to have a life."

_____ John, who had dropped out of school in the tenth grade, earned his high school equivalency diploma.

_____ He then worked at Delancey Street's moving company and eventually was promotd to the head office.

_____ "I finally have a future," he says.

Michael Ryan, "They Earn Their Way Back," *Parade* (November 8, 1987). Reprinted by permission of the author and the author's agents, Scott Meredith Literary Agency, Inc., 845 Third Avenue, New York, New York 10022.

Each of the following sentence groups is a paragraph. However, the sentences are out of order. Write a capital T in front of the topic sentence. Remember: the topic sentence does not state a fact or detail. It is general enough to cover the ideas in the rest of the paragraph. Sometimes it can be a question.

_____ You won't find its fashions on the racks of Bloomingdale's or Saks Fifth Avenue.

_____ It produces "premade funeral fashions."

__T__ Vera Lee Garment Co. makes clothes you'd just die to wear.

_____ That is, Vera Lee makes clothes for dead people.

_____ It operates out of a small yellow building in a residential neighborhood.

__T__ The company makes about 125 styles of burial apparel.

_____ Vera Lee is headquartered in Fort Worth, Texas.

_____ The styles range from frilly nightgowns and dresses ($47 to $100 wholesale) to sober business suits ($75 to $80).

_____ In 1989, the company sold about 400 dresses a week.

__T__ Gloom hangs over parts of the fashion industry this season, but business for Vera Lee is lively.

_____ It racked up total sales of about $1 million for the year.

_____ Owner Kathye Kellow says the company intends to expand into new areas of the country this year.

_____ It will add five or six salespeople.

__T__ As the company's sales increased, profits rose.

_____ Why wouldn't they choose a favorite old dress or suit?

_____ Many of the deceased had been in nursing homes for years.

__T__ Why would anybody buy a Vera Lee original for a loved one's eternal rest?

_____ They don't have any dress-up clothes left.

_____ Buying a new outfit saves family members a painful search through the deceased's closet.

_____ Some funeral homes display Vera Lee styles side by side with matching caskets.

__T__ Good marketing helps, too.

_____ A lot of times a family will see a dress and say, "That's Mom."

_____ Fashion takes a back seat to practicality.

_____ Suit pockets and zippers are fake.

__T__ This branch of the apparel industry operates with its own set of rules.

_____ Waists are elastic: one size fits most.

_____ Dresses are fitted with Velcro fastenings down the back.

WRITING THE TOPIC SENTENCE

To start your paragraph, you have chosen a topic and stated your attitude toward it. Before you write a first draft, you need a topic sentence for your paragraph. Your topic sentence should do the following:

1. Name your topic;
2. State an opinion or purpose; and
3. Be worded as a complete sentence.

In addition, it should be neither too general nor too limited. Charlotte tried a couple of possibilities that needed rethinking:

One possibility: **I'd like to change a lot of things about myself.**

She has focused on a key verb, "change." However, "a lot of things" is general and vague. Charlotte hasn't decided what to tell the reader in the paragraph. She needs to decide where she's going with her topic.

Another possibility: **I'm short and plump, a 36-year-old wife and mother going back to college.**

This sentence is specific and limited. But it doesn't tell us *why* Charlotte is writing the paper. She shouldn't throw this sentence away, however. She might fit it into her paper later.

A better possibility: **I would like to raise my self-esteem by changing my physical appearance.**

This gives Charlotte a plan for writing the first draft of her paragraph.

EXERCISE 2.5

We have suggested several possible topic sentences for each of the following paragraphs. Three out of each four choices are faulty. In the blank before each one, indicate whether it is

TL: Too limited
TG: Too general
OP: Off the point or
TS: A well-focused topic sentence.

Here is a paragraph without *a topic sentence:*

He is a dynamic performer and a prolific writer and producer. During the last decade Prince has been a great influence in the music industry. He also has shown an unusual capacity for bringing beautiful and talented young women to the spotlight.

We have labeled possible topic sentences for this paragraph for you.

___TL___ Prince writes great music. (**Too limited:** Prince is more than just a musician.)

___TG___ Prince is just superb. (**Too general:** The sentence fails to tell how Prince is different from other famous people.)

___OP___ Prince has become very wealthy. (**Off the point:** The paragraph says nothing about how well-paid Prince is.)

___TS___ Most would agree that Prince has great artistic talents. (The paragraph will define the word "talents" as performing, writing, *and* producing.)

1. She was a pretty girl who liked to act. When Vanity left, she was replaced by Apollonia (Patty Kotero), who gave herself a new name. Then Sheila E, another pretty and talented girl, emerged. Up and coming is Jill Jones, the newest princess.

___TL___ Vanity was a lead singer in a rock group.

___TS___ One of the first to be noticed by his fans was Vanity.

___TG___ Fans like pretty girls.

___OP___ Prince's agent gave him some advice.

2. Several are racially mixed. Each was ambitious and talented before she met Prince. Each has been romantically involved with the young superstar. In addition, each remains very, very close and loyal to Prince.

___TL___ Each has a light complexion.

___OP___ Sheila E is a hot female drummer.

___TG___ They are dynamite girls.

___TS___ These four women have several things in common.

3. Sheena joined Prince when he toured Europe last summer. He surprised her with a $1 million "love nest" in Paris. He also gave her flowers, jewelry, and clothes. "The happiest times I've ever had in my life are when I'm with Prince," she said. "He's the only one who can give me everything I need."

___TL___ Sheena is a Scottish-born pop singer.

___TS___ Another talented woman linked to Prince is Sheena Easton.

___OP___ They say Prince is a "generous, wonderful gentleman."

___TG___ Sheena has a great personality.

4. "Somehow, somewhere he finds the good in everybody. He sort of brings it out," says Jill. At the same time, he has a very different relationship with each of his girls. They must understand that music is the primary focus. "When he gets tired of a situation, he lets you know," comments Jill.

___OP___ Prince doesn't do drugs.

___TG___ Prince is always looking around.

___TS___ Prince has an incredible knack for attracting beautiful, fresh talent.

___TL___ Jill has known Prince for six years.

5. She was 17. Jill's mother, a former singer, was Teena Marie's manager. Her Italian father was a drummer. ''Prince was wearing those little bikini pants and boots,'' remembers Jill. ''We got along fine, but I didn't think one way or another about him. I had a boyfriend then. That's probably why he found me interesting.''

___TG___ Jill said, ''Oh, my goodness.''

___OP___ Prince lives a very clean life.

___TL___ Jill was singing backup for Teena Marie.

___TS___ When Prince and Jill met, it was a real interesting time to meet him.

6. She accepted his invitation to move to Minneapolis. There, she sang ''background curtain'' for *Vanity 6*. As part of Prince's purple family, she was included in the highly successful *Purple Rain* movie. In it she portrayed the sassy, bleach-blonde nightclub waitress.

___TL___ Jill sang on his *1999* album and appeared in the video.

___OP___ Apollonia portrayed Prince's leading lady in *Purple Rain*.

___TG___ Jill has a pretty voice.

___TS___ The two kept in touch after the tour.

7. ''I've never been his girlfriend,'' she insists. ''We're basically really good friends.'' She adds that she has been like a mother to Prince. And he has been like a father to her. ''Right now I'm more like his little sister,'' she says. ''He's a lot more protective now. He pretty much watched me grow up, and I'm still kind of a brat.''

___TL___ Jill wants to keep the ''child innocence'' he finds in her.

___TS___ Jill and Prince have been through a lot of trials and tribulations, but that just makes for a good friendship, she says.

___TG___ Jill is more than just a pretty face.

___OP___ Sheila E made the album *Glamorous Life*.

''Prince's Intriguing Women,'' *Ebony* (November 1987)

EXERCISE 2.6

The paragraphs that follow lack topic sentences. Write a topic sentence for each paragraph. Each of them should either

- *Signal the reader as to what will come later, or*
- *Sum up the rest of the paragraph.*

We have provided clues in the form of boldface questions. In some cases, part of the topic sentence has been supplied.

EXAMPLE: They are the lovable pair of geezers who hawk Bartles and Jaymes wine cooler from their porch. ''Ed took out a second mortgage on his house, wrote to Harvard for an M.B.A., and now we're preparing to enter the wine cooler business," intoned Frank in the first of a series of more than thirty commercials that always end with him humbly thanking the viewers for their support.

TOPIC SENTENCE: **[How well known are Bartles and Jaymes?]**
By now, almost everyone who watches television is familiar with Frank Bartles and Ed Jaymes. _____

    1. Frank and Ed are fictional characters portrayed by novice actors. The two people really behind Bartles and Jaymes are not innocent rubes, but two of the shrewdest, most aggressive, most secretive, and most feared men in the wine business—Ernest and Julio Gallo.

TOPIC SENTENCE: **[How is the popular impression misleading?]**
But don't let the commercials fool you. _____
_____

    2. And with one-year-old Bartles and Jaymes, [TOPIC SENTENCE] _____
_____
It is one of the few bright spots in an industry suffering from flat sales. That coup, which reversed a two-year decline for Gallo, was only the latest of the remarkable string of successes that allowed the E. & J. Gallo winery to grow from a shed in the Great Depression into the world's largest winery. And the cooler's success has left the stunned competition gaping in awe.

TOPIC SENTENCE: **[How have the commercials affected Gallo's sales?]**
And with one-year-old Bartles and Jaymes, the Gallo brothers have stormed into first place in the booming wine cooler business. _____

    3. At the sprawling complex in Modesto that looks more like a refinery than a vineyard, [TOPIC SENTENCE] _____
_____ as they share ownership. Julio handles grape-growing, purchasing, and wine production. Ernest handles sales and marketing. The two sides of the operation are run almost like separate companies, former employees say. Julio and his staff occupy the first floor of the company's two story administrative building and Ernest and his staff the second, and the two staffs are not supposed to talk directly to one another.

TOPIC SENTENCE: **[How do the Gallo brothers handle the management of the winery?]**
At the sprawling complex in Modesto that looks more like a refinery than a vineyard, the brothers share managerial duties. _____

    4. Ernest Gallo demands [TOPIC SENTENCE] _____
_____ . One story told is that Ernest was having lunch with top executives at a Modesto restaurant and felt he was not served fast enough. The whole table immediately left the restaurant, their meals uneaten, never to patronize the restaurant again.

TOPIC SENTENCE: **[What quality does Ernest demand from his associates?]**

Ernest Gallo demands perfection from those around him.

_____

5. Mr. Gallo also [TOPIC SENTENCE] _____

_____ . A few months ago, Ernest got wind that two long-time Gallo executives had discussed joining another winery. He fired them on the spot, even though one was the son of the man who had served as Ernest's right-hand man for thirty years.

TOPIC SENTENCE: **[What other quality does Ernest demand from his associates?]**

Mr. Gallo also demands absolute loyalty.

UNIFYING THE PARAGRAPH

Sentences within a paragraph often follow a predictable order. A topic sentence may emphasize the **What?** or the **Why?** or the **When?** of the topic. Writers will then use one of several ways to develop the rest of the paragraph:

- **Time:** Moving from earlier to later times
- **Space:** Moving from inner to outer, down to up, or around
- **Order of importance:** More to less, less to more important, or back and forth
- **Cause and effect:** The effects of some causes, the causes of some effects
- **General and specific:** A general category followed by specific examples
- **Comparison and contrast:** Likenesses and differences

The topic sentence for the paragraph below is this:

For bloodhounds, life is full of disappointments these days.

This **topic sentence** prepares us for a list of specific reasons _why_ bloodhounds are being disappointed these days. The order of the rest of this paragraph is jumbled. Decide what order the sentences should follow:

(1) German shepherds, Doberman pinschers, and Labrador retrievers get the glamour jobs sniffing out drugs, bombs, and terrorists. (2) The only work that the sheriff's department in DuPage County, Illinois could find for a bloodhound named Nosy Britches earlier this summer was tracking a four-year-old boy who was lost—in the yard next door, it turned out. (3) Despite centuries as members of the dog elite—toiling for royalty, tracking escaped convicts, starring in books and movies—bloodhounds are no longer top nose. (4) Meanwhile, Bear, a German shepherd with the Chicago police department, found $37,000 in

cocaine payoffs and a burglary suspect. **(5)** Bloodhounds are lucky if they get to track lost children.

Now, we'll put these sentences back in order and tell why it is the proper order:

> **(3)** Despite centuries as members of the dog elite—toiling for royalty, tracking escaped convicts, starring in books and movies—bloodhounds are no longer top nose.

This sentence **compares and contrasts.** It gives examples of past glories (the opposite of disappointments). It also defines the bloodhound's main talent: its keen "nose."

> **(1)** German shepherds, Doberman pinschers, and Labrador retrievers get the glamour jobs sniffing out drugs, bombs, and terrorists.

This sentence moves from the general term "top nose" to specific examples of breeds. It also contrasts them with bloodhounds.

> **(5)** Bloodhounds are lucky if they get to track lost children.

This sentence adds another contrast between bloodhounds and other breeds.

> **(2)** The only work that the sheriff's department in DuPage County, Illinois could find for a bloodhound named Nosy Britches earlier this summer was tracking a four-year-old boy who was lost—in the yard next door, it turned out.

This sentence gives a specific example of work for dogs: child-tracking.

> **(4)** Meanwhile, Bear, a German shepherd with the Chicago police department, found $37,000 in cocaine payoffs and a burglary suspect.

The final sentence in the paragraph is another contrast. Its example contrasts a boring bloodhound's job—child-tracking—with a shepherd's glamorous job.

This paragraph mostly compares and contrasts. It uses specific examples as it moves back and forth between bloodhounds and other breeds.

EXERCISE 2.7

We have rearranged the sentences in the paragraphs below. Put them back in the proper order and list the numbers in order in the space below each paragraph. Then explain why you chose the order you did.

(1) They are squat, round, and unusually homely. **(2)** All things considered, they aren't easy to love. **(3)** They have floppy ears, heavy jowls, and the dog world's longest snout. **(4)** Bloodhounds that feel bad about all this can't console themselves by looking in the mirror.

Proper Order and Reasons Why:

Order: 4, 1, 3, 2. Reasons: (4) gives main idea by suggesting that bloodhounds are not handsome; (1) provides specific judgments about their homeliness; (3) provides specific examples of their homeliness; (2) sums up a general impression.

(1) Earlier in this century, bloodhounds helped capture members of the feuding Hatfield and McCoy families in the eastern Kentucky mountains. (2) But the features that make them so unattractive are the very ones that make them great trackers. (3) The long snout helps pick up scent, and the constant drooling intensifies it. (4) The ears and jowls drag on the ground and stir up scent. (5) Sandy and Little Red, bloodhounds in Pikeville, Tennessee, tracked down James Earl Ray, the killer of Martin Luther King, Jr., when he escaped from Brushy Mountain State Prison in 1977.

Proper Order and Reasons Why:

Order: 2, 4, 3, 5, 1. Reasons: (2) provides a transition to contrast bloodhounds' homely appearance with their tracking abilities; (4) provides anatomical reasons why they track so well; (3) tells how bloodhounds pick up scent after it is stirred up; (5) and (6) provide celebrated examples of the use of bloodhounds to track down famous fugitives.

(1) In 1958 Cuban dictator Fulgencio Batista thought so highly of some American bloodhounds that he sought their help in tracking down a guerrilla named Fidel Castro. (2) American bloodhounds have found work in other countries, too. (3) Who can say with certainty that a bloodhound or two wouldn't have forestalled the takeover? (4) And within months Mr. Castro had seized control of the country. (5) Their owner refused the request.

Proper Order and Reasons Why:

Order: 2, 1, 5, 4, 3. Reasons: (2) provides a transition from the use of American bloodhounds here at home to their use in a foreign country; (1) qualifies the topic sentence by telling who, when and where; (5) tells of the owner's negative response; (4) recounts the result of Batista's inability to track down Castro; (3) concludes the paragraph with a question.

(1) Bloodhounds don't attack, aren't good at jumping fences, are too bulky to work in crowded areas like airports. (2) Now there are breeds which are far more versatile, it seems. (3) "Bloodhounds will just sit down on the floor and stare at you," says a customs official at O'Hare International Airport in Chicago. (4) At most airports, Doberman pinschers and Labrador retrievers sniff for drugs. (5) "Ask a bloodhound to climb ladders and scale six-foot walls and it doesn't have the agility," says Kenneth Burger of the Chicago police force, which uses German shepherds instead. (6) According to the Miami police, bloodhounds don't have much of a nose for drugs and bombs.

Proper Order and Reasons Why:

Order: 2, 1, 6, 5, 4, 3. Reasons: (2) sums up with a contrast to the preceding paragraph; (1) provides a series of examples of skills which bloodhounds lack; (6) adds another detail of a skill lacked by bloodhounds; (5) adds another specific

Section Four: Using Transitional Devices

Transitional words hold sentences together within paragraphs. They show readers that ideas are closely related. If transitions are left out, we usually notice, as in this example:

> Avon Products, Inc., is courting America's baby boomers. The cosmetics company hasn't charmed as many women 22 to 40 years old as it would like. Avon has projected too classy an image.

When we add words to *connect* or *sum up*, the paragraph reads much more smoothly:

> Avon Products, Inc., **like most advertisers,** is courting America's baby boomers. **But so far** the cosmetics company hasn't charmed as many women 22 to 40 years old as it would like. **The problem, critics contend, is that** Avon has projected too classy an image.

One of the easiest ways to link thoughts together in a paragraph is to use formal transitions.

- Some of these words point out an example or illustration:

    first, to illustrate, for example, for one thing, thus, for instance

- At times, these words tell us another point is coming:

    in addition, similarly, next, above all, again, finally, and, also, too, then, second, equally, for another thing, furthermore, moreover

- Then too, transitional words may sum up or repeat in similar words:

    to sum up, consequently, in other words, as a result, in fact, so, therefore, accordingly, of course, indeed

- Finally, such words may indicate a contrast or difference:

    by contrast, but, however, still, yet, on the contrary, on the other hand, nevertheless

EXERCISE 2.8

We have left out the transition words in the account that follows. Choose a transition from the lists above to fill each of the blanks below. Commas usually separate these transitional words and phrases from the rest of the sentence.

Some of the weirdest people in the world assembled one morning last week in the Empire State Building. _____ For example _____ , there were the

Tattoo Man, the Grapecatcher, the Apple Peeler, the Dribbler, the Most Married Couple, and the Most Versatile Human. They were in New York to show why they are weird enough to be in the 1992 *Guinness Book of Records*. ____To illustrate____ , Tattoo Man Walter Stiglitz of North Plainfield, N. J., wore a skimpy black Speedo bikini. He had an Elvis on his back and an Elvis on his leg. ____Furthermore____ , he had Conway Twitty and Loretta Lynn on one hip and a self-portrait on his foot. He got his first tattoo when he was 13.

On May 27, Paul Tavilla caught in his mouth a black Ribier grape (with seed). It had been thrown 50 mph from 327 feet away. ____Moreover____ , in 1988 he captured air honors, catching one traveling at 110 mph, dropped from Boston's John Hancock Tower.

____Also____ , Apple Peeler Kathy Wafler Madison of Wolcort, N.Y. peeled a 20-ounce cooking apple 2,068 inches in 11½ hours on October 26, 1976. She used a special jackknife with multiple paring edges. ____In addition____ , she preserved the peel under glass, wrapped in mailing paper. It looks like a hairnet.

____Finally____ , Most Married Couple Carol and Richard Roble, 53 and 64, of Hempstead, Long Island, have been married 51 times. She's an accountant. He's a retired truck driver. ____To sum up____ , they started in 1969 and have been married in all 50 states and the District of Columbia—always on November 30.

Section Five: Writing the First Draft

As you review your prewriting, include or add important details, facts, and examples. When you have finished your prewriting and topic sentence, write a first draft. Develop one main idea in 10 to 15 sentences. Your draft may total 100 or 250 words after you have rewritten it once or twice. Later, you will probably add and delete, maybe moving ideas around and substituting words.

You may not use everything you jotted down. It's easier to cut your draft than to add to it. Once you've finished, review your notes. Check your subject, audience, and purpose.

Start your draft with your topic sentence. Try to write continuously without pausing. Use the ideas and details you generated in your prewriting. New ideas may occur to you along the way. Work them in. While you may wish to look back at what you have written, don't pause to cross out or rewrite. Don't stop to look up words in a dictionary. If you can't spell a word, guess at it. Then mark it in some way, perhaps by circling it and writing a small "*sp*" above it.

If you can't think of the *exact* word, use a synonym that comes quickly to mind, or leave a blank. In this version, you're trying to shape your ideas and fill in with details. One or more revisions will follow; in the final revision, you will correct your spelling, punctuation, and grammar. When you finish your first draft, give it a short title.

We've left Charlotte's first draft unchanged, mistakes and all. Her paper looks like this:

Changing Me

I would like to improve my self-esteem by changing my physical appearance. I'm too short, and therefore have a hard time finding clothes to fit. All the clothes I buy are too long and must be cut off and helmed. The sleeves on blouses and coats are always too long. Petite dresses, coats and clacks are much more expensive to buy. When I drive my car, it's hard for me to see over the wheel. Sometimes I drive faster than I should, I know, I need to change my driving habits. I also have a bad eating habit that I need to change. I eat sweets all the time. I like: cakes, fudge, candy bars, hot apple pie with vallina ice cream on top, bananna splits and cookies. If I had it in my power to change anything I wanted to, it would be to change the whole world's attitude about peace. Peace would bring people together and I personally think that would be wonderful. I'd love for everyone to be happy. I guess, I'll just have to change the things I can and wish my best to the world.

Section Six: Revising the Paragraph

ANALYZING THE FIRST DRAFT

Once you have completed a draft of your paragraph, analyze it closely. Read it aloud to a friend or classmate, or ask someone else to read it—even several readers, if possible. Remember that you have been struggling to shape your ideas. In the process, you have probably made mistakes in grammar and mechanics. It's too soon to call attention to these flaws; they should be corrected later. For now, you will work on clarity, conciseness, and concreteness.

Use the list of questions below, which we have applied to Charlotte's draft. (Even though it's too early to stress correctness, her spelling and punctuation errors are distracting, aren't they?)

1. *What ideas, statements, or phrases are particularly well-stated?*

Charlotte's expression is forceful and orderly. She is honest with herself and the reader. She admits that being short and plump bothers her. She includes specific detail about her difficulty in finding clothes that fit. She also provides an appealing list of tasty foods she can't resist. Near the end, she states an idealistic wish for peace. This tells the reader she is concerned with others, not just with herself. At the same time, it doesn't directly support her topic sentence.

2. *Where does the reader need more (or less) information?*

Charlotte needs to clarify her sense of audience, purpose, and situation. She tells us nothing about her age, family situation, job, finances, or reasons for going to college. These details would help establish a stronger kinship with other women, other people like her. Although she discusses her problems honestly, she needs to outline some possible solutions. Why is she so short on money, time, and power? What can she do about it, specifically? Then too, her discussion of world peace is quite abstract and long-range: she should drop this topic in favor of solutions to her personal problems.

EXERCISE 2.9

Apply the following questions to your own first draft (or ask someone else to do so):

1. What ideas, statements, or phrases are particularly well-stated?
2. Where does the reader need more (or less) information?

A FIRST REVISION

Your first rewrite involves more than recopying your draft, changing words here and there. It will require some additions, deletions, rearrangements, and substitutions. Some of these changes may be minor, but others will be rather drastic. Charlotte's rewrite looks like this:

After working as a teachers' aide for eight years, I returned to college part-time. Like many other women in their thirties, I married and started a family right out of high school. As I begin taking college courses, I have also begun thinking about improving how I look and act. **[TOPIC SENTENCE]** Since I am too short and plump, I would like to improve my physical appearance. To do so, I need to change a bad eating habit. I eat sweets all the time, even more now that I'm going to school part time and working full time too. I like: cakes, fudge, candy bars, hot apple pies with vallina ice cream on top, bananna splits and cookies. When I'm studying, I can't help thinking about that creamy milk chocolate, those crunchy peanuts and almonds; that fragrant steam rising from a tangy, hot, deep-dish apple pie with smooth, french vallina ice cream melting on top drives my crazy. So I snack constantly. Maybe I should take up jogging or aerobic dancing. I could use exercise and dieting. These would take my mind off food and get my weight down. However, I've never succeeded in reducing my weight before because I've tried to do it alone. Maybe if I joined a club like Encore, for older students, I'd find other people with the same problem. We could encourage each other to reach our goals.

Once you have revised your paper, it is time to analyze it more closely. We've applied a list of questions to Charlotte's rewrite to help her improve it further:

1. *Do the first two or three sentences make clear how the writer will proceed in the paper? If so, has the writer followed this plan? If not, how should the writer change the organization?*

The writer's shortness and weight bother her. Older than most students, she has married, raised children, and entered the work force. She would like to improve both her personal appearance and her social life. She has followed this plan in her paragraph, moving from personal to group purposes and actions.

2. *Where should the writer add or substitute more specific examples, reasons, or details?*

The writer might tell the reader her exact height and weight. She doesn't explain specifically why she went back to college. What does she hope a college degree will do for her personal development, self-esteem, family and financial situation? She could also describe how it feels to crave sweets, to be really hungry, what appeals to her about those sweets she munches on, what foods she thinks are superior to her snacks, and so on. However, she should select only the most important of these details and reasons, to preserve the conciseness of her paragraph.

Roget's Thesaurus provides an extremely useful source of synonyms and antonyms: words that mean the same and words that mean the opposite. However, you shouldn't use it for your first draft; development and organization are more important here than word choice. For instance, Charlotte emphasizes "change" in her paper. Her *Thesaurus* lists synonymous verbs, including *alter, adapt, adjust, vary, revamp, reshape, improve, better, turn the tide, turn over a new leaf,* and so on. Using synonyms for this key word would help her vary her expression and keep the reader's interest.

3. *Which sentences can be made more concise and forceful by making subjects the doers or changing passive verbs to more active, lively ones?*

Charlotte is wordy and repetitive when she writes, "As I begin taking college courses, I have also begun thinking about improving how I look and act." To avoid repeating the "begin taking . . . begun thinking," she could write, "Beginning college made me think about improving my appearance." Also, she could link cause and effect more closely. Instead of writing "I eat sweets all the time, even more now that I'm going to school part time and working full time too," she might say, "Attending school part-time while working full time is quite tiring. To cope, I constantly eat sweets."

34

4. *Which sentences should be combined with other ones, or short-ened by being broken up?*

After the series that begins, "To do so, I need to change a bad eating habit," she might say, "Maybe I should jog or begin aerobic dancing, using exercise to take my mind off food and reduce my weight."

5. *What devices like connectives, synonyms, and pronouns has the writer used to tie his or her ideas together? What additional devices should the writer use?*

Charlotte uses connectives like *when, so, maybe,* and *however*. But she needs more transitional words and phrases like *to begin with, further-more, also, next, therefore, thus, as a result,* and *finally* to tie her ideas more closely together.

She also uses synonyms like *other people* and *each other* for "older students," *courses* for "college," *exercise* for "jogging or aerobic dancing," and *snack* for "eating." She should look over her paper for repetitions and synonyms that focus more firmly on her topic.

Finally, she should vary pronouns such as "they" and "these" with others like *she, he, it, this, that, some,* or *another*.

6. *Does the paper end with a conclusion that summarizes, raises a new but related issue, or recommends some specific change?*

Charlotte's paper would profit by ending with a sentence like one of the following:

a. With careful planning and a well-chosen support group, I should be able to improve both my appearance and my social life. (sums up).

b. It would help me to know how other married women manage to dress attractively, stay slim, hold down a full-time job, go to school part-time, and meet new people too (raises a new but related issue).

c. Maybe if my husband and sons took over more household tasks, I'd have more time for myself and more patience with my problems (recommends a change).

Now have a peer or classmate (preferably several of them) apply these questions to your draft, or analyze it yourself.

1. Do the first two or three sentences make clear how the writer will proceed in the paper? If so, has the writer followed this plan? If not, how should the writer change the organization?

   _____

   _____

2. Where should the writer add or substitute more specific examples, reasons, or details?

   _____

   _____

3. Which sentences can be made more concise and forceful by making subjects the doers or changing passive verbs to more active, lively ones?

_____

_____

4. Which sentences should be combined with other ones, or shortened by being broken up?

_____

_____

5. What devices like connectives, synonyms, and pronouns has the writer used to tie his or her ideas together? What additional devices should the writer use?

_____

_____

6. Does the paper end with a conclusion that summarizes, raises a new but related issue, or recommends some specific change?

_____

_____

Section Seven: Final Editing

Apply the questions we have listed above to your own work, or ask someone else to do so. Then rewrite. Once you have finished this version, clean up your grammatical problems, punctuation errors, and misspellings. The following questions should be helpful in this last stage:

1. *What kinds of grammatical problems need to be solved?*

Be sure that your subjects and verbs agree. Don't shift tenses or number as you move from nouns to pronouns or arrange your nouns or verbs in a series.

2. *What kinds of punctuation errors need to be corrected?*

Charlotte tends to overpunctuate. Or she neglects setting off transitions with commas. She may use a comma when she needs a semicolon. She knows that a colon often introduces a list, but she uses it improperly in "I like: cokes, . . ."

3. *What misspellings should be corrected?*

Charlotte reveals several spelling problems. She reverses syllables in "vallina" and doubles single consonants in "bananna." If you have troublesome spelling problems, list them by type in a special section in your journal.

Answer the following questions as you edit your own paper. In addition, look over a previous paper you have written in this class or for another class. Check particularly closely for those errors you have made before.

1. *What kinds of grammatical problems need to be solved?*

   _____

   _____

2. *What kinds of punctuation errors need to be corrected?*

   _____

   _____

3. *What misspellings should be corrected?*

   _____

   _____

EXERCISE 2.10

Each of the following topics can be developed into a paragraph. For the one you choose, write a specific, focused topic sentence. Then develop it with concrete, closely related illustrations. Be sure to generate ideas, plan the organization and support, revise, and edit before you consider your paragraph complete.

1. The postal service recently found several hundred letters written by servicemen in 1944 but never delivered. Imagine you are writing a letter to a close friend or spouse. He or she will read it thirty years from now. What would you say?

2. When is the first time you ever went into a hospital? Try to recall the smells, your feelings, the things that were said.

3. Someone has said that in the movies and on TV swimming pools sometimes stand for other things. They stand for things like:

   - An uncertain future (*E.T.*)
   - Newfound status (*Top Gun*)
   - Becoming young again (*Cocoon*)
   - Boy-meets-girl (*Witness*)

   What incident or object in your life has special meaning? Describe it, and tell what it means to you.

4. When did you get caught doing something you shouldn't have done? How did you react? What should you have done?

5. How do you feel about speaking before a group? Describe a time when you did so. How did you feel before, during, and after?

6. If you could design a special place to relax in, where would it be? What could people do there? How would it resemble and how would it differ from other such places?

7. Which of your personal traits do you consider to be the most outstanding? Do other people think so too?

8. What person from your own or an older generation have you most wanted to be like?

Unifying Paragraphs

A paragraph has unity—that is, it holds together—in two ways. First, the sentences follow one another in a predictable order. They are most often arranged by **time, space,** and **order of importance.** At the same time, a reader expects sentences to be linked together. Each sentence is related to the one it follows, as well as to the one that follows it.

Section One: The Unity of Time

To a certain extent, audiences read narratives for action. Incidents follow one another closely. Each one often causes the one which follows it. When readers know the order of the happenings, they can see the action clearly in their minds' eyes. The following paragraph is ordered by time, or **chronology:**

> When Elvis died on August 16, 1977, the *Inquirer* flew staff members to Memphis. Then they set up headquarters in a boarding house. The reporters were instructed to find a "blockbuster" scoop, something to eclipse the emerging stories about the King's drug habit. One staffer came up with the idea of a photograph of Presley in his coffin. That was it. The night before the funeral, reporters bought a number of cameras. Next, they handed them out to "mourners" along with a liberal sprinkling of cold, hard cash. The day after the funeral, the command center was littered with snaps of the King lying in state. The next issue of the *Inquirer* went on sale with Elvis's corpse on the cover. It quickly became the newspaper's all-time biggest (at the time) seller.

- The paragraph begins by telling the reader the topic: "When Elvis died on August 16, 1977."
- The writer follows chronology in arranging the sequence of actions. They are described in the order in which they happened.
- The order of the events is signaled by transitional words or phrases: **when, then, before, next, after,** and **at that time.** The writer uses these words to help the reader move from one event to the next.

EXERCISE 3.1

The sentences are out of order in each of the paragraphs below. Renumber them in the correct time *order in the spaces provided. Underline transitional words like* when, then, after, before, *or* at last *that remind us of the right order.*

A. __2__ Being a natural prankster, he bought a fleet of shabby wrecks.

__5__ He <u>now</u> has 26 thriving branches all over America.

__4__ To his surprise, there was an insatiable demand for them.

__1__ <u>When</u> David Schwartz left college in 1972, he set up Rent-a-Wreck as a joke.

__3__ He looked forward to watching people's faces as they took their choice of dented junkmobiles.

B. __3__ They had taken off from a base in Fort Lauderdale on December 5, 1945.

__2__ A New York City-based company discovered the remains of five Navy Torpedo bombers.

__1__ The Bermuda triangle <u>recently</u> lost an important bit of mystery.

__4__ They were never seen again.

__5__ The planes turned up in 740 feet of water about 20 miles off Fort Lauderdale.

C. __1__ Sixteen students clad in cooks' blouses take notes as chef Kathy Shepard begins her lecture.

__3__ <u>Then</u> she picks up a slab of fish and shows how to get it ready for the sauté pan.

__6__ It's their dinner that night.

__5__ The trout had better be edible.

__2__ "I want to see lots of color on the plates," she says of the stir-fry.

__4__ <u>After</u> the demonstration, the students will try to duplicate Shepard's movements.

EXERCISE 3.2

Choose one of the following topics for your own paragraph. Complete the suggested topic sentence, and tell how you feel about it. Then generate some ideas by making a list, clustering, or answering the reporter's questions: **Who? What? Where? When? Why?** *and* **How?** *Arrange the details in terms of time. Work in transitional words or phrases such as these:*

first	to illustrate
for example	for one thing
thus	for instance
in addition	similarly
next	above all

Paragraph A: **One problem I encountered recently was** . . . . *Tell what the problem was, and why it bothered you. When did it happen? Describe what happened in detail. Tell how you solved it or failed to do so.*

Paragraph B: **One thing I am most proud of accomplishing is** . . . . *Tell what you accomplished and how you did it. Why did you think of it as important? How did it make you proud? Tell how long it took you to do it. Use transitions to make the time order apparent to your reader.*

Paragraph C: **One thing members of my own age group are doing is** . . . . *What are members of your age group doing, and how do you feel about it? Describe the behavior in detail, putting the focus on one particular incident. Arrange the sentences according to time order.*

Section Two: The Unity of Space

Writers often describe a person, place, or thing. To appeal to readers, they need to place their details in space order. To describe a **place:** imagine how it looks from above. Then move toward, into, or through the place from outside to inside, from front to back, or from general to specific. Here is an example of descriptive writing:

The largest of the known cactus species, the saguaro is found in the Sonoran Desert. It can reach heights of up to fifty feet in its over 200 years of growth. Its shallow roots extend radially, like interlaced wire spokes, as far as sixty-five feet in all directions. These roots form an effective plumbing system for the saguaro. When it rains, the network of roots sponges up water at a rapid rate. After a summer cloudburst, the saguaro may absorb a ton of water. A mature saguaro may weigh over ten tons, of which four-fifths may be water. The cactus is well prepared for the dry months that follow the rain.

- The paragraph begins with a topic sentence which tells us the name of the largest cactus and where it grows.
- The paragraph organizes its detail by *space:* looking first at its height, then at its roots, and finally explaining its weight and makeup.
- The writer uses words that repeat earlier similar words, such as *these roots* and *the cactus* for "saguaro." It also uses transitions such as *when* and *after* to indicate changes in time.

The following paragraph describes a person:

An essentially neat man, Bernie rose from his cleared desk, feeling a pronounced sense of well-being and achievement. In his middle forties, he had never cut a dashing figure. He was small and his face was round as a pumpkin, a fact particularly apparent now that he had lost most of his graying hair. Glasses over his large eyes gave him a somewhat startled look, yet the success of recent years had produced a certain confidence in his manner. If you looked carefully past the lenses of those glasses, you would look into the eyes of a man who had made his way nicely and who expected to go a touch farther.

This paragraph lacks a topic sentence. Sum up what you think it ought to be:

Although Bernie did not look impressive, he was self-confident.

How does the paragraph move from part to part of Bernie's appearance? *It deals first with his size and shape, then with his hair, his glasses, and then his eyes.*

What transitional words does the writer use? *He uses phrases such as now and if.*

EXERCISE 3.3

The details are out of order in each of the lists below. Renumber them in the correct space order in the spaces provided.

A. A person [CLUE: The paragraph moves through visual details, from the top down, to dress, movements, and sound]

 6 a high, metallic voice

 3 a gold chain with a dangling cross

 1 a long face, like a sheep's

 5 quick, birdlike movements

 4 dressed in black

 2 brown, dull hair, carefully arranged

B. A place [CLUE: The paragraph moves from outer to inner, large to small]

 3 a city made of sugar cubes

 1 mountains in the blue distance

 5 matchstick figures hustling along morning pavements

 4 cars crawling like colored beetles

 2 a city between the sea and the mountains

C. An object [CLUE: The paragraph moves from large, outside visual details to the inside, from specific to general]

 5 most of the interior ripped out

 3 stickers advertising motor oil and parts

 1 painted orange

 6 only one seat—for driver

 2 body work banged up all over

 4 instrument panel replaced by a few dials

EXERCISE 3.4

Choose one of the following topics for your own paragraph. Complete the suggested topic sentence, and tell how you feel about it. Then generate some ideas by making a list, clustering, or answering the reporter's questions: **Who? What? Where? When? Why?** *and* **How?** *Arrange the details in terms of space. Work in transitional words or phrases such as these:*

over	under	in front of	behind
next to	beyond	on top of	underneath
beside	to the left	on the right	farther out

Paragraph A: **The place I most remember is . . . .** *List a set of details in order. Use transitions to help the reader move through the paragraph.*

Paragraph B: **The famous person I most admire is . . . .** *Write down examples of the person's appearance, dress, and mannerisms.*

Paragraph C: **My favorite object is . . . .** *Let the reader know your point of view. Choose specific details that help you describe the object vividly.*

Section Three: The Unity of Importance

Writers often tell a story in the order of importance. They may move from less important details to more important, building tension until the end of the paragraph. Such paragraphs hold the attention of the reader, who knows that the examples are moving toward a climax:

Thomas Nuttall (1786–1859) was a pioneer botanist. As an explorer, however, he was almost permanently lost. During his expedition of 1812, his colleagues had to light beacons to help him find his way to camp. One night he failed to return and a search party went out. As the searchers approached him in the darkness, Nuttall thought they were Indians and he tried to escape. His rescuers chased him for three days through bush and river. Finally, he accidentally wandered back into the camp. On another occasion, Nuttall was lost again and lay down exhausted. A passing Indian, instead of scalping him, picked him up, carried him three miles to the river, and paddled him home in a canoe.

- A topic statement appears near the beginning of this paragraph: *Thomas Nuttall, a pioneer botanist . . . was almost permanently lost.*
- The writer develops the topic with three incidents, each more surprising than the one before. Being chased by rescuers is more surprising than the lighting of beacons. At the end, it is most surprising that Nuttall was rescued by one of the Indians he deeply feared.
- The details are linked by transitions such as *during, one night, as the searchers approached him, finally,* and *again.*

In expository writing, your reader needs to know your organizing topic or principle. As you jot down details related to a topic, think about their importance. If you want to build suspense or a growing sense of comedy, begin with a minor detail. Then arrange your examples so that they lead in order to the most important at the end.

In addition, try arranging your facts or details with the most important one first. Then follow it with your other examples. Look over the paragraph below:

Wendy's has square hamburgers to look different from McDonald's. They look bigger, use less condiments, and are custom made. First, every time a Wendy's hamburger is turned on the grill, the patty is pressed. It might end up thinner, but it is still large in area. Next, if you order a quarter-pounder with "the works" at both places, you will notice the condiments more at McDonald's. Wendy's wants you to think McDonald's has something to hide. Finally, when Wendy's hit upon the "old fashioned" slogan, it meant that the customer was always supplied a custom-made sandwich.

In what three ways does Wendy's make its hamburgers look bigger than McDonald's?

They are pressed thinner, have fewer condiments, and are custom made.

What transitions help the reader see the paragraph move from one reason to another?

First, but, next, finally.

EXERCISE 3.5

Arrange the ideas in the following lists in the order of importance, moving from most to least important. Then decide whether the paragraph would be more effective if the order were reversed.

A. If you compare sets of measuring spoons or cups, they probably won't hold exactly the same amount of liquid. **[CLUE: Which of the reasons is most likely to happen?]**

___3___ Hot water in the dishwasher warps these instruments.

___2___ Consumers never bother to test the accuracy of their measuring instruments.

___1___ The workmanship is often shoddy.

B. Most movie theaters do not pop their own popcorn. **[CLUE: Consider the impact of each one on a theater's profitability.]**

___3___ Equipment can get messy and smelly.

___1___ Theater managers must train employees not to wreck the corn poppers.

___4___ Prepopped corn is uniform in size and taste, unlike homemade popcorn.

___2___ Theaters never run out of prepopped corn.

C. Seat belts are seldom installed on school buses. **[CLUE: Consider cost and impact]**

  __4__ More students die getting on and off buses than riding them.

  __2__ In the hands of a teenager, a seat belt buckle is a lethal weapon.

  __5__ The money could be better spent on training bus drivers.

  __3__ Installing them would make school buses more expensive.

  __1__ Children refuse to wear them.

EXERCISE 3.6

Decide how to arrange the details for the topics listed below, and tell why this is the best arrangement.

EXAMPLE: I always liked living in a big city.

Type of arrangement: Space

Purpose: To describe places from the city's center to near the city limits.

Type of arrangement: Time

Purpose: To illustrate things that could be done from morning to late night.

Type of arrangement: Order of importance

Purpose: To list the things I liked from trivial to most significant.

A. My (friend, relative) influenced me more than anyone else.

 Type of arrangement: Order of importance

 Purpose: To list influences in order either from least to most—to achieve a feeling of suspense—or from most to least.

B. (Name individual) is my favorite performer.

 Type of arrangement: Time

 Purpose: To describe the times the writer heard the performer live, on a recording, or on TV.

C. I decided to go to college for several reasons.

 Type of arrangement: Order of importance.

 Purpose: To list reasons in order, either from least to most important, or from most important to least important.

Section Four: Linking Sentences with Transitions

In addition to unifying sentences by placing them in order, writers link them by the way they use words. We usually notice when **coherence**—the glue that holds sentences together—is missing. These methods of linking ideas include the following:

- Using transitional words or phrases;
- Repeating important words;
- Using pronouns to refer back to important words; and
- Substituting synonyms for key words.

Writers use special words to hold sentences together within paragraphs. These **transition words** show readers that ideas are closely related in meaning. If they are missing, the reader may find the sentences confusing and hard to follow, as in this example:

More old people than younger ones eat at cafeterias. Cafeterias are located in downtown areas, where old people live. Seniors dine out more than the population at large. Older people have more money to spend. Seniors mention price as the number one reason they like cafeterias.

When we add transition words to *connect* or *sum up,* the paragraph reads much more smoothly:

More old people than younger ones eat at cafeterias. *First,* cafeterias are located in downtown areas, where old people live. *Contrary to popular belief,* seniors dine out more than the population at large. Older people *also* have more money to spend. *Most importantly,* seniors mention price as the number one reason they like cafeterias.

One of the easiest ways to link thoughts together in a paragraph is to use formal transitions (we have starred* the conjunctions).

Some of these words point out an example or illustration:

first, to illustrate, for example, for one thing, thus, for instance

At times, these words tell us that another point is coming:

in addition, similarly, next, above all, again, finally, and*, also, too, then, second, equally, for another thing, furthermore, moreover

Then too, transitional words may sum up or repeat in similar words:

to sum up, consequently, in other words, as a result, in fact, so*, therefore, accordingly, of course, indeed

Finally, such words may indicate a contrast or difference:

by contrast, but*, however, still, yet*, on the contrary, on the other hand, nevertheless

EXERCISE 3.7   *Choose a transition from one of the lists above to connect the sentences below to one another.*

1. There are logical reasons why the music for ice dancing is often so bad. *For one thing,* competitive skaters are mostly in their teens and twenties. _____ However _____ , judges are mostly middle-aged and older.

2. _____ In some cases _____ , coaches select the music for skaters; _____ in others _____ , skaters select their own.

3. _____ Usually _____ , it is a collaborative process between the two. _____ But _____ music must always be selected that will impress judges, _____ even if _____ the arrangement probably won't bowl over audiences.

4. Skating judges need not have any musical training. _____ In fact _____ , they are often untrained musically.

5. Skaters may need to please judges from Japan, Germany, and Canada. _____ As a result _____ , you had better not offend any of them.

6. Prominent skaters have been punished for their choice of music. _____ For example _____ , Judy Blumberg and Michael Seibert were not awarded a medal in the 1984 Winter Olympics. A judge felt that "Scheherazade" was inappropriate for ice dancing.

7. There is no rule against vocal recordings in free-skating. _____ However _____ , no one dares defy the common law.

8. The restriction on vocal selection hurts skaters in two ways. _____ For one thing _____ , they can't use the best version of a given song. _____ In addition _____ , skaters and coaches are forced to find an all-instrumental version of a song.

9. Ice dancing music is usually better than free-skating music. _____ To illustrate _____ , free-skating includes more acrobatic leaps and spins.

10. Music must be found to favor these movements. _____ Thus _____ , the selection of good material is much more difficult.

48

11. Many skaters are just kids. _____Consequently_____ , they don't know how to interpret music.

12. Their coaches may not understand their limitations and strengths. _____As a result_____ , the students may ignore the music.

13. The skaters and their coaches are really trying to find the best music possible for their performances. _____Nevertheless_____ , fate has made this a difficult task indeed.

Section Five: Linking Ideas with Pronouns and Synonyms

Along with transitions, pronouns or synonyms may connect one sentence to another. These words refer to earlier words or phrases. Writers replace one word with another one having the same or similar meaning. The paragraph below replaces "Jack Dittemore" with **synonyms** and **pronouns:**

When **Jack Dittemore** shows up at a bank, depositors and bank officials have reason to be nervous. **Mr. Dittemore** isn't an auditor or a bank robber. But **he** has been a customer at three of the 32 Oklahoma banks that have failed since 1982. The most recent collapse came last month. The **55-year-old Oklahoma City resident** was on **his** way to the veterinarian to pick up his sick cat when **he** noticed a commotion outside Citizens National Bank & Trust Co., where **he** had an account. Sure enough, federal regulators had declared the bank insolvent. By that time, however, **he** had become used to such occurrences. **He** had moved his account to Citizens National when another bank had failed.

- This paragraph uses synonyms like *Mr. Dittemore* and *the 55-year-old Oklahoma City resident* to replace the original subject, "Jack Dittemore." It also uses substitutes for the word "fail"—words like *collapse, insolvent,* and *occurrences.*
- The paragraph also replaces Dittemore's name with pronouns such as *he* and *his.*

Synonyms also extend and define words in a paragraph:

New fast-food companies like Rally's in Louisville, and Burger Street and Flyers, both in Dallas, are building tiny restaurants with stripped-down menus and take-out-only service. **This new generation of hamburger restaurant** is taking a **bare-bones approach.**

Synonyms link the second sentence to the first:

- "This new generation of hamburger restaurant" restates words like "Rally's . . . Burger Street and Flyers."
- "A bare-bones approach" restates "tiny restaurants with stripped-down menus and take-out-only service" in different words.

EXERCISE 3.8

Read over the following paragraphs. Then pick out the synonyms and pronouns that replace the italicized words and list them below.

A. Almost 10 percent of all *sheets* produced are defective. However, customers love to buy them. Even the ritziest department stores stock irregulars. And they don't hide these flawed goods in the basement.
   This paragraph also refers to "sheets" as them, irregulars, and flawed goods.

B. The ritual of eating *ham* around Easter time predates Christianity. Pagans buried fresh pork legs in the sand by the sea. The pork was cured by the constant "marinating" of the salt water. The preserved meat was then cooked over wood fires.
   This paragraph also refers to *ham* as pork legs, pork, and preserved meat.

C. The *Kodak Brownie* was introduced in 1900, providing cameras for the masses. This handy gadget combined ease of use with a comfortable price. The camera sold for a buck, a roll of film for 15 cents.
   This paragraph also refers to the Kodak Brownie as a handy gadget and a camera.

EXERCISE 3.9

In the following paragraph, use synonyms or pronouns in the blanks instead of the proper names "Samuel Patch" or "Steve Brodie."

For sheer idiocy, few human endeavors can compare with high-altitude jumping. This sport was in vogue, believe it or not, during the 1800s. The fad started with *Samuel Patch* of Pawtucket, Rhode Island. In 1827 _____Patch_____ announced that _____he_____ would dive off the Paterson bridge. Authorities tried to arrest _____the fellow_____ for _____his_____ own good, but _____he_____ eluded them and plunged 90 feet into the swirling Passaic River. When _____he_____ bobbed up alive, Samuel Patch was a national hero. _____His_____ next challenge was Niagara Falls. Feet first, _____the daredevil_____ jumped from a precipice on Goat Island—and survived. _____He_____ then turned to the treacherous Genesee Falls. A crowd cheered _____ him _____ as _____ the chap _____ made a running leap into "the abyss" below, a distance of 125 feet. That was on November 18, 1829. They found _____ the boy's _____ body on March 17, 1830. *Steve Brodie,* a (use a phrase meaning "a stupid seller of newspapers") _____ foolhardy newsboy _____ from New York City, then took to jumping— first from the Brooklyn Bridge into the East River. _____ He _____ lived and was acclaimed (use a phrase meaning a grown-up risk-taker) _____ "the man who took a chance." _____ Brodie capitalized on _____ his _____ fame by touring variety halls and theaters recreating _____ his _____ famous leap. With a cry, _____ "I'll _____ save the girl," _____ he _____ would hop six feet from a cardboard bridge down onto the stage.

Section Six: Linking Ideas by Repeating Important Words

In addition to using transitions and substitutions to link sentences together, writers often **repeat** important words or ideas:

Spain dominates the sale of green olives in the United States for two reasons. Olive farming is so important to the Spanish economy that olive production is heavily subsidized by the government. Also, California olive farmers don't try to compete with Spain. They can sell all the ripe olives that they harvest.

- The word *olive* (or its plural) is repeated five times in this paragraph.

To avoid boring the reader with too many repetitions, writers often replace key words with synonyms (words which mean approximately the same):

The Forest Service recently collected $20,000 from the Idaho Boy Scouts after a campfire burned a 115-acre forest. As more people build houses in the woods, fires threaten more lives and homes. Forest fires last year destroyed 1,400 homes, more than double the previous year. And firefighters were so busy saving homes during a major North Carolina fire this spring that the fire spread wildly through the woods.

- The word *fire* is repeated six times, including once as part of the word "firefighters," and once as part of the word "campfire."
- The word *forest* is also repeated once.

51

- The paragraph also uses synonyms to add variety to word choice. For example, *woods* is substituted for *forest*, and *destroyed* is used as a synonym for *burned*.

EXERCISE 3.10

Underline the repeated words in the following sentences. If the paragraph substitutes synonyms or pronouns for key words, circle them. Note: The first synonym for x's is the phrase "symbols of affection."

A. Those cute little *X's* we put on Valentine's Day cards did not begin as symbols of affection. They were substitutes for signatures in the Middle Ages, when most people couldn't write. But the X was also used by well-educated people. Even kings and queens signed with the X as a symbol of good faith. In some cultures an X became a binding oath.

B. During World War II, when oils and fats were in short supply, artificial detergents were hastily developed. By 1953, artificial detergents, led by Procter & Gamble's Tide, supplanted soaps as the United States' favored cleaning agent. Detergents were not only more effective in cleaning than simple soaps; they also relieved many of the hard water washing problems. That is because they are chemically built to resist hard water minerals.

C. "Gourmet" popcorn is a hybrid. It is bred to pop bigger than ordinary yellow kernels. "Regular" popcorn averages an expansion ratio of 35–38 times. However, the best hybrids average over 40. Makers of "gourmet" popcorn also claim that their product is less tough than regular popcorn.

EXERCISE 3.11

A. Complete the following sentence: Maturity consists of _____ . How do you define it: by your age, or by the decisions you make? What other words can you substitute for "maturity"? Develop this idea in a paragraph, linking your ideas by repeating words, and by using synonyms and pronouns.

B. Complete the following sentence: The most admirable person I know is _____ . Explain how you feel about this person and why. Then write a paragraph which defines or illustrates this person's qualities. Link your sentences by repeating words, and by using synonyms and pronouns.

REVIEW EXERCISE 3.12

Writers link ideas in paragraphs by placing sentences in order, by using transitions, by repeating words, and by using synonyms and pronouns. Look over each of the paragraphs below. Then answer the questions that follow each of them.

A. Yossarian had everything he wanted in the hospital. The food wasn't too bad, and his meals were brought to him in bed. There were extra rations of fresh meat, and during the hot part of the afternoon he and the others were served chilled fruit juice or chilled chocolate milk. Apart from the doctors and the nurses, no one ever disturbed him. For a little while in the morning he had to censor letters, but he was free after that to spend the rest of each day lying around idly with a clear conscience.

Joseph Heller, "The Texan"

What synonyms are used for "food"?
meals, rations, fresh meat, chilled fruit juice, chilled chocolate milk

What transitional words and phrases does the paragraph use?
during, apart from, for a little while, after that

What pronouns does the paragraph use to refer to "Yossarian"?
he, his

B. A hard or leathery shell is what differentiates a nut from a seed. The cashew is a seed, not a nut. The cashew is the seed of a pear-shaped fruit, the cashew apple, which is itself edible. The cashew seed hangs at the lower end of the fruit, vulnerable and exposed. Cashews grow not on trees, but on tropical shrubs, similar to sumac.

What ordering principle does the paragraph follow?
Order of most to least importance. It first defines the cashew as a kind of seed, tells where on the plant the seed is located, and, finally, tells what kind of plant it is found on.

Which words are repeated in this paragraph?
nut, seed, cashew, and fruit

What synonyms for what words does the paragraph use to link ideas to one another?
seed for cashew, pear-shaped fruit for apple, shrub for sumac

C. A cheap chest of drawers stood against the wall. She showed them a closet holding a few frayed dresses. A gold-faced clock ticked. Another row of pictures, faded relatives, were lined up in front of the mirror on the chest. A double bed was against the door. A blue chenille spread covered the bed. A pair of cracked shoes stood underneath.

Sol Yurick, "The Siege"

What order does the paragraph follow?
The order of space. The paragraph describes the appearance of the room as the eye might record the objects in it.

What transitional words does the paragraph use to show the relationship of objects to one another?

against, another, in front of, on, underneath

D. Mr. Michael Murphy, a 22-year-old draftsman from Stevenage in Hertfordshire, set off in August 1975 to cycle around the world. During the next two years he was robbed by Yugoslavian peasants, stoned by tribesmen in the Khyber Pass, and nearly frozen to death in a blizzard. When he finally arrived back in England in April 1977, he had only to collect his bike at Heathrow Airport and cycle the last 40 miles home. After 25,000 miles he confidently expected to make it back to Stevenage. His hopes were crushed, as was his bicycle, by a conveyor belt joining the plane to the customs hall. He had to hitch a lift home.

What order does the paragraph follow?

The order of time, summing up the mishaps that Murphy suffered over a two-year period.

What transitions does the paragraph use to link incidents?

during, when, finally, after, as, joining

What synonyms and pronouns does the paragraph use to refer back to Murphy?

draftsman, he, his

What synonyms does the paragraph use for the idea "to travel"?

set off, cycle, arrived back, make it back, hitch a lift home

Developing
with Examples

A paragraph may be developed with examples. It may begin with a topic sentence dealing with an emotion, perhaps, or a problem. The paragraph then illustrates the topic with several examples or incidents. These examples may take place in time, as in a narrative, or in space. Sometimes you may choose to arrange them in order of importance. With this approach, writers don't deal with a single incident in depth. Rather, they use several instances to develop a particular point.

Section One: Choosing a Topic

Below is a list of possible topics for an example paragraph. Choose one that particularly interests you.

- Several things frightened me as a child.
- Many people of college age are forced to grow up very quickly.
- The most important trait in my personality is . . . .

Section Two: Generating Ideas

Before beginning to write a paragraph using examples, take a few moments to generate some ideas. This is called *prewriting*. The first chapter in this book, "Generating Ideas," takes up several ways to get started. One of the simplest yet most effective ways to put down thoughts is to list ideas in a scratch outline. Write your topic at the top of a sheet of paper. Then begin listing general aspects of the topic. As you move along, fill in details following each aspect. This approach resembles brainstorming, but is more structured.

My First Registration

First day
 Signed up for courses
  Tried to get five courses
  Got only three of them
Second day
 Hard to find books
 Stood in long lines
 Paid for books, tuition & fees
  Each book cost at least $40
  Tuition and fees cost $900
 Spent about $1,100 of my savings
Third day
 Had to drop-and-add courses
 Hard to work new courses into my schedule

Trial Topic Sentence: My first registration was not only frustrating, but expensive.

Order of Examples: In the paragraph, as in the scratch outline, the student would arrange the examples on the basis of time. The paragraph would deal with the first, second, and third days in order.

Section Three: Planning and Organizing the Paragraph

An example paragraph starts with this topic sentence:

The kids who grew up on "Star Trek" can't find their way around Earth.

The paragraph begins by summing up an idea. To make the initial idea clear, the writer needs to illustrate it—to provide examples. This paragraph develops the idea above with several examples:

The kids who grew up on "Star Trek" can't find their way around Earth. Americans can dial direct to England, but only half can find it on a map of Europe. They can fly almost anywhere in the United States for a few hundred dollars, but they put New York State in 37 places on both coasts. When they look for the United States itself, they spot it in China, Australia, Brazil, the Soviet Union, India and Botswana. For people who are supposed to be leaders of the free world, Americans are geographically dumb.

Joan Beck, *Chicago Tribune*

What can Americans do?
They can dial direct to England and fly almost anywhere in the United States for a few hundred dollars.

What are Americans unable to do?

They are unable to find England, New York State, and the United States on a map.

How is Ms. Beck's paragraph ordered?

It is ordered by importance, least to most. She and most readers would consider finding England less important than locating the United States.

What transitions does Ms. Beck use to link her ideas together? (Check "Section Four: Using Transitional Devices" in Chapter 2, p. 30, if needed.)

but, when, and *for*

The examples in this kind of paragraph may be ordered by time, space, or order of importance. In order to write her paragraph, Ms. Beck probably organized her thoughts like this:

Trial Topic Sentence: Americans are geographically dumb.

After deciding to develop this idea, she may have thought of a more colorful way to begin her paragraph. She may have decided to remind her readers of "Star Trek," a popular television series. She expanded on her idea with examples, possibly with a scratch outline which looked like this:

First Example: Finding England on map of Europe
  Most dial direct
  Half find it
Second Example: Finding New York State
  Fly anywhere in United States
  Put New York State 37 places on both coasts
Third Example: Finding the United States
  Confuse it with six other locations in world

Finally, she used her original idea to sum up at the end of the paragraph.
  A paragraph may also use *time* to order its examples:

At the hospital Alexander studied the mushrooms which may have poisoned the victims. Scraping off minute spores, he exposed them to an iodine solution. Under the microscope the small, round spores gradually turned bluish. That was bad. It indicated the presence of a complex sugar that can be found in poisonous mushrooms. He then mashed a piece of cap onto newspaper and applied a drop of hydrochloric acid. A sky-blue halo appeared around it. That was worse. It suggested a particularly dangerous toxin. Neither test was conclusive. Then he looked at an uncooked mushroom. One look was all Alexander needed. It was *Amanita phalloides,* the death cup—one of the world's most lethal mushrooms. Fields roared off to Portland's Bess Kaiser Hospital.

Jack Fincher, "Transplant Emergency"

What general statement serves as the topic sentence?

At the hospital Alexander studied the mushrooms which may have poisoned the victims.

What examples does the writer give to support the topic sentence?
Scraping and testing spores, mashing and testing a cap, looking at an uncooked mushroom.

How does the paragraph use *order of importance* as well as *time* to arrange its examples?
After mentioning two tests which fail to show the problem conclusively, the paragraph takes up the third, crucial test which does solve it: the appearance of the poisonous mushroom. This leads to a final climactic action: roaring off to the hospital.

A paragraph may also use *space* to order its examples:

Nearly everybody has a creek in his past, a confiding waterway that rose in the spring of youth. A park ranger's voice softens as he talks of a boyhood creek in Louisiana where he swam and fished. A conservationist's eyes sparkle as he recalls building dams on Strawberry Creek in the California of his youth. An Ohio woman feels suddenly at home again as she remembers catching crayfish in the creek behind her parents' house. Nothing historic ever happens in these recollected creeks. But their persistence in memory suggests that creeks are bigger than they seem.

Peter Steinhart, "The Enchantment of Creeks"

What general statement serves as the topic sentence?
Nearly everybody has a creek in his past.

What examples does the writer give to support the topic sentence?
The writer uses examples of creeks remembered by a park ranger, a conservationist, and an Ohio woman.

How does the paragraph use *space* to arrange its examples?
It uses an example from each of three regions of the United States: Louisiana (the South), California (the West), and Ohio (the Midwest).

Section Four: Using Transitional Devices

In addition to ordering your examples, you need to link them with transitional devices. (Check "Section Four: Using Transitional Devices" in Chapter 2, p. 30, if needed.) Look over the following list:

Transitional Devices to Link Examples

for instance, for example, one of these, yet, another, in particular, first (second, third, finally), next, also, then, to sum up

Note: Do not overuse these devices in a paragraph.

Read over the example paragraphs below. Underline the topic sentence. Following each one, list the examples used. Then put down the transitions you find. Note: Look for transitional phrases not included in the list.

A. I keep a file labeled "Remarkable Letters." A man wrote to propose his revision of the yearly calendar, with nine days of the week instead of seven. Another reader wrote to inform me of annual duck races in New Mexico. A woman wrote to complain that ever since the moon had gone into the sign of Sagittarius, her television reception had been poor. What should she do? The moon will enter Capricorn in two days, I told her, and you might check with your television repairman if that doesn't clear things up.

Martha White, "Dog Days, Cat Nights and Pogonips"

What examples does the writer give to support the topic sentence?

Changing the calendar, duck races in New Mexico, a supposed link between astrology and poor TV reception.

What transitions link the examples?

another, and, if

B. Ravaged by amyotrophic lateral sclerosis (Lou Gehrig's disease), Stephen Hawking is unable to talk or to move anything except his eyes and three fingers of his right hand. But, oh, how the man can think. His mind cruises among black holes, white holes, time reversals and universes that dance on the head of a pin. A mathematics professor at Cambridge University and now author of the best-seller *A Brief History of Time,* he scoots around in a motorized wheelchair and communicates through a word processor hooked up to a voice synthesizer. Married in 1965, this father of three fairly bubbles with zest. "When one's expectations are reduced to zero," he explains, "one really appreciates everything one does have." What Hawking does have is a rare and wonderful consolation. From his wheelchair, on a clear day he can see Forever.

People Weekly

What examples does the writer give to support the topic sentence?

The way Hawking's mind works, the way he gets around and communicates, the way he appreciates what he has and can do.

What transitions link the examples?

but, now, married in 1965, from his wheelchair

EXERCISE 4.2

In the following paragraphs, each one of the examples should be closely related to the topic sentence beginning the paragraph. Each of the topic sentences is followed by a list of examples. Check the example that doesn't fit.

A. Last spring my Sunday-school teenagers wrote, produced, and performed their own rock opera based on the Book of Acts.

_____ 1. Kristy and Amy devised dance steps.

_____ 2. Eric electrified us with his guitar riffs.

_____ * 3. The Bible includes many incidents which students can dramatize.

_____ 4. Dong Han confounded everyone by singing on key.

B. No one wanted to miss NASA's launch of three astronauts in mankind's first attempt to land on the moon.

_____ 1. Nearly a million people had come to watch the launch of Apollo 11.

_____ * 2. Even at 3 a.m., this Wednesday morning was hot and muggy.

_____ 3. Many had sweated in bumper-to-bumper traffic from Cocoa Beach to Titusville the night before.

_____ 4. The headlights of almost 300,000 cars cut through the darkness.

C. The oceans are the main source of humidity, but plants and human activity also pour moisture into the air.

_____ 1. In one day, a five-acre forest can release 20,000 gallons of water, enough to fill an average swimming pool.

_____ 2. A dryer extracts moisture from wet clothes, adding to humidity.

_____ 3. Every time we exhale, we expel nearly one pint of moist air into the atmosphere.

_____ * 4. "Humidity" is a measure of the moisture that air can hold.

D. Parents can get kids to help at home by managing the family's time better.

_____ 1. Make an inventory of what has to be done.

_____ 2. Break each task into 15-minute segments.

_____ * 3. One child promised to take care of the lawn, but did nothing for three weeks.

_____ 4. Assign the work to each family member according to his or her preferences.

E. Columnist Bob Greene describes his profession.

_____ * 1. He is a devoted husband and father.

_____ 2. He talks with people and notices things.

_____ 3. He does not lift heavy objects or manufacture widgets.

_____ 4. He puts it all on paper for strangers.

F. On August 14, the Perseids appear, a great shower of meteors.

_____ 1. They are swifter and brighter than most other shooting stars.

_____ * 2. The moon is a natural satellite of the earth, visible by reflection of sunlight.

_____ 3. The largest Perseids leave long, incandescent trails that slowly melt away.

_____ 4. They are visible from about July 17 to August 17, and on peak nights appear one every few minutes.

G. I use a 35-millimeter camera for night photography.

_____ * 1. It takes ten or twenty minutes for the pupils of the eye to adjust to darkness.

_____ 2. Any camera with a time-exposure setting and fast film will do.

_____ 3. I open the lens as far as it will go and focus at infinity.

_____ 4. I make exposures of five to thirty minutes throughout the night.

EXERCISE 4.3

Answers will vary.

For each of the topics below, write out at least one example that develops it. Be as specific as possible, using complete sentences for your example.

A. Any number of incidents can make me lose my temper.

Example: The last time I registered for college, three of the courses I needed were closed out.

B. Although most laundry detergents are basically the same, many of their ads try to make each one look different.

Example: An ad for "Snuggle" fills an enormous bed with colorful quilts, children playing happily, and their stuffed animals.

C. My childhood was unusual in a number of ways.

Example: Because my father was in the military, we lived in thirteen different places in fifteen years.

D. I liked (or disliked) some of my teachers in high school.

Example: One of my teachers, Ms. Harriman, assigned us interesting topics in a speech class and helped us develop our vocabularies.

E. The voters of this state often show poor judgment in the politicians they elect.

Example: During the last election, the voters reelected a candidate who had been convicted of vote-buying several years before.

F. Children can be taught how to make friends easily.

Example: Initially, they should walk up to a strange child, exchange names, and ask the stranger about himself or herself.

G. People often say personal or embarrassing things to complete strangers.

Example: A stranger on a bus once told me all the details about the delivery of her first child.

H. The costs of clothing have risen over the last five or ten years.

Example: A simple sports shirt which once sold for $2.95 now costs six or seven dollars.

Section Five: Writing the First Draft

Using your topic sentence and the examples you have ordered, write a first draft. Here is an example of a draft written by a student using the topic sentence: *I will never regret the decision to leave home.*

I will never regret the decision to leave home. Since leaving home, I have had this feeling of relief. Relief from the rules. I have also been relieved emotionally. No more do I feel as if I have to prove anything to anyone but myself. A number of events have occurred in my life recently that really put allot of emotional strain on me. The most recent being my girl friend breaking up with me. I became really depressed with no one that I could talk too who would understand how I'm feeling. Another problem is with my dad being in a wheelchair and always being depressed make it harder for me. Since I have moved out, I feel free from all the curfews and rules that I had at my parents home. All of my old friends don't believe I can handle the bills and expenses of moving out but I know if I put my mind to it I can do anything. So far after I pay my share of the bills I don't have much money left. I also know it will only get harder before it can get better. Moving out hasn't completely washed my blues away, but it has helped me to start my own life. There are still alot of things I get confused about. I have begun to get my life back in order and have new dreams I want to accomplish. Some of the dreams at the top of my list are buying a new truck or maybe taking a cruise. No matter how hard things get for me, this is one decision I will never regret making.

Section Six: Revising the Paragraph

Apply the questions in the checklist below to your first draft, or have a friend or classmate do it. We have applied them to the student draft.

1. *Which examples used in the paragraph are most specific and interesting?*

The writer uses specific examples such as his resentment of curfews, his father's disability, breaking up with his girlfriend, problems with being on his own, and his dreams for the future.

2. *Has the writer focused on the topic sentence, or do some of the examples deal with other topics?*

Some of the examples deal with the writer's relief at leaving home: feeling free of curfews and rules, the way his disabled father depresses him.

63

However, he also mentions problems that still bother him. And he brings in examples of dreams he holds for the future. The writer can handle only one of these topics adequately in a paragraph.

3. *Suggest a topic sentence that would help the writer focus on a topic more clearly and narrowly. The writer might use one of the following topic sentences:*

> I have recently felt stressed by a number of recent events in my life.
>
> OR
>
> Even though I solved some problems by leaving home, I now must deal with new ones.
>
> OR
>
> Now that I have left home, I have dreams for the future which I want to accomplish.

4. *How should the writer organize the examples?*

The writer should consider ordering the examples in time. For example, if the writer wants to deal with recent problems, he or she might handle them in the order in which they occurred. Or the writer could deal with them in their order of importance: moving from trivial to most important problems.

5. *What serious mechanical or other problems should the writer solve while rewriting the first draft?*

The writer has a serious problem with fragments such as (1) "Since leaving home, I have had this feeling of relief. Relief from the rules," and (2) "The most recent being my girlfriend breaking up with me."

The first one contains a fragment lacking a subject and verb. The writer could correct it by combining the fragment with the preceding sentence:

Since leaving home, I have had this feeling of relief from the rules.

While the second one needs a verb, it is also wordy. The writer could correct it like this:

Most recently, my girlfriend broke up with me.

If you have repeated difficulty with fragments, look at Chapter 20, "Fragments," for a more extended treatment of this problem.

The writer also misspells "a lot" two ways, in both cases as one word: "allot" and "alot." Since the word is often misspelled, he needs to make a note of it, perhaps in his journal.

He also omits an apostrophe to show possession in the phrase "at my parents home." Since the plural word "parents" expresses possession of "home" and ends in *s*, the writer should add an apostrophe: *parents'*.

If you have difficulty punctuating possessive words, look at Chapter 30, "Minor Punctuation Marks."

Apply the questions in the revision checklist below to your own writing, or have a friend or classmate do it.

64

1. Which examples used in the paragraph are most specific and interesting?
2. Has the writer focused on the topic sentence, or do some of the examples deal with other topics?
3. If necessary, suggest a topic sentence that would help the writer focus on a topic more clearly and narrowly.
4. How should the writer organize the examples?
5. What serious mechanical or other problems does the writer need to solve?

Using your analysis of your first draft, rewrite it. A revision of the student draft follows (we have underlined the new topic sentence):

<u>Several recent events in my life really put a lot of emotional strain on me.</u> Moving into an apartment has been more expensive than I had planned. Along with two roommates, I am now renting a small apartment for $350 a month. Each one of us buys his own groceries and cooks for himself. We also divide up the expenses for power and water. After I pay my share of the bills, I don't have much money left. However, I have begun to get my life back in order and set goals I want to accomplish, like buying a new truck or maybe taking a cruise. Moving out hasn't completely washed my blues away, but it has helped me to start my own life.

Section Seven: Final Editing

Once you have finished, clean up the grammatical problems, errors, punctuation, and misspellings. The following questions should be helpful in the final stage of your writing process:

1. Have I corrected the kinds of grammatical errors I often make? (Look back over earlier papers you have written; then check this one for mistakes like subject–verb agreement, misplaced modifiers and the like.)
2. Have I corrected the kinds of punctuation errors I tend to make?
3. Have I corrected the kinds of words I usually misspell?

Section Eight: Further Topics

1. When being forced to speak before a group, I experience a number of feelings, such as . . . .
2. The best ways to please my (spouse, children, parents, or whoever) are . . . .
3. The most (peculiar, interesting, exciting) date I ever had was . . . .
4. The task I most (like, dislike) at work is . . . .
5. The most fun I ever had with a (friend, group) was . . . .

Describing a
Place or Person

Writers use description to present an impression of a person, place, or thing in living, specific detail. Your own writing should appeal to several of the senses. Bring in action, sound, color, touch, smell, textures, and feelings wherever they fit. Physical, sensuous detail adds interest and vividness to descriptive writing. Writers use it to enhance the description of people, places, or things.

Here is an example of a *character* drawn by F. Scott Fitzgerald. We have underlined especially appealing *visual* details:

At eighteen, . . . Anson was tall and thick-set, with a clear complexion and a healthy color. . . . His hair was yellow and grew in a funny way on his head; his nose was beaked—these two things kept him from being handsome.

"The Rich Boy"

- Fitzgerald emphasizes details that the reader can see.
- These details first stress the size and shape of Anson's body, his complexion, and then his hair and nose.

Joyce Carol Oates describes a *place*:

It's the "Lakeside Bar." That big old building with the grubby siding, and the cinder driveway that's so bumpy. . . . There is a custard stand nearby with a glaring orange roof.

"Four Summers"

- Oates's description stresses feelings and impressions: the building's age and grubbiness, with a bumpy cinder driveway.
- Her last detail—the "glaring orange roof" is strikingly visual. It hurts her eyes.

Kay Boyle describes *objects*:

From his lounging chair he could . . . finger the parched stems of the geraniums. The south, and the Mediterranean wind, had blistered them past all belief. They bore their rosy top-knots or their soiled white flowers balanced upon their thick Italian heads.

"Rest Cure"

68

- Boyle's flowers resemble people irritated by thirst ("parched") and scorched by the sun ("blistered").
- She compares the flowers to "thick Italian heads."

In the paragraph below, James Baldwin describes both a room and his feelings about it. In the process, he gives it personality:

The room I lived in was heavy ceilinged, perfectly square, with walls the color of chipped dry blood. Perhaps because the room was so hideous it had a fantastic array of light fixtures: one on the ceiling, one on the left wall, two on the right wall, and a lamp on the table beside my bed. My bed was in front of the window through which nothing ever blew but dust. It was a furnished room and they'd thrown enough stuff in it to furnish three rooms its size. Two easy chairs and a desk, the bed, the table, a straight-backed chair, a bookcase, a cardboard wardrobe; and my books and my suitcase, both unpacked; and my dirty clothes flung in a corner. It was the kind of room that defeated you. It had a fireplace, too, and a heavy marble mantelpiece and a great gray mirror above the mantelpiece. It was hard to see anything in the mirror very clearly—which was perhaps just as well—and it would have been worth your life to have started a fire in the fireplace.

"Previous Condition"

1. What is Baldwin describing?

   He is describing the room he lives in, along with its furnishings and his belongings.

2. What words would best describe Baldwin's *feelings* about this room?

   It is run-down, ornate, crowded, messy, and depressing.

3. We have listed a few of Baldwin's sentences below. Label each detail according to the sense it appeals to, whether *sight, touch, hearing, smell,* or *feeling.* We have done one of them for you.

                   touch   sight   sight
   a. The room I lived in was heavy ceilinged, perfectly square, with walls
          sight   touch touch sight
   the color of chipped dry blood.

                               feeling   feeling   sight
   b. Perhaps because the room was so hideous it had a fantastic array of
      sight   sight   sight   sight
   light fixtures: one on the ceiling, one on the left wall, two on the right
               sight
   wall, and a lamp on the table beside my bed.

      sight   sight   touch
   c. My bed was in front of the window through which nothing ever blew
      touch
   but dust.

            sight   touch sight   sight   sight
   d. It had a fireplace, too, and a heavy marble mantelpiece and a great
     sight sight   sight   sight
   gray mirror above the mantelpiece. It was hard to see anything in the
     sight
   mirror very clearly. . . .

69

4. What terms does Baldwin use—transitions and prepositional phrases—to guide our eyes around the room?

on the ceiling, . . . on the left wall, . . . on the right wall, . . . on the
table, beside my bed, in front of, through which, in it, in a corner, above
the mantelpiece, in the mirror, in the fireplace

5. How does Baldwin organize his paragraph? That is, how does he move around in *space*?

_____ Front to back

_____ Outside to inside

___*___ Outer to inner to outer

Baldwin moves from outer parts of the room—walls and light fixtures—to
inner aspects—the bed and furniture—and then to outer parts again: the
mirror and fireplace.

Section One: Choosing a Topic

To begin your descriptive paper, invent a topic or choose one of these:

- A person who has impressed you: a friend, relative, co-worker, athlete, entertainer, or teacher
- A pet, an animal in a zoo or movie, an unusual tree or flower or insect
- Someone who is "a free spirit," who is afraid of something, or who has a closed mind

Section Two: Generating Ideas

Before beginning to write your descriptive paragraph, take a few moments to generate some ideas. This is called *prewriting*. One of the simplest yet most effective ways to put down thoughts is to cluster. Get started by putting your topic in the center of a blank sheet of paper. Then think of ideas that your topic suggests. Add them around your central topic. Circle the new details or examples, and connect them with lines or arrows. After finishing your cluster, write a trial topic sentence.

Here is an example of a cluster a student drew to describe a visit to an old plantation house:

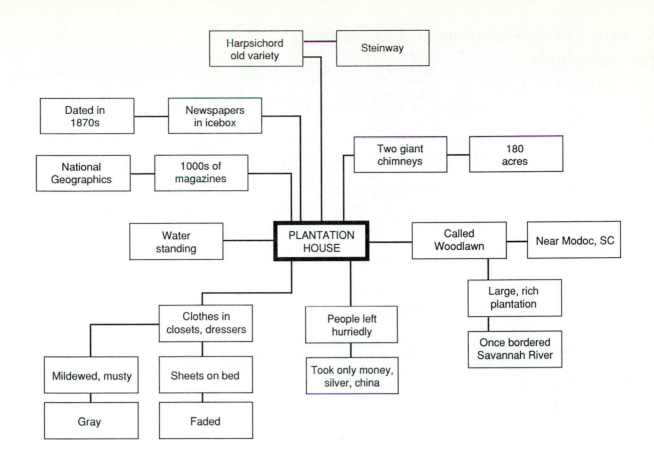

Trial Topic Sentence: A visit to an old, deserted house on a plantation called Woodlawn gave me an eerie feeling.

Many writers use another prewriting device, making a brief, informal *outline* before writing a draft. You may find a simple grouping of words or phrases most helpful. The student who visited the deserted plantation could have made the following short outline:

History and location of plantation
    Date constructed
    Size
    Location
House (neglected)
    Furnishings
    Newspapers
    Mantle pieces
Barn
    Cotton gin
    Crates—labels
    Sled—more newspapers

WRITING A TOPIC SENTENCE

When you have completed your prewriting, write a topic sentence for your own paragraph. In it, you should

- Include your topic;
- State your opinion or purpose about your topic; and
- Word it as a complete sentence.

In addition, it should not be either too general or too limited.

> *One possibility:* I like to look around the rural South Carolina countryside.

This attempt is quite general and vague. The writer hasn't told the reader what to expect in the rest of the paragraph or how he will order it. He needs a clearer sense of direction.

> *Another possibility:* In 1981 I visited an old plantation home near Modoc, South Carolina.

This is too specific and limited to serve as a topic sentence. The writer hasn't indicated the impression his subject made on him. However, he may want to fit these facts into the paper later.

> *A better possibility:* In the spring of 1981, my visit to a decaying old plantation home near Modoc, South Carolina, gave me an eerie feeling.

This is much improved. Joe has not simply given us a fact. He has stated an *opinion* or *attitude* toward his subject. To develop this idea, he will need supporting information. These details should emphasize his general impressions of *decay* and *eeriness*.

ORGANIZING THE PARAGRAPH

Here are some guidelines to help you organize your descriptive paper. To describe a **place:**

Imagine how it looks from above. Then move

- toward
- into and/or
- through the place

from

- outside to inside
- general to specific

- most important to least important, or
- least important to most important.

You may move from one side to the other or circle the area, as in the diagram below:

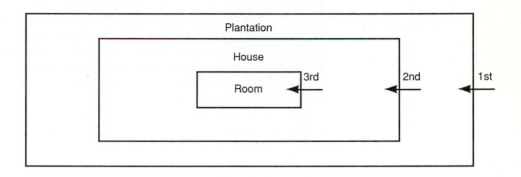

To describe a **person,** begin at the head and work down, or begin at the feet and work up:

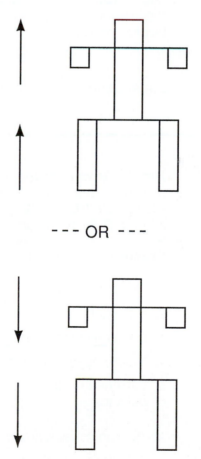

Your movement in space reflects the importance of the details you plan to list—most to least, or least to most.

The sentences in the following descriptive paragraph have been placed out of order. Read it over; then place the sentences in order.

(1) Among other things, it is the meeting place of migratory birds coming from north and south. **(2)** Big Sur has a climate of its own and a character all its own. **(3)** It is also the home of the redwoods; one encounters them on entering from north and one leaves them on passing southward. **(4)** It is a region where extremes meet, a region where one is always conscious of weather, of space, of grandeur, and of eloquent silence. **(5)** The grizzly bear is no longer to be found here, but the rattlesnake is still to be reckoned with. **(6)** It is said, in fact, that there is a greater variety of birds to be found in this region than in any other part of the United States. **(7)** From November to February are the best months, the air fresh and invigorating, the skies clear, the sun still warm enough to take a sun bath. **(8)** In summer, when the fogs roll in, one can look down upon a sea of clouds floating listlessly above the ocean; they have the appearance, at times, of huge iridescent soap bubbles, over which, now and then, may be seen a double rainbow. **(9)** At night one can still hear the coyote howling, and if one ventures beyond the first ridge of mountains one can meet up with mountain lions and other beasts of the wild. **(10)** On a clear, bright day, when the blue of the sea rivals the blue of the sky, one sees the hawk, the eagle, the buzzard soaring above the still, hushed canyons.

Henry Miller, "Big Sur"

Sentence numbers in order: <u>2, 4, 1, 6, 3, 9, 5, 10, 8, 9</u>

The details you use to support your main ideas should all be relevant. They should all contribute to the impression you introduce at the beginning. For each of the topic sentences below, one of the details does not fit. Check the letter in front of the one that does not fit.

EXAMPLE: This stocky man was going hurriedly towards the subway.

1. passable-looking
2. with short black hair and small eyes
✓ 3. <u>research chemists are sometimes absent-minded</u>
4. a high, open forehead
5. buttoned up to the chin in a Burberry coat and walking with feet turned outward

A. The room was sparsely furnished.

1. lit by a dim globe
2. cot, a folding chair, a small table, old unpainted chests
3. no closets
4. a small sink with a rough piece of green, institutional soap on its holder
✓ 5. <u>You could smell the soap across the room</u>

B. She was a big woman, with a rough appearance and dress.

    1. a weatherbeaten but unwrinkled face

✓ 2. <u>her kitchen was primitive</u>

    3. her lips were held tightly together

    4. her eyes looked out with a curious dulled brightness

    5. She wore a formless garment of some gray coarse material, rough-dried from washing.

C. I had settled in to observe the beaverworks.

    1. a huge conical lodge made of branches and plastered mud

    2. a 150-foot dam that created a pond of about four acres

✓ 3. <u>the fresh breeze blew briskly</u>

    4. The pond was blanketed with fragrant waterlilies and yellow bullheads in matted profusion.

    5. Narrow bands of open water were laid out in a pattern through the carpet of lilies.

D. Cooper, a tall, thin fellow, seemed to be about thirty.

    1. a sallow face all of one tone, without a spot of color

✓ 2. <u>Warburton disliked him from the first.</u>

    3. He had a large, hooked nose and blue eyes.

    4. His large skull was covered with short brown hair.

    5. He had a weak, small chin.

E. A small boy is being read to on a winter's night in 1936 in Halifax, Nova Scotia.

    1. He is warm from a hot bath.

    2. He wears striped, flannel pajamas and a thick woolen dressing gown with a tasseled cord.

    3. He has dropped off his slippers to slide his bare feet between the cushions of the sofa.

    4. Outside, a salty wind blows snow against the panes of the windows.

✓ 5. <u>Books were rare and expensive then.</u>

F. Terry Becker is hardly your garden-variety environmentalist.

✓ 1. <u>Americans have become concerned with the environment.</u>

    2. He is a man of salty conversational style.

    3. He is 35 years old, six feet tall, weighing 250 pounds.

    4. He has a wind-lashed complexion.

    5. A reddish-gray beard sprouts from his chin like an untamed whisk broom.

G. Jonathan Gurr, who is dyslexic, spent his first eight grades in an Alexandria, Virginia private school.

    1. "I was a basket case," he remembers.

    2. "The teachers seemed to think that if they yelled at me, I would learn something."

✓ 3. <u>Dyslexia is not a disease.</u>

    4. "I was put in classes with the troublemakers who weren't learning anything."

    5. "But my mother kept telling me I was smart; she gave me confidence."

H. Everything you needed to know about Art Rooney was in his face.
   1. It was disarmingly out of kilter.
   √ 2. He owned the famous Pittsburgh Steelers.
   3. The eyes were warm.
   4. The mouth loved to wrestle all at once with a smile and his ever-present cigar.
   5. He regarded each new acquaintance, whether governor or garbage man, with the "expression of a little boy who has just been handed a puppy."

EXERCISE 5.3

Answers will vary.

A number of topics for descriptive paragraphs have been listed below. Write in at least five details for each one. Whenever possible, include language that reflects action, sound, color, touch, smell, textures, and feelings. Make sure that each detail fits the topic.

A. The large house was beautifully furnished and kept up.
   1. The living room was spacious.
   2. To the left as one entered was a long table.
   3. The largest part of the living room centered around a fireplace.
   4. On the right were some bookshelves and a piano.
   5. The roses on the piano were reflected in the polish of the broad top.
   The details reflect the words "furnished" and "kept up."

B. The farmer was a big man, with a weatherbeaten face and worn clothes.
   1. his belt slung low about his hips
   2. looked at least thirty
   3. had a hot, red face
   4. wore muddy blue pants
   5. had on an old military coat which was stained and patched
   The details reflect the words "weatherbeaten face" and "worn clothes."

C. Jane Doe is an average American woman.
   1. better educated than ever before
   2. going to live longer
   3. shorter (five feet four), heavier (144 pounds), and older (33) than most people on TV
   4. has seven or eight credit cards
   5. spends from two fifths to one half of her income on food and shelter
   The details reflect the words "average," "American," and "woman."

D. _____ , the famous (movie, television, entertainment) star, is easily recognizable.
1. is a skinny, gawky man
2. wears a t-shirt under an unbuttoned vest and a beat-up hat
3. bounces around with zest
4. utters strange sounds like "va-va-va-voom"
5. forever drives his co-star into a rage

The details reflect the words "famous" and "easily recognizable."

E. My friend's dog is lovable despite its origins.
1. owner ordered a pup from an Alaskan breeder
2. had expected a huskily built, game-hunting line of Airedale
3. got a pathetically scrawny creature
4. dog was all legs and feet
5. the pup was ugly but all affection

The details reflect the words "lovable" and "origins."

EXERCISE 5.4   *Choose the paragraph you handled best in the previous exercise. Write a topic sentence that reflect the details you have written. Then place the details in order, explaining why you chose this sequence.*

Section Four: Using Transitional Devices

As you describe a scene or character, you will arrange your details in order: inside to outside, top to bottom, large to small, or some other spatial sequence. You may also choose to list specific examples by importance—lesser to greater, for instance. To help your reader follow your description, use transitional words or phrases:

> over, under, around, between, to the left, in front, in back, at the top, next to, across from, nearby, on the opposite side

(Check "Section Four: Using Transitional Devices" in Chapter 2, if needed.)

Section Five: Writing the First Draft

Choose a topic from the list in Section One of this chapter, or from Section Eight, at the end. Generate a list of details that appeal to the senses, and place them in order. Cross out details that don't fit. Using your topic sentence and the examples you have ordered, write a first draft. Here is an example of

a draft written by a student using the topic sentence: *In my grandparents'
yard stands a unique, historical, white church that is still in use today.*

A Unique White Church

<u>In my grandparent's yard stands a unique, historical, white church that is still
in use today.</u> This church is very special to me because my great-grandfather
used to preach in this church. Right beside their barn sits this old white church
that were build during the year of 1850. The church sits on about two thirds
of an acre. the entire front yard is mostly gravel rocks, for parking. A few big
oak trees are standing throughout the front. Directly behind the church there
are seven graves. The graves are so old that they have begun to sink in. They
have markers there dating back to 1750. This proves there was possibly another
church here before this one was built. Anyway, looking at the church, you can
see the discolored white paint beginning to chip. The roof is missing several
shingles. In front stands a set of thick, white doors. As you enter the church,
the old, musky smell of cedar fills your nose, like a furniture store. Everything,
including the walls, floors, seats and platform was made of cedar. The well-
preserved wood has a beautiful, glossy shine. Ten rows of seats fill the church,
five on each side of the isle. The eight narrow windows catch your attention.
However, you can barely see out of them, because of it's thick, gloomy glass.
A peaceful feeling overcomes you that is hard to describe. You can hear the
echo as you speak; the slightest pin drop sounds like a microphone had amplified it. I can feel my great-grandfathers' presence. Today, this unique church
is still in use every Sunday, with a population of twenty-five people including
my grandparents. Sometimes, they occasionally dress in their long pioneer
dresses and fancy hats with flowers stuck in the top of them. Thus church is
queit a view.

Section Six: Revising the Paragraph

Apply the questions in the checklist below to your own writing, or have a
friend or classmate do it. We have applied them to the student draft.

1. *Which examples used in the paragraph are most specific and
interesting? How do they appeal to the senses?*

The writer uses specific examples that appeal to the various senses.
She appeals to our sense of *sight* with her examples of chipped paint, missing
shingles, the thick, white front doors, the shiny wood walls and seats, the
thick glass windows, the costumes of present-day worshipers. She appeals
to *smell* with the musty odor of cedar, to *texture* with the gravel in the front
yard, to *sound* with the echo of voices.

2. *Has the paper focused on the topic sentence, or do some of the
examples deal with other topics?*

Most of the paragraph deals with the appearance of the church and
its grounds. Other details relate to the uses of the church by present-day
worshipers, which, while interesting, probably belong in another paragraph.
Still another paragraph could be devoted to the graveyard in back of the
church.

3. *If necessary, suggest a topic sentence that would help the writer focus on a topic more clearly and narrowly. For example:*

"In my grandparents' yard stands a unique, historical, white church." While more limited, this sentence is still difficult to read because the writer piles up adjectives: *unique, historical, white.* She could simplify it by adding a prepositional phrase:

In my grandparents' yard stands a white church with unique historical significance.

4. *How should the writer organize the examples?*

Her paragraph begins outside the front of the church, moving from the roof at the top to the doors at eye level. Rather than moving directly inside the church through these doors, she takes up details of the graveyard (which she should consider leaving out of this paragraph). Finally, her conclusion is rather vague and weak.

5. *What serious mechanical or other problems does the writer need to solve?*

Her third sentence includes a noun—verb agreement problem:

"Right beside their barn sits this old white church, that *were built* during the year of 1850." She may have meant the plural helping verb "were" to refer to the barn *and* church. However, the reader cannot tell.

She also has problems with both pronoun reference and possession in the sentence discussing the church windows: "However, you can barely see out of them, because of *it's* thick, gloomy glass.

She means the "glass" to refer to the plural "windows"—not one window's glass. She should have used *their* instead of the singular contraction *it's.* Many writers have trouble remembering that *it's* with an apostrophe is a contraction of *it is.* The possessive *its* has no apostrophe. It takes possession with -s like *his, hers,* and *theirs.*

She also misspells the words *isle* (aisle) and *queit* (quiet).

Apply the questions in the revision checklist below to your own writing, or have a friend or classmate do it.

Revision Checklist

1. Which examples used in the paragraph are most specific and interesting?
2. Has the paper focused on the topic sentence, or do some of the examples deal with other topics?
3. Suggest a topic sentence that would help the writer focus on a topic more clearly and narrowly.
4. How should the writer organize the examples?
5. What serious mechanical or other problems does the writer need to solve?

Using your analysis of your first draft, rewrite it. A revision of the student draft follows (we have underlined the new topic sentence):

A Unique Church

In my grandparents' yard stands a white church with unique historical significance. This church is very special to me because my great-grandfather used to preach in this church. Right beside their barn sits this old white church that was built in 1850. The church sits on about two-thirds of an acre. The entire front yard is mostly gravel for parking. A few big oak trees stand in front. The roof is missing several shingles. On its front, the discolored white paint is beginning to chip. As you enter the thick, white doors, the old musky smell of cedar fills your nose, like a furniture store. Everything was made of cedar, including the walls, seats and platform. The well-preserved wood has a beautiful, glossy shine. Ten rows of seats fill the church, five on each side of the aisle. the eight narrow windows catch your attention. However, you can barely see out of them because of their thick, gloomy glass. You can hear the echo as you speak. The slightest pin drop sounds like a microphone had amplified it. As I sense my great-grandfather's presence, a peaceful feeling overcomes me.

Section Seven: Final Editing

Once you have finished, clean up the grammatical problems, punctuation errors, and misspellings. The following questions should be helpful in the final stage of your writing process:

1. Have I corrected the grammatical errors I often make? (Look back over earlier papers you have written. Then check this one for mistakes like subject—verb agreement and misplaced modifiers.)
2. Have I corrected the punctuation errors I tend to make?
3. Have I corrected the words I usually misspell?

Section Eight: Further Topics

- A ghost town, a church, a public square in America or another country
- A store or mall, a museum or library
- A treasured object or collection
- Your favorite clothing
- A painting or statue
- A remarkably handsome or ugly face
- Someone you envy enough to trade lives with
- The one item you would most want to save from a destructive fire
- The person you would most value as a dinner guest

CHAPTER

6

Long ago in a galaxy far away . . .

Narrating an Incident

A narrative presents an action or happening, usually one involving people. It goes on in a particular time and place. Audiences read narratives partly for their action. They experience a parade of incidents that follow one another closely. Each is often *caused* by those which came before. Knowing what is happening helps readers visualize the action clearly.

The reader also wants to know the writer's *feelings* about the action—whether the writer feels happy, embarrassed, or sad. We like to find out how the actors' emotions change as the action moves along in time.

A narrative also should appeal to our senses—of vision, hearing, touch, smell, even taste. In this way, we can identify with the people in the narrative. We can put them in their place. We also like knowing how people look, how they speak. A few words of dialogue—whether spoken or thought—make them come to life on the page.

Read over the following example:

He pulled into a little dead Martian town, stopped the engine, and let the silence come in around him. He sat, not breathing, looking out at the white buildings in the moonlight. Uninhabited for centuries. Perfect, faultless, in ruins, yes, but perfect, nevertheless.

He started the engine and drove on another mile or more before stopping again, climbing out, carrying his lunch bucket, and walking to a little promontory where he could look back at that dusty city. He opened his thermos and poured himself a cup of coffee. A night bird flew by. He felt very good, very much at peace.

Perhaps five minutes later there was a sound. Off in the hills, where the ancient highway curved, there was a motion, a dim light, and then a murmur.

Tomas turned slowly with the coffee cup in his hand.

And out of the hills came a strange thing.

It was a machine like a jade-green insect, a praying mantis, delicately rushing through the cold air, indistinct, countless green diamonds winking over its body, and red jewels that glittered with multi-faceted eyes. Its six legs fell upon the ancient highway with the sounds of a sparse rain which dwindled away, and from the back of the machine a Martian with melted gold for eyes looked down at Tomas as if he were looking into a well.

Ray Bradbury, "August 2002: Night Meeting"

EXERCISE 6.1   *Answer the following questions about the Bradbury selection.*

1. Sum up the main idea of this selection in a sentence:
   Just after Tomas drove into a dead Martian town, a Martian riding an insect-like vehicle came out of the hills and joined him.

2. Where and when does this incident take place? How much time passes?
   This incident takes place somewhere on Mars, as indicated by the twice-repeated adjective "Martian,"; at night, indicated by "in the moonlight" and "a night bird flew by." No indication of year, month, or day appears, except in the piece's title. Perhaps fifteen minutes elapse. We are told midway in the selection that five minutes pass while Tomas sits looking at the city and drinking coffee.

3. How does the central character feel about the action? Find words that emphasize his feelings:
   At first bored, the central character—Tomas—is startled by a strange, un-canny occurrence, the appearance of an original inhabitant of the town. Tomas appreciates the beauty of the Martian town, which he twice terms "perfect." He likes solitude—being alone in a vacant landscape.

4. What action verbs does Bradbury use?
   He describes his characters' actions with verbs like "pulled into," "stopped," "let," "sat," "started," "drove," "stopping again," "climbing out," "walk-ing," "opened," and "poured." "Perhaps five minutes later" is his only explicit reference to time. When the Martian appears, Bradbury uses terms like "there was a *motion,* a dim light, and *then a murmur.*" We are told the legs of the machine "fell upon" the ancient highway.

5. How does Bradbury appeal to the senses?
   Vision: the *white* buildings in the *moonlight,* looking back at the city, a *dim light,* the *jade-green* Martian machine, *indistinct,* countless *green diamonds winking* over its body, and *red* jewels that *glittered with multi-faceted eyes, melted gold* for eyes, *looking* down at Tomas as if he were *looking into a well*

   Sound: the *silence* coming in around him, a *sound* and then a *mur-mur,* the sounds of a sparse rain which dwindled away.

   Taste: Bradbury mentions the lunch bucket and the coffee several times. The term "dusty"—applied to the city—may appeal to taste, smell, and touch.

Feeling: <u>The Martian machine rushes through the *cold air* with a sound like a *sparse rain* (appealing to two senses, hearing and feeling).</u>

Smell: <u>Perhaps the references to coffee and to rain may appeal to this sense.</u>

6. How does Bradbury describe the Martian's appearance, especially his face? <u>The Martian is described with similes of jewels—jade, diamonds and rubies—insects, rain, and a precious metal—gold—applied mostly to his vehicle. The intensity of his stare is described as though looking into a well.</u>

Section One: Choosing a Topic

As in the Bradbury selection, few narratives can be developed adequately in a single paragraph. However, many of the paragraphs in your narrative are likely to be quite brief. Some of them will be only a sentence or two. To select a topic for a narrative, choose a personal experience. Think of an incident that occurred during a brief period of time—perhaps only five or ten minutes—with no interruptions. Avoid difficult devices such as flashbacks. Invent a topic for your narrative, or complete one of these:

- When I was (caught in a storm or had an auto accident), I . . . .
- During a (trip or visit), I met _____ , who made a great impact on my life.

Section Two: Generating Ideas

Before writing this narrative, generate some ideas. Brainstorming works well with the narrative. One writer chose to handle her experience of a storm. Her list of details may have looked like this:

Topic:	A summer thunderstorm made me nervous
Overview:	Thunderstorm, afternoon, my house, nervous feelings
Outside, before:	Lightning, thunder, clouds, wind
Beginning of storm:	rain poured, power lines swayed
Inside house:	lights flickered, radio static, fear increased
Afterward:	feelings of relief, sun came out

Each one of these details grows out of her chosen topic and supports it.

Section Three: Planning and Organizing the Paragraph

STATING THE MAIN IDEA

Narratives seldom, if ever, include topic sentences. However, stating the main idea of your narrative will help you organize it even though you may not include it as a formal topic sentence. The writer who generated ideas about a summer thunderstorm stated her main idea like this:

> As a summer thunderstorm approached my home that afternoon, I became very nervous.

What is the topic of this narrative?
The writer will narrate her reactions to a summer thunderstorm as it reaches her home.

What are the writer's feelings about the storm?
She is nervous and frightened.

What are the time and place of the incident?
It occurs in the summertime at her home.

USING TIME TO ORGANIZE THE NARRATIVE

Narratives are usually organized according to *time* order. One incident follows another.

EXERCISE 6.2

Read over the jumbled paragraph below. Decide how the sentences should follow one another in time, and write the numbers in the correct order.

(1) He had been traveling for some seven hours, he believed. **(2)** He walked on steadily, avoiding the light snow wherever possible, keeping to the cover of trees when he could. **(3)** In another hour he should be close to his prepared hideout. **(4)** When the first feeble rays of sunlight showed themselves, he was well on his way. **(5)** However, he doubted that at any time he had done as much as three miles in an hour. **(6)** The mutter of the distant helicopter had been prodding at him for several minutes before it came to his attention. **(7)** The walking was precarious and he had tried to move on rocky, snow-free surfaces when possible. **(8)** He beat his hands together and tried rubbing his legs to keep the blood alive. **(9)** Quickly, he eased back into the trees, merging carefully with a tree trunk. **(10)** The cold was intense. **(11)** He waited, listening. **(12)** When it came within view, it was flying very low, and it just barely cleared the nearest ridge. **(13)** Meanwhile, the sound of the motor came closer and closer. **(14)** Such a copter would probably carry three men. **(15)** At this distance and in the still cold he could hear it for some time before he saw it. **(16)** It came in, flying no more than a hundred to a hundred and fifty feet off the ground, following the same stream he had followed. **(17)** It muttered on by, heading up for the ridge he must cross to get to his hidden camp. **(18)** It came on, and when it passed he could see the faces of the men inside, although he could make out no features. **(19)** His camp was at most five miles off and a good place to hide. **(20)** He would need three arrows for three fast shots, and then he must try to get away.

Louis L'Amour, Last of the Breed

Sentence numbers in order: <u>2, 4, 1, 5, 7, 3, 6, 9, 11, 10, 8, 13, 15, 12, 14, 16, 18, 17, 20, 19</u>

EXERCISE 6.3

All of the details in a narrative should support the main idea. In each of the following lists put together by brainstorming, one detail does not fit the topic. Find the detail that is out of place and underline it.

A. Disney's Magic Kingdom affected a small part of nature.
1. Planners turned island into bird sanctuary.
2. Planted island with bamboo and palms, plants from India and China.
3. Populated island with robot birds, with a few real ones thrown in.
4. <u>Condominiums and steak houses put up near cow pastures.</u>
5. Living birds attracted hundreds of others.

Does not make a direct impact on nature.

B. Bob Wiley attaches himself to his new shrink, Leo Marvin.
1. Bob arrives uninvited at psychiatrist's summer house.
2. He finds family not functioning well.
3. <u>Wisconsin located in Midwest.</u>
4. The "Good Morning America" visit is disaster.
5. Leo tries to kill Bob.

Location irrelevant to Bob's attachment.

C. As a child, I did everything I could to delay scary bedtime.
1. Afraid spies from Russia lurking outside window.
2. <u>Toys 'R' Us is place family usually shops.</u>
3. Shiver at thought Dracula lurking under bed.
4. Piled stuffed animals on bed near place I would be sleeping.
5. Tried to turn off light, leap into bed before room dark.

Linked to childhood but not to "scary bedtime."

D. Delivery of child was first time I was hospitalized.
1. First day, just wanted to sleep, get over trauma.
2. <u>Hospital located on east side of city.</u>
3. Second day not fun, watching soap operas, but boring.
4. Asked parents to bring real food, fried chicken, macaroni & cheese.
5. Hated the frequency of nurses checking on me.

Location irrelevant to writer's feelings about hospitalization.

EXERCISE 6.4

Answers will vary.

We have listed several ideas for narratives. List several incidents which would support each idea in chronological order. Appeal to the senses, leaving out details that don't support the main idea.

A. My (name of relative, acquaintance) showed his/her temper when he/she
  1. slammed lunchbox on table
  2. yelled for a cold beer
  3. kicked a chair across room
  4. began throwing plates against wall
  5. threw silverware to floor

B. My (relative, friend) helped me out when he/she
  1. rented me a car and lent me some money
  2. gave me a sympathetic cheering up
  3. referred me to a friend for a lead on a job
  4. donated a suitcase full of clothes of right size
  5. packed me a snack

C. An unfair moment occurred when
  1. boss found me reading in back room
  2. late at night, no customers in shop
  3. had cleaned up and straightened out store
  4. began criticizing me for laziness
  5. fired me on the spot

D. I most appreciated working with my (relative, friend) when
  1. big set of orders came in late, just before holiday
  2. friend, relative decided to stay on job with me
  3. one of us packed boxes while other one answered phone
  4. didn't finish until 3:00 in the morning
  5. managed to set record for one day's production

Section Four: Using Transitional Devices

Writers use transitions to help us follow a narrative's movement through time. Such terms provide the readers with signposts to indicate *how* and *when* particular actions take place.

Transitions to Show Continuity

then, next, furthermore, moreover,
at that moment, in addition, above all,
finally, because, while, suddenly, consequently

Transitions to Show Contrast

but, still, yet, however,
by contrast, nevertheless

EXERCISE 6.5

In the following selection, fill the blanks with transitions from the lists above:

I recently saw a traffic accident when a 1984 Mustang went off the road and into nearby trees. It had just stopped raining; _____consequently_____ , the roads were wet. _____When_____ the car came down Dorchester road at over 50 m.p.h., a dog wandered out onto the road. _____At that moment_____ , the driver slammed on his brakes, losing control of his car. He _____consequently_____ slid wildly into the trees ahead. The car hit a tree head on and _____then_____ rolled over against another tree, _____finally_____ trapping him in the car.

EXERCISE 6.6

Answer the following questions about the narrative in the previous exercise:

1. What overall impression does the writer give of this incident?
    He seems to feel that it is sudden, frightening, and yet somehow predictable.

2. What details does the writer include to support the overall impression?
    wet roads, recent rain, car going 50 m.p.h., wandering dog, slamming on brakes, sliding wildly, hitting tree, rolling, trapped driver

3. How much time goes by in this narrative?
    Perhaps no more than thirty or forty seconds

Section Five: Writing the First Draft

Get started on your narrative by choosing one of the topics in Section One of this chapter, or by inventing your own. Fill in the blanks below:

Main idea: _____

Your feelings about it: _____

_____

A tentative title: _____

A list of important incidents in order:

_____

_____

_____

_____

Rodney handled his narrative this way:

> *Main idea:* While I was relaxing in the sand near Miami Beach, all of a sudden a plane flew over me, in distress.
>
> *His feelings about it:* I was surprised, shocked, and inspired to take action.
>
> *A list of important incidents in order:*
>
>   plane getting lower and lower
>
>   flames shooting out of engine
>
>   plane crashed in sea 60 feet from shore
>
>   as plane sunk, companions and I rescued people
>
>   waiting boat took us back to shore

Here is the narrative Rodney based on this list:

As I relaxed under a hot sun on the warm, brown sand near Miami Beach, a plane suddenly flew over me, in distress. The privately-owned plane called "Amie" began descending rapidly. It was like a wounded bird about ten feet in the air. It was gliding as the demon, red flames danced from its fuel compartment. The beach got totally quiet. They watched the plane come down. It got eight feet, five feet, three feet, one foot. Suddenly "bang," it collapsed. Two men and I dashed into the ocean and swam to the plane. It crashed about sixty feet from the shore. Two men and a woman was unconscious inside. We swam to the front of the plane. We tore off the door, causing it to sink. A big mistake! We dashed under water, into the plane and grabbed the victims. When we reached the surface, a man and a woman waited patiently in their boat. They were going to take us back to shore. An ambulance was waiting to take the victims to the hospital. My vacation ended two days later, but it was everything my travel agent said it would be. It was rewarding, adventurous, and exciting.

Section Six: Revising the Paragraph

After you have written your narrative, apply the questions in the checklist below to help you revise. We supply answers that refer to Rodney's narrative above.

1. *Do the first two or three sentences make clear how the writer will proceed in the paper? If so, has the writer followed this plan? If not, how should the writer change the organization of his or her narrative?*

Rodney alerts us to his main idea—a plane crash—in his first few sentences. After telling us what happened, he describes his reactions. He and others help rescue the passengers.

His actions follow one another in time, like this:

- Sitting on a beach
- Seeing a plane in trouble
- Seeing the plane crash
- Rushing out to the plane
- Pulling out the passengers
- Getting the victims to shore
- Summing up his feelings

A few details may be missing. He might tell how the people on the beach reacted as they watched the plane fall. Later, he could move the location where the plane crashed to an earlier sentence.

2. *Where should the writer add or substitute more sensory examples, reasons, or details?*

Rodney could add details regarding the plane's shape, sound, color, and direction of flight. He could also describe the sounds and sight of the plane's crash, details about rescuing the passengers, and the appearance of the waiting boat and its owners. He also might tell how his helpers looked and what they did and said. He might explain his reasons for helping rescue the victims.

3. *What devices like connectives, synonyms, and pronouns has the writer used to tie his or her ideas together? What additional devices should the writer use?*

Rodney links his ideas with a few connectives like *as, when,* and *but.* However, he should consider more terms like *at that moment, then, just afterwards, next, finally,* or *to sum up.* He could replace the word "plane" with words such as *craft* or *Amie.* And he could substitute other words for his companions, such as *fellow helpers* or *rescuers.*

4. *Does the narrative reach an effective, satisfying close?*

Rodney brings his narrative to a satisfying close. However, he could make it crisper by combining his last two sentences and substituting a more vivid verb:

My vacation ended two days later, having been everything my travel agent promised: rewarding, adventurous, and exciting.

5. *What serious mechanical and other problems should the writer solve while rewriting the first draft?*

In "They watched the plane come down," Rodney doesn't indicate who *they* refers to. He can solve this problem by telling us that "The bathers got totally silent," or giving the word *they* a clear antecedent.

His singular verb doesn't agree with his plural subject in "Two men and a woman *was* unconscious inside." He should replace *was* with *were*.

Apply the questions in the revision checklist below to your own writing, or have a friend or classmate do it.

Revision Checklist

1. Do the first two or three sentences make clear how the writer will proceed in the paper? If so, has the writer followed this plan? If not, how should the writer change the organization?

2. Where should the writer add or substitute more sensory examples, reasons, or details?

3. What devices like connectives, synonyms, and pronouns has the writer used to tie his or her ideas together? What additional devices should the writer use?

4. Does the narrative reach an effective, satisfying close?

5. What serious mechanical or other problems should the writer solve while rewriting the first draft?

Using the results of this analysis, rewrite your first draft.

Section Seven: Final Editing

Once you have finished, clean up the grammatical problems, punctuation errors, and misspellings. The following questions should be helpful in the final stage of your writing process:

1. Have I corrected the grammatical errors I often make? (Look back over earlier papers you have written. Then check this one for mistakes like subject–verb agreement and misplaced modifiers.)

2. Have I corrected the punctuation errors I tend to make?

3. Have I corrected the words I usually misspell?

Section Eight: Further Topics

1. An unforgettable vacation I once took
2. A request for money that I had difficulty making (or granting)

3. The most frightening experience I ever had
4. A time when a person from another generation influenced me
5. Once when I received an unforgettable beating (physically or in a game or contest)
6. An occasion when I took a dangerous chance
7. The worst or best job I ever had
8. A moment of disaster, embarrassment, or shame
9. A turning point between childhood and adulthood
10. An occasion when I made a good or bad decision

Describing
a Process

Descriptions of a process may emphasize one of two approaches: *how to do* something, or *how something happens.* In the first approach, a writer may give someone directions on how to repair something that is broken, how to get to a location, or how to set up an apparatus. Sometimes, others may ask us how to find a new video store or cook a favorite recipe. Frequently, we need to follow directions in order to put a child's toy together or operate an automatic teller machine. By doing what the directions tell us, step by step, we can do a job without other help. Like the narrative, the process description may consist of more than one paragraph. Many of these paragraphs may be quite short, however.

In the second approach, a writer may describe how and perhaps why some process takes place: the way some animal or insect develops, the stages through which a star passes, or a chemical process. The reader is more interested in comprehending this process than in controlling or duplicating it.

Read over the following paragraph:

An oyster has an irregular shape. The valves are rough and their lips hard to find. Crooked and wrinkled, the hairline crack between the valves can't be widened with the blade of a knife; the point must enter first. Furthermore, a big Chincoteague [from the Chincoteague Islands, Virginia] doesn't fit the left hand. One must hold the animal slanting against the edge of the kitchen sink and poke around, seeking the slot by touch as much as by sight. It takes painful practice. When the knifepoint finds a purchase, push carefully and quickly before the oyster realizes what's afoot and gets a firmer grip on itself. Push in the wrong place—it's easy to mistake a growth line for the groove—and the knife takes a life of its own. It can skid and open up your hand. This delicate work requires patient agility to find the groove, push the knife in, then slit the muscle and open the critter without losing too much juice. Restaurants serve oysters on their flat shell. It's better to throw that one away and lay the delicacies on a bed of crushed ice in the roundest half-shell which holds its delicious liquor. Sprinkle each one with lemon juice—a healthy oyster will wriggle the slightest bit at this to prove it's alive—lift the dishlike shell to the lips, and drink the oyster down. It's a delicious, addicting experience.

Philip Kopper, "How to Open an Oyster," *The Wild Edge*

Answer the following questions about the paragraph you just read:

1. The paragraph lacks a topic sentence. Write one that briefly sums up the main ideas of the paragraph.
   It takes practice to open, serve, and eat a Chincoteague oyster.

2. List the steps necessary to carry out the process Kopper describes.
   One must hold the oyster carefully, find the crack between the shells, insert the knife blade, slit the muscle, open the oyster, sprinkle each oyster with lemon juice, and drink the oyster down.

3. What equipment, workspace, and materials are necessary to carry out this process?
   An oyster opener will need lots of fresh, live oysters still in the shell; a kitchen sink; an oyster knife or other type of short, pointed knife; crushed ice; and the roundest half-shell.

4. How does Kopper (a) warn you that a particularly difficult step is coming up, or (b) tell you how to solve a hazardous problem?
   He warns that because of the oyster's shape, the valves are hard to find and open; you must use the point of the knife and not the blade, hold the oyster against the edge of the sink, poke around slowly and carefully, avoid mistaking a growth line for a groove, act quickly when you find the groove, and try not to spill the liquor inside. He also suggests serving the oyster on the rounded, not the flat, shell, and drinking it down.

5. What key words does Kopper use for the oyster and its parts to tie the paragraph together? List them below.
   For the oyster and its parts, he uses other words such as *a big Chincoteague, the animal, the critter, the delicacies, it, each one, a healthy oyster, the dishlike shell.*

6. What transitional words does Kopper use to indicate that certain steps in the process are beginning or ending?
   first, furthermore, as much as, when, before

Section One: Choosing a Topic

Invent a topic or choose one of those listed below. Don't pick something too long and involved, like "Building Your Own Atom Bomb for Fun and Profit." And avoid something too brief, like "Inserting an Opener into Your Favorite Beverage Can."

- How to cook or bake your favorite dish (chili, tacos, candy, or whatever)

- How to communicate with language
- How to be more sensitive and observant
- How to start your own school
- How to choose a television program

Section Two: Generating Ideas

Once you have chosen a topic, you need to generate ideas for your process paragraph. Several approaches are useful at this stage. First, identify your purposes and audience. Then consider your materials and equipment, with their costs. List the steps involved in the process.

One student chose the topic "How to Set Up a Fish Collection." First, she guessed at her purposes and audience:

1. *What are your purposes?*

Mostly as hobby, also for entertaining children, for a conversation piece; to make living area more lively; always liked watching fish in restautants, banks, and dentists' aquariums; might link with careers in biology, teaching, or interior decorating.

2. *Who is your audience?*

People like me who like pets, but who may lack space and/or lots of money; people interested in zoology, interior decorating, art, bright colors; people who may not like the noise or mess that goes with furry pets.

To decide on equipment, materials, and costs, she brainstormed, including both questions and possible answers:

Collecting Fish

Aquarium and accessories
   what size? 20 gallon?
   heater

pump

fish net

filter

food

Scenic background

  algae plants

  colored rocks for bottom

Book of information on fish

Equipment—costs and sources?

  budget—how to afford—$75 maximum?

  garage sales

  want ads

  pet stores

Fish

  color

  varieties

  size

Section Three: Planning and Organizing the Paragraph

After prewriting, arrange your ideas in *time order*, group them, and number the groups. Cross out steps which are irrelevant, and write in steps you may have forgotten:

1. Buy equipment and materials

   - aquarium
   - top
   - filter
   - colored rocks
   - algae plants
   - scenic background
   - heater
   - fish
   - food

2. Wash and fill aquarium

   - Use mild detergent
   - Take impurities out of water

3. Install equipment

   - filter
   - aquarium top
   - pump
   - heater

4. Put in colored rocks, scenic background, algae
5. Regulate temperature
6. Put fish in aquarium
7. Feed fish
8. Clean aquarium regularly

Write a topic sentence—for example: *To collect fish, you should gather materials and equipment, install them in the aquarium, and care for your fish.*

EXERCISE 7.1

Answers may vary.

We have provided several topic sentences for process paragraphs. Suggest enough steps for each paragraph to finish describing the process. Place the steps in the proper time order.

A. The only way to judge a contractor is to get references and look at his work.
   Scour neighborhood for houses under renovation.
   Ask homeowners whether the contractor kept them informed and listened to their questions and suggestions.
   Above all, ask about the contractor's attention to detail and commitment to finishing the work.

B. It is easy to calculate percentages.
   The first step is to know what you're looking for. Take this example: only 60 of 160 club members have signed up for a meeting, and you want to know what percentage of the membership is present.
   Stating the problem in words helps: 60 is what percent of 160?
   Next, remember this simple hint: the number following "of" is the number you divide by to find the percentage.
   Thus, you divide 160 into 60 and your answer is .375, or 37.5 percent.

C. Waiting in airports is one of the most trying features of modern life, so be prepared.
   One man I know takes a word game along with him and asks strangers to play the game with him.
   Some people work on their laptop computers.
   One woman goes through a stack of catalogs methodically, turning down the corners of the pages, filling out order blanks.
   A friend works crossword puzzles.
   I always carry a paperback.

D. How do parents produce well-rounded, happy kids who live up to their potential?

The parents are successful in their jobs, but are not swept up in the pursuit of success.

They don't spend a lot of money and time frantically checking kids into every ballet, hockey, swimming, and modern language class within a 50-mile radius.

They always give their children their time and attention.

They make study their No. 1 priority.

The children are not allowed to have after-school jobs.

E. Unending patience is the secret of success in training any animal.

Never strike an animal, but instead constantly repeat instructions.

Use rewards for accomplishments and mild rebukes for failure.

Consistency is important—presenting yourself every day to an animal in the same way.

Most animals respond to a consistently firm, quiet tone.

Another type of process paragraph describes how something happens or takes place:

Pale green when hatched, the caterpillars eat many times their weight in leaves, passing in three weeks through five larval stages. Each larva then transforms itself into a jade-green chrysalis wearing a necklace of shiny gold dots, and hangs for a week or two from the milkweed. Finally, a Monarch butterfly wriggles out and clings tremulously awhile to the plant, shaking its wet wings.

What process is being described in this paragraph?

The writer explains how a caterpillar becomes a Monarch butterfly by passing through stages.

How many stages does the writer describe in this paragraph?

The writer describes three stages: (a) the larval stage(s) (b) the chrysalis stage, and (c) the butterfly stage.

What words or phrases does the writer use to signal the reader at each stage?

The writer uses words and phrases such as "when hatched," "then," and "finally."

EXERCISE 7.2

The paragraph below describes a process so the reader will understand it better. The sentences have been jumbled. Decide how to reorder them. List the numbers in the correct order below. To help you out, we have underlined terms and phrases which describe each step and stage for the reader.

(1) Now I have two things cooking, prime ribs and potatoes, at different times and temperatures, and they both have to be watched very closely. **(2)** With my work area set up, I must make clarified butter and garlic butter. **(3)** The garlic butter is for stuffing escargots [snails]. **(4)** Preparing food for the sauté line at the restaurant where I work is a hectic two-hour job. **(5)** The first thing I do is to check the requisition for the day and order my food. **(6)** I come to work at 3:00 p.m., knowing that everything must be done by 5:00 p.m. **(7)** In the meantime, I must put three trays of bacon in the oven. **(8)** Then I have to clean and season five or six prime rib roasts and place them in the slow-cooking oven. **(9)** The bacon needs very close watching, too, because it burns very easily. **(10)** After this, I clean and season five trays of white potatoes for baking and put them in the fast oven. **(11)** Now I have prime ribs, potatoes, and bacon all cooking at the same time—and all needing constant watching. **(12)** These also go into an oven for baking. **(13)** Now I have prime ribs, baking potatoes, bacon, and popovers cooking at the same time and all of them needing to be closely watched. **(14)** The other half of the ground meat mixture will be used to stuff mushrooms. **(15)** Next, I make popovers, which are unseasoned rolls. **(16)** Now I make au jus, which is served over the prime ribs, make the soup for the day, and cook the vegetables and rice. **(17)** I have to prepare veal, cut and season scampi, and clean and sauté mushrooms and onions. **(18)** Half of the ground meat will be mixed with wild rice and will be used to stuff breast of chicken. **(19)** I have to make ground meat stuffing also. **(20)** Is it any wonder that I say preparing food for the sauté line at the restaurant where I work is a very hectic two-hour job! **(21)** In the meantime, I check the prime ribs and potatoes, take the bacon and the popovers out of the oven, and put the veal and chicken into the oven. **(22)** This and sometimes more has to be done by five o'clock. **(23)** Then I heat the bordelaise sauce, make the special for the day, and last of all, cook food for the employees. **(24)** The clarified butter is for cooking liver, veal, and fish.

Sentence numbers in order:

4, 6, 5, 8, 10, 1, 7, 9, 11, 15, 12, 13, 2, 24, 3, 19, 18, 14, 17, 21, 16, 23, 22, 20

EXERCISE 7.3

Several paragraphs describing processes appear below. The sentences are out of order. These paragraphs also include some irrelevant details. Number the sentences in the correct order, and underline details that don't belong.

A. When I am selling someone a product, I get my energy up in several ways.

    3   Sometimes I walk around for a few minutes, to get my heart pumping.

    2   I think about the goals of the meeting—mine and the other person's.

    1   Before I meet someone, I usually sit quietly, collect my thoughts, and breathe deeply.

    5   I focus on the other person and try to find things to like about him or her.

    4   Once I go through that doorway, I no longer think about myself.

A generalization that adds
nothing to a description of
the process.

_____ <u>Selling is important to my family's welfare.</u>

B. In 1962, the Mescalero Indians purchased a mountainous area next to the reservation that it hoped to turn into the southernmost ski resort in the United States.

___4___ The resort featured a 250-room hotel, a 200-acre man-made lake, tennis courts, and a golf course.

___3___ In 1975 the Mescalero opened a $11-million luxury resort called Inn of the Mountain Gods.

_____ <u>Indians are descendants of people who crossed the land bridge from Asia many thousands of years ago.</u>

___2___ Yet within two decades the ski resort had to be expanded—from one lift to eight—because it was so jammed each weekend.

___1___ Some BIA officials predicted the venture would fail, for Indians had never before been in the ski business.

C. Lehigh University has agreed to protect students by trying a pilot door-alarm program.

___3___ A building-wide alarm sounds in case of intrusion.

___5___ This simple measure may be the obstacle preventing another burglary, rape, or murder.

___4___ Also, exterior doors are wired to signal police if they are propped open.

_____ <u>Lehigh enjoys a high reputation for its academic program.</u>

___2___ A machine records the time and the identify of each card user.

___1___ In this program, keys are replaced with plastic cards.

D. In recent decades, mountain bluebirds have suffered from a shortage of suitable nesting sites.

___4___ Eventually over 150 volunteers put up, and continue to tend, more than 18,000 boxes throughout the state.

Irrelevant to the process
of installing boxes for
nesting sites.

_____ <u>Mountain bluebirds are a beautiful but rare bird.</u>

___2___ Art talked timber companies into donating wood.

___5___ Other volunteers are putting up boxes in Idaho, Wyoming, Utah, Nevada, and Washington, as well as in Alberta and British Columbia, Canada.

___3___ He also got high-school shop classes to pre-cut the lumber.

___1___ In the mid-1970s, Art Aylesworth and others formed a group—Mountain Bluebird Trails—to build nesting boxes.

E. Impatient people don't like to waste time.

___3___ They don't allow for the possibility of delay or the unexpected.

___6___ When an appointment absolutely can't be missed, it pays to allow ridiculous amounts of time.

Irrelevant to process of
avoiding the waste
of time.

_____ <u>Impatient people have been labeled "Type A" personalities.</u>

___4___ It is better to provide a margin for error.

2	They budget the exact number of minutes that a journey or task should take.
5	The more important your appointment, the more time should be alloted.
1	They cut things too close.

Section Four: Using Transitional and Pointing Devices

Since a process must happen in time, writers use transitional devices to tie ideas together. They lead their readers from point to point in the following ways:

- *Using transitional terms:*

    first, second, third, finally, now, then, next, also, after, during

- *Repeating the same words or using synonyms, or counting things:*

    In one of the paragraphs above, the writer describes the stages of a Monarch butterfly as first a "larva," then a "chrysalis," and finally a "butterfly."

- *Pointing out:*

    Use words such as *this, that, these, those,* and so on.

Section Five: Using Forceful Action Words

Use imperative verbs when giving instructions. Imperative verbs are commands that leave out the pronoun "you." If the writer of the paragraph on cooking were *instructing* the reader rather than *describing* a series of actions, he or she would need to use more forceful verbs. For instance, instead of saying "Then I heat the borderlaise sauce," the writer would put the verb first, imperatively: "*Heat* the bordelaise sauce." We use imperative verbs to speak with authority. These verbs also tell the reader to do something at a particular time.

Make your directions more forceful by applying these tests:

1. Avoid empty words or repetition that *does not link thoughts together.* Cross out unnecessary words.

2. If a sentence gives a direction, put an imperative verb at the beginning and leave out the subject:

    Not: Now I make the popovers.

3. Rewrite the sentence:

    Make the popovers.

Here is another example:

1. Identify and cross out empty words:

    First, ~~the fish collector~~ buys an aquarium and filter.

2. Put an imperative verb at the beginning of the sentence, right after a transitional term:

    Buys

3. Rewrite the sentence:

    First, buy an aquarium and filter.

EXERCISE 7.4

The following sentences on quail hunting develop this topic sentence:

Athletic outdoor types will find quail hunting tremendously exhilarating and exciting.

Improve these sentences by doing these things:

1. Identify and cross out empty words.
2. Put an imperative verb at the beginning of the sentence.
3. Rewrite the sentence.

EXAMPLE: They should wear the right clothing, pick the best equipment, and keep simple directions in mind.

1. Identify and cross out empty words.

    ~~They should~~ wear the right clothing, pick the best equipment, and ~~keep~~ simple directions in mind.

2. Put an imperative verb at the beginning of the sentence.

    Select *wear, pick,* and *follow* (instead of the weak *keep*).

3. Rewrite the sentence.

    Wear the right clothing, pick the best equipment, and follow simple directions.

1. Your clothing must be warm and tough.

Identify and cross out unnecessary words.
~~Your~~ clothing ~~must be~~ warm ~~and~~ tough.

Select an imperative verb:
Wear

Rewrite the sentence:
Wear warm, tough clothing.

103

2. You need to have pants that will shed briars and small prickly weeds.

Identify and cross out unnecessary words.
~~You need to have~~ pants ~~that will shed~~ briars ~~and small prickly weeds.~~ [small

prickly weeds are the same as "briars"]

Select an imperative verb:
Wear and Buy

Rewrite the sentence:
Wear briar-proof pants.

3. Along with these pants, you need to obtain a hunting vest in order to store your game as you walk along. You can usually obtain these materials at a sporting goods shop.

Identify and cross out unnecessary words.
~~Along with these pants, you need to~~ obtain a hunting vest ~~in order to~~ store

your game ~~as you walk along.~~ ~~You can usually obtain these materials~~ at a

sporting goods shop.

Select an imperative verb:
obtain

Rewrite the sentence:
Also, obtain a hunting vest at a sporting goods shop to store your game.

4. You also need a shotgun. Your shotgun and shotgun shells can be purchased at any arms store and will cost about $300. Your ammunition can also be purchased at the arms store. The type of shot that is most preferred is number 8 dove and quail.

Identify and cross out unnecessary words:
~~You also need a shotgun.~~ Your shotgun and shotgun shells ~~can be purchased~~

at any arms store and will cost about $300. ~~Your ammunition can also be~~

~~purchased at the arms store.~~ ~~The type of shot that is most~~ preferred ~~is~~ number

8 dove and quail.

Select an imperative verb:
purchase

Rewrite the sentence, combining where necessary:
Purchase your shotgun and preferred number 8 dove and quail shot at any

arms store for about $300.

5. Then you need to find dogs that are trained in the art of quail hunting. The dogs may be the single most important item to any true bird-hunter because they do all the work while you take part in all the pleasure.

Identify and cross out unnecessary words:
~~Then you need to~~ find dogs ~~that are~~ trained in ~~the art of~~ quail hunting. ~~The~~

~~dogs may be the single~~ most important ~~item to any true bird-hunter~~ because they do all the work while you ~~take part in all the~~ pleasure.

Select an imperative verb:
find

Rewrite the sentence, combining where necessary:
Most important, find trained quail-hunting dogs to do all the work.

Section Six: Writing the First Draft

To write your own process paragraph, choose a topic from Section One of this chapter. Then go through these steps:

- Decide on your purpose(s) and audience.
- Decide on equipment, materials, and costs (brainstorming works well for this).
- Make a list or informal outline of the process, step by step in time. Scratch out ideas that don't support your topic.
- Group the steps and number the groups.
- Write a topic sentence for your instructions.

Write your paragraph, either describing a process or giving directions. If you are giving instructions, use forceful imperative verbs. We have included a student's first draft below. Note that he has described a process rather than giving instructions.

Finding a New Home

Trailors are ideal living units which come in all sizes and colors. They can be extravagent with hot tubs, built in fireplaces, sunken living rooms, and show-case bedrooms. Unfortunately, these come with price tags which would pay for any degree at a decent college. What I needed was a solid, no frill or fuss, two bedroom and one bath unit.

Now my next step was to find this perfect mobile home that fit my needs and my budget. I was looking for payments that didn't exceed one weeks pay and didn't require a large down payment.

I started shopping on Gordon Highway and found a large selection of homes to chose from. After endless trips up and down trailor boulevard, I met a crafty eyed salesman who I started wearing down. He had a set price and I had a set price. The only difference was a few minor dollars that numbered in the hundreds and was in my favor. This war between the price raged for days and then went into weeks. At last a deal was made and I was the proud owner of a three bedroom and two bath mobile home.

The rest of this story is history. My trailor sits snugly on my land and has its own power pole and septic tank. The trailor also sports a blue interior with matching sofa and chair. None of this was an easy task but, as I sit in my new found bliss. I take pride in my new home that secures not only a home for me but, also for my little boy. A home which holds the possibilities of many future projects. At last a place to call my own again!

Section Seven: Revising the Paragraph

After you have described your process, apply the questions in the checklist below to help you revise. We supply answers that refer to the writing above.

1. *Does the first sentence or two state the writer's topic and plan? If not, how should the writer change the organization?*

The writer tells us he needed a trailer, but doesn't say why, or mention his topic soon enough. He should consider beginning his writing with a topic sentence like this: "Since a divorce left me financially strapped, I needed a cheap, basic trailer to put on my own land."

2. *Does the writer include all the reasons and details the reader needs? Are they in the right order?*

We do not know how much the writer has to spend: he fails to tell us in the first paragraph. When he mentions it in the second paragraph, he limits his monthly payments to "one week's pay," with no dollar amount. He also needs to tell the reader earlier in the paper how he prepared his property for the trailer, and that he needed it for only two people—himself and his son. He also needs to describe the trailer sooner, when he first sees it.

3. *How has the writer linked his or her ideas together? What devices like connectives, synonyms, and pronouns has the writer used? Which of these devices should the writer use?*

He should indicate his starting point more clearly, signaling his intentions with words or phrases like *initially,* or *to begin with,* or "*after* my divorce." He introduces his second step awkwardly with the words, "Now my next step was . . . ," instead of the terser *next* or *second.* He does uses synonyms for "mobile home" like *living unit* and *trailer.*

4. *Sets of directions do not always need a conclusion. They may end with the direction that completes the process. However, an effective, satisfying close will sometimes improve a process paper. Does the example above have one?*

The writer concludes his paragraph with several interesting ideas:

- He takes pride in his new home for himself and his little boy.
- His home provides a place for future projects.
- He now has a place he can call his own.

5. *What serious mechanical or other problems should the writer solve while rewriting the first draft?*

Three of the last four sentences are fragments. One of these can be easily corrected by omitting the unneeded connective *which* in the following sentence:

This home *which* holds the possibilities of many future projects.

The other two sentences need added subjects and verbs.

None of this was an easy task, *I think*, as I sit in my newfound bliss. At last *I have* a place to call my own again!

As for spelling and mechanics, he misspells "trailer" as "trailor" and "extravagant" as "extravagent." He also omits the apostrophe to show the possessive for "week" in "week's pay."

Apply the questions in the revision checklist below to your own writing, or have a friend or classmate do it.

Revision Checklist

1. Does the first sentence or two state the writer's topic and plan? If not, how should the writer change the organization?
2. Does the writer include all the reasons and details the reader needs? Are they in the right order?
3. How has the writer linked his or her ideas together? What devices like connectives, synonyms, and pronouns has the writer used? Which of these devices should the writer use?
4. Does the writing have a conclusion? If a conclusion would improve it, how should it be written?
5. What serious mechanical or other problems should the writer solve while rewriting the first draft?

EXERCISE 7.5

The student-written process paper above is a description. Turn it into a set of directions by using imperative verbs. Find the needed verb in each sentence, or guess what it should be. Then begin sentences, where needed, with verbs that command the reader.

Section Eight: Final Editing

Once you have finished, clean up the grammatical problems, punctuation errors, and misspellings. The following questions will help you finish the process of writing your paragraph:

1. Have I corrected the grammatical errors I often make? (Look back over earlier paragraphs you have written. Then check this one for mistakes like subject—verb agreement, misplaced modifiers, and the like).
2. Have I corrected the punctuation errors I tend to make?
3. Have I corrected the words I usually misspell?

Section Nine: Further Topics

- How to conduct an experiment
- How to take or develop photographs
- How to make a simple car or home repair
- How to carry out some sport like fishing, hunting, or bird-watching
- How to win at some game
- How to drive defensively
- How to ruin a date
- How to fail a course
- How to destroy a new car
- How to put off doing things as long as possible
- How to make a boring task exciting

Early warning signs: The Mad Bomber wins the fourth grade Science Fair

Defining a Term

A definition of a word places an idea or an object in a *class*. Then it tells how it *differs* from other members of the class or group. A botanist would define peanuts as peas, grouping them with vegetables. Anabolic steroids are synthetic compounds that mimic testosterone, we are told. The writer Mike Royko considered naming his son Rocko. This name would define him as a future tight end or maybe a linebacker. The boy would get through college free, maybe turn pro and make a lot of money, Royko speculates. These definitions all place an item in a category or *class*. Here is the topic sentence of a definition paragraph:

> The mad bomber appears to be an obsessive/compulsive personality.

Here is the complete paragraph:

The mad bomber appears to be an obsessive/compulsive personality. The attention to detail in his bombs likely carries through to most of his life. His home or apartment is meticulously organized. He dresses neatly. He is a list-maker. He likely drives a well-maintained older car. In many respects he is the ideal neighbor or tenant: quiet, creating no disturbances, paying his rent or mortgage on time. Though his age is hard to predict, he could be in his mid or late 30s. His letters indicate high intelligence and good schooling. The bomber is very likely a loner. He generally has difficulty dealing with other people, especially females. If he has a girlfriend, she is likely much younger.

Andrew Hilburn, "Help Find This Mad Bomber"

In what classes does the writer place mad bombers?
In classes such as obsessive/compulsive personalities with attention to detail, ideal neighbors or tenants, people who are well-educated.

What characteristics make mad bombers different from the classes they seem to fit?
They not only make bombs; they are often loners who can't deal well with other people, especially women.

Sometimes the terms to be defined are general and abstract. No yardsticks exist to measure them, no scales to assess their exact weights. However, speakers still use intangible terms like *courage, determination*, or even *the pits* or *stressed out* to convey meaning. In the absence of scientific measurements, such terms can still be defined. These definitions make meanings clear by the use of examples or anecdotes, like this definition of *a class act:*

By "class act," I mean any behavior so virtuous that it puts normal behavior to shame. It was a class act, for instance, when Alexander Hamilton aimed high and fired over Aaron Burr's head. Benjamin Guggenheim performed a class act on the *Titanic* when he gave his life jacket to a woman passenger and then put on white tie and tails so he could die "like a gentleman." That same year, 1912, Capt. Lawrence Oates became frostbitten and lame on Robert Scott's ill-fated expedition to the South Pole. Rather than delay the others in their desperate trek back from the Pole, he went to the opening of the tent one night and said, "I am just going outside and may be some time." He thereupon walked to his death in a blizzard. Certainly a class act.

John Berendt, *Class Acts*

Into what larger classes or groups could "class acts" be placed?
"Class acts" could be placed in groups such as acts involving *self-denial, nerve, determination,* and *fortitude.*

What traits set "class act" apart from the larger groups in which the term could be placed?
It is set apart by its emphasis on individual rather than group actions, on the near-certain chance of death as a consequence, on loyalty to an invisible code of conduct.

Section One: Choosing a Topic

Begin your definition paragraph by choosing a topic. Remember: you will define it by first placing it in a class. Then you will tell how it differs from other members of the same class. Some possible topics:

- An excellent repair person, a dynamic preacher, an effective classroom teacher
- Human traits such as honesty, conceit, greatness, reverence, genius, enthusiasm
- Possible role models: a sports figure like Chris Evert or Jack Nicklaus, an evangelist like Billy Graham, a politician like Pat Schroeder or Mario Cuomo
- Behavior patterns or types: lowbrow, redneck, clothes horse, world beater, nag, dreamer, social climber, wacko

Section Two: Generating Ideas

To develop your definition paragraph, you need to generate ideas. Use an approach like brainstorming, list-making, a scratch outline, or clustering. Refer back to Chapter 1, "Generating Ideas," for help on this. If you decide to brainstorm, write your topic at the top of a blank sheet of paper. Then list all the ideas you can associate with your topic, in random order. The brainstorm below lists ideas linked with a common ailment, the aching back.

The Aching Back

May start with carrying luggage through an airport

Simple, easy movements, like bending over to tie shoes

May be just a passing twinge

Widespread ailment—like the common cold

Perhaps felt in one place, then radiates all over the body

Sometimes long-lasting

May feel like the stab of an ice pick

Could hit unsuspecting people

Often causes excruciating pain

Big cause of lost work time

Tentative Topic Sentence: An aching back may strike suddenly, causing excruciating pain.

In what class does the writer place "an aching back"?

It is placed in a class with other pains that strike the human body.

How do back pains differ from other kinds of pain?

They strike suddenly and are often excruciating.

Section Three: Planning and Organizing the Paragraph

To organize your paragraph, make a plan. One good way involves using a scratch outline. Include details from your brainstorm and add others as they occur to you or perhaps from your reading. After generating ideas for a paragraph about an aching back, the writer could make a plan like this one:

Topic Sentence: An aching back strikes suddenly, causing excruciating pain.

First Causes: strikes suddenly

Hits unsuspecting people
    As they bend over to tie their shoes
    As they carry luggage through an airport
May strike in one place
May be only a twinge
Can cause excruciating pain, like an ice pick

Later Effects: radiates over entire body

Slightest movement hurts
    Lifting coffee cup may be painful
    Hard to turn over in bed
May be long-lasting, very painful
    Eighty percent of all Americans—about 200 million people—will have aching backs
    More than 15 million will suffer backaches chronically
    After the common cold, the biggest cause of lost work time

---

EXERCISE 8.1

Read over the following paragraph, and answer the questions that follow.

The now-conventional retirement age of 65 originally grew out of the Social Security Act of 1935. But in 1935, the average 65-year-old American male could expect to live another 12 1/2 years. Today, according to Victor Fuchs of the National Bureau of Economic Research, that is the remaining life expectancy for a 72-year-old man. Fuchs argues that it makes more sense to define "elderly" in terms of the number of years remaining on one's life rather than the years already lived. In that case, the standard retirement age would be pushed up seven years to age 72.

Dan Cordtz, *Financial World*

In what *class* is the word "elderly" usually placed?
In a class measured by the number of years already lived, like "teenager" or "adult"

How does the writer redefine the idea of "elderly"?
The writer defines elderly both in terms of what it *is* and what it *is not*. It is defined in terms of years of life remaining, not years already lived.

What details does the writer use to define his term?

He uses comparison and contrast: in 1935, the average 65-year-old American male could expect to live another 12 1/2 years. Today, a 72-year-old man can expect to live the same length of time.

What conclusion does the writer draw?

Retirement age should be pushed up from 65 to 72.

EXERCISE 8.2

Make a scratch outline for the paragraph on retirement above.

Topic: Changing the Retirement Age

Outline:

The Social Security Act of 1935
   Set retirement age of 65
   In 1935, average 65-year-old American male would live another 12 1/2 years
Change in life expectancy since 1935
   Today, 72-year-old man will live 12 1/2 years
   Could push up standard retirement age seven years to age 72

EXERCISE 8.3

Read over the following definition paragraph and answer the questions that follow.

What is a newspaper lead? It is the first paragraph of a story intended to seduce the reader into finishing the entire piece. The lead on an article in *Capper's* about a publication that has urged its readers to go in for hugging: "The *Farmer's Almanac* has gone hug wild." From the *Philadelphia Inquirer*: "After going around in circles, the California Senate decided not to make the square dance the official state dance." In a *National Geographic* news feature: "To some 15 million Americans who suffer through the seasonal agonies of hay fever, pollen is unquestionably something to be sneezed at."

What term is defined?

The newspaper lead

In what larger category is the term placed?

Paragraphs of newspaper stories

What examples of effective leads does the writer use?

Leads about hugging, the California state dance, and pollen

EXERCISE 8.4

Some topic sentences for definition paragraphs appear below. Select one and generate some ideas for it. Then plan how to organize it, and write a topic sentence for it.

- It is the exceptional person who stops to help the woman maneuvering her kids and groceries up the staircase.
- A family project can be stimulating if you choose one that everyone enjoys.
- Change is the most changeless thing in the universe.
- Providing guidance is very different from giving orders.
- A family business is very rewarding.

EXERCISE 8.5

Write a paragraph about a champion in some area of life, sports, entertainment, religion, education, or business. In this paragraph, define one of the following terms relating to championship: talent, training, character, equipment, coaching, winning. Begin by placing someone you consider a champion in a class. Define one of the qualities above or another that you consider crucial to his or her success. Then develop your paragraph with examples, synonyms, likenesses, or contrasts.

Section Four: Using Transitional Devices

A number of transitional devices will show readers that another example or illustration is coming:

first, to illustrate, for example, for instance
in addition, similarly, next, above all, again, finally, also, too, then, second, equally

Other transitional devices will indicate a contrast or difference:

by contrast, but, however, still, yet, on the contrary, on the other hand, nevertheless

Section Five: Writing the First Draft

Write the first draft of your definition paragraph. To do so, go through the following process:

- Choose a topic from Section One of this chapter or invent your own.

- Use brainstorming, outlining, or some other prewriting device to generate details and reasons to support your paragraph.
- Design a plan to use your reasons or details.
- Base a topic sentence on these ideas.
- Give your paragraph a title.

Here is a student example of a definition paragraph:

Mother Nature with a Touch of Man

If I could design a special place to relax, it would be a combination of many things. First, it would have all the excitement of Myrtle Beach. You could hear the video games from the pavilion and smell the salt off the ocean. There would be ladies all around. In the background would be mountains covered with green foliage. Occasionally, you would catch a glance of a buck eating or maybe a mother racoon and her family. This special place of mine couldn't be special if it didn't have my most favorite fishing hole there. With the water coming from the rocks and a cool breeze, the water is always fresh and relaxing. The rocks the water runs down would shine in the sun, and I would be right in the middle of it all. I could swim in the ocean, lie under a tree on top of a mountain or fish until my back and legs are so tired I wouldn't be able to stand any more. This place of mine would not have any pollution or busy cars travelling through the middle of it. The people would all get along and not have a worry in the world. During the day the sun would always shine and at night when the stars come out you could either walk on the beach or do a little catfishing, all depending on what type of mood you were in. When you finally lie down to go to sleep, you'll fall asleep to the sound of the water flowing softly down the rocks or maybe the crickets singing a song. No matter how it is you would rest as if you were on a cloud, because you will be very tired after the days activities. People want come here not because of a tourist trap or a vacation but to be free, to be themselves. They will leave all their worries and fears on the other side of the mountain. There will be no credit cards or debts. No laws except for the ones mother nature has laid out for us to follow. Life will be simple an sweet and all you have to do is sit back watch and enjoy.

Section Six: Revising the Paragraph

Apply the questions in the checklist below to your own writing, or have a friend or classmate do it. We have supplied the answers for the sample paragraph above.

1. *Does the first sentence or two state the writer's topic and plan? Does it clearly define the term? If not, how should the writer change the plan of organization?*

The writer tells the reader that he plans to define a special place to relax. He then tells us vaguely that this place is "a combination of many things." However, he needs a plan. He should define his special place by summing up its aspects in order.

If he had made a plan, he would have listed the traits that make his own place *special.* His topic sentence or statement might read: "My own

116

special place to relax would resemble Myrtle Beach. It would be close to unspoiled nature: the mountains, beach, and lakes for recreation. By coming here, friendly people would leave their worries behind."

2. *Does the writer include all the reasons and details the reader needs? Are they in the right order?*

The writer needs to make some choices. He could carefully select details to illustrate the ideas in his statement: (a) his special place's *physical traits*; (b) the *people* who go there, and (c) what his special people would *do.* Or he could focus on one of these ideas, and list details that illustrate it.

3. *How has the writer linked his or her ideas together? What devices like connectives, synonyms, and pronouns has the writer used?*

The writer uses terms like *first, occasionally, this place of mine, during the day, when the stars come out,* and the weak *no matter how it is.* He repeatedly refers to himself with the first-person pronoun *I.* He should consider synonyms for people like himself such as *vacationers* or *lovers of nature.*

4. *A definition paragraph often needs an effective, satisfying close. Does the student example above have one?*

The student closes with a rather rambling summation: "Life will be simple and sweet. All you have to do is to sit back, watch and enjoy." His conclusion would be clearer and more concise if he wrote, "To enjoy the simple sweet life in my special place, you need to do no more than sit back, watch and enjoy."

5. *What serious mechanical or other problems should the writer solve while rewriting the first draft?*

He improperly uses a comma to separate the dependent clause from the opening independent clause in "No matter how it is you would rest as if you were on a cloud , because you will be very tired after the days activities." In addition, the word *days* should be possessive with an apostrophe: after the *y* if singular: day ' s; after the *s* if plural: days '.

The next-to-last sentence is a wordy fragment: "No laws except for the ones mother nature has laid out for us to follow." It has no subject or verb. If these were added, the sentence would read; "*We would follow* no laws except for those laid out by Mother Nature." Since <u>M</u>other <u>N</u>ature is a personification, both words need to be capitalized. The writer has also misspelled the word "and" as "an" in the phrase "simple an[d] sweet."

Apply the questions in the revision checklist to your own writing, or have a friend or classmate do it.

Revision Checklist

1. Does the first sentence or two state the writer's topic and plan? Does it clearly define the term? If not, how should the writer change the plan of organization?

2. Does the writer include all the reasons and details the reader needs? Are they in the right order?

3. How has the writer linked his or her ideas together? What devices like connectives, synonyms, and pronouns has the writer used?

4. A definition paragraph often needs an effective, satisfying close. Does your example have one?

5. What serious mechanical or other problems should the writer solve while rewriting the first draft?

Section Seven: Final Editing

Once you have finished, clean up the grammatical problems, punctuation errors, and misspellings. The following questions will help you finish the process of writing your paragraph:

1. Have I corrected the grammatical errors I often make? (Look back over earlier papers you have written. Then check this one for mistakes like subject–verb agreement or misplaced modifiers.)

2. Have I corrected the punctuation errors I tend to make?

3. Have I corrected the words I usually misspell?

Section Eight: Further Topics

- An efficient salesclerk or a good cash register operator
- Personality traits such as sneakiness, repulsiveness, or incompetence
- A business executive like Lee Iacocca, a writer like Joyce Carol Oates or Stephen King, a singer like Willie Nelson, an actress like Julia Roberts
- A personality type such as "new kid on the block," nitwit, dreamboat, airhead, role player

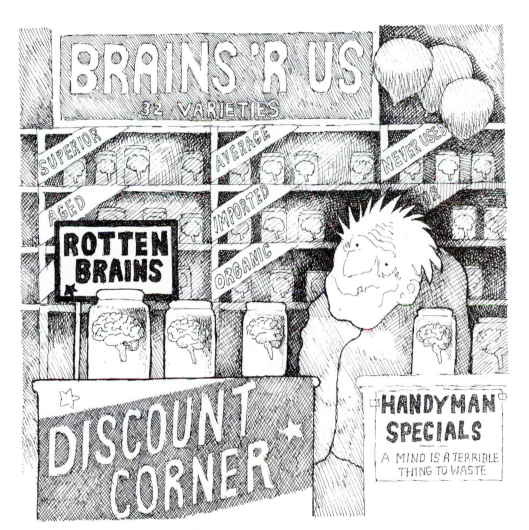

Igor spots a bargain

Dividing
and Classifying

SECTION ONE: Choosing a Topic
SECTION TWO: Generating Ideas
SECTION THREE: Planning and Organizing the Paragraph
SECTION FOUR: Using Transitional Devices
SECTION FIVE: Writing the First Draft
SECTION SIX: Revising the Paragraph
SECTION SEVEN: Final Editing
SECTION EIGHT: Further Topics

Division and classification involves two processes. You begin with a topic: an object, a person, or an idea. You then use division to separate the topic into smaller groups. For example, cars might be divided into types such as sports, transportation, and luxury vehicles. In a supermarket, you might divide food into types like chilled, frozen, canned, fresh, and dried. A comic once divided food by national origin: "It's fun to eat in America, the melting pot. Yesterday I had a Mexican omelette for breakfast, egg foo young for lunch, ravioli for dinner, and sukiyaki for a snack. Late at night I ate the only American thing—a Rolaids." They are all foods, but national origin sets them apart from one another.

On the other hand, you use classification to place objects, persons, or ideas together in groups. You gather or bunch them on the basis of similarities. You might group Manet and Picasso as modern painters, or group a Chrysler and a Ford together as American-made cars.

Division or classification writings may often be limited to eight or ten sentences. However, you may wish to break them up into separate paragraphs of two or three sentences each to emphasize the different groups or aspects.

The following paragraph mostly *divides* the group called "squirrels" into smaller groups. Read over the paragraph and answer the questions that follow.

Taxonomists divide the North American tree squirrels by their physical characteristics into well over 50 species, but I divide them into country squirrels, suburban squirrels, and city squirrels. Country squirrels can scurry around a tree so cleverly that predators don't even know they are there. In the suburbs squirrels not only rob bird feeders but also have been known to watch television. In the city, squirrels have been seen waiting for traffic to stop before crossing the street.

A.B.C. Whipple, "Those High I.Q. Squirrels"

EXERCISE 9.1

Answer the following questions about this paragraph.

1. The writer first refers to the way zoologists classify squirrels. He then invents

his own classification system. Into how many groups does he divide squirrels? What are they?

He divides squirrels into three groups: country, city, and suburban squirrels.

2. What basis does the writer use for his divisions?

The locations where they are found.

3. How does the writer justify his first grouping, "country"?

Country squirrels hide cleverly behind trees.

4. How does the writer justify his second grouping, "suburban"?

Suburban squirrels not only rob bird feeders, but watch TV.

5. How does the writer justify his third grouping, "city"?

City squirrels watch for traffic to stop before crossing the street.

6. What plan has the writer designed for his paragraph?

He first invents three groupings for squirrels based on their locations. Then he provides an example or two of squirrel behavior to justify his use of location for his groupings.

This paragraph limits itself to three types of squirrels. After naming his groups, the writer deals with each one in order. His system of division is based on a single, simple pattern: *location.* He could have added more places, such as *wilderness* or *junkyard,* for example. When he organizes his paragraph, he chooses a particular order:

1. Country (squirrels' normal habitat)
2. Suburbs (someplace in-between nature and people)
3. City (closest to large groups of people)

The paragraph below *classifies* by finding a crucial similarity between individual items or terms:

There are only a few words our boy has in his vocabulary. *More* is probably the foremost and means anything from fun to food. *No* is also a front-runner—he hears it so much he naturally repeats it at every opportunity. *Hello, Bye-Bye, Momma* and *Daddy* make up his standard casual conversation, and that's about the size of it. Except for one word. By far his most distinguished and seldom used expression is *wow.* He only says "wow" when something impresses him: If Dad lets a frying pan catch on fire. If we hit the ditch on the way to town. If the house were to burn down around him, I'm confident he would sum it all up with "Wow."

What do the italicized words above have in common, allowing the writer to place them in the same class or group?

All these italicized words make up the vocabulary of the writer's child.

How does the writer *divide* as well as *classify*?

The writer sets one word, "wow," apart from all the other words in his son's vocabulary, giving examples to add emphasis.

In what order does the writer place his examples?

The writer moves from least to most important, leaving the most important word for last.

Section One: Choosing a Topic

Choose one of the following topics for a paragraph that either divides or classifies:

- Impressions that teachers have made on you
- Conditions leading to (or interfering with) success in school, work, or personal relationships
- Turning points in your life, past or future

Section Two: Generating Ideas

To generate ideas for your paragraph, respond to the questions below. Write the topic you have chosen at the top of a piece of paper. Decide whether to divide or classify. Then divide your topic into three or four aspects. Write them down. Finally, design a topic statement based on these notes:

Topic: _____

Basis of paragraph design: _____ Division _____ Classification _____

Categories (if division):

_____

_____

_____

_____

Topic Statement: _____

_____

Section Three: Planning and Organizing the Paragraph

In organizing division and classification paragraphs, writers arrange their examples *logically*, using one or more of these bases:

- Order of importance (most to least, or least to most)
- Time (early to later)
- Place (inner to outer, or outer to inner)
- Size (smaller to larger, or larger to smaller)

EXERCISE 9.2

Read the paragraph below and answer the questions that follow it.

The crowd roars as the team takes the field. Some on this day will suffer lifelong injuries, but probably *not* the athletes. Surprisingly, those most at risk are members of the band, who practiced before the game in a room so small that the clarinetist sat with his head almost inside the mouth of the tuba. Next at risk are the fans, screaming cheers and blasting noisemakers in a stadium where the sound level can exceed that of a jet during takeoff.

Lowell Ponte, "How Noise Can Harm You"

1. What kind of paragraph is this—division or classification?
   It is a *division* paragraph which divides "some on this day" into groups.

2. How many groups are named in the paragraph? What are they?
   Three groups may suffer injuries at athletic events. Of these three, two groups are likely to be injured by noise: the members of the band and the fans.

3. On what basis does the writer divide these groups?
   The writer classifies them on the basis of the likelihood of hearing injury from noise: from greatest, the band; to somewhat less likely but still great, the fans; to least likely, the athletes.

EXERCISE 9.3

In the following lists, all the items but one belong in a single grouping or classification. *Find the item that does not fit and cross it out. In the blank after each list, indicate the basis for grouping the remaining items.*

Examples:

Canaries	Beef
~~Dogs~~	Chicken
Parrots	~~Tuna~~
Parakeets	Pork
Basis for grouping: birds	Basis for grouping: types of meat

Pain relievers	Foreign languages
Bandages	~~Freshman composition~~
Salves	Business administration
~~Coffee~~	Nursing
Basis for grouping: found in medicine cabinet	Basis for grouping: related courses

123

Beach wear   Automobile magazines
~~Brightly colored clothes~~   Newspapers
Party apparel   Scholarly journals
Formal outfits   ~~Editorial pages~~
Basis for grouping: _degree of_   Basis for grouping: _types of_
formality   _publications_

~~Twinkies~~   Double beds
Vegetables   ~~Comfortable~~
Fruits   King-size beds
Meats   Bunks
Basis for grouping: _basic food_   Basis for grouping: _size and type_
                                    of bed

EXERCISE 9.4

Nearly all groups of items can be grouped or classified in more than one way. For example, restaurants can be classified in ethnic groups (Mexican, German, Chinese) or by cost (cheap, moderate, and expensive). Both groupings are useful, depending on the writer's purpose and the needs of the audience. Think of at least two ways in which each of the categories below can be grouped:

Group	Types of Classification
EXAMPLE	
Employees	A. Years of experience
	B. Highest degree, years of education
1. College students	A. Major
	B. Grade point average
2. Movies	A. Audience ratings
	B. Country of origin
3. Professional sports	A. Level of popularity
	B. Size of teams
4. Motels	A. Location
	B. Cost
5. Computers	A. Speed and capacity
	B. Maker

EXERCISE 9.5

Several groups of people or objects are listed below. Think of a way in which each group can be classified. Then suggest several types of classification for

Answers may vary. each approach. Finally, write a topic statement that sums up the type of grouping you have chosen for each list of items.

Group	Basis for Grouping	Types
EXAMPLE:		
Children who misbehave	Means of disciplining	1. Punishment 2. Bribery 3. Encouragement

Topic Sentence: Children who misbehave may be disciplined by punishment, bribery, or encouragement, of which the last one works best over the long run.

1. Investing money	Forms of investment	Real estate Stock market Precious metals

Topic Sentence: People often invest money in real estate, the stock market, and precious metals.

2. Restaurants	Fast food	Hamburger Chicken Seafood

Topic Sentence: Fast food restaurants include hamburger, chicken, and seafood restaurants, in order of popularity.

3. Recreation	Outdoor	Golfing Tennis Skiing

Topic Sentence: Many people enjoy various types of outdoor recreation: golfing, tennis, and skiing.

Section Four: Using Transitional Devices

Your choice of transitional devices will emphasize dividing and grouping, as you move from specific to general, or as you provide specific examples:

first of all, for one thing, second, also, next, another, in addition, moreover, furthermore, finally, last of all

Section Five: Writing the First Draft

Write the first draft of your division or classification paragraph. Follow these steps:

- Choose a topic from Section One of this chapter or invent your own.
- Decide which type of paragraph you plan to write, *division* or *classification.*
- Use brainstorming or some other prewriting device to generate details and reasons to support your paragraph.
- Design a plan to use your reasons or details.
- Base a topic sentence on these ideas.
- Give your paragraph a title.

Here is a student example of a division paragraph. We have underlined the topic statement:

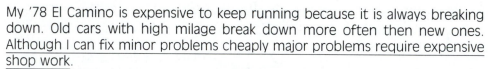

Keeping Up With My Car Is Very Expensive

My '78 El Camino is expensive to keep running because it is always breaking down. Old cars with high milage break down more often then new ones. Although I can fix minor problems cheaply major problems require expensive shop work.

I do some of the usual maintenance on the car myself. I change the oil and filter every 3,000 miles. Also, I have replaced the power sterring pump and fuel pump. Fixing these minor problems has saved me a good bit of money. But it's nothing compared to what I saved by rebuilding the engine with a friend of mine.

Even though I saved a considerable amount of money by rebuilding the engine, it was a lot of hard work. I never realized so much was involved. I had to search around for all the parts that would be replaced like pistons, rings, gaskets, and bearings. I also had to take the heads and block to the machine shop to get reworked. At least I learned a lot about how an out of date Chevy eight cylinder engine looks and works. I also don't have to worry about the engine breaking down because its all new.

My car has had a lot of expensive shop work done to it also. The front end is aligned about once every other month. It is also expensive to have the transmission rebuilt or everything in the front end replaced. Both of which I have had done. But when it does I've got to fork out the cash to get it out.

As you can tell this car cost a lot more than it is worth. But its got to be done for me to have transportation; whether I fix it myself or, pay a mechanic to do it. I wish I could get a little economy car that never breaks down. I would have so much money to spend on other things. I also would not be bothered with the expense of fixing my car.

Section Six: Revising the Paragraph

Apply the questions in the checklist below to your own writing, or have a friend or classmate do it. We have supplied the answers for the sample paragraph above.

1. *Does the first sentence or two state the writer's topic and plan? Does it clearly define the term? If not, how should the writer change the plan of organization?*

The writer states his topic in his title and third sentence. However, he has omitted some information here: he also needs to buy parts and work on the car himself with help from a friend. His topic statement should include this information.

His plan has three parts, based on the type of work involved, and the amount of help needed: (1) Doing routine work himself, (2) doing more complicated repairs with help from a friend, and (3) handling the most complicated repairs by paying professionals.

2. *Does the writer include all the reasons and details the reader needs? Are they in the right order?*

The writer includes all the necessary examples. However, he needs to tell whether he can handle the front end repairs with a friend, or whether they need professional help; he should then group them accordingly. He needs to do the same with transmission repairs.

3. *How has the writer linked his or her ideas together? What devices like connectives, synonyms, and pronouns has the writer used?*

The writer overuses the word *also*, along with words such as *even though*, *but*, and *as you can tell*. More variety would appeal to the reader. He should make greater use of transitions such as *second*, *in addition*, *third*, and *finally*. He does substitute synonyms for his *'78 El Camino* such as *old car* and *out of date Chevy*, while using an antonym to better define it: *little economy car*.

4. *A division or classification paragraph often needs an effective, satisfying close. Does this example have one?*

The writer explains why he needs the car—for transportation—and repeats the reason repairs are expensive. He also puts his present expenses in perspective: he'd rather own a cheaper, more reliable car to save time and money.

5. *What serious mechanical or other problems should the writer solve while rewriting the first draft?*

The writer includes two fragments. The first of them, "Both of which I have had done," needs a subject and verb: "I have had both of them done." He separates a second fragment from an earlier clause with a semicolon: ; whether I fix it myself or, pay a mechanic to do it." He could solve this problem by replacing the semicolon with a comma, while removing the comma after the conjunction *or*,: "But it's got to be done for me to have transportation, whether I fix it myself or pay a mechanic to do it. (We have also solved the problem with the misspelled *it's*.)

The writer also fails to set off an introductory subordinate clause with a comma: "But when it does, I've got to fork out the cash to get it out." He leaves out a helpful comma after a transitional phrase: "As you can tell, this car cost a lot more than it is worth." In the same sentence, he may have made a noun—verb agreement error. He may mean the present tense *costs* in, "As you can tell, this car costs a lot more than it is worth."

He also misspells several words, using *then* for *than* and *sterring* for *steering*.

Finally, the paper tends to be wordy and repetitious. He could omit the repetitive clause, "Even though I saved a considerable amount of money by rebuilding the engine." He could also omit a sentence like, "I never realized so much was involved." Instead of writing, "My car has had a lot of expensive shop work done to it also," he could have written, "In addition, my car has needed expensive shop work." Solving these and other wordiness problems would reduce the length of the paper to a more manageable paragraph.

Apply the questions in the revision checklist below to your own writing, or have a friend or classmate do it.

Revision Checklist

1. Does the first sentence or two state the writer's topic and plan? Does it clearly define the term? If not, how should the writer change the plan of organization?

2. Does the writer include all the reasons and details the reader needs? Are they in the right order?

3. How has the writer linked his or her ideas together? What devices like connectives, synonyms, and pronouns has the writer used?

4. A division or classification paragraph often needs an effective, satisfying close. Does your example have one?

5. What serious mechanical or other problems should you solve while rewriting the first draft?

Section Seven: Final Editing

Once you have finished, clean up the grammatical problems, punctuation errors, and misspellings. The following questions will help you finish the process of writing your paragraph:

1. Have I corrected the grammatical errors I often make? (Look back over earlier papers you have written. Then check this one for mistakes like subject—verb agreement or misplaced modifiers.)

2. Have I corrected the punctuation errors I tend to make?

3. Have I corrected the words I usually misspell?

Section Eight: Further Topics

- Kinds of status symbols (cars, clothes, neighborhoods, clubs)
- Parties (political and social)

- Religious devotion (or lack of it)
- Career paths right for you
- Dream (and nightmare) houses or apartments
- Types of commercials, TV programs, or films
- Compliments or criticisms

Linking Causes and Effects

A cause and effect paragraph traces events in time. Why did our car sputter and stop? What health problem makes us feel unwell? Why is a particular movie or music star so popular? What causes changes in the weather? As in narrative and process paragraphs, effects follow causes in time order.

Sometimes a writer will isolate an effect in order to trace several causes. At other times, a writer will be more interested in the way a cause leads to several effects. Sometimes, of course, a writer will balance causes and effects. Here is a cause-and-effect paragraph with the topic sentence underlined:

Nothing posed a more serious threat to the bald eagle's survival than a modern chemical compound called DDT. Around 1940, a retired Canadian banker named Charles L. Broley began keeping track of eagles nesting in Florida. Each breeding season, he climbed into more than 50 nests, counted the eaglets and put metal bands on their legs. In the late 1940s, a sudden drop-off in the number of young produced led him to conclude that 80 percent of his birds were sterile. Broley blamed DDT. Scientists later discovered that DDE, a breakdown product of DDT, causes not sterility, but a fatal thinning of eggshells among birds of prey. Applied on cropland all over the United States, the pesticide was running off into waterways where it concentrated in fish. The bald eagles ate the fish and the DDT impaired their ability to reproduce. They were not alone, of course. Ospreys and pelicans suffered similar setbacks.

Jim Doherty, ''The Bald Eagle and DDT''

EXERCISE 10.1

Answer the following questions about the paragraph above.

1. Is the writer more interested in causes or in effects, or does he balance them fairly evenly?

   The writer traces effects to their causes, but balances them fairly equally.

2. In what order does the writer deal with causes and effects?

   The writer begins with effects—the drop in the number of young eaglets

   produced in the late 1940s. He then moves to causes—DDE, a breakdown product of DDT, leading to thin eggshells. At the end, he returns to another effect of these causes, the inability of ospreys and pelicans to reproduce.

3. How many steps are there in the chain of causes leading to the final effect—the failure of eagles to reproduce? What are they?

There are at least five steps: (1) farmers applied DDT to cropland, (2) the pesticide ran off into waterways, (3) DDT concentrated in fish, (4) bald eagles and other birds ate the fish, and (5) DDT (or its byproduct DDE) caused thin shells.

The following paragraph written by a student deals mostly with *effects*. We have underlined the topic sentence:

<u>After awakening Saturday morning with a hangover and shortness of breath, I realized that I had to stop smoking cigarettes.</u> My friend Lisa and I had visited my sister in Savannah, Georgia. The night before, when we had all gone out, I consumed too many drinks and cigarettes. While walking to the kitchen the next morning, I could barely breathe and I had a bad headache. After taking a couple of aspirins, my headache felt a lot better; however, I still had shortness of breath. Lisa didn't feel bad, so she drove home. She smokes a lot of cigarettes, probably two packs daily. Lisa's cigarettes had begun to smell real good. When the aroma got under my skin, I had to light one up. After taking two drags, my lungs felt weak and congested, so I threw it out the window. I had thought about quitting for a while. Finally, I decided to do something about it. I threw my full pack of Salem Lights out the window. I quit: no more smoking.

EXERCISE 10.2   *Answer the following questions about the paragraph above:*

1. What *effects* does the paragraph deal with?

The writer deals with two sets of effects. The first set is shortness of breath and a headache; the second set is smoking after smelling the smoke from someone else's cigarettes.

2. What *cause(s)* does the paragraph deal with?

The writer identifies the causes as smoking too much, resulting in shortness of breath, and smoking again after smelling another person's smoke. Finally, pain in her lungs leads her to give up smoking entirely.

133

Section One: Choosing a Topic

To get started on your cause and effect paragraph, invent a topic or choose one of these:

- Why your favorite writer, musician, or artist is so good or so popular
- How television teaches people the right (or wrong) language, values, or eating habits

Your topic: _____

Section Two: Generating Ideas

Once you have chosen a topic, generate ideas to develop it. Some good ways to do this include clustering or brainstorming. To brainstorm, write your topic at the top of a sheet of paper. If you start with a *cause*, list all the *effects* you can think of. If you begin with one or more *effects*, try to think of all the possible *causes*. Think about why some action or situation causes or results from another thing or situation. List reasons, facts, details, or examples below each subtopic. As you go along, consider what order these details should follow. After you have finished your list, refine your order by drawing lines and arrows, or by circling details. You can always insert examples that come to you later. Once you have finished generating ideas, write out a topic statement.

One student, Evelyn, placed her topic, a cause, at the top of a list of (mostly) effects.

Toyota Starlett died
Had really been dependable
Over 100,000 miles
Long time no car
Had to repair its transmission
   $350 cost estimated
Social life curtailed
   Quiet evenings at home
   Watched much TV
Did more studying
   Test grades went up
   Last English composition improved
Arranged temporary transportation
   Friends rescued me for two days
     Mary picked me up in the morning
     Julie took me home in the evening

Tentative Topic Idea: When my Toyota Starlett died, the effects on my life were both good and bad.

EXERCISE 10.3

Answers will vary.

The following topic deals with an effect. Fill in reasons and examples for the topic idea, "People weaken on the threshold of success for a number of reasons."

EXAMPLE:

Reason: Physical cravings

Details: Desires for food, alcohol, love

Reason: Lack of willpower

Details: Stopped going to work early after three days; after first week, began taking two or three hours for lunch

Reason: Bad luck

Details: Family sickness, loss of money or job, betrayal by friends

Reason: Emotional distress

Details: Began drinking two cases of beer a weekend, striking spouse and children

EXERCISE 10.4

We have listed both supporting reasons and details below. Mark the reasons with an R *and the details with a* D.

Topic Idea: States have adopted official symbols for a number of reasons.

__R__ Some states have wanted to seem different or unusual.

__D__ Arizona has official neckwear (the bola).

__R__ Utah wanted to commemorate a miraculous event.

__D__ Minnesota has an official mushroom (the morel).

__D__ Minnesota has an official symbol of peace (the morning dove).

__D__ It all began in 1892, when the state of Washington designated an official flower.

__D__ Pennsylvania was the first to adopt an official state insect.

__D__ Connecticut has a state ship (*USS Nautilus*).

__D__ South Carolina has a state dance (the shag).

__R__ Presidential politics comes into play when states adopt a state song favored by a prominent politician.

__D__ West Virginia has three state songs.

__D__ Virginia has a state shellfish (the oyster).

Once you have generated a list of reasons and details to support your topic, place them in the order of their importance.

EXERCISE 10.5

We have provided both causes and effects below, along with supporting details. Identify the causes or effects and put them in the order of importance from most to least important. Then arrange the details under the cause or effect they support. Finally, write a new topic sentence.

Topic A: Being Unemployed Caused Me Severe Problems

Depression

Financial problems

Long delay in receiving benefits

Altering clothing instead of buying new: making dresses into blouses, pants into skirts

Lack of self-confidence

Fruitless job interviews

Confusion

Psychological problems

Son's college tuition payments hard to make

Standing in lines

Coping with bureaucracy of Unemployment Bureau

Falling behind in rent, then paying back rent

Buying hamburger instead of steak, spreading two pounds over three meals

Bewilderment: wondering why this happened to me

Most Important Effect: Financial problems

Detail 1: Falling behind in rent, then paying back rent

Detail 2: Son's college tuition payments hard to make

Detail 3: Buying hamburger instead of steak, spreading two pounds over three meals

Detail 4: Altering clothing instead of buying new: making dresses into blouses, pants into skirts

Less Important Effect: Psychological problems

Detail 1: Depression

Detail 2: Confusion

Detail 3: Lack of self-confidence

Detail 4: Bewilderment: wondering why this happened to me

Least Important Effect: Coping with the bureaucracy of the Unemployment Bureau

Detail 1: Long delay in receiving benefits

Detail 2: Fruitless job interviews

Detail 3: Standing in lines

New Topic Sentence: Losing my job resulted in problems with money, my feelings, and coping with the unemployment bureaucracy.

Topic B: Kids Can Be Taught to Love Reading (Causes)

Students get what they can out of their reading
Instructor gives no exams on dictionary use
Students are encouraged to read lots of books
Students are told to read only for pleasure
Students need not finish books
Students are not forced to look words up
The instructor holds no contests
Students are encouraged to find out where words come from, how they changed over years
Students are encouraged to browse in a good dictionary
Students are encouraged to look up odd or forbidden words
Instructor asks no vocabulary questions
Teacher gives no etymology quizzes
Instructor encourages students to read books

Most Important Cause: Instructor encourages students to read books

Detail 1: Students are encouraged to read lots of books

Detail 2: Students are encouraged to read only for pleasure

Detail 3: Students get what they can out of their reading

Detail 4: Students need not finish books

Detail 5: The instructor holds no contests

Less Important Cause: Students are encouraged to browse in a good dictionary

Detail 1: Students are not forced to look words up

Detail 2: Students are encouraged to look up odd or forbidden words

Detail 3: <u>Students are encouraged to find out where words come from, or how they changed over the years</u>

Least Important Cause: <u>The instructor gives no exams on dictionary use</u>

Detail 1: <u>Instructor asks no vocabulary questions</u>
Detail 2: <u>Teacher gives no etymology quizzes</u>

Topic Sentence: <u>Kids can be taught to love reading if the teacher encourages them to read books they like, influences them to browse in a good dictionary, and does not test them on their reading.</u>

Topic C: A Record Snowfall in the City Creates Changes (Effects)

People walk more
The airports close
People can't go out
People speak and smile
The city becomes more beautiful
A blanket of white covers everything
They watch a lot of TV
People treat one another differently
Ugliness is hidden
The availability of transportation changes
The birthrate rises nine months later
People become more friendly to strangers
The streets are empty of cars
People recognize the power of nature
The city becomes quiet

Most Important Effect: <u>People can't go out</u>

Detail 1: <u>They watch a lot of TV</u>
Detail 2: <u>The birthrate rises nine months later</u>
Detail 3: <u>People recognize the power of nature</u>

Less Important Effect: <u>The availability of transportation changes</u>

Detail 1: <u>People walk more</u>
Detail 2: <u>The streets are empty of cars</u>
Detail 3: <u>The city becomes quiet</u>
Detail 4: <u>The airports close</u>

Next-to-Least Important Effect: <u>People treat one another differently</u>

Detail 1: <u>People become more friendly to strangers</u>

Detail 2: <u>People speak and smile</u>

Least Important Effect: <u>The city becomes more beautiful</u>

Detail 1: <u>A blanket of white covers everything</u>

Detail 2: <u>Ugliness is hidden</u>

Topic Sentence: <u>Under a heavy snowfall, city people must stay inside, have difficulty finding transportation, treat one another differently, and notice the city's beauty.</u>

Section Four: Using Transitional Devices

Transitional devices will help you link your causes and effects together. They lead your readers from point to point in time, as in narrative and process paragraphs:

first, second, third, finally, now, then, next, also, after, during

You should also use words and phrases which tell your reader *how* and *why* events occur:

consequently, as a result, thus, therefore, because

Section Five: Writing the First Draft

Write the first draft of your paragraph, emphasizing either causes or effects, or balancing between them. Follow these steps:

- Choose a topic from Section One of this chapter or invent your own.
- Decide which type of paragraph you plan to write, *cause* or *effect*, or evenly balanced between them.
- Use brainstorming, clustering, or some other prewriting device to generate details and reasons to support your paragraph.
- Design a plan to use your reasons or details.
- Place your reasons in order of importance, from most to least important, or least to most important. Do the same for details or examples you use as support for your reasons.
- Base a topic sentence on these ideas.
- Give your paragraph a title.

Based on these early steps, write the first draft of your paper. Brian wrote the first draft of a paragraph below:

At nineteen, Patrick loves the taste of alcohol and the speed of cars. He is a junior in college and an active member in the community. When Patrick drinks alcohol and drives his car fast, he is irresponsible. His habits cause him to take unnecessary risks. If he does not take control of his life, he might cause a terrible accident. When Patrick gets in his car, a gray 300ZX, he drives very fast. He loves to speed and to pass cars at illegal points in the road. He loves the sense of being in the fresh air and driving about 100 miles per hour. For example, last year at Christmas, he left my house like he had an appointment. His tires were smoking and the smell of fresh rubber could be detected. When he drinks and drives, he loses his sense of control over life. He does tasks to endanger his life. For example, last New Year's night, Patrick drank about ten cans of beer. His eyes were blood shot red. He walked like he could not see where he was going because he fell over everything. When he tried to start his car, he left it in gear. Moving, the car hit a tree. On the way home, he passed a police officer going 110 miles per hour. The policeman stopped him for speeding. When the policeman asked for his license, he passed out. He went to jail. When Patrick drives his car and drinks, he is irresponsible. If Patrick does not become more responsible, he might do something that he might regret.

Section Six: Revising the Paragraph

Apply the following questions to your own writing, or have a friend or class-mate do it. We have applied them to Brian's paragraph.

1. *Does the writer stress cause or effect, or does he or she balance them? Does the first sentence or two state the writer's topic and plan? If not, how should the writer change the organization?*

Brian is stressing the *effects* of heavy drinking. He should begin his paragraph with his topic sentence, rather than bringing it in later. To create it, he should combine his third and fourth sentences, like this:

When Patrick drinks alcohol, he drives his car too fast, taking unnecessary risks.

This new topic sentence creates a tighter link between cause (drinking) and effect (driving fast), while adding a comment to show how the writer feels about it: "taking unnecessary risks."

2. *Does the writer include all the reasons and details the reader needs? Are they in the right order? Should any reasons or details be left out?*

Brian includes enough reasons and details in the right order. He moves from details of Patrick's drinking and driving to a particular incident. How-ever, Brian fails to relate an early sentence to his primary concern, the link between Patrick's drinking and driving: "He is a junior in college and an active member in the community."

140

Brian should either omit these details or explain them. Does Patrick act more responsibly when he is sober? Does he hide his misbehavior from others? Then too, we don't know the most important likely results of Patrick's arrest, such as a heavy fine, loss of driving privileges, and an increase in insurance premiums.

3. *How has the writer linked his or her ideas together? What devices like connectives, synonyms, and pronouns has the writer used?*

Brian uses words such as *when, if, for example,* and *on the way home* as transitional devices. Using more such words and phrases would link his sentences together more smoothly. He also replaces the name *Patrick* with the pronouns *he* and *him*. However, he needs synonyms for *Patrick* such as *alcoholic adolescent, risk-taker,* and perhaps *boozer* or *speedster*.

4. *A cause and effect paragraph often needs an effective, satisfying close. Does Brian's paper have one?*

No. Brian brings his paragraph to a close by repeating sentences he uses in the first part of his paragraph. However, Brian has already told the reader that Patrick acts irresponsibly. Patrick probably already regrets his arrest, jailing, and other consequences of speeding while drunk. Brian should add a more specific conclusion to account for these details.

5. *What serious mechanical or other problems should the writer solve while rewriting the first draft?*

Brian's paper includes no serious mechanical, spelling, or punctuation errors. However, he could write more concisely. He could replace a phrase like "to pass cars at illegal points in the road" with "to pass cars illegally." Instead of "he loses his sense of control over life," he could write simply, "he loses control." He needs to look over his writing closely for empty words and phrases. Then he should replace or omit them.

Apply the questions in the revision checklist to your own writing, or have a friend or classmate do it.

Revision Checklist

1. Does the writer stress cause or effect, or does he or she balance them? Does the first sentence or two state the writer's topic and plan? If not, how should the writer change the organization?
2. Does the writer include all the reasons and details the reader needs? Are they in the right order? Should any reasons or details be left out?
3. How has the writer linked his or her ideas together? What devices like connectives, synonyms, and pronouns has the writer used?
4. A cause and effect paragraph often needs an effective, satisfying close. Does your paper have one?
5. What serious mechanical or other problems should the writer solve while rewriting the first draft?

Section Seven: Final Editing

Once you have finished, clean up the grammatical problems, punctuation errors, and misspellings. The following questions will help you finish the process of writing your paragraph:

1. Have I corrected the grammatical errors I often make? (Look back over earlier papers you have written. Then check this one for mistakes like subject–verb agreement or misplaced modifiers.)
2. Have I corrected the punctuation errors I tend to make?
3. Have I corrected the words I usually misspell?

Section Eight: Further Topics

- Why political or social scandals are so interesting
- What makes us courageous or afraid
- Changes caused by (you or an acquaintance) going to college.
- What do you look for when you converse with people? What kinds of topics do you usually discuss, and why?
- What would induce you to give up life as you know it and face the unknown?
- Does lots of money make people complacent and unwilling to accept risks? Explain.
- If a computer error gave you too large a paycheck, would you report it? Explain why.

On the one hand, I can give you the west wall with its gleaming limestone and sunny exposure. On the other hand, I can offer you the north wall with its quaint charm and enchanting vistas.

Comparing and Contrasting

When we compare two persons, places, or objects, we look for *likenesses* or similarities. When we contrast them, we look for *differences*. Should I marry Frank or Lorenzo? Do I buy a sporty, brightly painted two-seater sports car, or should I settle for a more sedate four-door sedan in an appealing shade of gray? Do I save for a skiing vacation in Colorado or charge it? This chapter will deal with both techniques—comparison and contrast.

The following paragraph mainly *compares*:

Minor imperfections are one key to a man's distinctiveness. Case in point: A boyfriend—ordinarily dignified—showed up for a party in a kilt and knee socks, announcing that it was his family tartan. Glimpsing his pale, skinny legs, I bit my tongue lest I utter something . . . well, untoward. But he said, "I wanted a chance to show off my elegant legs!" His whole character seemed distilled in that gesture. I smiled for weeks after. A friend who married a hot-shot lawyer remembers, "On the first date, I learned that he could ride out rough hours and stiff client demands. On the second, I learned that what he couldn't ride was a bicycle. *That's* when I decided to give him a chance." We can bristle at quirks, or we can cherish them. Why not cherish?

Robin Reif, *Glamour*

What words in the topic sentence signal the writer's intention to stress *similarities*?

The words "one key" tell us that the writer will deal with likenesses.

What two different items are being compared, and in what way?

Women are comparing the lovable foibles they have found in two different men.

This paragraph mainly *contrasts*:

Americans have been retiring earlier and earlier. In 1948 close to half of all American men 65 or older were still working. Today only 16 percent of men in this age group remain in the labor force. The share of American men between 55 and 64 who have left the labor force has jumped from 13 percent in 1960 to 33 percent in 1988. More than half of all Social Security pensioners now claim

144

their benefits the minute they're eligible, at age 62, even though they receive only 80 percent of what they would get by waiting until they're 65.

What information about the *past* does the writer provide about retirement?
More than forty years ago, half of 65-year-old American men were still working. Thirty years ago only 13 percent of American men between 55 and 64 had retired.

What contrasting information about the *present* does the writer provide about retirement?
Only sixteen percent of 65-year-old men still work. Thirty-three percent of American men between 55 and 64 have retired. More than half of American workers claim social security benefits at age 62 instead of waiting until 65.

How does the writer organize the paragraph to make the contrast clear?
The writer contrasts two periods of time by swinging back and forth between past and present.

Why did the writer place these contrasting facts in this order?
He wanted to emphasize the present, using the past to make his figures more meaningful.

Before writing his paragraph, the writer probably designed it this way:

Topic Idea: Retirement rates for elderly American men 30 to 40 years ago and now.

Contrasting Points:	Then	Now
Percent of 65-year-old men still working	half	16%
Percent of American men between 55 and 64 retired	13%	33%
Social Security pensioners claiming benefits at 62	none or few (?)	half

By putting together his paragraph this way, the writer makes his point clearly and emphatically: American men are retiring sooner, in larger numbers, than ever before.

Here is another contrast paragraph:

Some regard the squirrel as a nuisance—utility companies, for example. The squirrel has found the metal in electrical cables useful for grinding its incisors, thereby occasionally causing power outages. But the squirrel has many defenders. According to one naturalist, because the squirrel is such a difficult target for marksmen, early American squirrel hunters became the best sharpshooters in the world. And during the American Revolution, it was the militiaman with his rifle who played a key role in winning the war.

How does the writer signal his intentions in the opening sentence?
While "some" regard the squirrel as a nuisance, "others" may not.

Instead of seesawing back and forth between contrasts, the writer develops one point fully. Then he develops a contrasting point. What are these points? The squirrel makes itself a nuisance by cutting electrical cables. However, it provided good training for American sharpshooters.

Section One: Choosing a Topic

To get started on your comparison and contrast paragraph, invent a pair of topics or choose one of these:

- A salesperson and a shopper
- A small town and a large city
- Simple food and fancy foods

Your topics: _____

Section Two: Generating Ideas

Once you have chosen to compare or contrast two objects, people, or ideas, decide on your approach. Do you want to stress similarities or differences? Or do you want to balance them? Then put each topic at the top of parallel columns. Under each topic, make a list of details, examples, and illustrations that will help you develop your topic. Stephanie decided to compare and contrast two small objects: a toy wooden elephant and a plastic tool called a "magicutter." She generated ideas by making notes on the similarities and differences she saw in her two objects:

Points of Similarity	A. Wooden Elephant	B. "Magicutter"
1. Small	Fits in palm of hand	Fits in palm of hand
2. Easily lost	Light weight	Light weight
3. Affordable	Priced under $3.00	Priced under $3.00

Points of Contrast		
1. Place of origin	Straw Market, Nassau	Augusta Federal Savings
2. Attractiveness	Tan with row of stripes along the side	Odd-shaped, scissors-like piece of blue plastic
	Two small tusks with two small baskets on each side	Small copper blade swivels against plastic section to cut paper
		Silver script on front says "Augusta Federal Savings"

| 3. Durability | Will last for years | Blade on cutter will wear down, making it useless |
| | A collector's item | Will be thrown away |

Stephanie then based her topic statement (two sentences) on her notes:

My wooden elephant and magicutter are both small, easily lost, and affordable. Unlike my magicutter, however, my wooden elephant is "foreign," more attractive, and more durable.

Stephanie still doesn't know whether to stress similarities or differences, or to handle both of them. However, making notes was a necessary beginning. If these details will fit into a paragraph, she can use most or all of them. If not, she can select the best or most important of them. She is now ready to plan the organization of her paragraph.

Section Three: Planning and Organizing the Paragraph

When writing a comparison or contrast paragraph, you must choose between two approaches. You may decide to move back and forth repeatedly. This approach may be best if you treat a number of details. It sets up a predictable pattern for the reader to follow:

Topic One: Aspect A → Topic Two: Aspect A

Topic One: Aspect B → Topic Two: Aspect B

Topic One: Aspect C → Topic Two: Aspect C

Or you may choose to develop one point fully before going on to the next one. This plan works well if you deal with only two similarities or differences.

Point One

• Aspect A

• Aspect B

• Aspect C

Point Two

• Aspect A

• Aspect B

• Aspect C

At times, you may want to insert a paragraph break between each of the points being compared or contrasted.

Look over Stephanie's notes in the section above. By generating ideas, she has learned how she feels about the two objects. She can probably handle all the details she has generated in a long paragraph. For the design of this paragraph, she can choose between two plans. The likenesses between her two objects are more important than their differences, she believes. Regardless of her plan for the paragraph, she will begin by summing up the similarities between the two objects.

What is one way for her to organize the rest of her paragraph?

She can organize the rest of her paragraph by describing all of her elephant's traits one by one. She can then describe all of her magicutter's traits.

In a second possible approach, Stephanie would also sum up the similarities between the two objects.

Following this alternate plan, how would she organize the rest of her paragraph?

She would organize the rest of her paragraph by seesawing between the two objects. She would identify the elephant's origin and then the origin of the magicutter. Then she would describe the elephant's appearance and that of the magicutter. Finally, she would describe the elephant's durability and move from there to the lasting qualities of the magicutter (or lack of them).

What conclusion should Stephanie write for her paragraph?

Long after the magicutter has worn out, the owner will consider the elephant a collector's item.

Write your own comparison and contrast paragraph by following this process:

Pair of people, objects, or ideas to be compared and contrasted:

_____

_____

Points of Similarity	Person or Object A	Person or Object B
1. _____	_____	_____
2. _____	_____	_____
3. _____	_____	_____

Points of Difference

1. _____	_____	_____
2. _____	_____	_____
3. _____	_____	_____

Way of planning development:

_____ comparison only

_____ contrast only

_____ *both* comparison and contrast

Your plan:

_____ Deal with all of one item's traits before describing the other item's traits

_____ Seesaw between the items, dealing with one trait of each before deailing with a trait of the other

Topic statement or sentence: _____

_____

EXERCISE 11.1

Read the following paragraph and answer the questions.

Free trade makes the world economy more efficient by allowing nations to capitalize on their strengths. The United States has an advantage in food production, for instance, while Saudi Arabia has an advantage in oil. The Saudis could undertake massive irrigation to become self-sufficient in food, but it is more economical for them to sell oil and purchase food from us. Similarly, we could become self-sufficient in petroleum by squeezing more out of oil shale. But it is much less costly to buy some of our oil from Saudi Arabia. Trade between our two countries improves the standard of living in both.

1. Does the writer compare or contrast, or do both?
   The writer mainly compares the *strengths* of two countries, the United States and Saudi Arabia, though these strengths involve two different commodities, food and oil.

2. What words in the first two sentences signal the writer's plan of organization?
   The writer signals an emphasis on comparison by repeating the same words for both countries: "has an advantage in." The writer also connects the ideas with the word "while," meaning "at the same time."

3. What plan of organization does the writer follow?
   The writer deals first with the United States, then with Saudi Arabia, then returns to the United States.

4. What transitions does the writer use to help us move from idea to idea?
   more, similarly, much less, between our two

EXERCISE 11.2

Read over the following paragraphs and respond to the questions.

Often, the difference between an emotionally strong child and a weak one is how well parental expectations match the child's capabilities. One child, Tim, could not do what his father wanted—stick to a task for hours on end. "You

149

have no character," the father raged, "no willpower." Finally, the boy decided his father was right—he had no character, nothing. So he simply gave up, dropping out of school and drifting as an adult.

Another family came close to the same disaster. Their daughter was born with a difficult temperament, intense and explosive. The parents labeled her a "rotten kid," and she played the part by developing behavior problems at school. Then, at age eight, she showed signs of musical and dramatic talent. As teachers praised her, the girl's parents decided her explosiveness was nothing more than an "artistic temperament." Once they began to focus on her strengths, the girl flourished.

1. How does the topic sentence signal the writer's emphasis in this paper—comparison or contrast?

   The first sentence uses the word "difference," and then assigns names to the two categories: the "emotionally strong child" and the "weak one."

2. What aspects of a "weak" child does the writer describe?

   The "weak" child's father expected too much of him. The father always reminded the son that the son wasn't measuring up.

3. What saves the "strong" child from a wasted life?

   Though condemned by her parents, the "strong" child encounters teachers who encourage her. They praise her musical and dramatic talents. Impressed by this praise, her parents change their views. They now see her behavior problems as "artistic temperament."

4. How has the writer designed the paper to deal with this contrast?

   The writer first sums up the key differences. He treats one type of child—the "weak" one—first. He then takes up the contrasting type of child, the "strong" one.

5. What transitional devices does the writer use?

   The writer uses words like *one child, finally,* and *so* to link word groups describing the "weak" child. He then uses words like *another, then, as,* and *once* in the section that treats the "strong" child.

EXERCISE 11.3

Answers will vary.

We have listed a number of topics for comparison or contrast paragraphs below. Invent two topic sentences for each one. Emphasize comparison in one, and contrast in the other.

EXAMPLE: The homebody and the wanderer.

Comparison Topic Sentence: The homebody and the wanderer both have predictable habits.

Contrast Topic Sentence: The homebody is far more predictable than the wanderer.

150

1. The social superstar and the average person.

Comparison Topic Sentence: The social superstar and the average person both need the approval of others.

Contrast Topic Sentence: The social superstar is much more poised and outgoing than the average person.

2. The same person first poor and then rich.

Comparison Topic Sentence: The same person first poor and then rich has the same fears and insecurities.

Contrast Topic Sentence: A poor person who becomes rich may select a new car, house, and friends.

3. High school and college students

Comparison Topic Sentence: High school and college students have similar attitudes towards friendship.

Contrast Topic Sentence: College students often study harder than high school students, and the cost of their education is higher.

4. Parents and children

Comparison Topic Sentence: Parents and children often look and sound the same.

Contrast Topic Sentence: Children usually wear brighter, gaudier clothing than their parents.

5. Broad-minded and prejudiced people

Comparison Topic Sentence: Broad-minded and prejudiced people may live in the same town and attend the same church.

Contrast Topic Sentence: Broad-minded people associate with a wider range of personalities than prejudiced people do.

EXERCISE 11.4

Answers will vary.

We have listed possible topics for comparison and contrast paragraphs below. Choose one of them. Then write two or three sentences that give examples or details illustrating the topic. Include transitional devices where useful.

EXAMPLE:

1. My biology [or other class] instructor teaches quite differently than my history [or other class] instructor.

151

Illustrating sentence: Whereas my biology instructor uses slides and specimens to illustrate her lectures, my history instructor writes on the chalkboard, often outlining his lectures.

2. Frank [or another person] and his wife, Georgina, [or another name] look and act in similar ways.

Illustrating sentence: Both Frank and his wife are very serious at all times, without much sense of humor. Neither of them sees anything funny in a minor mishap such as a broken dish, an overflowing washer, or a stalled car. At the same time, they are both rather disorganized and usually late for appointments.

3. Adults and children tend to choose different types of gifts.

Illustrating sentence: Adults tend to favor useful or decorative gifts such as clothing, tools, live plants, and jewelry. Children, on the other hand, prefer toys, sports equipment, candy, and games.

4. The career I eventually chose was quite different from (an) earlier choice(s) in life.

Illustrating sentence: At various times in my life, I wanted to be a policeman, a doctor, a farmer, and a veterinarian. However, during my second year in college, I finally decided to become a social worker, with the opportunity to help people in trouble.

EXERCISE 11.5

The following essay uses several paragraphs to both compare and contrast two cities. After reading it, answer the questions that follow.

New Castle, Delaware: During the first half of the seventeenth century, when the nations of Europe were squabbling over who owned the New World, the Dutch and the Swedes founded competing villages ten miles apart on the Delaware River. Not long afterward, the English took over both places and gave them new names, New Castle and Wilmington.

After a century and a half the two villages grew apace, but gradually Wilmington gained all the advantages. It was a little closer to Philadelphia, so when new textile mills opened, they opened in Wilmington, not in New Castle. There was plenty of water power from rivers and creeks at Wilmington, so when young Irénée DuPont chose a place for his gunpowder mill, it was Wilmington he chose, not New Castle. Wilmington became a town and then a city—a rather important city, much the largest in Delaware. And New Castle, bypassed by the highways and waterways that made Wilmington prosperous? New Castle slumbered, ten miles south on the Delaware River. No two villages with such similar pasts could have gone such separate ways. And today no two places could be more different.

Wilmington, with its expressways and parking lots and all its other concrete ribbons and badges, is a tired old veteran of the industrial wars and wears a vacant stare. Block after city block where people used to live and shop is broken and empty.

New Castle never had to make way for progress and therefore never had any reason to tear down its seventeenth- and eighteenth-century houses. So they are still here, standing in tasteful rows under ancient elms around the original town green. New Castle is still an agreeable place to live. The pretty buildings of its quiet past make a serene setting for the lives of 4,800 people. New Castle may be America's loveliest town, but it is not an important town at all. Progress passed it by.

Poor New Castle.

Lucky Wilmington.

Charles Kuralt, "Two Towns in Delaware"

1. Kuralt does not state a thesis for his contrast essay. We must guess. Sum up his thesis in a sentence or two.
   Although industrialization made Wilmington, Delaware, richer and bigger than New Castle in the name of "progress," Wilmington has lost its attractiveness, wealth, and people. In contrast, New Castle preserves the beauty, dignity, and peacefulness Wilmington has lost.

2. What is Kuralt's purpose?
   He may want to encourage readers to preserve rather than destroy attractive elements of the past, to consider not only *how* to do something but *why*: to improve the quality of our lives.

3. What similarities does Kuralt see between New Castle and Wilmington?
   Both have deep roots in history, having been founded in the early years of our country by immigrants. Both are Delaware towns. Both are within ten miles of one another on the banks of the same river.

4. What differences does Kuralt see between the two towns?
   An industrialist saw commercial possibilities for Wilmington that New Castle lacked: ample water power and closeness to Philadelphia. Consequently, Wilmington grew larger than New Castle, but then deteriorated, leaving it with ugly concrete structures like expressways and parking lots, a loss of residents, and economic depression.

   New Castle, on the other hand, preserved the beautiful houses which were—presumably—destroyed by industrialization in Wilmington. It stayed small and beautiful, a good place to live, while Wilmington grew large and ugly. Ultimately, the desire to make money which made Wilmington grow also destroyed it, driving its residents away.

5. How does Kuralt organize his contrast essay?
   He seesaws back and forth, dealing first with the common origins of both towns, then taking up Wilmington's growth and prosperity in contrast to

Section Four: Using Transitional Devices

Writers handle *similarities* or likenesses with transitional devices such as these:

at the same time, similarly, also, just as, like, every, each of, both, as well as, in the same way

Writers stress *differences* or contrast with these transitional devices:

however, on the other hand, although, unlike, but

Use a variety of these devices, depending on your approach to a topic.

EXERCISE 11.6
Answers will vary.

The paragraph below lacks transitional devices. As a result, it is hard to read. Add transitional devices where needed. Try to vary your choices.

The British version of English is fairly polite and well mannered. American English, ___on the other hand___ , has vitality, and it has guts. ___While___ British English is a slow-pitch softball, American English is a major-league spitball. ___Unlike___ British English, which seems confined by well-worn rules, American English is a boisterous language with a life of its own. British English ___once___ dominated polite usage, ___but___ America is leading the way now.

Section Five: Writing the First Draft

Write the first draft of your paragraph, emphasizing either comparison or contrast, or balancing them. Follow these steps:

• Choose a topic from Section One of this chapter or invent your own.

154

- Decide which type of paragraph you plan to write, *comparison* or *contrast*, or both evenly balanced.
- Use one of the patterns in Section Three to generate details and reasons to support your paragraph.
- Design a plan to use your reasons or details. Either develop one topic fully before going on to the next, or seesaw between the topics.
- Base a topic sentence on these ideas.
- Give your paragraph or paper a title.

Darla wrote the following comparison and contrast draft:

Although Liz and Darla are good friends, they handle dress and housekeeping quite differently. Liz is a perfect housekeeper. She dresses neatly, makes good grades, and keeps everything organized. Darla, on the other hand, dresses sloppy, keeps a dirty room, and her grades are not so good.

Liz keeps her house immaculate. You cannot find anything dirty or out of place in her house. Liz also has a very neat personal appearance—dress pants, shirt to match, and casual flat shoes with socks to match. She never leaves her house without her eyeshadow, blush, lipstick, and face make-up. Liz has brown hair to her shoulders that is always combed and styled. Organization and cleanliness are important to her in her lifestyle.

On the other hand, Darla is not a clean housekeeper. You can go in her room at almost anytime of the day and find it in total disarray. Shoes are all over the floor, make-up laying around, and empty hairspray containers here and there. Compared to Liz, Darla is not a neat dresser. She wears jogging pants and torn t-shirts. Darla has long, tangled brown hair. Darla thinks there is a time and place for organization and cleanliness.

Although Darla and Liz are so opposite, they still have a lot in common. They love to get together to shop, eat, and exercise. Darla and Liz are always there for each other. When they get together to shop at the mall, eat Chinese food, or exercise, they have a great time together. Although Liz and Darla are opposite, they still pass a good time together and have a good friend relationship. They are the female version of the Odd Couple.

Section Six: Revising the Paragraph

Apply the questions in the checklist below to your own writing, or have a friend or classmate do it. We have applied them to Darla's paper.

1. *Does the writer stress comparison or contrast, or does he or she balance them? Does the first sentence or two state the writer's topic and plan? If not, how should the writer change the organization?*

Darla tells the reader in the first paragraph that she plans to deal with two friends' dress and housekeeping. She then deals with Liz's dress and housekeeping in its own paragraph. She then treats Darla's dress and housekeeping habits. Finally, she treats the less important similarities between them.

2. *Does the writer include all the reasons and details the reader needs? Are they in the right order? Should any reasons or details be left out?*

155

Darla includes all the necessary examples and details, but she is careless about putting them in the right order. In her topic sentence, she mentions dress and housekeeping in that order. However, she handles these two aspects randomly in the last two sentences of her introduction. And she reverses this order in the development of the two paragraphs that follow. Her treatment of illustrating details should be consistent with the order set up in her topic sentence.

3. *How has the writer linked his or her ideas together? What devices like connectives, synonyms, and pronouns has the writer used?*

She uses terms such as *although, on the other hand, also, compared to Liz, so opposite, still have a lot in common.* She also uses their names, *she,* and *they* refer to them. However, she needs a wider range of transitions in her work, such as *conversely, in the same way, similarly,* and *in contrast.* She could also use more synonyms such as *these two women* or *both students.*

4. *A comparison and contrast paragraph often needs an effective, satisfying close. Does this student paper have one?*

She uses the term *the odd couple* effectively in her conclusion.

5. *What serious mechanical or other problems should the student writer solve while rewriting the first draft?*

She makes an early parallelism error in the first paragraph when she writes: "Darla, on the other hand, *dresses sloppy, keeps a dirty room,* and *her grades are not so good.*" While she uses two parallel verbs, *dresses* and *keeps,* the third part of her series is a clause rather than a predicate: "her grades are not so good." She should change the last part in the series to a predicate, "and *makes* poor grades."

A similar problem emerges in this sentence: "Shoes are all over the floor, make-up laying around and empty hairspray containers here and there." Since she begins this series with a clause, she should add verbs to the second and third word groups, perhaps synonyms of *lie* and *litter:* "Shoes *lie* all over the floor, make-up is *strewn* around, and empty hairspray containers *litter* the room." This revision is both more accurate and more forceful.

She also misspells "appeare̲nce," uses *laying* when *lying* is appropriate, uses the adjective *sloppy* instead of the adverb *sloppily* to modify the verb *dresses,* and is occasionally wordy. For instance, she writes, "Liz has brown hair to her shoulders that is always combed and styled." A more concise rewrite would read, "Liz always combs and styles her brown, shoulder-length hair." Similarly, she should combine these two short, choppy sentences: "Liz keeps her house immaculate. You cannot find anything dirty or out of place in her house." Her rewrite would read, "Nothing is dirty or out of place in Liz's immaculate house."

Apply the questions in the revision checklist below to your own writing, or have a friend or classmate do it.

1. Do you stress comparison or contrast, or do you balance them? Does the first sentence or two state your topic and plan? If not, how should you change the organization?

2. Do you include all the reasons and details the reader needs? Are they in the right order? Should any reasons or details be left out?

3. How have you linked your ideas together? What devices like connectives, synonyms, and pronouns have you used?

4. A comparison and contrast paragraph often needs an effective, satisfying close. Does your paper have one?

5. What serious mechanical or other problems should the writer solve while rewriting the first draft?

Section Seven: Final Editing

Once you have finished, clean up the grammatical problems, punctuation errors, and misspellings. The following questions will help you finish the process of writing your paragraph:

1. Have I corrected the grammatical errors I often make? (Look back over earlier papers you have written. Then check this one for mistakes like subject—verb agreement or misplaced modifiers.)

2. Have I corrected the punctuation errors I tend to make?

3. Have I corrected the words I usually misspell?

Section Eight: Further Topics

- Someone's greatest success and greatest failure
- Being well-prepared and being caught off guard
- College and professional sports
- Vacationing and loafing
- Gullibility and skepticism
- Generosity and stinginess

Persuading
an Audience

Change our lifestyles or diets and live longer, we are told. Vote for this candidate or that bond issue. Come to a meeting and discuss schools or taxes. We enjoy the free exchange of ideas in our society. As citizens, we must often choose between people or proposals. Read the following persuasive paragraph and answer the questions that follow.

Today Lyme disease is reaching epidemic proportions. The disease has spread to 43 states, with 90 percent of all cases in Connecticut, Rhode Island, Massachusetts, New York, New Jersey, Wisconsin, and Minnesota. It is also found in Europe, Asia, and Australia. Everyone, including the Centers for Disease Control, agrees that the roughly 5,700 new cases reported to the CDC last year was a fraction of the true count. With several thousand people infected every year, Lyme disease now surpasses Rocky Mountain spotted fever as the most prevalent tick-borne disease in the country. About half of the people infected develop a rash and, sometimes, a fever. The disease may also involve arthritic-like symptoms in the knees or other large joints. The riskiest period for Lyme disease infection is late spring and summer, when people spend a lot of time outside. That's also when the deer tick is about the size of a poppy seed, making it difficult to detect. "It can't be stressed too much that early diagnosis and treatment will prevent the progression of Lyme disease in the overwhelming majority of cases," says Dr. Allen C. Steere, of the New England Medical Center in Boston.

John Pekkanen, "The Mounting Toll of Lyme Disease"

EXERCISE 12.1

Answer the following questions about the preceding paragraph.

1. The author makes a claim in the topic sentence. A *claim* is an assertion that he believes can be proven. What is it?
   Lyme disease is now reaching epidemic proportions.

2. The author supports his claim with facts. What are these facts?
   The disease has spread to 43 states.

   90 percent of all cases were in Connecticut, Rhode Island, Massachusetts,

New York, New Jersey, Wisconsin, and Minnesota.

It is also found in Europe, Asia, and Australia.

Roughly 5,700 new cases were reported to the CDC last year, a fraction of the true count.

3. The writer seems to be responding to an implied argument against his claim—an argument that he does not spell out. What might this argument be?

Some may argue—the writer suggests—that Lyme is not an important disease, even among those borne by ticks.

4. The writer further supports his claim by referring to authorities. He does so to provide a credible, trustworthy basis of opinion. Who are these authorities?

The Centers for Disease Control, and Dr. Allen C. Steere of the New England Medical Center in Boston.

5. How does the writer define Lyme disease?

He describes symptoms which include a rash, fever, and arthritis-like pain in the joints.

6. When is the most likely time for people to get Lyme disease, and why?

The most likely time to get Lyme disease is in the late spring and summer, when people are outside, and when the tick is small and difficult to detect.

7. The paragraph's conclusion extends the author's claim. It suggests a remedy to the problem stated earlier. What is it?

Early diagnosis and treatment will prevent most people from suffering the effects of Lyme disease.

Before writing this paragraph, the writer may have put together the following outline:

Topic Sentence: Today Lyme disease is reaching epidemic proportions (**claim**).

1. Spread of disease:
   a. In this country (**facts**)
   b. Abroad (**facts**)
2. Seriousness of epidemic
   a. 5,700 cases each year, a fraction of true count (**fact, authority, response to opposition**)
   b. Surpasses number of cases of Rocky Mountain spotted fever (**example, response to opposition**)

3. Symptoms

    a. Rash (**example**)

    b. Fever (**example**)

    c. Arthritic-like symptoms (**example**)

4. Riskiest period is late spring and summer

    a. Most people are outside (**reason**)

    b. Deer tick is small (**reason, fact**)

5. Need for early diagnosis and treatment (**reason, authority; completes the claim**)

To sum up, each item of support backs up the claim: facts, reasons, authority, response to opposition, examples. Each point also leads to the conclusion, which completes the claim.

Section One: Choosing a Topic

To get started on a persuasive paragraph, invent an interesting topic or choose one of the following:

- Certain courses should (should not) be required for a major or a college degree
- The law should (should not) treat adolescents the same way it treats adults
- Drunk drivers should (should not) be punished more severely than they are today.

Section Two: Generating Ideas

STATING A CLAIM

Persuasion is an effort to change the attitudes of others. After you argue a position persuasively, hearers may not be ready to share it. However, they should at least be open to considering your view. A persuasion paragraph should develop a main idea or *claim:*

> A claim states a belief that some change in attitude, action, or law would or would not be beneficial.

Your claim should be *both*

- **Definable**, and
- **Arguable**

162

First of all, a claim must be *definable.* To define things or qualities, you must tell the following:

- What it is, and
- What group it fits in

Ambrose Bierce used this approach to define a "cabbage" as "a vegetable about as large and wise as a man's head." The process of defining is also discussed in Chapter 8, pages 110–11. Your definition may also include such details as the following:

- What you do with it, or what it looks like; and often
- What it is not (an opposite or antonym)

"A hammer," you might say, "is a hand tool for striking. It has a handle attached to a heavy, rigid head."

This definition does the following:

- Names the tool: a "hammer"
- Places the hammer in a class: "hand tools"
- Tells what you do with it: "striking"; and
- Describes it: "a handle attached to a heavy, rigid head"

As our earlier chapter on the defining paragraph points out, a paragraph or essay will sometimes be needed to fully define objects or qualities.

In addition, a claim must be *arguable.* It must be debatable for or against, pro or con. Those on both sides of an issue should be able to cite reasons, examples, facts, or authorities to support their views. To be arguable, a claim must first be definable. Some views are too fuzzy or figurative to be arguable. Most people would agree, for example, that college is a pleasant place for many high school graduates. No one would object to an ad calling a movie "a breathtaking panorama, a life and time unlike any other, the greatest story ever told." However, indefinable statements are not arguable.

Therefore, some types of claims should be avoided, such as the following:

- Those that everyone agrees with
- Those that consist entirely of figures of speech
- Those that are not supportable with facts
- Those that simply state facts

No one could argue with the claim that one's grandfather was an alien from Mars. While all the terms are definable, no evidence could possibly be cited to prove the claim. No one could debate a Department of Labor estimate made in 1974 that there would be 4,300 new jobs for psychologists in 1975. One could resolve any such argument by checking the relevant government publication.

EXERCISE 12.2

Look over the claims below. Decide whether each one is both definable *and* arguable. *Then explain why it is or why it is not. For example, consider the claim that "All used cars should carry a list of all known defects." The terms* used cars *and* defects *are both* definable. *Since buyers and sellers might both cite reasons or facts to bolster their differing views, the claim is also* arguable.

1. To build a fire in a man's heart, wear something black . . . anything black.

Definable? _____ Yes ___X___ No   Why or why not?

While the color black is definable, "to build a fire in a man's heart" is a figure of speech. It is not meant to refer literally to incineration.

Arguable? _____ Yes ___X___ No   Why or why not?

Only by replacing the metaphor with a definable claim could this statement be made arguable.

2. Twelve months a year, Steve Wade and Ernest Paine punch, brand, and drive 2,200 head of cattle across 500,000 acres of land.

Definable? ___X___ Yes _____ No   Why or why not?

This statement of fact is definable. It numbers months, cattle, and acres, all of them with widely accepted meanings.

Arguable? _____ Yes ___X___ No   Why or why not?

The statement includes no opinions or claims about which anyone might disagree. It simply lists facts.

3. When your birthday is April Fools' Day, you learn very quickly to be ready for anything.

Definable? _____ Yes ___X___ No   Why or why not?

The speaker could presumably prove that his or her birthday is April Fool's Day. However, "ready for anything" is too general to be defined.

Arguable? _____ Yes ___X___ No   Why or why not?

Since "ready for anything" is an overstatement, the term "anything" would need to be replaced with a specific, definable situation to be arguable.

4. Motorists who drop litter on highways should be deprived of their driver's licenses.

Definable? ___X___ Yes _____ No   Why or why not?

The primary terms are all definable: "motorists," "litter," "highways," and "driver's licenses."

Arguable? ___X___ Yes _____ No   Why or why not?

This proposition is arguable. Others might disagree as to whether littering is an offense serious enough to warrant the loss of one's driver's license.

5. Humankind is unwittingly altering the earth's climate by inserting too much carbon dioxide into the atmosphere.

Definable? __X__ Yes _____ No Why or why not?
Key terms like "humankind," "climate," "carbon dioxide," and "atmosphere" are all definable.

Arguable? __X__ Yes _____ No Why or why not?
Both scientists and lay people disagree about how much carbon dioxide is too much, how much of it emanates from man-made sources, and whether these presumed changes affect the earth's climate. Moreover, whether these presumed changes are dangerous or could or should be halted are arguable.

6. If God were all-powerful, he wouldn't allow horror and pain in his universe.

Definable? _____ Yes __X__ No Why or why not?
Terms such as "horror and pain" are too emotional to be defined. Reasonable people might also disagree about definitions of "God."

Arguable? _____ Yes __X__ No Why or why not?
Unless the terms are defined or quantified to everyone's satisfaction, the assertion cannot be debated.

7. Dinosaurs may have been warm-blooded, with the right-sized brains for reptiles of their body size.

Definable? __X__ Yes _____ No Why or why not?
Scientists can define terms such as "dinosaurs," "warm-blooded," "brains," and "body size."

Arguable? __X__ Yes _____ No Why or why not?
Because only fossil remains exist, scientists may reasonably disagree about the temperature of dinosaurs' blood and the approximate size of their brains.

8. War, and preparation for war, is the primal curse now afflicting the human race.

Definable? _____ Yes __X__ No Why or why not?
While "war" and "the human race" are definable, "primal curse" (as a metaphor), "afflicting," and perhaps even "preparation for war" are not.

Arguable? _____ Yes __X__ No Why or why not?
The proposition is not arguable until the metaphorical words are replaced with definable ones.

9. Anyone who has worked longer than a year knows that any job quickly loses most of its glamour.

Definable? _____ Yes __X__ No Why or why not?
While the terms "longer than a year" and "job" are definable, "glamour" refers too closely to emotions to be definable.

Arguable? _____ Yes __X__ No Why or why not?
The statement itself relies too heavily on the feelings of the speaker to be arguable.

SUPPORTING A CLAIM

To decide whether your argument can be supported, generate backing for it. Decide whether your claim is best justified by *citing facts or examples, appealing to authority, predicting results, responding to an opposing view, giving reasons,* or *appealing to the emotions and senses.* Your purpose and audience will affect your choice of type of backing.

1. *Facts and examples* give your claim credibility. They also interest your reader. Edward O. Wilson uses facts to compare male and female athletes:

> Male champions are always between 5 and 20 percent faster than women champions: in 1974 the difference was 8 percent in the 100 meters, 11 percent in the 400 meters, 15 percent in the mile, 10 percent in the 10,000 meters, and so on through every distance. Even in the marathon, where size and brute strength count least, the difference was 13 percent. Women marathoners have comparable endurance, but men are faster—their champions run twenty-six five-minute miles one after another.

By piling up facts, Wilson gives force and inevitability to his facts. While he does not cite a source for his facts, a reader could easily check them in a reference work such as the *Encyclopedia of Sports.*

Jacob Bronowski gives *examples* to link science and art:

> The great ages of science are the great ages of all the arts, because in them powerful minds have taken fire from one another. . . . Galileo and Shakespeare, who were born in the same year, grew into greatness in the same age. When Galileo was looking through his telescope at the moon, Shakespeare was writing *The Tempest,* and all Europe was in ferment, from Johannes Kepler to Peter Paul Rubens, and from the first table of logarithms by John Napier to the Authorized Version of the Bible.
>
> "The Reach of Imagination"

You must make sure that the facts and examples fit your claim, however. It would be wrong to compare men swimmers with women tennis players. It would also be misleading to use Babe Ruth as an example of a great American golfer.

2. *Appeals to authority* also help support your claim, especially if the authority is someone whose testimony is reliable. The name of a well-known individual or organization lends prestige or substance to an argument. The following paragraph cites a medical expert to support a claim:

> The acne drug that recently became famous for its ability to smooth wrinkles may also prevent skin cancer, says Dr. Albert Kligman, a professor of dermatology at the University of Pennsylvania in Philadelphia. The drug is tretinoin, a derivative of vitamin A.

Most readers consider a professor at a well-known university a reliable authority. However, some appeals to authority seem suspect or biased. We tend to discount support of a Democratic candidate for office by the Americans for Democratic Action. A product may use the testimony of an entertainer to influence us. However, a popular singer or actress is probably not an expert or authority. Exceptions exist, however. An entertainer may testify truthfully that a product enhanced his or her success.

3. *Predicting results* of a certain action may also persuade the reader, particularly if an action is carried out by an expert or authority. If a certain cause takes place, an effect can be reliably predicted:

> A new portable heart-lung machine has taken the terror out of some high-risk heart procedures, says Dr. Paul Overlie, a cardiologist in Lubbock, Texas. Called the Bard Cardiopulmonary Support System (CPS), it uses a narrow catheter threaded through the leg's femoral vein up to the heart and another through the femoral artery. The system shunts blood to an external machine, where it is oxygenated, warmed and pumped back into the body. The small insertion area in the leg usually heals quickly.

In this technique, an expert sets a *cause* in motion—use of a CPS to reroute blood from the body to an external machine. This has a clear *effect:* oxygenating the blood, warming it, and pumping it back into the body.

4. *Responding to opposition* or objections may keep the reader from opposing a claim. The following sentences describe a politician's use of this device:

> As astonishing as it might have appeared in the dark days of 1981, France and Mitterand were still together five years later. The franc was strong, inflation had been throttled, the Communists were out of government, and the Socialists themselves took on an air of moderation. "Only imbeciles never change their minds" goes an old French proverb, and change has been a way of life for François Mitterand in the more than four decades of his extraordinary political career.

The writer tries to persuade us that despite Mitterand's socialist allegiances, he managed the French economy and political system with great skill. He did so by taking opposing views into account.

5. *Giving reasons* appeals to our need for logic. It tells us **why** we should do or believe something:

> Exercise is great for your heart. A fifteen-minute workout, three times a week, can help raise you HDL "good cholesterol" while lowering your LDL "bad cholesterol." And it can help you reach and maintain your ideal weight—an important part of a heart-health program. Consult your doctor before beginning any exercise program.

The writer explains the value of exercise by pointing to its positive effects on health and appearance.

6. Finally, *appeals to the emotions and senses* are also very persuasive. The following ad uses both of these devices:

> Introducing the anything, anywhere SaladShooter. Electric slicer-shredder. The point-and-shoot sensation that slices, chops, grates,

shreds. Now cordless, too, with power to do big jobs. Presto Salad-Shooter slicer-shredder, the way to make great salads, and much, much more. Shred cheese to top a pizza, even hard fresh Parmesan for fettucini. Chop nuts to top a dessert, shred potatoes for perfect hashbrowns. Shoots right where you want, no extra bowl to clean. Easy cleanup. Just wipe the base, the rest is dishwasher safe.

This ad appeals to *emotions* like our desire for power, for mastery. It also appeals to our *sense* of taste by listing appetizing foods such as shredded cheese, pizza, Parmesan, fettucini, chopped nuts, shredded potatoes, and hashbrowns.

EXERCISE 12.3

Read the following paragraph and answer the questions.

Have a good laugh. When you do, says Dr. William Fry, a Stanford Medical School psychiatrist, your lungs, heart, back, and torso get a good workout, and your arm and leg muscles are stimulated. After a good laugh, your blood pressure, heart rate, and muscle tension subside, leaving you relaxed.

1. What *claim* is this paragraph making?
   The paragraph claims that laughter is good exercise, relaxing the laugher.

2. What types of support does the paragraph use?
   The paragraph cites authority, a Stanford psychiatrist; gives reasons by listing the results of laughter; and appeals to the senses by telling how much better a laugher feels after laughing.

3. What is the first result of laughter?
   Your lungs, heart, back, and torso get a quick workout.

4. What is the second result of laughter?
   Your arm and leg muscles are stimulated.

5. What is the third result of laughter?
   After a good laugh, your blood pressure, heart rate, and muscle tension subside.

6. What is the final result of laughter?
   It leaves you relaxed.

7. What transitional words does the paragraph use?
   when you do, and, after, leaving

EXERCISE 12.4

Read the following paragraph and answer the questions.

We have a completely distorted view of life's real perils. The chance of dying in a commercial airplane crash is just one in 800,000. You are more likely to choke to death on a piece of food. You are twice as likely to be killed playing a sport as you are to be stabbed to death by a stranger. And the chance of dying of a medical complication or mistake is tiny (one in 84,000). You take a far greater risk riding in a car. One in 5,000 of us die that way. But don't be too alarmed. The chance of having a fatal car accident on any one occasion is just one in four million—practically negligible. The problem is that we use the car so much—the ordinary person makes about 50,000 trips in a lifetime—that the possibility of coming to grief sometime, somewhere, is vastly heightened.

1. What *claim* is this paragraph making?

We exaggerate the chances of dying in an airplane crash, from a stabbing, or from surgery.

2. What types of support does the writer cite for the claim?

The writer responds to opposing views, gives reasons, and cites facts and examples.

3. What facts downplay the danger of dying in an airplane crash?

The chances are one in 800,000, less than the danger of choking to death on a piece of food.

4. What facts downplay the danger of being stabbed to death?

We are twice as likely to be killed playing a sport.

5. What facts downplay the danger of dying in surgery?

The chances of dying this way are one in 84,000, less than the chances of a fatal car accident.

6. What fact minimizes the danger of dying in a car accident?

The chances of death in a car accident are one in four million.

7. What fact *increases* the danger of a possible car accident?

The ordinary person makes about 50,000 car trips in a lifetime, increasing the chances of an accident during one of them.

8. What transitions does the writer use to link ideas?

twice as likely as, far greater, just, that, sometime, somewhere

---

EXERCISE 12.5

Answers will vary.

A writer persuades the reader by using several kinds of support for claims: citing facts or examples, appealing to authority, predicting results, responding to opposing views, giving reasons, appealing to the senses, *and* invoking emotion. *Write an example of one of these supports for each of the following claims. Some library research will be necessary. Identify the kind of support you have cited.*

EXAMPLE: American automakers are having difficulty competing.

SUPPORT: Sales of imported Japanese automobiles now amount to more than 20 percent of the American market. **(fact)**

1. Citizens of the United States file more lawsuits than citizens of any other country. *(fact)*.

Support: The United States has one attorney for every 360 citizens.

2. Children should be taught to handle their personal finances. (Consider the *kind of authority* who could support this claim.)

Support: According to Lois O'Connor, a financial consultant at the investment firm of Shearson Lehman Hutton, too many people enter adulthood without a basic knowledge of personal finance.

3. All women should avoid breast cancer by regularly scheduling mammograms. *(predicting results)*

Support: It is possible to cure almost 100 percent of breast cancers if they are found and treated before they spread.

4. Eating right does more to improve a person's outlook than taking tranquilizers and antidepressants. (Respond to *opposing view*—the use of drugs to handle depression—by citing facts, examples, results, or authority.)

Support: Carbohydrates are a sort of "comfort food," says University of Chicago Medical School psychologist Bonnie Spring. Eating protein sustains alertness and mental energy. Three to four ounces of fish, chicken, or veal can bring about this effect.

5. The will to succeed is part of the American spirit. *(appeal to emotions)*

Support: You can dream your own dream of success; you are free to innovate; you can create new ideas and services.

6. Use Loving Care to cover gray hair. *(appeal to the senses)*

It's as gentle to the hair as shampoo. It bathes each strand of hair with beautiful, natural-looking color. With 23 shades to choose from, it's easy to match your own natural color.

AVOIDING FALLACIES

Although persuasion often relies on emotion and feelings, the argument should be clearly and logically expressed. Sometimes, links between ideas become unclear or muddled. In such cases, writers may fall into logical fallacies, such as the following:

An *overgeneralization* is a statement that goes far beyond the available evidence. It oversimplifies. Often, the facts do not justify a particular conclusion. For example:

U.S. schools fail to teach basic skills to half the nation's children, according to a Labor Department report. Deprived of skilled workers, *many of the country's largest companies will soon go bankrupt.*

Comment: Although the example cites an authoritative estimate, the conclusion is too broad and sweeping. The final statement ignores other economic factors. It also leaves out training programs operated by businesses to improve their workers' skills.

The *either/or* fallacy limits choices to only two possibilities. It ignores other options:

To protect their profits, American olive growers must either be subsidized by the government or be protected against foreign imports.

Comment: This claim ignores American olive growers who have succeeded without government help, as well as changes in the domestic market, among other evidence.

The *post hoc* fallacy comes from the Latin *post hoc, ergo propter hoc,* which means "After this, therefore because of this." It oversimplifies. One action followed another in time. Therefore, it claims, the first action caused the second one, ignoring other causes:

Everyone who meditates becomes more relaxed. I know this is true. *Soon after I made my mind go completely blank, I slept better than I had in weeks.*

Comment: After meditation, the speaker slept well. This is the only link. The speaker may also have exercised, drunk a glass of warm milk, or bought a new mattress. Other causes are overlooked.

A *non sequitur* is a conclusion that does not logically follow from the stated cause:

Just after I'd had my car painted, a drunk motorist ran into it, totaling it. *I'll never spend money on an expensive paint job again.*

Comment: The accident indeed followed the paint job in time. However, drunkenness is a more logical cause for the accident than painting the car.

A *false analogy* compares an unfamiliar concept to a familiar image. The fact that a likeness appeals vividly to the senses does not constitute proof:

A decade ago you got into a field within a company and saw the future ahead of you *like a well-mapped road.* Everybody who went into business at that time succeeded.

Comment: The analogy between the future and "a well-mapped road" is easy to visualize. However, it does not prove that everyone who entered the work force a decade ago was successful.

An *ad hominem* argument (meaning "to the man") is a personal attack on a person. It shifts a hearer's attention from an issue to someone's shortcomings:

In the Australian parliament, it has been reported that an opposition senator asked a government official about social security fraud. In the process he called him a grub, a parasite, and a leech.

Comment: A person's past misdeeds may reflect on his or her present trust-worthiness. However, name-calling proves nothing.

The *bandwagon fallacy* involves support by rich or famous people for products or candidates:

Famous rock stars Mildred Hooch and Freddy Winch owe their sparkling white dentures to Mor-Smylz. Shouldn't you try it too?

Comment: Companies often pay celebrities to endorse their products, whether they use the products or not. Political campaigns recruit celebrities too. However, entertainment stars usually know little more about products or candidates than a lay person.

EXERCISE 12.6

Answers will vary.

Each statement below is untrue or illogical. Explain why, referring to the types of support listed above.

1. Television has made divorce more acceptable in American society. In 1950, at the dawn of television, the divorce rate was 2.6 per 1,000 Americans. By 1983, it had jumped to five per thousand; nearly half of all marriages were ending in divorce.

Untrue or illogical because:

This is an overgeneralization that oversimplifies. Not only television, but changes in American society made divorce more acceptable. These changes range from the increasing mobility of the population to the undermining of settled patterns of work, family, and neighborhood.

2. People who are extremely sick don't want to know what's wrong with them. One woman who was the sole support of three children died slowly of inoperable cancer. She never asked anyone about her diagnosis.

Untrue or illogical because:

This is overgeneralization. One instance provides too little evidence about the needs and desires of all terminally ill patients. Moreover, in the example cited, the woman may have wanted her doctor or other health care professional to raise the issue first.

3. Famous vaudeville stars George Handsome and Marilyn Gorgeous drink sparkling new Yuppy Cola. Shouldn't you buy it too?

Untrue or illogical because:

This is the bandwagon effect. The celebrities may not know or care anything about the product. Wise consumers should check analyses of products by reliable consumers' organizations and read labels closely.

4. After a black cat crossed my path, my brother criticized my golfing swing,

a Doberman snapped at my heels as I walked by, and nobody could change a fifty at the Quik Shop. I should have avoided that cat.

Untrue or illogical because:

The cat did not cause the speaker's problems by crossing his or her path. This is a non sequitur.

5. When I was sixteen, my parents had a particularly violent argument about the washing machine, which had broken down. Now they're divorced. If I want my marriage to last, I'd better buy a reliable brand of washing machine.

Untrue or illogical because:

This is a non sequitur because the parents' quarrel about their washing machine was not the only cause of their divorce. Other factors must have contributed too.

6. Professor Ben Tuffmoniker must be a great classroom teacher. He looks so debonair driving that little sports car around town.

Untrue or illogical because:

In this non sequitur, Professor Tuffmoniker's dashing appearance is unrelated to his ability to present material effectively in the classroom.

7. We must either limit television watching to two hours a day or become a nation of passive, numb people who can't interact with others.

Untrue or illogical because:

People may not be as inactive and socially incompetent as this either/or statement implies.

8. Advertisers are using every gimmick they can think of to make us buy things. If we consumers were deer, a closed season would be declared on us to protect an endangered species.

Untrue or illogical because:

In this false analogy, the writer compares advertisers hunting consumers to hunters killing deer. Consumers are better able to resist the power of advertisements (which, in any case, are never fatal), than deer are able to evade hunters.

Section Three: Planning and Organizing the Paragraph

After you have chosen or invented a topic, write it below. Your topic may be a general phrase; for example, "Early Retirement for the U.S. Military."

Topic: _____

To develop your topic into a claim, tell *who, why,* and *what*—for example: "In order to protect unsuspecting consumers, record companies should warn them that lyrics contain explicit references to sex or violence."

Your thesis or claim: _____

_____

Support your claim by *citing facts or examples, appealing to authority, predicting results, giving reasons, appealing to the senses,* or *invoking emotion.* For instance, a writer might demand that warnings be placed on tapes to alert buyers. To support her claim, the writer might quote an authority who states that 80 percent of today's heavy metal musicians use offensive lyrics in their music. The list of offensive topics includes sex, violence, drugs, alcohol, and references to the occult. She might further argue that obscene language taints the minds of young children.

List three or four pieces of evidence below. Identify your sources, if possible:

Item: _____

Item: _____

Item: _____

Item: _____

To better persuade your audience, consider evidence that opposes your view. For instance, the writer who wants companies to label records should be aware of other views. Some people prefer raunchy lyrics. Then too, her proposal could lead to censorship or performance bans. Finally, much great literature contains references to sex, violence, drugs, and alcohol.

Evidence opposed to your view:

Item: _____

Item: _____

Your answer to opposing view(s):

Item: _____

Item: _____

Section Four: Using Transitional Devices

You will need transitions to lead your readers from point to point in time, as in narrative and process writing:

first, second, third, finally, now, then, next, also, after, during

You will also need to use words and phrases telling your reader *how* and *why* events occur:

consequently, as a result, thus, therefore, because

Section Five: Writing the First Draft

Based on the ideas you have generated, write the first draft of your paragraph. Follow these steps:

- Choose a topic from Section One of this chapter or invent your own.
- State your claim, indicating your position on your topic.
- Generate reasons and details to support your claim.
- List opposing views.
- State a response to opposing views.
- Give your paragraph a title.

Theresa wrote the following persuasion paragraph:

Many people feel that the handicapped aren't capable of holding a job or being independent. However, the independence of handicapped persons is often restricted by limits on their mobility. These people include paraplegics and quadraplegics, as well as those with multiple sclerosis. People have forgotten that one of our greatest presidents was confined to a wheelchair after a few years in office. Certainly, President Roosevelt was quite capable of holding a job. Transportation for the handicapped is also limited, and parking places designated for the handicapped are often ignored by able-bodied citizens. The handicapped have often been denied access to air travel. My mother, who has been a paraplegic for 30 years, has flown all over the United States. She was chairman of the board of the Salt Lake Citizen's Congress, and was expected to speak at a convention in Washington. She was denied her flight because she was handicapped and didn't have a chaperon. This cost the SLCC thousands of dollars. Definately, discrimination in this manner must be halted. Until 1987, persons confined to wheelchairs weren't allowed access to public transportation. During that year, wheelchair lifts were provided for certain busses in the Salt Lake area. However, not all busses have this device to enable the handicapped to ride. I feel that this too, is discrimination. If a person in West Valley needs to get to downtown Salt Lake, he or she must call a UTA van to pick them up, which is not always available at the time they are needed. Handicapped parking zones have been located in almost every supermarket, shopping mall, or entertainment center. Yet when there aren't any close parking places at hand, many people will park in a designated area for the handicapped. If these places are illegally taken, the handicapped person must find two spaces together to have enough room to get out. I feel that the key for helping this situation lies in education. If people only realized what problems were arising due to their ignorance, discrimination in the work force would cease.

Section Six: Revising the Paragraph

Apply the questions in the checklist below to your own writing, or have a friend or classmate do it. We have applied them to Theresa's paper.

1. Does the first sentence or two state the writer's claim and plan? If not, how should the writer change the organization?

The writer makes her claim clear, along with the organization of the rest of the paragraph, by the end of the seventh sentence. However, she has failed to state her claim at the beginning of the paragraph: "Congress (or a state legislature) should give the handicapped more independence by improving their access to travel by plane, bus and car." She follows this unstated plan in the rest of her paragraph.

2. *A claim may be supported by* citing facts *or* examples, appealing to authority, predicting results, responding to opposing views, giving reasons, appealing to the senses, *or invoking emotion. What kinds of persuasive support does the writer include, and in what order?*

The writer first provides a significant *example:* President Roosevelt did his job despite his disability. In a second *example*, she cites her mother's difficulty in arranging air travel. Her personal example also *appeals to emotion*, especially to the feelings of readers who have a handicapped relative. She then cites several *facts* which apply to her own city: (a) the city was required to equip buses with lifts in 1989, (b) but not all buses have yet been so equipped. She then *predicts a result:* the handicapped often have difficulty arranging alternative transportation. Finally, she *predicts* the unfortunate *results* when people park illegally in spaces reserved for the handicapped.

3. *How has the writer linked her ideas together? What devices like connectives, synonyms, and pronouns has the writer used?*

She uses terms like *however, also, often, because, definitely, during, too, if,* and *when* to show relationships between ideas. She also uses synonyms to refer to her subjects as *paraplegics, handicapped persons,* and *persons in wheelchairs.* She could also use the term *physically disabled.*

4. *A persuasion paragraph often needs an effective, satisfying close. Does the student paper above have one?*

In her close, the writer indicates that the public needs to be better educated about the special needs of handicapped citizens. This conclusion is a persuasive addition to her earlier emphasis on legislation.

5. *What serious mechanical or other problems should the writer solve while rewriting the first draft?*

She misspells *definitely* as "definately," a common error. She also includes a shift in number and misplaced clause when she writes "If a person in West Valley needs to get to downtown Salt Lake, he or she must call a UTA van to pick them up, which is not always available at the time they are needed." Her sentence would be more readable if all her references to persons were plural: "If *people* in West Valley need to get to downtown Salt Lake, they must call a UTA van to pick them up." This rewrite ends with the word "up." Her next complete sentence might read: "However, these vans are not always available when needed." She should also omit the wordy phrase, "I feel that . . . ."

Apply the questions in the revision checklist below to your own writing, or have a friend or classmate do it.

176

1. Does the first sentence or two state the writer's claim and plan? If not, how should the writer change the organization?

2. A claim may be supported by *citing facts or examples, appealing to authority, predicting results, responding to opposing views, giving reasons, appealing to the senses,* or *invoking emotion.* What kinds of persuasive support does the writer include, and in what order?

3. How has the writer linked her ideas together? What devices like connectives, synonyms and pronouns has the writer used?

4. A persuasion paragraph often needs an effective, satisfying close. Does your paper have one?

5. What serious mechanical or other problems should the writer solve while rewriting the first draft?

Section Seven: Final Editing

Once you have finished, clean up the grammatical problems, punctuation errors, and misspellings. The following questions will help you finish the process of writing your paragraph:

1. Have I corrected the grammatical errors I often make? (Look back over earlier papers you have written. Then check this one for mistakes like subject—verb agreement or misplaced modifiers.)

2. Have I corrected the punctuation errors I tend to make?

3. Have I corrected the words I usually misspell?

Section Eight: Further Topics

- All college graduates should (should not) be required to be computer literate.

- All governmental bodies should (should not) be required to open all their meetings to the public.

- This college should improve its policies on (registration, graduation, library use, book purchases, parking, grading, etc.).

- The right of Americans to own weapons should (should not) be severely restricted.

- Terminally ill Americans should (should not) be given the right to end their lives.

- Women should (should not) be allowed to serve in combat roles in the armed services.

Sentence Consistency

Your writing should always be **consistent.** This means that you should focus on the following:

- Use the same *tense* throughout a piece of writing. Do not shift back and forth between present and past tense **unless** actions require you to do so.
- Use the same *person*, especially within and between sentences. Do not shift between first, second, and third person.
- Use the same *number*, especially within and between sentences. Do not shift between singular and plural.
- Balance similar elements within a *series:* words, phrases, and clauses.
- Use either direct or indirect quotations within the same sentence. Do not mix them.

Section One: Keeping Tense Consistent

When you begin writing a paper, decide which tense you plan to use: past, present, or future. Then stick to it. See Chapter 22, "Verb Agreement: Past Tense," p. 338, for more information on changes in tense. This is an example of an inconsistent tense shift:

> For almost an hour the hiker had *tossed* and *turns* in her sleeping bag while her father and her brother *dozed* peacefully in theirs.

This sentence begins with past-tense *tossed*, shifts to present-tense *turns*, and then shifts back to past-tense *dozed.* The verbs could be made consistently past tense:

> For almost an hour the hiker had *tossed* and *turned* in her sleeping bag while her father and her brother *dozed* peacefully in theirs.

This sentence consistently uses the past-tense verbs *tossed, turned,* and *dozed.* Or they could be made consistently present tense:

> For almost an hour the hiker *tosses* and *turns* in her sleeping bag while her father and her brother *doze* peacefully in theirs.

This sentence consistently uses the present-tense verbs *tosses, turns,* and *doze.*

At times, however, the sense of the sentence will require a shift between tenses, as in these examples:

He *used to be* fat; now he *is* thin.

The transition *now* signals the change from past to present tense.

He *walks* now, but he hopes he *will ride* soon.

The conjunction *but* signals a change from present to future tense.

EXERCISE 13.1

Write in the correct form of the past-tense verb in parentheses in the blank.

EXAMPLE: Queen Victoria (is) _____ born in London in 1819 and (has) _____ an unhappy childhood.

ANSWER: Queen Victoria <u>was</u> born in London in 1819 and <u>had</u> an unhappy childhood.

1. Because her father (dies) _____ had died _____ when she (is) _____ was _____ a baby, she (is) _____ was _____ under the supervision of Sir John Conroy, who (hope) _____ hoped _____ to make the child weak and dependent on him.

2. Victoria (have) _____ had _____ to sleep with her mother, and she never (descends) _____ descended _____ the stairs alone nor (speaks) _____ spoke _____ to any other person alone.

3. Conroy also (organizes) _____ organized _____ long and exhausting tours of the British Isles, which frequently (make) _____ made _____ the child ill.

4. Victoria (marries) _____ married _____ her first cousin, Albert, with whom she (falls) _____ fell _____ madly in love.

5. Albert, however, (is) _____ was _____ very straitlaced and (sets) _____ set _____ the moral tone for the kingdom.

6. When he (dies) _____ died _____ at the age of 42, Victoria (goes) _____ went _____ into deep mourning and (insists) _____ insisted _____ that Albert's rooms (are) _____ were _____ maintained as if he would return.

7. Each morning, she (have) _____ had _____ his clothes
   (lay) _____ laid _____ out for him, and each evening she
   (has) _____ had _____ fresh water placed in his basin.

8. Finally, Benjamin Disraeli, the Prime Minister, (flatters)
   _____ flattered _____ and (coaxes) _____ coaxed _____
   her out of seclusion.

9. To the delight of her subjects, she once more (takes)
   _____ took _____ part in public ceremonies and even (begins)
   _____ began _____ dancing again.

10. In 1897, the entire country (celebrates) _____ celebrated _____ her
    Diamond Jubilee, and she (drives) _____ drove _____ in state to St.
    Paul's Cathedral through streets (pack) _____ packed _____ with
    millions of cheering subjects.

EXERCISE 13.2   *Write in past-tense verbs above all the present-tense verbs.*

                                   fought
The students at the University of California at Santa Cruz fight for a long time
                              wanted
to get the mascot of their choice. The students want the banana slug as their
           was   **lived**
mascot. Their choice is a bright yellow mollusk that lives on fungus and debris
  left   **needed**
and leaves a nasty trail of slime. The school, invited to join the NCAA, needs an
                              preferred
official mascot and team name. Most of the students prefer the slug, which
  saw   **insisted**
they see often on campus during the rainy season. But the Chancellor insists
         was   **rebelled**
that the sea lion is more appropriate. The students rebel quickly. Bobby and
              was
the Slugtons, a rock group, is formed, and their song, "The Slugs are Back,"
became   **wore**   **wrote**
becomes popular. Students wear slug T-shirts, and alumni write letters in favor
                      represented
of the slug. To the students, the slug represents the uniqueness of a school
    had
that has no fraternities, sororities, or athletic scholarships and no grades
            requested   **gave**   **allowed**
unless the student requests them. The chancellor finally gives in and allows the
                 could
students a mascot with whom they can empathize.

EXERCISE 13.3   *Identify all the past-tense verbs in the following paragraph and write the present tense in above them.*

                                  brings
The macrobiotic diet brought the individual into harmony with life and the
           rejects
universe. It rejected all commercial foods as well as most animal products. Beef
               are   *are*
and dairy products were forbidden, as were tomatoes, potatoes, and eggplant.
         is   *are*
Green tea was the preferred drink. All foods were raised within a hundred-
                               are   *is*
mile radius of the consumer and were fresh and whole. Refrigeration was
                                              warns
discouraged. However, the American Medical Association warned that a macro-
     can
biotic diet could lead to anemia, calcium deficiency, scurvy, and malnutrition.

EXERCISE 13.4
Answers will vary.   *In the following passages, write in verbs above the line to eliminate inconsistencies.*

                                                had gone, were going
Driving across Illinois, we stopped at an old general store. We felt as if we going
                                     walked
back in time as we walk on the wooden sidewalk up to two benches on the

porch. One bench was labeled "Democrat," the other "Republican." Unaware
                                          sat
of the political leanings of the area, my wife sits down on the "Democrat"
                                                glanced
bench. A farmer in well-worn overalls came out of the doorway and glances

briefly at her while continuing down the steps to his truck. "Don't let folks
                                            called
catch you sittin' there during tomato season!" he calls over his shoulder, and
drove
drives off.

Section Two: Keeping Person Consistent

Use the same *person*, especially within and between sentences. Do not shift
between first, second, and third person.

- First person includes the singular *I* and the plural *we*. It is used in informal writing, especially narrative.
- Second person for both singular and plural addresses the reader as *you*. It is often used in descriptions of processes, especially to give directions. In other cases, however, writers should generally avoid the use of *you* or *your*.
- Third person includes the singular *he*, *she*, and *it*, as well as the plural *they*. It is preferred for more formal writing. Third person also includes all nouns, such as *person* or *people*, *student* or *students*.
- All indefinite pronouns are considered third person. They include all pronouns ending in *-one* or *-body*, such as *someone* or *somebody*, *anyone* or *anybody*, *everyone* and *everybody*, *no one* and *nobody*. Do not shift from a third-person indefinite pronoun such as *anyone* or *someone* to second-person *you*.

Inconsistent person: When *they* need calcium in *their* diet, *you* drink more milk.

This sentence shifts from third-person *they* and *their* to second-person *you*. This problem can be corrected in three ways:

1. When *they* need calcium in *their* diet, *they* drink more milk.
2. When *you* need calcium in *your* diet, *you* drink more milk.
3. When *people* need more calcium in *their* diets, *they* drink more milk.

The first example uses third person consistently, with *they*, *their*, and *they*. The second example uses second person consistently, with *you*, *your*, and *you*. The third example uses third-person plural consistently, with *people*, *their*, and *they*.

EXERCISE 13.5

Answers will vary.

Write in the correct nouns or pronouns to give the following sentences consistency of person.

1. Early in this decade, aside from pregnant women, (you) ___they, few people___ hardly gave calcium a second thought.

2. Shoppers could fill (your) ___their___ entire shopping carts with products boasting their calcium content.

3. One researcher noted that middle-aged nuns were excreting more calcium than (you) ___they___ were taking in.

4. As a result, they had poor bone density and were putting (yourselves) ___themselves___ at risk of osteoporosis.

5. Those with high calcium intake were not losing parts of (your) ___their___ bone.

184

6. Ads began proclaiming that you could ward off osteoporosis merely by increasing (their) _____your_____ calcium intake.

7. However, most Americans are not protecting (yourselves) _____themselves_____ because (you) _____they_____ don't have the facts.

8. The normal young adult woman has about 1,000 grams of calcium in (your) _____her_____ body.

9. Normal young adult males have 1,500 grams in (your) _____their_____ bodies.

10. Teenage girls who consumed more calcium retained more in (your body) _____their bodies_____ .

Section Three: Keeping Number Consistent

Use the same *number*, especially within and between sentences. Do not shift between singular and plural. Choose one or the other. Then stay with it in your paragraph or paper.

Inconsistent number: *We* walked a narrow trail through brush so thick that *I* could see only six feet on either side.

In this sentence, the plural pronoun *we* shifts to the singular pronoun *I* later in the sentence. This problem can be corrected in two ways:

1. *I* walked a narrow trail through brush so thick that *I* could see only six feet on either side.
2. *We* walked a narrow trail through brush so thick that *we* could see only six feet on either side.

The first example uses the singular *I* consistently. The second example consistently uses the plural *we.*

EXERCISE 13.6   *Correct any shifts in number in the following sentences.*

1. Soon Plotkin found the first item on (their) _____his_____ want list.

185

2. He collected samples and dropped (it) _____them_____ into (their) _____his_____ pack.

3. The sun was high now, (their) _____its_____ rays ricocheting off the leaves above us.

4. Plotkin held up some plants that a shaman had handed (them) _____him_____ .

5. He has eaten an anaconda and a giant rodent, but he doesn't like the taste of (it) _____them_____ .

6. They looked down on the river and trees as (it) _____they_____ glistened in the sun.

7. The conversation began to wander as (they) _____it_____ always did.

8. The shaman reputedly could transform (themselves) _____himself, herself_____ into a jaguar.

9. The Indians will soon be civilized. (He) _____They_____ will wear (a coat) _____coats_____ and (tie) _____ties_____ in a few years.

10. They will drink a medicinal potion if (he has) _____they have_____ an incurable illness.

Shifts of person and number often occur in the same sentences.

Inconsistent number and person: In *your* roundabout way, *one* collects rare and exotic plants.

In this sentence, the second-person, possibly plural *your* shifts to the third-person, singular *one*. This problem can be corrected in the following ways:

1. In *your* roundabout way, *you* collect rare and exotic plants.
2. In *their* roundabout way, *they* collect rare and exotic plants.

EXERCISE 13.7

Correct any shifts between person and number in the following sentences. Write in your corrections above the line. Make sure your language is consistent.

a. The age of plastic started when America hit the road after World War

                                    motorists
II. Oil companies issued cards so you wouldn't have to carry cash. But the

modern charge card was born in 1949, when Frank McNamara found
         himself   *his*
themselves short of cash. His wife had to come in and pay your bill. He related

the story to his partner, and they came up with an idea: people would join a
                    them   *meals*
club letting you charge a meal.

                                                                their streets
            b. Out in the suburbs, people have no sidewalks along one's street. They
                            their lives
don't consider sidewalks part of your life. Families get to know one another
                    they   *a visitor, others* (s) *he, she, they are*
better when you have sidewalks. Without them, you feel as if one is intruding.
                                                    they reach
A sidewalk is a place for children to ride tricycles before one reaches maturity.
                                                their
The experts skated along in swinging strides, your wheels clicking. There was
                            beginners   *his, her, one's falls*
usually a strip of grass where the beginner could cushion their fall. Boys passing

the home of a girl would talk loudly and hit one another, hoping to impress
 her
them.

Section Four: Balancing Elements
Within a Series

Balance similar elements within a *series:* words, phrases, and clauses. Using
a parallel structure for similar words or word groups makes them easier to
read. Compare the following nonparallel groups of sentences with parallel
versions:

Nicotine is one of nature's poisons, is used in pesticides, and not *being* healthy to humans.	Revised: Nicotine *is* one of nature's poisons, *is* used in pesticides, and *is* not healthy for humans.

The revised version of the sentence balances the repeated verb "*is . . . is
. . . is.*"

Few parents read their children a story, help with their homework, or just *to talk* with them.	Revised: Few parents *read* their children a story, *help* with their homework, or just *talk* with them.

The revised version balances parallel verbs: "*read . . . help . . . talk.*"

| The children were happy, confident, and *being* self-assured. | Revised: The children were *happy, confident,* and *self-assured.* |

The revised version balances descriptive words: "*happy . . . confident . . . self-assured.*"

| The manager told the clerk to total his accounts, to pick up new supplies, and *loading* a new computer program. | Revised: The manager told the clerk *to total* his accounts, *to pick up* new supplies, and *to load* a new computer program. |

The second version places a series of *to* words in balance: "*to total . . . to pick up . . . to load.*"

| High school dropouts work at unskilled jobs. Unemployment is a problem for many of the rest. | Revised: High school dropouts work at unskilled jobs. Many of the rest are unemployed. |

As revised, the sentences use similar word order: "*dropouts work . . .* and *many . . . are.*"

EXERCISE 13.8   *Each of the following sentences is unbalanced in some way. Rewrite the problem part of each sentence so that the parts are parallel.*

EXAMPLE: The strange cloud seemed alive, writhing, and *to seeth.*
seething

1. Some people banged on pots and pans. <del>Old tires were burned by others</del>.
   Others burned old tires.

2. Locusts settled on acacia trees, covered the ground like a carpet, and <del>filling</del> the evening air.
   filled

3. Tree branches had been stripped, palm fronds <del>were</del> scissored, and <del>they gnawed grass</del> to dust.
   had been
   grass had been gnawed to dust

4. The three-inch locusts hit me in the neck, face, and <del>struck my</del> arms.
   arms, not "struck my arms."

5. These insects devour natural vegetation, <del>eating</del> crops, and even <del>consuming</del> wool on a sheep's back.
   omit "eating"
   omit "consuming"

188

6. Swarms have been known to land on high mountains, to stay snow-covered for days and ~~taking~~ *to take* off again.

The second and third to's can be omitted.

7. Many Arabs still eat them grilled, ~~like to roast them~~ *roasted* or ~~smoking them~~ *smoked*.

8. Many food-lovers compare locusts to chicken or ~~find similarities to~~ shrimp.

compare locusts to chicken or shrimp.

9. Periodically, the locust's color changes from brown to yellow; ~~a lengthening~~ *lengthen*, and its legs shorten. ~~of its wings occurs;~~ and its legs ~~undergo shortening~~.

Periodically, the locust's color changes from brown to yellow, its wings

10. Rains in the southern Sahara bring locusts and ~~there is~~ famine.

bring locusts and famine.

EXERCISE 13.9

Answers will vary.

For each of the sentences below, fill in words that complete its parallel pattern.

EXAMPLE: You're at a cocktail party. *Your spouse is working late.*

1. You nod your head knowingly.
   Your friend blinks his eyes helpfully.

2. You are trying to work the buttons on your VCR.
   You don't have the faintest idea how to do it.

3. We believe that more information means more power.
   We suspect that it gives us less control.

4. We are at the tail end of an assembly line cranking out data.
   The line has no off button.

5. Men like movies with violence.
   Women like films with romance.

6. Never nod your head at something you don't understand.
   Practice asking people to clarify their statements.

7. More choices seem to produce more anxiety.
   Fewer options seem to create less freedom.

8. I acquire information by talking to an expert.
   Others learn by reading a book.

9. Some people are motivated by genuine curiosity.
   Others are driven by guilt or status-seeking.

10. I read only the magazines which interest me.
    I throw the rest out.

EXERCISE 13.10
Answers will vary.

Write five sentences below that use the suggested parallel structure.

1. Three parallel verbs: My father likes to cook, loves to eat, and hates to put on weight.

2. Two parallel clauses: The overweight man went into the fast food restaurant, and he ordered eighteen biscuits.

3. Two parallel prepositional phrases: The other guys do business with a bill of sales, not with a Bill of Rights.

4. Three parallel clauses: To satisfy customers, build a quality product, protect it, and treat patrons with respect.

5. A dependent clause beginning with *when, if,* or *which* followed by an independent clause: If beauty has its price, the competition is getting away with highway robbery.

EXERCISE 13.11

Underline faulty or wordy parallelism in the sentences below. Then rewrite the faulty part so that it is parallel with other words or word groups in the sentence.

Example of Faulty Parallelism: George and Nancy went to the circus, eating cotton candy, and pet the giraffes.

Rewrite: George and Nancy *went* to the circus, *ate* cotton candy, and *petted* the giraffes.

Example of Wordy Parallelism: Whispering Hills is filled with houses *that look Colonial, resemble Tudor designs, and have split-levels.*

Rewrite: Whispering Hills is filled with Colonial, Tudor, and split-level houses.

a colorless, odorless,

a. Many of these houses have high levels of radon, a gas that is colorless,
radioactive gas.
lacks any odor, and having radioactivity. One basement contained an alarming

3,500 picocuries per liter of air. A lifetime exposure to four picocuries is a cause
3,500 means a high probability of lung cancer
for concern, while there is a high probability that lung cancer may result from
finds
a lifetime exposure to 3,500. Radon rises from the soil, and finding its way
builds up
through house foundations, and building up to life-threatening concentra-
tested
tions. Contractors dug up the Watras cellar and test a variety of venting tech-
omit "to"
niques. If radon increases, the Watras family opens up windows and to sets
puts
electric fans going. Radon affects virtually every part of the nation and millions

190

millions of lives at risk
of lives are what it puts at risk. The EPA estimates that up to 20,000 lung cancer

deaths a year stem from long-term radon exposure, nearly as many as cigarette
                causes
smoking causing.

    b. The earth, it has been said, is the farmer's canvas. As you fly about the
                                                        surprising
plains of canvas, you behold giant sunflowers, which are brilliant, a surprise,
omit "they are"   uses a tractor, disk, mower, and two-
and they are grand. Artist Stanley Herd uses a tractor, employs a disk, operates
bottom plow
a mower, and utilizes a two-bottom plow as his brushes. With these tools
        maps   checks
he mapping his compositions from coordinates on a grid and checking their

accuracy from a plane. Some compare his work to the visionary work of Nazcas,
                flourished   left its mysterious
a culture that flourishing 1,500 years ago and whose mysterious markings were
markings
left on the desert landscape of Peru. Whenever Herd finishes a new work, local
customers immediately besiege local charter pilots
charter pilots are besieged by customers. They want to view it. Why does Herd

do it? He says we are all just temporary stewards of the land, and there is an
we have an obligation not to spoil it   do
obligation for us not to spoil it. "My earth pieces prove you can doing something
        omit "to"   leave no trace
beautiful, to stay in tune with the planet, and yet no trace is left.

Section Five: Keeping Quotations Consistent

Use either direct or indirect quotations within the same sentence. Try not to mix them. A comma sets off direct quotations, which are marked by quotation marks. The last set of quotation marks encloses the final punctuation marks, as in these examples:

> Her mother said, "See, Emily's a magician turning the baby into a frog."
>
> A Spanish proverb states, "Two great talkers will not travel far together."

Both of these examples include direct quotations. Note that the final quotation marks follow the periods after "frog" and "together."
The following examples report what was said without quotation marks:

> The businessman said he would never again criticize his wife for being late.

Stephen Jay Gould said that he became a scientist because he saw a dinosaur at a museum when he was five years old.

As in the example above, the word *that* often introduces indirect quotations.

Sentences that include *both* direct and indirect quotations should clearly identify the direct quotation with quotation marks.

Director Steven Spielberg said that *Poltergeist* is what he fears, and *E.T.* is what I love.

This sentence shifts inconsistently from indirect to direct quotation. The shift in person from third person *he* to first person *I* confuses the reader. This mistake can be corrected in one of two ways:

1. Director Steven Spielberg said that *Poltergeist* is what he fears, and *E.T.* is what *he* loves.

In this correction, the references to person are consistent, *he* and *he*.

2. Director Steven Spielberg said that *Poltergeist* is what he fears, and "*E.T.* is what *I* love."

In this correction, the direct quotation is set off from the indirect one by quotation marks. Three other changes occur:

- The pronouns change from *he* to *I*.
- The quotation marks prepare the reader for the change in person from *he* to *I*.
- The first word of a direct quotation is capitalized.

EXERCISE 13.12

The sentences below all include indirect quotations. Make all of the quotations direct, punctuating them correctly. Change words as necessary.

1. Lou Holtz said that he never learned anything talking.
   Lou Holtz said, "I never learn anything talking."

2. Someone said that love is like a violin.

   Someone said, "Love is like a violin."

3. John Ciardi said that you don't have to suffer to be a poet.

   John Ciardi said, "You don't have to suffer to be a poet."

4. Dwight Eisenhower said that a people that values its privileges above its principles soon loses both.

   Dwight Eisenhower said, "A people that values its privileges above its principles soon loses both."

5. The young student said that she had a great fear of strangers.

   The young student said, "I have a great fear of strangers."

EXERCISE 13.13   *The following paragraphs use quotations inconsistently. Rewrite the sentences to use either direct or indirect discourse correctly.*

As editor of my college paper, I had been sent to greet a distinguished writer. When he arrived, I managed to say "that I write too." He kindly replied then we'll have a lot to talk about.

As editor of my college paper, I had been sent to greet a distinguished writer. When he arrived, I managed to say, "I write too." He kindly replied, "Then we'll have a lot to talk about."

A sign in a park I've visited says there are no strangers in the world; "that there are only friends waiting to be met." At a party, you may be thinking "you're too shy for gatherings like this." Or you may tell yourself that a lot of people find parties boring, but I like them. In any case, it's better to say to yourself "you are shy" or I'm a stranger here than to seem unfriendly.

A sign in a park I've visited says, "There are no strangers in the world; there are only friends waiting to be met." At a party, you may be thinking, "I'm too shy for gatherings like this." Or you may tell yourself, "A lot of people find parties boring, but I like them." In any case, it's better to say to yourself, "I am shy" or "I'm a stranger here" than to seem unfriendly.

REVIEW EXERCISE 13.14   *Correct inconsistencies of tense, person, and number in the sentences below.*

1. My mother told me to eat my fish because it is brain food.
   ^{was}

2. When her daughter was studying for an exam, a nutritionist told her to eat
   herself
   tuna to keep you mentally alert.

   carries
3. When the nutritionist travels, she carried cans of tuna for snacks.

   their
4. What people put in your mouths can affect their mood and alertness.

5. The chemistry of the brain depends on whether you had lunch and what
   you
   they ate.

   you
6. If you pay attention to scientists' findings, I may well gain mental sharpness.

   you
7. After you drink one or two cups of coffee, I will be more alert.

   they
8. After they drink three cups of coffee, you will feel less clear-headed.

9. Most people recognize the ability of the "three-martini lunch" to dull his
   their
   or her minds all afternoon.

10. People who eat bread, potatoes, and sweet desserts for lunch could not
    their
    keep his or her minds focused on work.

REVIEW EXERCISE 13.15

Solve problems of unbalanced elements within a series and inconsistent quotations in the sentences below.

calls
1. My nephew is away at college and calling home frequently.

   he called me
2. I didn't realize just how often I was called by him.

   got her answering machine
3. I called his mother the other day and her answering machine was gotten by me.

   operator that she couldn't come to the phone,
4. The taped message told the operator that she couldn't come to the phone,
   but would "accept collect calls from Steve." OR *operator that she couldn't*
   but I will accept collect calls from Steve.
   come to the phone, but that she would accept collect calls from Steve.

   ran
5. I stopped my car, jumped out, and running over to her.

   I traded keys with her and said, "Drive my car home."
6. I traded keys with her and said, drive my car home.

194

7. He high-tailed it to Alaska, working as a logger and a deckhand, *He high-tailed it to Alaska, worked as a logger and deckhand, married his* marries his *high-school sweetheart, and settled down in Homer.* high-school sweetheart, and in Homer was where he settled down.

8. The coach said he got all the film of the games and then I completed a *The coach said that after he got all the film of the games, "I completed* *a report on all the players."* report on all the players.

9. The film star said she auditioned for a job 45 years ago and I finally got it. *The film star said she auditioned for a job 45 years ago and "I finally got it."*

10. Writing a play is like getting on a high diving board, to jump, and hope *jumping* *hoping* there is water in the pool.

Answer Key

The following answers are included for every other question in the exercises in this chapter:

EXERCISE 13.1

2. Victoria had to sleep with her mother, and she never descended the stairs alone nor spoke to any other person alone.

4. Victoria married her first cousin, Albert, with whom she fell madly in love.

6. When he died at the age of 42, Victoria went into deep mourning and insisted that Albert's rooms were maintained as if he would return.

8. Finally, Benjamin Disraeli, the Prime Minister, flattered and coaxed her out of seclusion.

10. In 1897, the entire country celebrated her Diamond Jubilee, and she drove in state to St. Paul's Cathedral through streets packed with millions of cheering subjects.

EXERCISE 13.2

The students wanted the banana slug as their mascot.

The school, invited to join the NCAA, needed an official mascot and team name.

But the Chancellor insisted that the sea lion was more appropriate.

Bobby and the Slugtons, a rock group, was formed, and their song, "The Slugs Are Back," became popular.

To the students, the slug represented the uniqueness of a school that had no fraternities, sororities, or athletic scholarships and no grades unless the student requested them.

EXERCISE 13.3

It <u>rejects</u> all commercial foods as well as most animal products.

Green tea <u>is</u> the preferred drink.

Refrigeration <u>is</u> discouraged.

EXERCISE 13.4

We felt as if we <u>were</u> <u>going</u> back in time as we <u>walked</u> on the wooden sidewalk up to two benches on the porch.

Unaware of the political leanings of the area, my wife <u>sat</u> down on the "Democrat" bench.

"Don't let folks catch you sittin' there during tomato season!" he <u>called</u> over his shoulder, and <u>drove</u> off.

EXERCISE 13.5

2. Shoppers could fill <u>their</u> entire shopping carts with products boasting their calcium content.

4. As a result, they had poor bone density and were putting <u>themselves</u> at risk of osteoporosis.

6. Ads began proclaiming that you could ward off osteoporosis merely by increasing <u>your</u> calcium intake.

8. The normal young adult woman has about 1,000 grams of calcium in <u>her</u> body.

10. Teenaged girls who consumed more calcium retained more in <u>their</u> <u>bodies</u>.

EXERCISE 13.6

2. He collected samples and dropped <u>them</u> into <u>his</u> pack.

4. Plotkin held up some plants that a shaman had handed <u>him</u>.

6. They looked down on the river and trees as <u>they</u> glistened in the sun.

8. The shaman reputedly could transform <u>himself/herself</u> into a jaguar.

10. They will drink a medicinal potion if <u>they</u> <u>have</u> an incurable illness.

EXERCISE 13.7

a. Oil companies issued cards so <u>motorists</u> wouldn't have to carry cash. His wife had to come in and pay <u>his</u> bill.

b. They don't consider sidewalks part of <u>their</u> <u>lives</u>. Without them, <u>others</u> <u>feel</u> as if <u>they</u> <u>are</u> intruding.
The experts skated along in swinging strides, <u>their</u> wheels clicking. Boys passing the home of a girl would talk loudly and hit one another, hoping to impress <u>her</u>.

EXERCISE 13.8

2. Locusts settled on acacia trees, covered the ground like a carpet, and <u>filled</u> the evening air.

4. The three-inch locusts hit me in the neck, face, and arms.

6. Swarms have been known to land on high mountains, stay snow-covered for days and take off again.

8. Many food-lovers <u>compare</u> <u>locusts</u> <u>to</u> <u>chicken</u> <u>or</u> <u>shrimp</u>.

10. Rains in the southern Sahara <u>bring</u> <u>locusts</u> <u>and</u> <u>famine</u>.

EXERCISE 13.9

2. You don't have the faintest idea how to do it.

4. The line has no off button.

6. Practice asking people to clarify their statements.

8. Others learn by reading a book.

10. I throw the rest out.

EXERCISE 13.10

2. Two parallel clauses: The overweight man went into the fast food restaurant, and he ordered eighteen biscuits.

4. Three parallel clauses: To satisfy customers, build a quality product, protect it, and treat patrons with respect.

EXERCISE 13.11

a. Radon rises from the soil, <u>finds</u> its way through house foundations, and <u>builds up</u> to life-threatening concentrations. If radon increases, the Watras family opens up windows and sets (<u>omit</u> "<u>to</u>") electric fans going.

   The EPA estimates that up to 20,000 lung-center deaths a year stem from long-term radon exposure; <u>only</u> <u>cigarette</u> <u>smoking</u> <u>causes</u> <u>more</u> <u>deaths</u>.

b. As you fly about the plains of canvas, you behold giant sunflowers, which are brilliant, <u>surprising</u>, and <u>grand</u> (<u>omit</u> "<u>they</u> <u>are</u>").

   With these tools he <u>maps</u> his compositions from coordinates on a grid and <u>checks</u> their accuracy from a plane.

   Whenever Herd finishes a new work, <u>customers</u> <u>immediately</u> <u>besiege</u> <u>local</u> <u>charter</u> <u>pilots</u>.

   "My earth pieces prove you can <u>do</u> something beautiful, <u>stay</u> (<u>omit</u> "<u>to</u>") in tune with the planet, and yet <u>leave</u> <u>no</u> <u>trace</u>.

EXERCISE 13.12

2. Someone said, "Love is like a violin."

4. Dwight Eisenhower said, "A people that values its privileges above its principles soon loses both."

EXERCISE 13.13

When he arrived, I managed to say, "I write too."

At a party, you may be thinking, "I'm too shy for gatherings like this."

In any case, it's better to say to yourself, "I am shy" or "I'm a stranger here" than to seem unfriendly.

REVIEW EXERCISE 13.14

2. When her daughter was studying for an exam, a nutritionist told her to eat tuna to keep <u>herself</u> mentally alert.

4. What people put in <u>their</u> mouths can affect their mood and alertness.

6. If you pay attention to scientists' findings, <u>you</u> may well gain mental sharpness.

8. After they drink three cups of coffee, <u>they</u> will feel less clear-headed.

10. People who eat bread, potatoes, and sweet desserts for lunch could not keep <u>their</u> minds focused on work.

REVIEW EXERCISE 13.15

2. I didn't realize just how often <u>he</u> <u>called</u> <u>me</u>.

4. The taped message told the operator that she couldn't come to the phone, but would "accept collect calls from Steve." OR The taped message told the operator that she couldn't come to the phone, but she would accept collect calls from Steve.

6. I traded keys with her and said, "Drive my car home."

8. The coach said that after he got all the film of the games, "I completed a report on all the players."

10. Writing a play is like getting on a high diving board, <u>jumping</u>, and <u>hoping</u> there is water in the pool.

Sentence Variety

Section One: Replacing Passive Verbs with Active Ones

Replacing the passive voice with the active voice will usually make your writing more forceful and direct. The active voice is briefer and less wordy than the passive voice. In the active voice, the subject carries out the action; it is the *actor.* In the passive voice, the subject receives the action. Verbs in the passive voice always combine a form of the verb *to be* (*is, are, was, were,* and so on) with a *past participle: is* built, *was* work*ed.* In the passive voice, the doer is no longer the subject of the sentence. The doer appears later in the sentence, or may be omitted. Consider these examples:

Active Voice: Frank built a purple house.

In this example, *Frank* is the subject. The verb *built* stresses the action that he took as the *actor* in the sentence.

Passive Voice: A purple house was built by Frank.

Passive Voice: A purple house was built.

In these examples, the subject *house* receives the action. It does not carry it out. The true *actor,* **Frank,** comes later in the first sentence. It is the object of the preposition *by.* The verb combines the helping verb *was* with the past tense *built.* The sentence focuses on the house, rather than on the builder.

The active voice offers writers these advantages:

The active voice is more direct and forceful, using fewer words.

Active: Ann writes in her diary daily.

Passive: Ann's diary is written in daily.

The active voice gets rid of awkwardness:

Active: Mostly, I record happy events.

Passive: Mostly, happy events are recorded by me.

The first example in each pair above is briefer and more to the point.

The active voice is more personal, less machinelike:

Active: The manager arranged his schedule.

Passive: The manager's schedule was arranged.

However, the passive voice has certain advantages too.

- Use the passive voice when the doer is unknown.

   The agency's regulations were created in 1961. (No one knows who did it.)

   The photocopier was stolen last night. (No one knows who did it.)

- Use the passive voice when the action or object is more important than the actor.

   The car's oil was last changed three years ago.

   The house was appraised recently.

   Ancient fossils have been found in the valley.

   No one knows or cares who carried out the actions described above.

- Use the passive voice to soften the tone or make the action more impersonal:

   The copier was left on last night. **NOT** Someone left the copier on last night.

   Thirty-four people in the accounting department were laid off. **NOT** Vice President Frank Sullivan laid off thirty-four people in the accounting department.

   These sentences avoid blaming anyone for mistakes or unpleasant actions.

In most instances, however, you will prefer to use active verbs. Your rough drafts will often use far too many passive verbs. In revision, you should make most of them active. Use this process:

1. Identify the **subject, verb,** and **actor** in each *passive voice* sentence, as in this example:

Most animals have been created (by nature) to fit the many faces of the land.

   Subject: *animals*

   Verb: *have been created* (*to be* helper + past tense)

   Actor: *nature*

2. Make the actor the subject of the *active voice* sentence, changing other words as necessary:

Nature has created most animals to fit the many faces of the land.

   The *actor,* **nature,** is the new subject. The new active verb is *has created.* Note that the verb *created* is past tense. However, the helping verb *has* is not a *to be* helper.

201

All the sentences below are written in the passive voice. Change all of them to active voice, using the process described above.

1. Moose have been adapted (by her) to marshes, squirrels to trees, camels to deserts.

   Subject: _____Moose_____ Verb: _have (has) been adapted_ Actor: _her (She)_

   Rewrite: _She has adapted moose to marshes, squirrels to trees, camels to deserts._

2. If nature is given an environment or situation, a creature will be evolved by her. *Note:* Since no one knows *who* or *what* gives something to nature, the first word group should be passive, as given here.

   Subject: _____creature_____ Verb: _will be evolved_ Actor: _her (she)_

   Rewrite: _If nature is given an environment or situation, she will evolve a creature._

3. As a result of this fitting, the sun is circled by some really unbelievable creatures.

   Subject: _____sun_____ Verb: _is circled_ Actor: _creatures_

   Rewrite: _As a result of this fitting, some really unbelievable creatures circle the sun._

4. One summer in Maine a sleek female horned grebe was seen by me.

   Subject: _____grebe_____ Verb: _was seen_ Actor: _me (I)_

   Rewrite: _One summer in Maine I saw a sleek female horned grebe._

5. Her three bobbing young were being herded to supper.

   Subject: _____young_____ Verb: _were being herded_ Actor: _(her) she_

   Rewrite: _She was herding her three bobbing young to supper._

6. Suddenly something was noticed by me through my binoculars.

   Subject: _something_ Verb: _was noticed_ Actor: _me (I)_

   Rewrite: _Suddenly I noticed something through my binoculars._

7. Her babies were being fed feathers by her from a deserted duck nest.

   Subject: _____babies_____ Verb: _were being fed_ Actor: _her (she)_

   Rewrite: _She was feeding her babies feathers from a deserted duck nest._

8. As the dry feathers were being stuffed into the gaping mouths, two or three pokes were made by her to get each one down.

   Subjects: _feathers_ Verbs: _were being stuffed_ Actors: _her (she)_
   pokes _were made_ _her (she)_

   Rewrite: _As she stuffed the dry feathers into the gaping mouths, she made two or three pokes to get each one down._

9. Finally, a dozen or so were worked down her own throat.

Subject: _____dozen_____ Verb: _____were worked_____ Actor: _____her (she)_____

Rewrite: _Finally, she worked a dozen or so down her own throat._

10. Then, sailing low on the water, she was seen to vanish among the plants.

Subject: _____she_____ Verb: _____was seen_____ Actor: _____she_____

Rewrite: _Then, sailing low on the water, she vanished among the plants._

11. It was later learned by me that feathers are what 60 percent of the grebe's diet consists of.

Subjects: _____It_____ Verbs: _____was learned_____ Actors: _____me (I)_____
_____feathers_____ _____are_____ _____60 percent_____

Rewrite: _I later learned that 60 percent of the grebe's diet consists of feathers._

12. When it was asked why by me, an answer from a biologist was, "A use for everything is found by nature."

Subjects: _____it_____ Verbs: _____was asked_____ Actors: _____me (I)_____
_____answer_____ _____was_____ _____biologist_____
_____use_____ _____is found_____ _____nature_____

Rewrite: _When I asked why, a biologist answered, "Nature finds a use for everything."_

13. "A strainer is how feathers act to prevent fishbones from entering and damaging the intestines."

Subject: _____strainer_____ Verb: _____is_____ Actor: _____feathers_____

Rewrite: _"Feathers act as a strainer to prevent fishbones from entering and damaging the intestines."_

Section Two: Varying Sentence Length

Varying the length of your sentences will also make your writing more forceful and emphatic. Your sentences should not all be long and complex. Nor should they all be brief. Beginning writers tend to overuse short, choppy sentences, as in this example:

> We were planning to go on my senior trip. It was to Miami Beach in June. The group included James, De Wayne, and me as the driver. I needed $400 dollars spending money. I asked my dad for permission to go. He was against the idea.

All the sentences in this paragraph are short and disconnected. The style seems immature. This revised version of the same paragraph varies the length of the sentences:

203

We were planning to go on my senior trip to Miami Beach in June. The group included James, De Wayne, and me. *I would drive.* Since I needed $400 dollars spending money, I asked my dad about the trip. *He opposed the idea.*

The revised paragraph is more forceful because it inserts the two short italicized sentences between longer ones. These brief sentences emphasize first the writer's role: "I would drive." The concluding short sentence shifts the reader's attention to the father's role: "He opposed the idea."

EXERCISE 14.2

The paragraph below is filled with short, choppy sentences. Combine them in any way you wish to vary the sentence lengths. You may add or drop words. However, do not change the basic meaning.

These creatures were black and white. People sought them all over. At least this was in Cuba and the southern United States. Just last week a report was made about them. Ivory-billed woodpeckers are a handsome species. They were believed for years to be extinct. They were spotted in a Cuban forest. "I thought, 'My God, I've seen it'," Dr. Lester L. Short said. He is chairman of ornithology at the American Museum of Natural History. He recalled a day in April. An ivory-bill crossed his path. It was before he could aim his camera. It was gone.

Rewrite: These creatures were black and white and were sought all over, at least in Cuba and the southern United States. Just last week, according to a report, two ivory-billed woodpeckers were spotted in a Cuban forest. The handsome species had been believed for years to be extinct. "I thought, 'My God, I've seen it'," said Dr. Lester L. Short, chairman of ornithology at the American Museum of Natural History. He recalled a day in April when an ivory-bill crossed his path. Before he could aim his camera, it was gone.

Section Three: Varying Sentence Beginnings

Writers also vary their sentence beginnings by using *-ly* words, *-ed* words, *-ing* words, *to* word groups, and prepositional phrases. These words usually modify (or *describe*) the subject or the action. They also reduce wordiness by connecting closely related ideas. When they open a sentence, they are set off by commas. The following examples illustrate the use of these words:

-ly word   West Perrine began changing.
It was quick.
Quickly, West Perrine began changing.

-ed word	Lee and Sara could finally afford a new house. They were elated. *Elated*, Lee and Sara could finally afford a new house.
-ing word	People went to sleep. They left their screen doors unlatched. *Leaving their screen doors unlatched*, people went to sleep.
to **word** **group**	Lee wanted to stay in town. She quit school for a factory job. *To stay in town*, Lee quit school for a factory job.
prepositional **phrases**	Children played tag. It was in the shadows of the street lights. *In the shadows of the street lights*, children played tag.

A prepositional phrase includes a preposition and its object (either a noun or a pronoun). Word groups such as *around the corner* or *up the street* are prepositional phrases:

Preposition	**Object**
around	corner
up	street
under	desk

Following is a list of frequently used prepositions:

about	beneath	in	through
above	beside	into	throughout
across	between	near	to
against	by	of	toward
among	during	on	under
as	except	onto	up
at	for	out	upon
behind	from	over	with
			without

EXERCISE 14.3

Combine the following short, choppy sentences by using the suggested openers. Leave out unnecessary words, and punctuate your revisions correctly.

1. Elephants are quite valuable.
   People hunt them for their tusks. (**-ed word**)

   Rewrite: Hunted for their tusks, elephants are quite valuable.

2. Most animals seek to escape the sun.
They shelter motionlessly. (**-ing word**).

Rewrite: Seeking to escape the sun, most animals shelter motionlessly. OR: Sheltering motionlessly, most animals seek to escape the sun.

3. Poachers hunt down the elephants.
They are relentless. (**-ly word**)

Rewrite: Relentlessly, poachers hunt down the elephants.

4. Small, wiry tribesmen scuttle crablike.
They want to avoid the low thorns. (**-to words**)

Rewrite: To avoid the thorns, small, wiry tribesmen scuttle crablike.

5. Elephants could become virtually extinct.
It could happen in less than fifteen years. (**prepositional phrase**)

Rewrite: In less than fifteen years, elephants could become virtually extinct.

6. Kimmi went off to college.
She was armed with her first checkbook. (**-ed word**)

Rewrite: Armed with her first checkbook, Kimmi went off to college.

7. Kimmi wrote a $200 check to her sorority house.
She subtracted the sum from her account. (**-ing word**)

Rewrite: Subtracting the sum from her account, Kimmi wrote a $200 check to her sorority house. OR: Writing a $200 check to her sorority house, Kimmi subtracted the sum from her account.

8. She patted her father on the back.
She was happy. (**-ly word**)

Rewrite: Happily, she patted her father on the back.

9. We went to a nearby playground.
We wanted to take pictures of the children. (**to word group**)

Rewrite: To take pictures of children, we went to a nearby playground.

10. I spent a great deal of time marking errors.
I was an English teacher. (**prepositional phrase**)

Rewrite: As an English teacher, I spent a great deal of time marking errors.

11. Fair weather involves high-pressure air masses.
It is composed of dry, stagnant air. (**-ed word**)

Rewrite: Composed of dry, stagnant air, high pressure air masses bring fair weather.

12. People observed the sky, winds, and clouds.
People made up sayings to remember the patterns (**-ing word**)

Rewrite: Observing the sky, winds and clouds, people made up sayings to remember the patterns.

13. High altitude cirrus clouds warn of coming rain.
This is typical. (**-ly words**)

Rewrite: Typically, high altitude cirrus clouds warn of coming rain.

14. The sun must shine through clear skies.
    This must happen in order for the fog to be burned off. (**to word group**)

    Rewrite: To burn off the fog, the sun must shine through clear skies.

15. You should check the upper atmosphere for wispy clouds.
    This should be done during fair weather. (**prepositional phrase**)

    Rewrite: During fair weather, check the upper atmosphere for wispy clouds.

16. They matched up a number of clues.
    They looked at the sky to do this. (**-ing word**)

    Rewrite: Looking up at the sky, they matched up a number of clues.

17. Old-timers didn't rely on a single rhyme to predict weather.
    This was wise of them. (**-ly word**)

    Rewrite: Wisely, old-timers didn't rely on a single rhyme to predict weather.

18. People should watch the barometer.
    This will help them to foretell the weather. (**to word group**)

    Rewrite: To foretell the weather, people should watch the barometer.

19. Plants release oils into the atmosphere.
    This happens whenever the humidity is high. (**prepositional phrase**)

    Rewrite: In a period of high humidity, plants release oils into the atmosphere.

Section Four: Combining Ideas with Coordination

CREATING A COMPOUND SENTENCE

Ideas may also be linked by means of coordinating conjunctions—words like *and, or, but, nor, so, yet,* and *for.* Adding a second complete thought to a simple sentence with one of these words results in a compound sentence. When you do this, the coordinating word must be preceded by a comma, as in the following examples:

> Our former parish was not wealthy, *and* our pastor depended on parishioners for upkeep of the church.
> I wanted a fantail goldfish, *but* all the fantails looked alike.
> I hadn't received any responses, *so* I called all the mothers.

Each of these examples uses a coordinating conjunction to connect two independent clauses, each with its own subject and verb. Each example places a comma before a coordinating word: *, and, , but,* and *, so.*

We discuss these principles further in Chapter 29, "The Comma."

EXERCISE 14.4

Choices of conjunctions
will vary.

Combine the pairs of simple sentences below into compound sentences. Insert a comma and use a coordinating word (and, or, for, but, nor, so, and yet) to link each pair of clauses.

1. Two cars collided in the parking lot.
   The drivers got out to survey the damage.

   Rewrite: Two cars collided in the parking lot, [and, so] the drivers got out to survey the damage.

2. My mother sent my son a water pistol.
   He headed for the nearest sink.

   Rewrite: My mother sent my son a water pistol, [and, so] he headed for the nearest sink.

3. I invited my friend Susan to dinner.
   She couldn't make it that evening.

   Rewrite: I invited my friend Susan to dinner, [but] she couldn't make it that evening.

4. No one spoke for a few minutes.
   The guide answered his question.

   Rewrite: No one spoke for a few minutes, [so, but, for] the guide answered his question.

5. We can eat oat bran.
   We can worry about cholesterol.

   Rewrite: We can eat oat bran, [or] we can worry about cholesterol.

6. Fiber is good for us.
   Moderate amounts discourage overeating.

   Rewrite: Fiber is good for us, [and] moderate amounts discourage over-eating.

7. All fibrous foods contain some fiber.
   The most concentrated supply is found in wheat bran.

   Rewrite: All fibrous foods contain some fiber, [but, yet] the most concentrated supply is found in wheat bran.

8. One doctor claimed that fiber protected against certain diseases.
   Scientists began to investigate.

   Rewrite: One doctor claimed that fiber protected against certain diseases, [and, so] scientists began to investigate.

9. Several studies have reported that oat products lower blood cholesterol.
   A Harvard study shows no such benefit.

   Rewrite: Several studies have reported that oat products lower blood cholesterol, [but, yet] a Harvard study shows no such benefit.

10. Fibrous foods hold water.
Fiber may also battle hunger.

Rewrite: Fibrous foods hold water, [so] fiber may also battle hunger.

CREATING A COMPOUND PREDICATE

You may also combine ideas by creating a compound predicate. This kind of sentence includes more than one verb, but does not repeat the subject before the second verb. Like compound sentences, these verbs may be linked by coordinating words like *and, or, but, nor,* and *yet.* However, no comma comes before the coordinating word. The resulting sentence is a simple one with two verbs:

The basketball player *stood* six foot ten **and** *weighed* 300 pounds.

The witness *closed* her mouth **but** *revealed* the truth.

The job *required* education **yet** *demanded* ability.

The examples above use compound predicates: one subject followed by two verbs. No comma precedes the coordinating words *and, but,* and *yet.*

EXERCISE 14.5

*Combine the pairs of simple sentences below into one sentence with a compound predicate. Use a coordinating word (*and, or, but,* and* yet*) to link each pair of verbs. Remember this time* not *to use a comma before the coordinating word.*

1. An optimist may be naive.
She may also wear rose-colored glasses.

Rewrite: An optimist may be naive and wear rose-colored glasses.

2. Bob visited the new plant in town.
He applied for a job.

Rewrite: Bob visited the new plant in town and applied for a job.

3. The new agents tested low in aptitude.
They rated high in optimism.

Rewrite: The new agents tested low in aptitude but rated high in optimism.

4. Some people cannot view some situations optimistically.
They cannot put a good face on them.

Rewrite: Some people cannot view some situations optimistically [and, or] put a good face on them.

5. Many people stop worrying.
When they do this, they start working.

Rewrite: Many people stop worrying and start working.

6. I reorganized the business.
I also ran the household.

Rewrite: I reorganized the business [and, yet] ran the household.

7. In the Bible, Job suffered repeated calamities.
He refused to lose hope.

Rewrite: In the Bible, Job suffered repeated calamities [yet, but] refused to lose hope.

8. Upbeat beliefs are helpful.
They don't change realities.

Rewrite: Upbeat beliefs are helpful [but, yet] don't change realities.

9. One woman benefited from a few close friends.
She also joined a support group.

Rewrite: One woman benefited from a few close friends [and, but, yet] also joined a support group.

10. Many people worry a lot about little things.
They learn to stop being afraid.

Rewrite: Many people worry a lot about little things [but, yet] learn to stop being afraid.

Section Five: Combining Ideas with Subordination

You may also combine a simple sentence with a dependent clause. This combination results in a *complex sentence.* Both clauses have subjects and verbs; however, only one of them—the independent clause—may stand alone. The dependent clause is set off by a comma *only* if it comes first. The following subordinating words may be used to link a dependent thought to an independent one:

after	if, even if	when, whenever
although, though	in order that	where, wherever
as	since	whether
because	that, so that	which, whichever
before	unless	while
even though	until	who, whoever
how	what, whatever	whose

A complex sentence improves your writing in these ways:

- It indicates that one idea is more important than another.
- It links short, choppy ideas.

Look over these complex sentences:

Because movie makers want to be taken seriously, they can't stay away from religious themes.

The dependent clause comes first. It begins with the word *because* and is separated from the independent clause with a comma.

Movie makers can't stay away from religious themes because they want to be taken seriously.

Both examples emphasize the idea in the independent clause: "Movie makers can't stay away from religious themes."

Here are other examples of complex sentences. All of them stress the idea in the independent clause.

Robert Duvall won an Oscar as a washed-up alcoholic *whose* life is transformed by religion.

Religion offers one subject *that* everyone considers serious.

The independent clause comes first in both examples above.

Although almost 58 million Americans went to the movies every week in 1950, today only 22 million do.

In this example, the independent clause beginning with *today* comes last.

Subordination is also handled in Chapter 20, "Fragments," and in Chapter 21, "Correcting Run-Ons and Comma Splices."

EXERCISE 14.6

Combine each pair of short sentences below into one sentence with a subordinating word or phrase from the list above. If the subordinate clause comes first, separate it from the rest of the sentence with a comma.

1. Some local actors in Medfield, Massachusetts put on a production of *The Music Dreaming Man.*
   It celebrates the life of one Lowell Mason.
   Rewrite: Some local actors in Medfield, Massachusetts put on a production of *The Music Dreaming Man,* which celebrates the life of one Lowell Mason.

2. I asked a bystander to pick out several towns.
   They lie on or close to the 40th parallel.
   Rewrite: I asked a bystander to pick out several towns [that] lie on or close to the 40th parallel.

3. I called up the library in each one to ask about anyone.
   His name might have caught the nation's eye.
   Rewrite: I called up the library in each one to ask about anyone whose name might have caught the nation's eye.

4. Eugene O'Neill had a daughter Oona.
   She married Charlie Chaplin.

   Rewrite: Eugene O'Neill had a daughter Oona who married Charlie Chaplin.

5. My next stop was Burlington.
   It was the birthplace of James Fenimore Cooper.

   Rewrite: My next stop was Burlington [because it, which] was the birthplace of James Fenimore Cooper.

6. Freda Ehmann developed a successful method for canning olives.
   They could be marketed commercially.

   Rewrite: After Freda Ehmann developed a successful method for canning olives, they could be marketed commercially.

7. I was growing up in the slums of North Philadelphia.
   Any kid who wanted to could get work.

   Rewrite: When I was growing up in the slums of North Philadelphia, any kid who wanted to could get work.

8. My father had deserted us.
   My mother needed help.

   Rewrite: Because my father had deserted us, my mother needed help.

9. I could sell people a shiny vacuum cleaner.
   I could get them to buy a share of stock.

   Rewrite: I could sell people a shiny vacuum cleaner [before, after] I could get them to buy a share of stock. OR Because I could sell people a shiny vacuum cleaner, I could get them to buy a share of stock.

10. I finished graduate school.
    I went back into the stock market.

    Rewrite: [After, When] I finished graduate school, I went into the stock market.

Section Six: Combining Ideas with Modifiers

A useful way to combine ideas is to link them with an -*ing* or an -*ed* descriptive phrase. The following sentences are combined with an -*ing* phrase:

> I wanted to start my own construction company.
> I went to college.

> **Combination:** *Wanting* to start my own construction company, I went to college.

In the first sentence, the verb *wanted* has been changed to an -*ing* phrase, "*wanting* to start . . ." The first subject, *I*, has been dropped. The *wanting* modifier tells the reader that both actions are going on at the same time. However, the sentence stresses the action described in the independent clause.

The idea "I went to college" is more important than the descriptive phrase "Wanting to start my own construction company." The modifying phrase is followed immediately by the word it refers to, *I*.

A comma separates the *-ing* word group from the word that it modifies, *I*.

Ideas can also be linked with a past participial *-ed* modifier, as in this example:

> He was scared he would go broke.
> He worked that much harder.

> **Combination:** *Scared* of going broke, he worked that much harder.

The first sentence has been changed to an *-ed* past participial modifier by deleting the helping verb *was* and the pronoun *He*.

The idea "He worked that much harder" is more important than the modifying word group, "scared of going broke." The modifying phrase is followed immediately by the word to which it refers, *he*.

A comma separates the *-ed* past participial word group from the word it modifies, *he*.

EXERCISE 14.7

Convert the first sentence in each of the following pairs to either an -ing or an -ed modifier. The word it modifies should follow the modifier directly. Punctuate correctly.

1. I washed the meat case.
   I might skip two or three wires on the grate.

   Combination: Washing the meat case, I might skip two or three wires on the grate.

2. A typhoon battered the ship.
   It wallowed in heavy seas.

   Combination: Battered by a typhoon, the ship wallowed in heavy seas.

3. I took off my trousers.
   I waded into the lake to look for the golf ball.

   Combination: Taking off my trousers, I waded into the lake to look for the golf ball.

4. The child was sucked through a flooded culvert.
   She fell into a roiling storm sewer.

   Combination: Sucked through a flooded culvert, the child fell into a roiling storm sewer.

5. I sold to laundries and hospitals.
   I became a salesman for bulk soap.

   Combination: Selling to laundries and hospitals, I became a salesman for bulk soap.

6. He was transfixed in the control room.
   He watched a daily talk show being broadcast.

   Combination: Transfixed in the control room, he watched a daily talk show being broadcast.

7. Michelle had been successfully dieting.
   She and her family moved from St. Louis to Atlanta.

   Combination: Having been successfully dieting, Michelle moved with her family from St. Louis to Atlanta.

8. Darlene was concerned about everyone but herself.
   She overate to cover up her anxiety.

   Combination: Concerned about everyone but herself, Darlene overate to cover up her anxiety.

9. She recognized a problem.
   She didn't pretend it would go away.

   Combination: Recognizing a problem, she didn't pretend it would go away.

10. She was feeling terrible.
    Yet she continued to eat with abandon.

    Combination: Though feeling terrible, she continued to eat with abandon.

Section Seven: Combining Ideas with Appositives

You can also vary your writing by using an appositive to combine short simple sentences. An appositive is a noun or word group that contains a noun and that renames another noun. Using an appositive rather than a subordinate clause makes a sentence flow more smoothly:

EXAMPLE:

A secondary education teacher joined the staff.
He was named Rhoney Williams.

Combining with a Subordinate Clause:

A secondary education teacher *who was named Rhoney Williams* joined the staff.

Combining with an Appositive:

A secondary education teacher, *Rhoney Williams*, joined the staff.
OR
Rhoney Williams, *a secondary education teacher*, joined the staff.

In the first example, the appositive is *Rhoney Williams*. The sentence stresses the idea in the main clause: *secondary education teacher*.

In the second example, *a secondary education teacher* is the appositive. The idea in the main clause is stressed: *Rhoney Williams*.

Appositives will give your writing flexibility because they can be moved around from the beginning to the middle to the end of sentences. Set them off by commas.

Archye Leacock had left Trinidad in 1972 for America.
He was a blind man.

Archye Leacock, *a blind man*, had left Trinidad in 1972 for America.
OR
Totally blind, Archye Leacock had left Trinidad in 1972 for America.

Now he was teaching piano.
He was a man in his thirties.

Now, *a man in his thirties*, he was teaching piano.
OR
A man in his thirties, he was now teaching piano.

Cyril wished to imitate his example.
It was an inspiring one.

Cyril wished to imitate his example, *an inspiring one*.

EXERCISE 14.8

Answers will vary, depending on which sentence is converted to an appositive.

Combine the following pairs of simple sentences by making one of them an appositive. Punctuate correctly.

1. Cyril ran his first marathon with a friend.
   His friend was a sighted Trinidadian.

   Combination: Cyril ran his first marathon with a friend, a sighted Trinidadian.

2. Anthony Salloum asked Cyril if he wanted to run in the New York City Marathon.
   Anthony was club president.

   Combination: Anthony Salloum, club president, asked Cyril if he wanted to run in the New York City Marathon.

3. His time was respectable for any runner on a first attempt.
   It was 3:47.

   Combination: His time, 3:47, was respectable for any runner on a first attempt.

215

4. He won the praise of Dick Traum.
   Dick was an amputee.

   Combination: <u>He won the praise of Dick Traum, an amputee. OR: Dick Traum, an amputee, praised him.</u>

5. If you ever get to New York again,'' said Traum, ''come train with us.''
   Traum was also founder of the Achilles Track Club.

   Combination: <u>''If you ever get to New York again,'' said Traum, founder of the Achilles Track Club, ''come train with us.''</u>

6. Meanwhile, Cyril achieved his fondest dream.
   It was his high-school equivalency diploma.

   Combination: <u>Meanwhile, Cyril achieved his fondest dream, his high-school equivalency diploma.</u>

7. Traum listened to an intriguing proposal from Dr. Richard Koplin.
   Koplin was the director of the Eye Trauma Center.

   Combination: <u>Traum listened to an intriguing proposal from Dr. Richard Koplin, director of the Eye Trauma Center.</u>

8. Dr. John Seedor told Cyril he would perform an operation.
   The operation would be a corneal transplant on the right eye.

   Combination: <u>Dr. John Seedor told Cyril he would perform an operation, a corneal transplant on the right eye.</u>

9. Raising the bandage, Cyril saw himself clearly for the first time in 15 years.
   He was a young man with a broad, handsome face.

   Combination: <u>Raising the bandage, Cyril saw himself clearly for the first time in 15 years, a young man with a broad, handsome face.</u>

10. Cyril told Traum he wanted to run in a new role.
    He would run as a guide for a blind runner.

    Combination: <u>Cyril told Traum he wanted to run in a new role, a guide for a blind runner.</u>

REVIEW EXERCISE 14.9

Combine the following series of simple sentences, using the following devices described in this chapter:

- Using *-ly* words, *-ed* words, *-ing* words, *to* words, and prepositional phrases.
- Creating a compound sentence with words like *and, or, but, nor, so,* or *yet.*
- Creating a compound predicate with words like *and, or, but, nor,* or *yet.*

- Creating a complex sentence by using subordinating words such as *after*, *when*, *because*, or others.
- Using an appositive.

Be sure to punctuate correctly.

Answers will vary.

1. I parked my jeep at the end of the road.
   The giant whale bones lay bleaching in the sun. **[subordination]**

   Combination: I parked my jeep at the end of the road where the giant whale bones lay bleaching in the sun.

2. Three months earlier I'd arrived at the U.S. Air Force base in Iceland.
   It was on January 6, 1963. **[appositive]**

   Combination: Three months earlier, on January 6, 1963, I'd arrived at the U.S. Air Force base in Iceland.

3. This assignment made us leave spouses and children behind.
   We also had to lower our profile. **[compound predicate]**

   Combination: This assignment made us leave spouses and children behind and lower our profile.

4. I spotted a boy watching me from a distant farmhouse.
   He was perhaps nine or ten. **[appositive]**

   Combination: I spotted a boy, perhaps nine or ten, watching me from a distant farmhouse.

5. He crossed the meadow.
   He stood at the wire fence that lined the beach. **[subordination or compound predicate]**

   Combination: After he crossed the meadow, he stood at the wire fence that lined the beach. [subordination] OR: He crossed the meadow and stood at the wire fence that lined the beach. [compound predicate]

6. I held a bag of candy toward him.
   He smiled and cupped his hands. **[subordination or coordination between clauses]**

   Combination: When I held a bag of candy toward him, he smiled and cupped his hands. [subordination] OR: I held a bag of candy toward him, so he smiled and cupped his hands. [coordination]

7. A sea bird nested in a shallow depression.
   It was mottled brown and gray. **[-ed word]**

   Combination: Mottled brown and gray, a sea bird nested in a shallow depression.

8. I leaned down to examine the bird.
   It refused to move. **[subordination]**

   Combination: I leaned down to examine the bird, which refused to move. OR: When I leaned down to examine the bird, it refused to move.

9. The boy jumped to his feet.
   He motioned me to follow. **[-ing word]**

   Combination: Jumping to his feet, the boy motioned me to follow. OR: Motioning me to follow, the boy jumped to his feet.

10. Val left the trail.
    He scampered down to the water's edge. **[-ing word, or compound predicate]**

    Combination: Leaving the trail, Val scampered down to the water's edge. [-ing word] OR: Val left the trail and scampered down to the water's edge. [compound predicate]

11. We entered a sheltered cove.
    Dun-colored seals dived from craggy rocks.
    They swam about in calm waters. **[subordination *and* compound predicate]**

    Combination: We entered a sheltered cove where dun-colored seals dived from craggy rocks and swam about in calm waters.

12. Val flashed a wide grin.
    He ran over.
    He handed me a wicker basket.
    He motioned me to the beach. **[-ing word and compound predicate]**

    Combination: Flashing a wide grin, Val ran over, handed me a wicker basket, and motioned me to the beach.

13. Others waved me on.
    I joined the hunt.
    I ignored the screeching terns.
    They dived at my head. **[subordination, -ing word, and subordination]**

    Combination: As others waved me on, I joined the hunt, ignoring the screeching terns that dived at my head.

14. At the first clutch, I scooped up both eggs.
    Val took one from me.
    He put it back. **[coordination, compound sentence, *and* compound predicate]**

    Combination: At the first clutch, I scooped up both eggs, but Val took one from me and put it back.

15. It was at the end of the day.
    I sat on the knoll with Val.
    I returned the islanders' waves. **[prepositional phrase, -ing word]**

    Combination: At the end of the day, I sat on the knoll with Val, returning the islanders' waves.

ANSWER KEY

The following answers are provided for every other question in the exercises in this chapter.

EXERCISE 14.1

2. *Subject:* creature   *Verb:* will be evolved   *Actor:* her (she)
Rewrite: If nature is given an environment or situation, she will evolve a creature.

4. *Subject:* grebe   *Verb:* was seen   *Actor:* me (I)
Rewrite: One summer in Maine I saw a sleek female horned grebe.

6. *Subject:* something   *Verb:* was noticed   *Actor:* me (I)
Rewrite: Suddenly I noticed something through my binoculars.

8. *Subjects:* feathers   *Verbs:* were being stuffed   *Actors:* her (she)
       pokes   were made   her (she)
Rewrite: As she stuffed the dry feathers into the gaping mouths, she made two or three pokes to get each one down.

10. *Subject:* she   *Verb:* was seen   *Actor:* she
Rewrite: Then, sailing low on the water, she vanished among the plants.

12. *Subjects:* it   *Verb:* was asked   *Actor:* me (I)
        answer   was   biologist
        use   is found   nature
Rewrite: When I asked why, a biologist answered, "Nature finds a use for everything."

EXERCISE 14.2

These creatures were black and white and were sought all over, at least in Cuba and the southern United States. Just last week, according to a report, two ivory-billed woodpeckers were spotted in a Cuban forest. The handsome species had been believed for years to be extinct. "I thought, 'My God, I've seen it'," said Dr. Lester L. Short, chairman of ornithology at the American Museum of Natural History. He recalled a day in April when an ivory-bill crossed his path. Before he could aim his camera, it was gone.

EXERCISE 14.3

2. Seeking to escape the sun, most animals shelter motionlessly. OR: Sheltering motionlessly, most animals seek to escape the sun.

4. To avoid the thorns, small, wiry tribesmen scuttle crablike.

6. Armed with her first checkbook, Kimmi went off to college.

8. Happily, she patted her father on the back.

10. As an English teacher, I spent a great deal of time marking errors.

12. Observing the sky, winds and clouds, people made up sayings to remember the patterns.

14. To burn off the fog, the sun must shine through clear skies.

16. Looking up at the sky, they matched up a number of clues.
18. To foretell the weather, people should watch the barometer.

EXERCISE 14.4

2. My mother sent my son a water pistol, [and, so] he headed for the nearest sink.
4. No one spoke for a few minutes, [so, but, for] the guide answered his question.
6. Fiber is good for us, [and] moderate amounts discourage over-eating.
8. One doctor claimed that fiber protected against certain diseases, [and, so] scientists began to investigate.
10. Fibrous foods hold water, [so] fiber may also battle hunger.

EXERCISE 14.5

2. Bob visited the new plant in town and applied for a job.
4. Some people cannot view some situations optimistically [and, or] put a good face on them.
6. I reorganized the business [and, yet] ran the household.
8. Upbeat beliefs are helpful [but, yet] don't change realities.
10. Many people worry a lot about little things [but, yet] learn to stop being afraid.

EXERCISE 14.6

2. I asked a bystander to pick out several towns [that] lie on or close to the 40th parallel.
4. Eugene O'Neill had a daughter Oona who married Charlie Chaplin.
6. After Freda Ehmann developed a successful method for canning olives, they could be marketed commercially.
8. Because my father had deserted us, my mother needed help.
10. [After, When] I finished graduate school, I went into the stock market.

EXERCISE 14.7

2. Battered by a typhoon, the ship wallowed in heavy seas.
4. Sucked through a flooded culvert, the child fell into a roiling storm sewer.
6. Transfixed in the control room, he watched a daily talk show being broadcast.
8. Concerned about everyone but herself, Darlene overate to cover up her anxiety.
10. Though feeling terrible, she continued to eat with abandon.

EXERCISE 14.8

2. Anthony Salloum, club president, asked Cyril if he wanted to run in the New York City Marathon.

4. He won the praise of Dick Traum, an amputee. OR: Dick Traum, an amputee, praised him.

6. Meanwhile, Cyril achieved his fondest dream, his high-school equivalency diploma.

8. Dr. John Seedor told Cyril he would perform an operation, a corneal transplant on the right eye.

10. Cyril told Traum he wanted to run in a new role, a guide for a blind runner.

REVIEW EXERCISE 14.9

2. Three months earlier, on January 6, 1963, I'd arrived at the U.S. Air Force base in Iceland.

4. I spotted a boy, perhaps nine or ten, watching me from a distant farmhouse.

6. When I held a bag of candy toward him, he smiled and cupped his hands. [subordination] OR: I held a bag of candy toward him, so he smiled and cupped his hands. [coordination]

8. I leaned down to examine the bird, which refused to move. OR: When I leaned down to examine the bird, it refused to move.

10. Leaving the trail, Val scampered down to the water's edge. [-ing word] OR: Val left the trail and scampered down to the water's edge. [compound predicate]

12. Flashing a wide grin, Val ran over, handed me a wicker basket, and motioned me to the beach.

14. At the first clutch, I scooped up both eggs, but Val took one from me and put it back.

Choosing
Effective Words

When talking informally with a friend, you might say, "Some company gave a party a while ago, and a lot of people went. It was awesome!" Vague statements in casual conversation give us few problems. If our friend doesn't understand, she'll ask some questions. When we have written something, however, our readers can't question us. We need to make our ideas clear. We should also use fresh, vivid language that catches their interest. Our first drafts focus on organization and support. We then revise these early efforts to make our word choice more specific and original.

Section One: Specific Language: Avoiding Generalities

As far as possible, good writers choose exact, precise words. They use them to replace vague generalities that call up no images in the reader's mind. Look over the following pairs of sentences and decide which one of each pair is more specific.

   a. Everyone was crying.
   b. Even grown men were snuffling, with tear-filled eyes.
   c. The car was easy to drive.
   d. The Lexis handled well in the curves, moving well on the wet road.
   e. My pet liked its food.
   f. My dog liked doggie treats and jerky bits.

Sentences b, d, and f are more specific and vivid. In sentence b, *grown men*, *snuffling*, and *tear-filled eyes* are more specific than *everyone* and *crying*.

EXERCISE 15.1   *Answer the following questions about the sentences above.*

1. What words does *d* use instead of *car* and *easy to drive?*
   It substitutes *Lexis* and *handled well in the curves, moving*

   well on the wet road.

2. Why are these words more exact?
   They describe the specific car model and exact road conditions: curving or wet roads.

3. What words does *f* use instead of *pet* or *food*?
   It uses *dog, doggie treats,* and *jerky bits.*

4. Why are these words more specific?
   They tell *what kind* of pet and food.

This vague account is quite general and dull:

When one girl was young, her mother gave her an allowance which she divided up. Her mother told her to follow the rules. One time, the girl spent all her money and called her mother for help. However, her mother wouldn't help her.

This version, however, is quite specific and detailed:

When Brooke Stephens was ten and growing up in Jacksonville, Florida, her mother gave her $5 a week, $1.75 of which was earmarked for bus fare and lunch. "If you lose your money," Brooke's mother told her, "you walk home." One week the girl spent all her allowance in a candy store; then she called home for a ride. "Mom made me walk home," recalls Stephens.

The revised version names the girl, tells the sums in dollars and cents, quotes exact words, and tells how the girl spent her allowance.

To make your writing more specific and vivid, replace dull, vague words with words that do the following:

- Sum up, count, measure, or resemble
- Tell what kind, what size, what color
- Quote people's exact words

Instead of referring to a *bad road,* for example, try using words like *bumpy, rough,* or *dusty.* Think of ways something smells: *smoky, sweet, fresh.* Replace a word like *moves* with *budges, shifts, plunges, lurches,* or *creeps.* For help in selecting fresh language, look up words in *Roget's Thesaurus of Synonyms and Antonyms.* This reference work helps you find words which mean the same as (synonyms) and words which mean the opposite (antonyms). Of course, your word choice will be influenced by context—the meaning of the sentences that include the word. Then too, word processing programs such as WordPerfect and Word include thesaurus utilities. When you place the cursor on a word and issue a command, the computer will list synonyms and antonyms on the screen.

EXERCISE 15.2

The sentences below offer choices between vague and more specific terms. Underline the most specific term available.

Example: The (function, party) for (Ivy League, Harvard) M.B.A.s was (outside, under the stars) at the (fancy, glittering) Tavern on the Green.

Party tells what kind of function, while Harvard is a particular member of the Ivy League. In addition, under the stars and glittering are both more visual and figurative than words such as outside and fancy.

1. The other party, for (students, people) from (another Ivy League school, the Wharton School of the University of Pennsylvania), was in (Morgan's exercise gym, a large room) in (a big place, the Exxon Building) amid (the stationary bicycles, a lot of exercise equipment).

2. When summer comes (Wall Street, the financial center) is (filled, overrun) with (students, people) who spend the (time, months) between the (first and second, beginning) years of business school in (good, prized) intern jobs.

3. These students are competing (furiously, hard) for eventual (permanent, long-lasting) jobs at (good, top) firms like Morgan Stanley.

4. Getting an (invitation, letter) is not hard—nearly every (so often, week night) students are invited to a (party, gathering) by one or another (financial institution, investment bank).

5. (Aggressive, forward) students try to use the parties to (move, jockey their way) onto the firm's formal (discussion, interview) schedule.

6. The (cocktail, drink) circuit has become a (good, important) recruiting (tool, thing).

7. Said a (high executive, vice president in charge of recruiting) at an investment bank, "Firms are renting (yachts, boats) and fancy (restaurants, places), competing with each other to provide the (best, most lavish) function."

8. Students (wanting, eager) to get offers from all the (top firms, best places) try to (ingratiate themselves, become friendly) with the (other people, recruiters).

9. With (ample buffets, lots of food), open bars, and (cold, frozen) smiles, the receptions seem like a (gathering, pledge party) at a (fraternity or sorority, college club).

EXERCISE 15.3

Many sentences like those below use dull, boring words. For each one, think of a more exact or vivid word to replace the general word in parentheses. Choose a word that fits the context—or meaning—of the sentence. Check the word in a dictionary or thesaurus, if necessary.

Answers will vary.

EXAMPLE: A young man with two babies in his arms was trying to go **[struggle]** through the door.

1. The (fast) _____foaming, rushing_____ ocean waves (come up) _____charge, surge_____ onto the beach.

2. Gerry was our new neighbor who just (came) _____moved, relocated_____ here from Canada.

3. A hungry diner (walked) _____strode, rushed_____ into the (small) _____diminutive, petite_____ Japanese restaurant.

4. Mary (thought) _____worried, fretted_____ constantly about getting her (boring) _____tedious, wearisome_____ household chores done after work.

5. Inside the shop, I (saw) _____glimpsed, sighted_____ a (big) _____huge_____ (foreign) _____oriental_____ gong.

6. Intrigued, I (walked) _____strolled, sauntered_____ up to it for a closer (look) _____glance, examination_____ .

7. The population of Lincoln, Vermont (is) _____hovers, fluctuates_____ around 900.

8. We (have) _____own, possess_____ three (tools) _____appliances, devices_____ and a home-improvement book.

9. I recently (looked) _____searched for_____ (work) _____employment, a position_____ in my campus newspaper's classifieds.

10. She took swimming lessons just to (see) _____glimpse, stare at_____ a (handsome) _____attractive, good-looking_____ young man.

11. One woman's husband (got up) _____rose, rolled out of bed_____ early and (put) _____placed, presented_____ a rose by her bedside.

12. For their anniversary, they decided to (cook) _____barbecue, grill_____ and (eat) _____feast on, devour_____ a couple of (good-tasting) _____luscious, sumptuous_____ steaks.

13. Couples who laugh at the same jokes are more likely to (be) _____stay, remain_____ together.

14. James (walked) _____raced, sprinted_____ away from the burning car, which was about to (blow up) _____explode_____ .

15. One evening a friend and I (went to) _____stopped, paused_____ at a newly opened restaurant.

Rewrite the following vague, general paragraph. Substitute or add more vivid, exciting verbs and descriptive words.

A man out West who called himself a healer made some people believe that their daughter did not need medicine. By tapping her body, he said, he could make the child get well. The girl soon died. He sent her parents a large bill for his help.

A man in Montana who called himself a nature healer convinced the parents of a 16-year-old diabetic girl that her daily insulin shots were unnecessary. By tapping his fingers on her chest, he said, he could stimulate their daughter's own insulin-making capacity. Three days later, the girl was dead. The healer billed her parents $6,350 for the treatment.

Section Two: Concise Language: Avoiding Wordiness

UNNECESSARY AND REPETITIOUS WORDS

Concise sentences are brief and forceful. They make their points without unnecessary repetition. In the following pairs of sentences, one is wordy and repetitious.

a. Imagine at the present time doing something like volunteering to be a surgeon, a pilot, or something of this sort.

b. Imagine volunteering to be a surgeon, a pilot, or a train engineer.

c. At this point in time, two people named Marian and Chuck took a nice trip for skiing in a place called Sun Valley, Idaho.

d. Marian and Chuck took a skiing trip to Sun Valley, Idaho.

e. On a really cold day in winter, two employees who obviously worked for a firm which was located in Wisconsin were sitting in the vicinity behind me on the plane.

f. On a cold winter day, two employees of a firm in Wisconsin [or *Wisconsin firm*] were sitting behind me on the plane.

Sentences a, c, and e are *wordy*. Versions b, d, and f are *concise* and forceful.

In sentence a, phrases such as *at the present time*, *doing something like*, and *something of this sort* add nothing to its sense.

Sentence c includes vague language: *At this point in time, two people named, nice,* and *in a place called.*

In sentence e, some words add nothing: *really, who obviously worked for, which was located in,* and *in the vicinity.*

To write concisely, avoid using the following:

- Words that *say nothing,* and
- Words that *repeat the same or similar words*

The following words are vague and empty. Avoid them, or replace them with more specific words:

---

area, aspect, field, factor, kind, quality, situation, sort, thing, bad, fine, good, important, nice, significant, actually, basically, completely, definitely, quite, very

---

The following phrases should be replaced with single, specific words:

Omit	Replace with
at the present time	now
at this point in time	now
by means of	by
for the purpose of	for
have the ability to	be able to
in the event that	if, when
in the vicinity of	near
on account of the fact that	if, because
until such time as	as
in regard to	about

EXERCISE 15.5

Some of the following sentences repeat words or phrases. Others use vague, empty words. Underline the unnecessary words.

EXAMPLE: At the present time my aunt deals with situations involving customer complaints.

1. On account of the fact that she and my uncle had had an argument with each other, he definitely wanted to make up.

2. Until such time as it was his turn, he was in the situation of waiting in the customer service line.

3. At the point of time when he had a secret, he basically whispered to her in her ear.

4. My uncle promised by saying to her he'd take her out to a nice dinner quite definitely that night.

5. Her face lit up as an aspect of her response, and she actually gave him a big kiss on account of her happiness.

6. The very next man in line stepped up for the purpose of speaking to her and sort of said, "I'm complaining about the same thing he was."

7. At the end of my <u>very</u> first day on a new route, I <u>had the occasion to</u> discover several <u>nice</u> items of clothing <u>obviously</u> left on my school bus.

8. <u>On account of the fact that</u> I had <u>basically</u> completed a plumbing call at a dentist's office, I <u>actually</u> gave my bill <u>for the purpose of payment</u> to the bookkeeper.

9. She <u>made the statement that</u> said that they would mail me a check <u>for purposes of payment</u>.

10. At that moment <u>in time</u> a sign <u>in the vicinity of</u> her desk <u>tended to catch</u> my eye.

11. I reached over and picked up the sign and <u>basically</u> turned <u>the thing</u> toward her.

12. It <u>significantly</u> read, ''Payment <u>definitely</u> expected <u>in the event that</u> services <u>are</u> rendered.''

13. <u>At that point in time</u> I <u>had the ability to leave</u> with my check.

THE DUMMY SUBJECTS *THERE* AND *IT*

We often begin spoken sentences with *there* and *it*. These words should point to a place (**there**) or a thing (**it**). If they do not, they are **dummy** subjects. They cannot be *actors* or *doers*. We must follow them with passive verbs like *it/was/were*. Here is an example:

> *There were* bills everywhere when an armored car spilled cash all over I-71.

The word *there* does not point to a place. Cross it out, along with the verb that follows it: "~~There were~~ bills everywhere . . ."

To revise the sentence, find a new, more active subject or *doer* later in the sentence: "bills." Then find or invent an active verb to follow it: "*flew*" or "*scattered*." Rewrite the sentence:

> Bills flew everywhere when an armored car spilled cash all over I-71.

EXERCISE 15.6

The following sentences all use dummy subjects, it *or* there. *Replace these words with subjects that* act *or* do. *Follow them with active, vivid verbs.*

1. It was the drama of firefighting that struck me at about the age of eight.
   Revision: The drama of firefighting struck me at about the age of eight.

2. There were errands to run to ingratiate myself with the men.
   Revision: I'd run errands to ingratiate myself with the men.

3. It was not long before the fire company adopted me.

   Revision: Before long the fire company adopted me.

4. From then on, there were dreams of my being a firefighter one day.

   Revision: From then on, I dreamed of being a firefighter one day.

5. It was a dream that I never outgrew.

   Revision: I never outgrew the dream.

6. It was as an adult that I joined the volunteer fire department.

   Revision: As an adult, I joined the volunteer fire department.

7. There was gear issued to me and training that I received.

   Revision: I was issued gear and received training. OR: The department issued me gear and trained me.

8. Finally, one evening there was a fire in a house on the west side of town.

   Revision: Finally, one evening a house on the west side of town caught fire.

Section Three: Original Language: Avoiding Clichés

Writers try to catch the interest of readers with fresh, novel language. Many familiar terms were once fresh when used in literature, advertising, or politics: "the cutting edge," "the real thing," "between a rock and a hard place," "a little learning is a dangerous thing," and countless others. With overuse, they seem tired and predictable. Which sentences below use language that you have often encountered?

    a. It's as certain as death and taxes.

    b. Industry is a better horse to ride than genius.

    c. His advice was as right as rain.

    d. The greatest of all arts is the art of living together.

In sentences a and c, "death and taxes" and "right as rain" have been overused. We scarcely notice them. When you are tempted to use a tired expression, replace it with your own more original version:

Cliché:	She was a *born loser*.
Fresher:	Her drooping shoulders and downcast eyes reflected despair.
Cliché:	He *had completely clammed up*.
Fresher:	He sat silently and gloomily.

EXERCISE 15.7

Answers will vary.

Cross out the clichés below. Write in fresher, more original language. Refer to a thesaurus if necessary.

1. I want to imagine myself free as a bird.
   Replace "free as a bird" with "where it's beautiful and quiet."

2. Roger punched the thug's lights out.
   Replace "punched . . . lights out" with "hammered the thug's skull."

3. The patient was sick as a dog.
   Replace "sick as a dog" with "breathing heavily and running a temperature of 104°."

4. She loved him for better or for worse.
   Replace "for better or for worse" with "deeply and passionately."

5. He heard the voices clear as a bell, and his spirits rose out of this world.
   Replace "clear as a bell" with "clearly and distinctly," and "out of this world" with "optimistically."

6. She looked down at the heels.
   Replace "down at the heels" with "penniless, unwashed, and shoddy."

7. When new, his car was bright as a penny, but now it is dull as dishwater.
   Replace "bright as a penny" with "gleamed brightly in the sun," and "dull as dishwater" with "lifeless and lackluster."

8. She was a pleasure to look at, with her clean-as-a-whistle hair and her milk-white skin.
   Replace "clean as a whistle" with "curly, blow-dried" and "milk-white" with "pure, healthy."

Section Four: Figurative Language: Metaphors and Symbols

Writers often clarify ideas with images or comparisons. They compare general terms with concrete objects—things we touch or see or hear. Fresh analogies help readers pick up ideas quickly:

The first in-room amenity in a hotel was probably a miniature bar of soap, and that was the standard until shampoo, shower caps, shoe mitts, and sewing kits began appearing regularly. In the 1980s, these basics were followed by lotions, bath gels, mouthwashes, shaving creams, razors, chocolates, shoe horns, shoe polish, suntan lotions, and even prepasted toothbrushes and vitamin pills.
   "It's *like a gas war*," said one hotel manager. "It's become *a giant monster*

taking over the world,'' said Daryl Hartley-Leonard, president of the Hyatt Hotels Corporation in Chicago.

This news report includes a clear, specific list of amenities supplied by hotels. It also makes the feelings of executives about growing competition easy to see with our mind's eye. It compares this runaway one-upmanship with a gas war or King Kong.

A *metaphor* suggests a relationship between two different things. A news report described a well-known preacher's run for national office:

> Some Republicans argue he will help the party by attracting new voters, but others fear he will scare some voters. *"This could drive a stake right through the heart* of new Yuppie Republicans,'' gloated one Democratic politician.

In this report a politician applies occult imagery to a confused political situation. People once believed that a vampire should be buried at a crossroads. A stake was driven through his heart to prevent him rising from the grave.

Another news report called a struggle by a government agency to obtain information on criminals "a *war of attrition.*" The writer meant that each side was trying to wear down the other side slowly.

A news item notes that "The Democratic Study Group plans a dinner honoring '**Jacknife Jack**' Brooks, '**Jugular John**' Dingell and '**Dangerous Dan**' Rostenkowski—the three toughest chairmen in the House." The account humorously refers to these three congressmen as bloodthirsty cutthroats.

EXERCISE 15.8

Answers will vary.

Each of the following sentences includes figurative language. Underline the figurative language. Rewrite the sentence in simple, literal terms. Then rewrite the sentence again, replacing the figurative language with your own figure of speech. Consider images drawn from the Old West, food, popular culture, warfare, sports, machinery, games, the cosmos, and so on.

EXAMPLE: Their conversations, and indeed their lives, sound *mind-bendingly* boring.

Literal: Their conversations, and indeed their lives, sound extremely dull and monotonous.

Figurative [animal]: Their conversations, and indeed their lives, sound so *piggishly boar-ing.*

1. Hallmark cards, the giant of the greeting card industry, is in a David-and-Goliath battle for a share of the card market.
   Literal: Hallmark cards, the giant of the greeting card industry, is in a David-and-Goliath battle [against smaller companies] for a share of the card market.

   Figurative: Hallmark cards, the General Motors of the greeting card industry, is in a race car and family sedan contest for a share of the card market.

2. Whether lawmakers will vote to cut off part of the hand that feeds their campaigns remains to be seen.

   Literal: Whether lawmakers will vote to cut off part of the hand that feeds [limit donations to] their campaigns remains to be seen.

   Figurative: Whether lawmakers will vote to start the countdown against the lobbyists who fund their campaigns remains to be seen.

3. IBM's flexibility has earned it the reputation among industry insiders as the "elephant that dances."

   Literal: IBM's flexibility has earned it the reputation among industry insiders as the "elephant that dances" [large company that moves nimbly].

   Figurative: IBM's flexibility has earned it the reputation among industry insiders as the brontosaurus that cavorts.

4. As its public image suffers from a recent drop in second quarter earnings, CBS is wielding an array of short-term and long-term weapons to blunt any further decline.

   Literal: As its public image suffers from a recent drop in second quarter earnings, CBS is wielding [making] an array of short-term and long-term weapons to blunt [management changes to slow down] any further decline.

   Figurative: As its public image suffers from a recent drop in second quarter earnings, CBS is launching an array of short-term and long-term craft to buoy up any further decline.

5. This is the story of how a man coped with the hand life dealt him.

   Literal: This is the story of how a man coped with the hand life dealt him [circumstances he encountered in life].

   Figurative: This is the story of how a man coped with the grounders life batted him.

6. Horsfalter put his story together like a detective, piecing together an enormous jigsaw puzzle.

   Literal: Horsfalter put his story together like a detective, piecing together an enormous jigsaw puzzle [solving the difficult problem].

   Figurative: Horsfalter put his story together like an astronomer, focusing his telescope on tiny pinpoints of light.

7. Harold Piepkorn won a long battle of attrition with his rivals for the affections of his beloved Florence Nightshade.

   Literal: Harold Piepkorn won a long battle of attrition [successfully overcame competition] with his rivals for the affections of his beloved Florence Nightshade.

234

Figurative: Harold Piepkorn won a long marathon with his rivals for the affections of his beloved Florence Nightshade.

8. His surprising hands, dark and hard-looking, were soft as a young girl's.
   Literal: His surprising hands, dark and hard-looking, were soft as a young girl's [extremely soft].

   Figurative: His surprising hands, dark and hard-looking, were soft as pigeon down.

9. His face was a mask of defeat.
   Literal: His face was a mask of defeat [he looked extremely depressed].
   Figurative: His face was a battlefield that armies had fought over.

EXERCISE 15.9
Answers will vary.

Complete the following sentences with similes. Remember: a simile includes the words like *or* as. *Be as creative as you can.*

EXAMPLE: My job is like *a commercial for a pain-killer*
a car which has just been totaled
a vacation in purgatory
being locked in a zoo.

1. Keeping up my car is like trying to fill up the Grand Canyon with money.
2. Falling in love is like stumbling into a hornet's nest.
3. Getting through college is like using a shovel to dig a ditch between San Francisco and Omaha.
4. My house looks like an eleven-car pileup on the expressway.
5. My family is like the cast of a sitcom.

**REVIEW
EXERCISE 15.10**
Answers will vary.

The following sentences are vague and general. Rewrite them, using more vivid verbs and descriptive words.

1. People have been doing new things.
   Special interest groups have been seizing the initiative.

2. Voters spoke to local politicians.
   Outraged voters lobbied and cajoled indifferent local politicians.

3. A number of people who lived in the area showed up to complain.
   An immense crowd of local citizens filled the huge hall to protest noisily.

235

4. The doctor was thinking of getting another answering service.
   The harried, overworked doctor racked his brain as he debated searching for another answering service.

5. The man sold his old car to a neighbor.
   The cunning, devious reprobate peddled his worthless wreck to an unsuspecting neighbor.

6. A small family walked through the mountains.
   Don Smith, his wife, Susan, and their children, David and Laura, hiked enthusiastically in California's Santa Ana Mountains.

7. An animal ran off with the child.
   A huge, famished mountain lion seized the child's head in its jaws and lumbered into the underbrush.

8. A truck dropped money on the road.
   An armored truck spilled cash in dark blue plastic bags all over I-71 in Columbus, Ohio.

9. I took the children off their chairs and cleaned them up.
   I yanked the half-pint culprits off their rickety stools and plunged their grimy hands and faces into soapy water.

10. His son talks a lot.
    His 13-year-old son, Ethan, has always been a noisy, nonstop chatterbox.

REVIEW EXERCISE 15.11

The following paragraph uses empty words, repeats words unnecessarily, and includes the dummy subjects there *and* it. *Underline words that can be omitted, and rewrite the paragraph more concisely.*

It is significant that Nancy's sleeping difficulties began on account of the fact that she went on vacation. At this point in time she blamed the aspect of noise in her motel room. But there was no improvement in the quality of her sleeping in the vicinity of her home. Instead of a situation of sleeping her usual six or seven hours a night, she basically had the ability to sleep just three or four. Nancy tried the technique of going to bed for the purpose of sleeping earlier. There was even the fact of her husband's breathing which significantly disturbed her. It was drinking a glass of wine at bedtime that definitely helped her fall asleep. It was her doctor who prescribed a pill for the purpose of sleeping. On account of the fact that she stopped taking the pills, it was worse sleeping for her than ever.

Rewrite: It is significant that Nancy's sleeping difficulties began on account

236

of the fact that [when] she went on vacation. At this point in time she blamed the aspect of noise in her motel room. But there was no improvement in the quality of her sleeping in the vicinity of her [did not improve at] home. Instead of a situation of sleeping her usual six or seven hours a night, she basically had the ability to sleep [slept] just three or four. Nancy tried the factor of going to bed for the purpose of sleeping earlier. There was even the fact of her husband's breathing which significantly disturbed her. It was drinking a glass of wine at bedtime that definitely helped her fall asleep. It was her doctor who prescribed a [sleeping] pill for the purpose of sleeping. On account of the fact that [When] she stopped taking the pills, it was worse sleeping for her [she slept worse] than ever.

Section Five: Writing Topics

Make some notes on one of the topics below. Use vivid, specific language and figures of speech. List as many as possible. Then write a topic sentence and develop your ideas into a paragraph.

1. Imagine a scene in full, vivid detail. Place it in reality or in some unreal locale. Create characters like yourself and perhaps others. Visualize an action which makes your characters come alive. Here is an example:

I am sitting crosslegged looking at the worst thing that ever came into my life. It's a wall. It's alive. It's a thick network of vines with the strength of King Kong and just as primitive. I've tried to defy my enemy and climb it, but the thorny, fingerlike branches tore at my hands unbearably painfully. I am surrounded and held captive. I am the fish, and it is the fish bowl. Even after I've located the sharpest of rocks and hammered away for hours, I've made only a small nick in it. It seems to smile and laugh when it sees defeat in my eyes.

2. Where would you like to spend time, either alone or with a close friend? Outside, perhaps near running water, with the smell of flowers? Or high in the sky, where the air is crisp? Inside a house or other building? "Look" from one side to another. Write down what your eyes "see" as you imagine this scene.

3. Pretend that you are putting together an ideal meal. It is one to which you would invite someone you deeply admire. Describe the smells of the food and its textures. How does it taste as you bite into it and chew it? What comments would you both make about it?

4. Pretend that you are standing on a street corner in your home town.

Identify and describe it. How does it look, sound, and feel at one of the following times:

- Sunday morning
- Saturday evening
- Noon on a weekday

In one of the time periods above, imagine that the seasons change before your eyes from winter, to spring, to summer, to fall.

5. Close your eyes. Imagine that you are listening to your favorite song. Who and what does it remind you of? What sort of place fits the lyrics best? What do you feel like doing?

6. Consider a difficult time in your life. Think of things that made you anxious. What sights or smells or sounds remind you of that time? What do you usually do to feel less anxious, more relaxed?

ANSWER KEY

We have provided answers to alternate questions in this chapter's exercises.

EXERCISE 15.2

2. When summer comes (*Wall Street*, the financial center) is (filled, *overrun*) with (*students*, people) who spend the (time, *months*) between the (*first and second*, beginning) years of business school in (good, *prized*) intern jobs.

4. Getting an (*invitation*, letter) is not hard—nearly every (so often, *week night*) students are invited to a (*party*, gathering) by one or another (financial institution, *investment bank*).

6. The (*cocktail*, drink) circuit has become a (good, *important*) recruiting (*tool*, thing).

8. Students (wanting, *eager*) to get offers from all the (*top firms*, best places) try to (*ingratiate themselves*, become friendly) with the (other people, *recruiters*).

EXERCISE 15.3

2. Gerry was our new neighbor who just (came) *moved, relocated* here from Canada.

4. Mary (thought) *worried, fretted* constantly about geting her (boring) *tedious, wearisome* household chores done after work.

6. Intrigued, I (walked) *strolled, sauntered* up to it for a closer (look) *glance, examination.*

8. We (have) *own, possess* three (tools) *appliances, devices* and a home-improvement book.

10. She took swimming lessons just to (see) *glimpse, stare* at a (handsome) *attractive, good-looking* young man.

12. For their anniversary, they decided to (cook) *barbecue, grill* and

(eat) *feast on, devour* a couple of (good-tasting) *luscious, sumptuous* steaks.

14. James (walked) *raced, sprinted* away from the burning car, which was about to (blow up) *explode.*

EXERCISE 15.5

2. Until *such time as* it was his turn, he was *in the situation of* waiting (waited) in the customer service line.

4. My uncle promised *by saying to* her he'd take her out to *a nice* dinner *quite definitely* that night.

6. The *very* next man in line stepped up *for the purpose of speaking* to her and *sort of* said, "I'm complaining about the same thing he was."

8. *On account of the fact that* (Upon) *I* had *basically* completed (completing) a plumbing call at a dentist's office, I *actually* gave my bill *for the purpose of payment* to the bookkeeper.

10. At that moment *in time* a sign *in the vicinity of* [on] her desk *tended to catch* caught my eye.

12. It *significantly* read, "Payment *definitely* expected *in the event that* [when] services *are* rendered."

EXERCISE 15.6

2. I'd run errands to ingratiate myself with the men.

4. From then on, I dreamed of being a firefighter one day.

6. As an adult, I joined the volunteer fire department.

8. Finally, one evening a house on the west side of town caught fire.

EXERCISE 15.7

2. Replace "punched . . . lights out" with "hammered the thug's skull."

4. Replace "for better or for worse" with "deeply and passionately."

6. Replace "down at the heels" with "penniless, unwashed, and shoddy."

8. Replace "clean as a whistle" with "curly, blow-dried" and "milk-white" with "pure, healthy."

EXERCISE 15.8

2. *Literal:* Whether lawmakers will vote to *cut off part of the hand that feeds* (limit donations to) their campaigns remains to be seen.
   Figurative: Whether lawmakers will vote to start the countdown against the lobbyists who fund their campaigns remains to be seen.

4. *Literal:* As its public image suffers from a recent drop in second quarter earnings, CBS is *wielding* [making] an array of short-term and long-term *weapons to blunt* [management changes to slow down] any further decline.

Figurative: As its public image suffers from a recent drop in second quarter earnings, CBS is launching an array of short-term and long-term craft to buoy up any further decline.

6. *Literal:* Horsfalter put his story together like a detective, *piecing together an enormous jigsaw puzzle.*
   Figurative: Horsfalter put his story together like an astronomer, focusing his telescope on tiny pinpoints of light.

8. *Literal:* His surprising hands, dark and hard-looking, were *soft as a young girl's* [extremely soft].
   Figurative: His surprising hands, dark and hard-looking, were soft as pigeon down.

EXERCISE 15.9

2. Falling in love is like stumbling into a hornet's nest.
4. My house looks like an eleven-car pileup on the expressway.

REVIEW EXERCISE 15.10

2. Outraged voters lobbied and cajoled indifferent local politicians.
4. The harried, overworked doctor racked his brain as he debated searching for another answering service.
6. Don Smith, his wife, Susan, and their children, David and Laura, hiked enthusiastically in California's Santa Ana Mountains.
8. An armored truck spilled cash in dark blue plastic bags all over I-71 in Columbus, Ohio.
10. His 13-year-old son, Ethan, has always been a noisy, nonstop chatterbox.

REVIEW EXERCISE 15.11

[Last half of paragraph] Nancy tried the factor of going to bed for the purpose of sleeping earlier. There was even the fact of her husband's breathing which significantly disturbed her. It was drinking a glass of wine at bedtime that definitely helped her fall asleep. It was her doctor who prescribed a [sleeping] pill for the purpose of sleeping. On account of the fact that [When] she stopped taking the pills, it was worse sleeping for her [she slept worse] than ever.

Designing
the Essay

An essay uses several paragraphs to develop points about a single idea, usually called a *thesis*. Like a topic sentence in a paragraph, the thesis states the writer's plan or purpose for the essay. A writer usually states a thesis in the first part of an essay, the *introduction*.

The *body* of the essay extends the thesis by making several points. These points are used as *topic sentences* in each paragraph of the body of the essay. Each of these topic sentences grows out of the central idea or thesis. These topic sentences are then supported with illustrations—details, facts, reasons, and so on. Finally, a writer wraps up an essay in a *conclusion*.

Section One: Choosing an Essay Topic

To get started on an essay, choose an interesting topic. Avoid boring or dull ones, for such topics seldom improve with age. If the topic doesn't inspire you, create a novel or offbeat approach. For example, suppose you are assigned this topic: "Ways of Responding to a Crisis." You may not remember ever acting heroically. However, you may recall a dinner-time "crisis." Just before your guests arrived, you took a casserole out of the oven. It slipped, falling upside down on the floor. Quickly, you slipped a cookie sheet under it. Then you flipped over the entire casserole, right side up, with contents intact. No one was the wiser, and no one got food poisoning. An anecdote such as this could help you define a key term in your assigned topic, "crisis." It could also give you a unique and humorous approach to the topic. Panic, inspiration, and harmless trickery could all play parts in your essay.

Choose one of the following topics to develop, or invent one of your own. When completed, your essay should include 4 to 6 paragraphs, totaling 300 or more words.

- Over the last few years, dating has changed in a number of ways.
- I have difficulty resisting several kinds of temptation.
- Several good ways to persuade people to cooperate include . . . .

Your choice of topic: _____

Section Two: Generating Ideas for the Essay

Chapter 1, "Generating Ideas," suggested a number of ways to generate ideas or *prewrite*. These include the reporter's questions, scratch outlining, clustering, and other techniques. Darlene used the reporter's questions—*who, what, where, when, why,* and *how*—to generate ideas for her topic, "Nursing in England." She expanded these simple questions at times, and her answers are notelike:

Who?	Member of health team, deeply respected, devoted woman, entrusted with vast responsibility
What does she do?	Makes many decisions: when wound healed, when to remove sutures; most familiar person to patients, in their view constantly; reports to doctor on observations
Where?	Her knowledge and skills are fully utilized by British hospital system, including doctors
When?	Nurses licensed to practice anywhere in Great Britain and in some countries abroad
Why?	Have practiced under socialized medicine since 1940s
How?	Nurse spends most of her time at patient's bedside, with less writing than in U.S.; no need to write charges and requests, since stocks of medicine kept in each ward; all charges met by "National Health"

Darlene then summed up the basis for her thesis:

In England the hospital nurse is given much responsibility; doctors rely on her, and she enjoys the confidence of patients.

To develop your topic, adapt the reporter's questions to the needs of your topic.

```
Who?
What?
Where?
When?
Why?
How?
```

When you have finished answering these questions, sum up the points you plan to use for your thesis in a sentence:

_____

_____

EXERCISE 16.1

Answers will vary.

We have listed several topics below. For each of them, generate a series of examples. Use the reporter's questions, brainstorming, or clustering to generate your illustrations. Then think of ways to group your examples and write a trial thesis.

1. Ways of Learning Something New

Examples: Imitating a dancing teacher, following written directions for putting together a bicycle, toy, or machine, using trial and error to repair a broken door handle, following cartoon figures in a magazine to build a step stool, watching a film telling how to clean a carburetor, listening to a tape that tells how to follow a computer program, asking a friend to tell you over the phone how to open a car door after you locked your keys inside

Ways to group examples: Using living people or "canned" advice; primarily visual, primarily oral, or a combination of the two

A possible thesis: Although I often learn something new by imitating or consulting an expert, I occasionally must rely on printed or audiovisual directions.

2. Harmless Toys

Examples: stuffed animals, puzzles, balls, playhouses, sticker books, nontoxic crayons, plastic dolls, model cars, cassette recorders, computer games, paper dolls, wooden blocks

Ways to group examples: cheap, moderately priced, or expensive; durable or consumable; passive or active

A possible thesis: My children much prefer cheap toys like wooden blocks, crayons, or puzzles to expensive plastic dolls or playhouses.

3. Kinds of Fraud

Examples: Selling a bridge you don't own, pretending you have a doctoral degree when you're a high school dropout, forging checks, counterfeiting money, sneaking out of a restaurant without paying the bill, using someone else's credit card illegally, saying a product is safe when a testing agency has proven it isn't

Ways to group examples: Oral and written fraud; crimes against property and crimes against people

A possible thesis: Although people who have lost money through fraud may recover their losses through court action, people whose health has been damaged by fraud have been more seriously hurt.

4. Kinds of Storms

Examples: storm, rain, wind, hail

Ways to group examples: Whether unexpected or predictable; whether over land or over sea; whether needed to water crops or coat ski slopes or unneeded; whether benign or dangerous

A possible thesis: Although the U.S. Weather Service usually predicts the weather correctly for broad regions of the country, it occasionally makes mistakes regarding specific locales.

5. Effects of Teachers and Students on Each Other

Examples: Teachers towards students: teaching students to add simple numbers, to read one- and two-syllable words, to be effective student council members, to speak courteously on the telephone, to use good personal hygiene, to understand adult behavior by observing the teacher, to learn to direct discussion by watching the teacher, to learn to judge others fairly by seeing how the teacher grades fairly

Ways to group examples: Educational, moral, and social values; basic and sophisticated skills; scholarship and leadership abilities

A possible thesis: While instructors teach students basic skills, they must also provide students with social poise and good judgment.

Section Three: Planning and Organizing the Essay

CHOOSING AN APPROACH TO YOUR TOPIC

To organize your paper, look back at your topic. If you have a choice, check the word group below that best explains what approach you want to take. If you are assigned an approach, check it:

_____ Tell a story

_____ Describe a person, place, or thing

_____ Explain to someone how to do something

_____ Place specific items in a group, or divide a group or concept into parts

_____ Define an idea, concept, or situation

_____ Trace the causes for an effect or the effects of a cause

_____ Compare and contrast people, objects, groups, or situations

_____ Persuade someone to change an attitude or take some action.

WRITING THE THESIS

Your *thesis* helps you plan your paper. It must be broader than the topic sentence of a paragraph. At the same time, it must be manageable within several paragraphs. If you began with a topic such as "Becoming a Stronger Person," you might narrow it to "Body Building" or "Nutrition Choices."

As you draft your thesis, ask yourself these questions:

1. *Is my thesis broad and encompassing enough?* Does it suggest several subtopics?

2. *Is my thesis clear and specific enough?* Avoid statements like "Young people find many things to do during summer vacation." This statement is too vague and general. At the same time, avoid mere statements of fact: "A car has up to 30,000 parts in a typical model." A sentence like this would be a fine start for an introductory paragraph; however, it is too narrow and factual for a thesis.

Here are some examples of well-focused thesis statements:

- My psychology teacher lectured more clearly, in a more logically organized way, than my history instructor.
- My attempts to study in college were thwarted by loud music, tempting quad activities, and the demands of a steady boyfriend.
- Accounting is a more appealing career path to me than outdoor recreation.
- My nephew reacted to Saturday morning TV in several interesting ways.

Unlike a single paragraph, an essay does not move directly from the thesis to supporting illustrations. The body paragraphs each take up topic sentences stemming from the thesis.

The diagram on page 247 shows how topic sentences for the body paragraphs grow out of the thesis:

The student essay below develops the topic "Different Bars Attract Different Folks." The thesis is underlined.

[Introduction]

Moods and personalities differ from person to person. Some people are very active and like to move around, while others are quiet and enjoy relaxed conversation. Still others crave entertainment. To reflect different types of patronage, bars could be designated discos, social clubs, and nightclubs.

[First Body Paragraph]

Discos attract active people who like to dance. For example, in New York, New York, mirrors border the brightly lit dance floor. The loud, all encompassing music crowds the dance floor with bodies moving to the beat. In a variation, the Electric Cowboy is a western type disco. The decor is rustic, topped by a neon cowboy, and crowds sway to the country rock music. An atmosphere of energy and excitement pervades the place.

[Second Body Paragraph]

Social clubs appeal to more laid back, conversational types. Big Kids has a quiet, relaxed atmosphere. While few people dance, patrons simply listen to

246

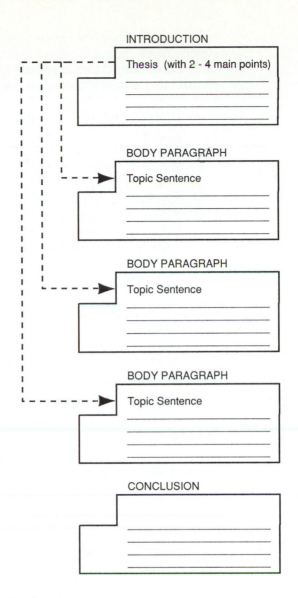

INTRODUCTION

Thesis (with 2 - 4 main points)

BODY PARAGRAPH

Topic Sentence

BODY PARAGRAPH

Topic Sentence

BODY PARAGRAPH

Topic Sentence

CONCLUSION

music or play video games. D. W. Fryes offers a wider variety of activities. Many people dance, but most of the building involves a lounging area with couches around a fireplace; a more active recreational area offers video games and a television. Despite the differences between these two bars, both offer a relaxed, slow-paced atmosphere.

[Third Body Paragraph]

With their floor shows, nightclubs appeal to people who enjoy live entertainment. The Honky Tonk is a western version offering an entertaining band. Patrons may dance in one area or move to a game room for other entertainment. Another variant, The Discotheque, offers female strippers; since they are the main attraction, no dancing area is provided. These nightclubs generate feelings of enjoyment and fun.

[Conclusion]

To sum up, bar designers must avoid replicating another already-established bar. Depending on the patronage they wish to attract, they must choose between creating a disco, social club, or night club. As a result, bars in the city offer an attractive range of dancing, socializing, and entertainment.

247

In this essay, the thesis lays out the writer's design for her classification essay. More information on this approach appears in Chapter 9, "Dividing and Classifying." In the body of the essay, each topic sentence takes up the points made in the thesis, in order:

Body Paragraph	Topic Sentence
First	Discos attract active people who like to dance.
Second	Social clubs appeal to more laid-back, conversational types.
Third	With their floor shows, nightclubs appeal to people who enjoy live entertainment.

- Each body paragraph takes up one of the three types of bars listed in the thesis.
- The topic sentences describe discos, social clubs, and nightclubs, in that order.
- Each body paragraph uses facts, details, and examples to support its topic sentence.
- The conclusion restates the thesis, while viewing bar design from owners' points of view.

EXERCISE 16.2

Deanna wrote an early draft in response to the question, "If you could live anywhere in the world, where would you choose?" She narrowed her topic from "California" to "California's Beaches and Mountains." Read over this draft and answer the questions that follow.

I've always dreamed that one day I would experience living in California. In fact, next year I hope to get a job at one of the resorts by the beach. Then maybe I could learn to surf and get an excellent tan. I visited California when I was in the sixth grade. We stayed at a rustic lodge in the mountains above San Bernardino for about nine days. We could throw snowballs at each other outside the lodge one day and then drive over to a sandy, warm beach by the ocean the next and go swimming. However, I realize that living at a place and vacationing there are two different experiences.

1. What is the main idea of this draft?
Deanna talks about vacationing at California's beaches, and mountains, hoping to live in California, but realizing that living in a place differs from vacationing there. Her paragraph lacks focus as it stands.

2. Suggest a new thesis for this draft, using two sentences if necessary.
If I could live anywhere in the world, I would choose California. I like the closeness of its snowy mountains to its hot, sandy beaches.

3. Is Deanna's approach broad and encompassing enough?
Her approach is broad enough for this paragraph; she needs a focus, however.

4. Is Deanna's approach clear and specific enough?
Deanna seems most interested in the variety she found in California. The cold,

248

snowy mountains are close to the warm, sandy ocean beaches. After rewriting her thesis, she should contrast the mountains with the beaches with more facts, examples and details. She should conclude her essay by stating a key difference or two between living and vacationing in a place.

EXERCISE 16.3

We have included several first drafts of student essays. Each of them has a weak thesis. Read them over. Then,

- Identify the topic,
- Narrow it down, and
- Suggest an improved thesis.

A. Choosing a major in college is an extremely important decision. The amount of demand for the field you choose is a major consideration. For instance, if you choose nursing, you can probably find a job easily. On the other hand, if you major in archeology, few jobs would be available. Also, you would need to think about location. If you planned to live in the western or northern U.S., you should probably major in business with an emphasis on heavy machinery rather than in textile chemistry, for instance. Finally, you need to decide whether to invest your time in your job or your family. A pediatrician or a church pastor would be on call practically twenty-four hours a day. A bank manager, on the other hand, leaves his job at 5:00 on Friday to enjoy the weekend with his family.

Subject: Careers or college majors

Narrowing: The most important factor influencing your choice of career or major

Thesis: Your choice of a college major should reflect market demand for your services, geographical preferences, and the amount of time you want to give your job.

B. A cashier can be viewed as a representative of the company she works for. It is required that she be friendly at all times and keep a smile on her face. When customers come through my checkout lane, I always smile and ask, "How are you today?" If a customer should ask a question relating to her store or her job, it's her duty to answer or have someone in charge do so. For example, when a customer complained that she couldn't find any chocolate candi-quick mix on the shelf, I didn't know what she meant. So I paged the co-manager, Mr. Solesbee. He assisted the customer by going to aisle five where the mix was and bringing it to the checkout counter. Also, she should be courteous at all times. One time, a lady who came through my lane asked for dye to color Easter eggs. In a courteous voice, I suggested that she turn around and look down. The coloring kits were on display about five steps behind her. A cashier must make a good impression on people. Her attitude reflects on the store where she works.

Subject: Work habits

Narrowing: The personality traits needed by a cashier

249

Thesis: <u>A good cashier should be friendly, well-informed, and courteous at all times.</u>

C. I work as a surveyor on a number of construction jobs. Sometimes, they are underbid or on a tight schedule. Or they may be closely budgeted. Or they may be all of these things. In these situations, people must work well under stress or be fired. On a construction job with 2,000 people, there are usually 25 to 30 surveyors. I am second in command over two construction sites. As a surveyor, I must make sure that everything on the drawings is where it is supposed to be. I check everything from removing the topsoil to locking the door, beginning to end. I also work closely with every craft on site. These include carpenters, electricians, pipefitters, plumbers, concrete finishers and laborers. All need supervision. I must either remember vast amounts of information, or I must be able to find the needed facts.

Subject: <u>Being a surveyor</u>

Narrowing: <u>Working under stress on a construction site</u>

Thesis: <u>As a surveyor on a construction site, I must supervise every craft and come up with information quickly.</u>

EXERCISE 16.4
Answers will vary.

The following essay attaches a plan to its thesis. Read it over and answer the questions that follow.

You will be relieved to learn that . . . science has now examined yet another habit which Americans indulge to excess: eating—specifically, the delights of eating crunchy, crispy things . . . Our delight has to do with noise, reports *Chemistry* (Vol. 50, No. 6) a bit breathlessly. Through . . . analysis of the sounds of green peppers, cookies, potato chips and so forth, three categories on the upper end of the noisy-crispy—quiet-not-crispy range can be specified.

- Wet-crisp, as when the living cells of celery or green peppers—filled with fluid under pressure—explode under the force of a tooth. The more pleasure, the louder the crunch.
- Dry-crisp, as when the air-filled brittle cells of crackers bend and break, then snap back to position. The vibrations build up into a sound pressure wave.
- Chip-crisp, as when a potato chip is broken by the teeth. Potato chips, only a few cells thick, are noisier (crispier) than you'd expect. Why? Being curved, they are repeatedly broken, which causes many crisp and noisy sounds.

James K. Page, Jr., "March of Science"

1. Into what categories does the writer divide crunchy, crispy things?
   <u>The writer has divided them into "wet-crisp," including celery and green peppers, "dry-crisp," including crackers, and "chip-crisp," such as potato chips.</u>

2. List other foods that make noise when people eat them, either because of the nature of the foods or because of the way their eaters behave.

Chewing gum, popcorn, soup, soft drinks, raw vegetables or fruits such as carrots, tomatoes, radishes, apples or grapes, corn on the cob, lobster, shrimp or crab in the shell, hard candy, peanuts, candy bars, cracker jacks, candy apples, pretzels, tacos, ice, popsicles, and so on, plus the wrappers and hulls of such foods.

3. Into what possible classifications or groups could you place the "noisy foods" you have listed for #2 above?

They could be divided into cooked and raw; appetizers, main dishes and desserts; dry and juicy; cheap and expensive.

4. On the basis of the groupings you have set up for #3 above, write a summary that groups and divides.

An example might read: Foods that make noise when eaten might include appetizers, main dishes, and desserts.

Section Four: Introductions, Transitional Paragraphs, and Conclusions

THE INTRODUCTION

The introductory paragraph leads an essay; it comes first. Writers use introductory paragraphs for a number of purposes. For example, writers sometimes expand on a thesis by summing up the essay to follow. This summing up gives them a handy plan. It also gives readers a clear idea of where the writer is taking them. Here's a good example of a *summary* introduction with the thesis underlined:

Guiding at its best in the north woods deserves to be called a profession and an art. Consider the requirements: the guide must know his region the way a man knows his own house. He must be thoroughly familiar with the habits of fish and game and the uses of rod and gun. He must be a good cook and a first-rate woodsman, ingenious enough to make the best of the materials at hand. He should be an expert canoe-man. But the list doesn't end there. His value is much increased if he is a good companion, a man with whom you can sit around the fire when the day's sport is over, and with whom you can enjoy talking. He needs tact, and the ability to bear with fools, and he must have a strong sense of responsibility.

J. Donald Adams, "The North Woods Guide"

This paragraph stands well alone. But the reader also glimpses the order in which the writer will develop his essay.

You also might begin an essay with a story or *anecdote* like the following. The thesis is underlined:

I had just fished the pool and was rounding a gradual bend upstream, wading slowly so as not to disturb the slow-moving clear water, when up ahead I noticed a gigantic bird atop a tiny, demure beaver dam, a creature almost too large to be real. He had his back to me and seemed to be peering intently into the pool on the other side of the dam. I froze, stood perfectly still as I watched him preside magnificently over the pond. I was only about fifteen or twenty feet away, and he was an elegant sight—a great blue heron.

Lucian K. Truscott IV, "The Great Blue"

You might try beginning your paper with a *question*. Both you and your reader should be interested in the answer, as in this example:

What will it be like to live in a predominantly metric nation?

Frank Kendig, "The Coming Changeover"

You might begin by *surprising* your reader, by turning an accepted idea on its head. The thesis is underlined:

Qwerty—in case you've been using it for so long that you have forgotten what it is—is the name for the standard typewriter keyboard. Q, W, E, R, T, and Y are the first six keys on the upper row of letters. Together they make up the traditional name for the keyboard. Qwerty even sounds faintly contemptible, and, after you learn the facts, it is.

Charles Lekberg, "The Tyranny of Qwerty"

Try beginning with an unreal or *fictional situation*. Your reader knows it is made up. The entire paragraph makes up this writer's thesis:

Out beyond our solar system there is a planet called Copernicus. It came into existence some four or five billion years before the birth of our Earth. In due course of time it became inhabited by a race of intelligent men.

James C. Rettie, " 'But a Watch in the Night': A Scientific Fable"

Sometimes, try an *analogy*. This draws a comparison or likeness between two things or concepts. The thesis is underlined:

For the moment—but only for the moment—it will be safe to assume that we all know what is meant by the word "word." I may even consider that my typing fingers know it, defining a word (in a whimsical conceit) as what comes between two spaces. The Greeks saw the word as the minimal unit of speech; to them, too, the atom was the minimal unit of matter. Our own age has learnt to split the atom and also the word.

Anthony Burgess, "Splitting the Word"

You may also come right out and tell the reader your *purpose* for writing. The thesis is underlined:

It wouldn't be quite true to say that "some of my best friends are hunters." Still, I do number among my respected acquaintances some who not only kill for the sake of killing but count it among their keenest pleasures. And I can think of no better illustration of the fact that men may be separated at some point by a fathomless abyss yet share elsewhere much common ground. To me, it is inconceivable that anyone can think an animal more interesting dead than alive. I can also easily prove to my own satisfaction that killing "for sport" is the perfect type of pure evil for which metaphysicians have sometimes sought.

John Strohman, "The Hunt"

EXERCISE 16.5

Write a practice introduction or two. Choose from these topics:

- Types of outdoor or indoor recreation
- Ways of responding to a crisis
- Conditions that make studying impossible

Answers will vary.

Topic: _____

Pattern: _____

Your introduction: _____

_____

TRANSITIONAL PARAGRAPHS

Sometimes, writers use a very brief one- or two-sentence paragraph as a bridge or transition between body paragraphs. When a one-line paragraph comes between longer ones, it catches our attention. Writers often use it for emphasis. William Saroyan has this in mind:

I bet my life that if I was not a published writer by the age of thirty, I would be nothing—a full refuser, and for that reason alone likely not to be permitted to live. The story that ended my apprenticeship contains within its swift short form the title: "Application for Permission to Live."

I had good luck.

Zav had good luck, too, for he was never not his own man, at any rate. If he didn't sing in opera, he damned well did in life.

"Meditations on the Letter Z"

THE CONCLUDING PARAGRAPH

Writers usually close a piece of writing with a *concluding paragraph.* In narrative or description, the last paragraph may simply present the last incident or detail in the story, or describe the last remaining part of aspect of a thing. In a process paper, it might describe the last step. However, in many writings, concluding paragraphs usually

- Sum up,
- Make a final point,
- Suggest a new question related to the essay topic, or
- Recommend some action to the reader.

In the concluding paragraph below, Robert Pirsig sums up:

And so in recent times we have seen a huge split develop between a classic culture and a romantic counterculture—two worlds growing alienated and hateful toward each other with everyone wondering if it will always be this way, a house divided against itself. No one wants it really—despite what his antagonists in the other dimension might think.

"Two Ways of Understanding"

Margaret Mead ends an essay on superstition by making a new point. It is linked closely to her original purpose, however:

Superstitions are sometimes smiled at and sometimes frowned upon as observances characteristic of the old-fashioned, the unenlightened, children, peasants, servants, immigrants, foreigners or backwoods people. Nevertheless, they give all of us ways of moving back and forth among the different worlds in which we live—the sacred, the secular and the scientific. They allow us to keep a private world also, where, smiling a little, we can banish danger with a gesture and summon luck with a rhyme, make the sun shine in spite of storm clouds, force the stranger to do our bidding, keep an enemy at bay and straighten the paths of those we love.

"New Superstitions for Old"

William Zinsser ends his discussion of respect for language by stressing audience:

Remember, then, that words are the only tools that you will be given. Learn to use them with originality and care. Value them for their strength and their infinite diversity. And also remember: somebody out there is listening.

On Writing Well

Section Five: Writing the First Draft

By this time, you have taken the following steps:

- Chosen your topic,
- Generated ideas about it,
- Written and narrowed your thesis, and
- Created a plan for your essay.

Look over your notes carefully. Then find an uninterrupted time and a quiet place to write a draft. Plan to write a page and a half or two quickly. As you write, don't pause to cross out or look up words. You can rewrite phrases or edit mistakes later. Put a check next to words or punctuation you aren't sure of. Correct them later. Devote a paragraph to each one of your subtopics or wait for revision.

Valerie decided to write a paper dealing with the question, "If I had three wishes, what would I ask for?" After prewriting, she wrote this draft:

If I had three wishes, first, I would choose to be a pediatric nurse. Secondly, I would like a creme colored brick home in the country. Finally, I would want a turquoise TR-7 sports car. By attaining these items, I would show my parents that I could be successful in life.

Since I favor working with small children, I would love to be a pediatric nurse. When children have to go to the hospital, they think the world has come to an end. They yearn to be securie, and they need to get well as soon as possible. I would reassure them and helping them get well. Also, I would be patient and understanding with them.

Moreover, because I am a nature-lover, I would prefer a home in the country. I could enjoy jogging without worring about careless motorists. For instance, Catherine was struck by a motorist who was preceeding at sixty miles per hour. Fortunately, she only got a badly bruised elbow. Also, I would have privacy from neighbors who love to interfere. For example, when a car comes to my house, my neighbor, Barbara, is always trying to see who is driving the car.

Finally, a turquoise TR-7 sports car would be nice. Although I do not want to be rich, I enjoy having a Triumph-Seven, which cost only seven-thousand dollars.

Although, one can not have everything they desire, I would be pleased to gain these items.

Section Six: Revising the Essay

To get help in rewriting your first draft, ask yourself the questions below, or ask a friend or classmate to do so. We have given Valerie some help on her first draft. This is not a good time to correct grammar, mechanics, and spelling problems (for instance, Valerie omits the *r* in "pedia~t~ric," and includes an unnecessary *i* in "secur~i~e"). However, these errors are distracting and will need to be corrected on the final editing stage.

1. *What ideas, sentences, and phrases are well expressed?*

Valerie states her thesis by putting her wishes in order: a career in nursing, a home in the country, and a car. Then she writes a paragraph for each one. She also provides some interesting detail: a friend struck by a careless motorist, and her nosy neighbor.

2. *Where does the reader need more (or less) information?*

The reader might like to know why she puts her wishes in the order she chooses, whether she can think of better reasons for wanting these things, whether she has had any specific experiences with sick children, where she'd like her home in the country to be and what it might look like, what her sports car might look like in detail, why it appeals to her.

She also needs to expand her conclusion. Perhaps she might tell how these wishes relate to marriage and a family, or to other, slightly less important wishes.

In rewriting your essay, keep your own (or your reader's) criticisms in mind. You need help and encouragement here, words to keep you writing. You don't need writer's block. Valerie rewrote her paper in response to the comments above:

If I had three wishes, first, I would choose to be a pediatric nurse. This is my long-time goal in life. Secondly, I would like a creme-colored brick home in the country. Finally, I would want a turquoise TR-7 sports car. By attaining these items, I would be happy and secure. I would also show my parents that I could be successful in life.

Since I favor working with small children, I would love to be a pediatric nurse. When children have to go to the hospital, they think the world has come to an end and yearn to be securie and need to get well as soon as possible. When I was younger, the little boy next door fell off his bicycle and gashed his knee. I heard his screams and ran to help. I am good at reassuring small children and helping them get well. Also, I would be patient and understanding with them.

Moreover, because I am a nature-lover and love my privacy, I would prefer a home in the country. My dream house would be pink with white columns in front, and stand back from the road behind a rolling lawn. Living away from town, jogging could be enjoyed without worring about careless motorists. For instance, Catherine was struck by a motorist who was proceeding at sixty miles per hour. Fortunately, she only got a badly bruised elbow. Also, I would have privacy from neighbors who love to interfere. For example, when a car comes to my house, my neighbor, Barbara, is always trying to see who is driving the car.

Finally, a turquoise TR-7 sports car would be nice. It should have deep blue carpeting, an AM/FM radio, a CB with forty-one channels, a cassette player and heating and air conditioning. My desire for nice things would be reflected by it. Although I do not want to be rich, having a triumph-seven, which costs only seven-thousand dollars, would be enjoyable.

Thus, if I were granted these desires, I would be content. With the nursery, I would gain satisfaction in a career. With the home in the country, I would be more active and have more privacy. With the car, I would attain assurance in my own capabilities, and I would have a very good car. Although all one's desires can not be attained, I would be pleased to gain these items.

After writing your second draft, analyze it. This time, look it over much more closely than you did before. Ask a friend or classmate (or several of them) to look it over too. We have listed some questions for you to ask. Our answers apply to Valerie's second draft.

1. *Do the first two or three sentences make clear how the writer will proceed in the paper? If so, has the writer followed this plan? If not, how should the writer change the organization?*

To organize her paper, Valerie lists her top three wishes as a *thesis statement.* She has put it together by restating the question in her own words. Then she takes up her wishes one at a time in the body of her paper. They follow the same order she used in her thesis. Each one is handled in its own paragraph. Her thesis is logical, and her organization is predictable.

2. *What does the reader already know about the subject? What would the reader want to know?*

Valerie seems to have several audiences in mind: mostly other young people, but also her parents and her instructor. She writes to young, ambitious people like herself. She thinks they share her desire for a profession. They want to help people; they want respect; and they want the rewards of success. She assumes they already know about medical people and their jobs. She also reflects common knowledge about country homes and sports cars. Her parents and her instructor would share these interests, she seems to think.

However, her audience would like *details* and *motives*. They could share her dreams more fully if they could see in their minds' eyes the work and rewards she hopes for. And they could identify better with her if they knew *why* she wants these things so badly.

3. *What is the topic of each paragraph? Can the reader find it easily?*

The paragraphs in Valerie's essay take up the topics she lists in her thesis, one at a time. She begins each paragraph with a topic sentence. Writers, we might note, often sum up the main idea of a paragraph in the first sentence or two. Two of her topic sentences tell both *what* and *why*. For instance, in the second paragraph her topic sentence states that she wants to be a pediatric nurse "since I favor working with small children." She also explains why she wants a country home. And, she suggests, a sports car would impress her parents.

4. *Where can the writer add or substitute more specific examples, reasons, or details?*

Valerie explains that she likes children, knows how to reassure them, and is patient. In the next paragraph, she needs to illustrate her interest in physical fitness and her desire for privacy. Finally, she describes her hoped-for sports car in some detail (she means a used TR-7). This is a good place to describe her feelings about owning and driving such a car.

Valerie should check a thesaurus of synonyms and antonyms for words that describe feelings of satisfaction, privacy, wealth, speed, and comfort.

5. *Which sentences can be made more concise and forceful—making doers the subjects and changing passive verbs to active, more lively ones?*

In the next-to-last paragraph, Valerie uses an awkward passive word group, "would be reflected." Since she refers to her car, she might make "it" the subject of a revised sentence. She should also replace inexact words like "reflect" and "nice." Her revision might read: "It would embody my desire for comfort and luxury."

Her last sentence in this paragraph sounds awkward, partly because she ends it with a linking verb and adjective: "would be enjoyable." She should use "I" as the subject of her main clause and follow it with an active verb: "Although I do not want to be rich, I would enjoy owning and driving a TR-7, which only looks expensive; a good used model costs less than $7,000."

Valerie's last sentence uses the passive verb group "can not be obtained." By making "nursing career" the subject, she can solve the problem: "Although all my wishes won't come true right away, a successful nursing career will give them to me soon."

6. *Which sentences should be combined with other ones, or shortened by being broken up?*

Valerie should tell the reader that she is listing her most important goal first. She could do so while combining the first two sentences in her essay: "If I had three wishes, I would first choose to be a pediatric nurse, my long-time goal in life." Or she might add emphasis by mentioning nursing last in this sentence: "If I had three wishes, I would first choose my long-time goal

257

in life: a career in pediatric nursing." The last two sentences in Valerie's introduction could also be combined: "Achieving these goals would give me the happiness, security, and success both my parents and I wish for me."

The second sentence in Valerie's second paragraph rambles rather shapelessly. She should break it up and restate it. Changing the second verb, "yearn," to an -ing word would add variety: "When children go to the hospital, they think the world has come to an end. *Yearning to be secure,* they need to get well as soon as possible."

Other wordy sentences in her essay could be shortened. For instance, she should replace a word group like "home in the country" with "country home," and so on.

7. *What devices like connectives, synonyms, and pronouns has the writer used to tie his or her ideas together? What additional devices should the writer use?*

Valerie effectively lists her wishes in the first paragraph in numerical order: "first, . . . second, . . . finally."

In the second paragraph, she links causes to effects with words like *since* and *when.* She refers to "small children" with words such as *children, they,* and *little boy. Also* begins her concluding sentence, but she should combine the last two sentences.

In the third paragraph, she helps the reader along with transitional terms or phrases such as *moreover, living away from town, for instance, also,* and *for example.*

She introduces her fourth paragraph by echoing *finally* from her first paragraph wish list.

Valerie begins her conclusion with *thus.* She goes on to repeat names of her wishes, "with nursing . . . with the home in the country . . . with the car," to begin sentences restating her reasons for each wish.

8. *Does the essay end with a conclusion that summarizes, raises a new but related question, or recommends some action by the reader?*

Valerie has chosen to simply summarize her wishes again. She could add interest to her essay by raising a new but related question (who would she like to share these wishes with?). Or she could suggest some actions to bring these wishes closer to fulfillment: studying hard in school or saving her money.

Have a peer or classmate (preferably several of them) apply these questions to your draft, or analyze it yourself. Your new insights should help you reshape your paper, improving its organization and sentence expression.

Revision Checklist

1. Do the first two or three sentences make clear how the writer will proceed in the paper? If so, has the writer followed this plan? If not, how should the writer change the organization?

2. What does the reader already know about the subject? What would the reader want to know?

3. What is the topic of each paragraph? Can the reader find it easily?

4. Where can the writer add or substitute more specific examples, reasons, or details?

5. Which sentences can be made more concise and forceful—making doers the subjects and changing passive verbs to active, more lively ones?

6. Which sentences should be combined with other ones, or shortened by being broken up?

7. What devices like connectives, synonyms, and pronouns has the writer used to tie his or her ideas together? What additional devices should the writer use?

8. Does the essay end with a conclusion that summarizes, raises a new but related question, or recommends some action by the reader?

Section Seven: Final Editing

Once you have finished rewriting your essay, edit it. Look over a paper you wrote earlier in this class. Check closely for errors you have made before. Then clean up the punctuation, grammatical and spelling problems in this paper. Answer these questions:

1. What grammatical problems need to be solved?
2. What punctuation errors need to be corrected?
3. What misspellings should be corrected?

Section Eight: Expanding a Paragraph into an Essay

At times, you may wish to expand a previously written paragraph into a longer, more detailed essay. The paragraph might have been a journal entry or a previous assignment in this course or some other. To base an essay on a paragraph, follow these steps:

- Develop a thesis by applying the reporter's questions. Think of several reasons *why?*, two or three aspects of *what? who? where?* or *when?*, a few ways *how?* Brainstorming, clustering, and other idea-generating devices work well too. Then decide which of your responses to these questions is most appealing to both you and the reader.

- Give the paper a title, set up a scratch outline of main topics, and sum them up in a trial thesis.

- Generate supporting details for each paragraph.

- Write a trial thesis and topic sentences, paying close attention to order and parallel structure. Rewrite your original paragraph as part of your new essay, perhaps as a body paragraph.

- Write a draft, revise, and edit as we described earlier in this chapter.

Jennifer decided to base an essay on this paragraph:

Since I love to read, I will try to pass this love on to my daughter. Although she is under two years old, I am already buying her books and reading to her. I feel that this is something that will help her throughout her life. Since my parents are not well educated, they did not encourage me to read often, as I plan to do with my daughter. For example, usually on a daily basis, I sit down with her and we "read" her books together.

APPLYING THE REPORTER'S QUESTIONS

Jennifer then applied the reporter's questions to topics her paragraph had raised:

Who?	My parents, me, my two-year-old daughter
What?	Good and bad memories, love of reading, my daughter's future, participating in school activities, feeling loved
Why?	To be close to my daughter, prepare her for future marriage (?), career (?)
When?	Now, during my daughter's school years
How?	Being there for my daughter, school activities, books and reading, making wise changes

SETTING UP A SCRATCH OUTLINE

After looking over the ideas she had generated, Jennifer set up the following scratch outline, following these steps:

1. She gave her paper a title.
2. She chose three subtopics.
3. She filled in with details and examples.

Raising My Child Differently

Reading to my daughter
  Unlike parents, who were uneducated
  Buying books and reading aloud
  Dr. Seuss, humorous poetry (Nash, Lear)
  Reading a daily habit
Her participation in school and community activities
  Father away driving truck, mother couldn't drive, depriving me
  Cheerleading, band, scouting
Being "there for my daughter at all times"
  Not being latch-key child, coming home to empty house
  Arranging my schedule to be there for daughter, even through college
  Fixing her snacks, helping her with homework

WRITING A TRIAL THESIS AND TOPIC SENTENCES

Trial Essay Thesis: My own childhood has shaped my concepts regarding the best ways to bring up children. While raising my own child, I will duplicate my parents' good ideas, but change bad ones. Specifically, I will read aloud to my daughter, encourage her to participate in group activities, and be home for her after school.

Topic Sentence #1: Since I love to read, I will pass this love on to my daughter by buying her books and reading to her. [Jennifer will use material from her original paragraph, along with new details and examples, here in the body of her essay]

Topic Sentence #2: To help my daughter feel comfortable in groups, I will encourage her to join activities at school and in the community.

Topic Sentence #3: Recalling my own loneliness, I will plan to be home with my child after school.

WRITE A DRAFT, REVISE, AND EDIT

To write a draft, revise, and edit, follow the steps we described earlier in the chapter.

Section Nine: Further Topics

- The best way to spend a vacation is to . . .
- The most memorable act of friendship I have ever experienced in my life is . . .
- The ideal shopping area would consist of . . .
- The activity which gives me most pleasure is . . .
- The most disturbing incident I have ever seen is . . .

Timed Essay Examinations

SECTION ONE: Preparing in Advance
SECTION TWO: Summarizing
SECTION THREE: Allocating Your Time
SECTION FOUR: Planning Your Essay
SECTION FIVE: Writing a Thesis for an Essay Exam
SECTION SIX: Prewriting Your Timed Essay
SECTION SEVEN: Writing Your Timed Essay
SECTION EIGHT: Proofreading Your Essay
SECTION NINE: Summing Up

Many instructors will give you written exams on lecture and text materials. None of these tests give you much time for prewriting or rewriting. In addition, you will often have only enough time for one draft.

Timed essay writing will require you to prepare carefully, be sure you understand the question, and organize your response. You will usually have only a limited amount of time to write a paper. Your ability to write quickly and clearly will count as much as your knowledge of the material.

Section One: Preparing in Advance

Many classes will ask you to summarize and comment on material you have studied earlier. To do well, you should prepare for the exam before it is given, following these steps:

1. Take notes on the main ideas in your instructors' lectures. The instructor may have emphasized a certain point of view toward particular concepts. Your notes will help you guess what questions will be included on the exam.

2. Underline or highlight topic sentences and important details in your textbook.

3. Pay special attention to helps in your textbook. These will often include such useful devices as

   • topic heads above paragraphs of written material,

   • chapter summaries at the end of each chapter

   • study questions

4. Practice summing up the main points of the text in your own words, rather than just memorizing.

Instructors will often ask you to summarize material from memory. Keep your summaries short, between 5 and 15 percent of the original. You will need to decide what to keep in and what to leave out.

Things to Put In:

1. Sum up the most important idea in the original material. This usually comes at or near the beginnings of paragraphs, essays, and chapters.

2. Include only the most important details—those needed to understand the material. Authors often identify words that do the following:

   • *Enumerate*—words such as **first, second, next**, and **finally**

   • Point to *cause and effect*—words such as **accordingly, as a result, because**, and **thus**

   • Point out *essentials*—words such as **basically, essentially, major**, and **significant(ly)**

   • Emphasize *conclusions* or *results*—signaled by words like **in conclusion**, or labeled, or placed in a separate paragraph or section

   • Put forth recommendations, telling why they are necessary or how to carry them out

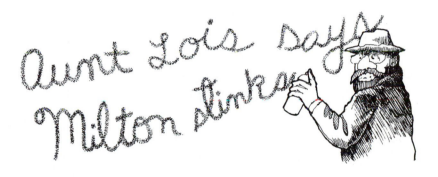

Things to Leave Out:

1. Unsupported opinions, witty remarks, irrelevant material
2. Minor details, examples, illustrations, and descriptions

EXERCISE 17.1

Sum up the following essay in four or five sentences. First, underline main ideas, looking for topic sentences. Then restate these ideas in your own words.

As an executive of a major company, Herman Cain has been known to give up a comfortable job to climb the corporate ladder. He once quit a vice-president's post to learn the fast food industry from the bottom up. In nine months, he went from a restaurant trainee to a regional vice-president.

But in 1986, Cain took on an even greater corporate challenge. He was named president of Godfather's Pizza, and by most accounts, it was an offer he could have easily refused.

At the time, the Omaha-based pizza chain was plagued with slumping sales, red ink, ineffective advertising and a spate of lawsuits from angry franchisees. Having just purchased Godfather's along with 300 Burger King restaurants, officials at the Pillsbury Co. weren't convinced the troubled chain could soon become profitable.

Enter Herman Cain. Within 18 months, he managed to erase his firm's woes and transform the once-ailing company into one of Pillsbury's most profitable restaurant chains. Profits have replaced the red ink, and, in the words of several food industry observers, Cain brought much-needed leadership to a poorly managed business.

Gone are the unprofitable franchises; Cain quickly cut the number of restaurants from 900 to just over 600. Sales have increased over the past year following a three-year period of decline. An innovative computer system in the Seattle market holds the promise of further reduction in home delivery time, and, like a band of guerrillas, Cain and his staff have introduced popular food items, such as a two-minute slice of pizza and a prepackaged salad that have ruffled the competition.

Cain admits that many of his ideas aren't new. But the 42-year-old executive says the resulting sales have rekindled an already heated contest among the nation's top pizza restaurants for the bulk of the $5 billion pizza market. "It's called competition," he says with some relish. "That's fun. It's like being in a fight. If you let them, they'll take the food off my table, out of the mouths of my kids, and put it in their pockets. That's the nature of competition."

With only 650 restaurants in 37 states, Godfather's Pizza currently ranks fourth in sales, trailing Pizza Hut, Domino's Pizza and Little Ceasar's Pizza Treat, Cain says. However, industry observers contend the chain's new business momentum soon will put it into third place. "They've been very innovative in finding their niche, and their sales numbers have been quite good," says John Mcmillin, a Prudential Bache Securities food analyst. "I estimate that they may earn on an operating basis close to $8 million this year, and I bet they *lost* $8 million a couple of years ago."

For Cain, the company's turnaround underscores an essential belief that has propelled him into the predominantly white ranks of running a major American business. "I've basically adopted the attitude that performance will be my barrier buster," he says. "If it means working a little harder, or that my performance has to be a little better, then, hey, that's the price you pay. It's a small price versus the price that was paid by those who died or were jailed so that I and others could have a chance."

Douglas C. Lyons, "The Godfather of Pizza," *Ebony*

Summary:

In 1986, Herman Cain was named president of Godfather's Pizza. The Omaha-based chain was plagued with slumping sales, red ink, ineffective advertising, and lawsuits from angry franchisees. Gone are the unprofitable franchises; sales have increased over the past year following a three-year period of decline. Godfather's Pizza currently ranks fourth in sales, but the chain's new business momentum may soon put it into third place. Cain calls this the nature of competition.

EXERCISE 17.2   *Summarize a chapter from a textbook you are now using.*

EXERCISE 17.3   *Summarize a lecture given recently in one of your courses. Limit your summary to half a page.*

Section Three: Allocating Your Time

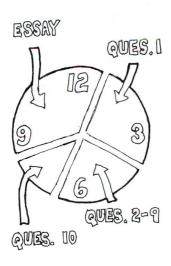

Instructors usually limit the time given to answer questions. You need to give yourself enough time to answer each question if there are two or more. Then too, you need to finish the test. If you are answering only one question, you need to decide how much time to spend on prewriting, writing, revising, and editing.

1. Divide your time between questions, answering the questions with the most points first. Your instructor may ask you to write on three questions, assigning 50 points to the first one, 30 points to the second, and 20 points to the third. Divide your time accordingly.

2. Keep track of your time. When you begin a particular question, make a note of the time you expect to finish it.

3. Leave space between your lines and leave wide margins. If you have time to go back over your answers, you can write in corrections or important details you left out.

4. If you are answering only one question, allocate 20 percent of your time for planning, 60 percent for writing, and 20 percent for rereading, revising, and correcting your mistakes. That is, break down a 50-minute writing assignment into 10–30–10.

Section Four: Planning Your Essay

As you read over essay questions, pay close attention to the approach(es) you are expected to take. Instructors use key words like *describe, define, explain, summarize, analyze, evaluate,* and *compare and contrast.* Here are some examples:

Define the concept of pasteurization.

Distinguish between nationalism and imperialism.

Identify the four Crusader states.

These key words have the following meanings:

Analyze	Divide into parts
Compare	Show similarities (*contrast* refers to differences)
Define	Tell what group a term belongs to, and then explain its parts
Describe	Provide a narration or a list of traits; the word *discuss* means much the same thing
Distinguish	Tell the differences between
Evaluate	Think of positive and negative aspects
Explain	Consider ways in which a topic can be discussed
Summarize	Provide the most important ideas, leaving out nearly all detail

EXERCISE 17.4

Decide which of the above approaches you should take for each of the following questions:

EXAMPLE: Tell what is meant by the Cluniac reform. Define

1. What can be done to reduce inner city drug use? Discuss

2. In a brief paragraph sum up the action in Stephen Crane's *The Red Badge of Courage*. Summarize

3. What is the difference between diesel fuel and gasoline? Distinguish or contrast

4. Discuss the causes of the Russian Revolution. Explain

5. Explain what is meant by *expressionism*. Define

6. Take a stand for or against abortion, giving reasons to support your stand. Evaluate

7. How are the plays of Henrik Ibsen and Bernard Shaw alike? Compare

8. What is the structure of a comet? Analyze

Here is a sample question: Focusing on *either* Africa *or* Asia after 1945, *describe* European domination of *one of these* regions, and *explain* how it was ended.

This question asks you to divide your attention in two ways.

1. You are asked to deal with one region or another in your response, *not both*.
2. You are asked to *describe* first with illustrations, and later to *explain* with *reasons*.

After you have decided what approach to take, follow these steps:

1. Begin by underlining key words: *either* and *one of these, describe* and *explain*.
2. Notice whether the question is broken down into parts.

EXERCISE 17.5

For each of the essay questions below, underline key words. Then divide the question into parts and explain what it is asking you to do.

A. Extracurricular activities may help or hinder the development of students' academic skills. Discuss.

Underline Key Words: <u>Extracurricular activities</u> may help <u>or</u> hinder the <u>development</u> of students' academic <u>skills</u>. <u>Discuss</u>.

How to Divide: Divide the response into two parts: a discussion of ways extracurricular activities help and ways they hinder students' academic skills.

What to Do: The question asks the student to <u>explain</u> both parts with reasons and illustrations.

B. The Vietnamese War came to an end in 1975. Explain the military, financial, and political costs of this war for the United States.

Underline Key Words: The <u>Vietnamese War</u> came to an end in 1975. Explain the <u>military</u>, <u>financial</u>, <u>and</u> <u>political</u> <u>costs</u> of this war for the United States.

How to Divide: Name and define each type of cost to the United States.

What to Do: The question involves first a definition of the three key costs, followed by a description of each one.

C. Students should be required to master computer skills before graduating from high school. Discuss.

Underline Key Words: Students should be <u>required</u> to <u>master</u> <u>computer</u> <u>skills</u> <u>before</u> <u>graduating</u> from high school.

How to Divide: After beginning with a short definition of key terms, students will describe and explain how this requirement should be applied.

What to Do: Students will define what is meant by <u>mastering</u> <u>computer</u> <u>skills</u>, explain what students need these skills for, and describe how students master them.

D. Contemporary architecture has been called "the most revolutionary visual

269

art'' of the twentieth century. Identify the most influential modern architects, and explain the effects of their buildings.

Underline Key Words: <u>Contemporary</u> <u>architecture</u> has been called ''the most revolutionary <u>visual</u> <u>art</u>'' of the twentieth century. Identify the <u>most</u> <u>influential</u> modern architects, and explain the <u>effects</u> of their buildings.

How to Divide: The first two parts—definition and identification—will be brief, followed by a longer explanation describing the influence of the modern architects in the order in which they were named.

What to Do: The students will define the term <u>contemporary</u> <u>architecture</u>, identify the most influential <u>modern</u> <u>architects</u>, and explain the effects of their buildings on their times.

E. Define Darwin's concept of evolution, and explain its effects on biological science.

Underline Key Words: Define Darwin's concept of <u>evolution</u>, and explain its effects on <u>biological</u> <u>science</u>.

How to Divide: The introduction—with definition and examples—will be brief, followed by a longer explanatory section.

What to Do: The students should provide a brief definition of evolution, followed by several examples of the effect of the theory.

Section Five: Writing a Thesis for an Essay Exam

When answering essay questions, create a *thesis*. This sets up a plan for you to follow in the paragraph or essay you intend to write. It also gives you credibility. Your reader will see that you understand how to limit and focus your discussion. For example, suppose you were asked to *define* the meaning of democracy in America. You should begin by restating the question as a thesis statement: "Democracy in America usually means equal opportunity for all, regardless of race, religion, sex, or national origin."

- The key words in this question are *define* and *democracy.*
- This question could best be developed in two parts: a brief definition of democracy, followed by a longer discussion including examples of its practice.

Asked to *analyze* the structure of a comet, you could write, "The structure of a comet consists of a head, or *coma*, a nucleus inside the coma, and a tail."

EXERCISE 17.6   *We have listed several examination questions below. Write a thesis statement for each, using the language of the question in a topic sentence even if you are not familiar with the question. Allow for agreement and disagreement.*

A. Compare and contrast the metric and English systems of measurement.

Thesis Statement: The metric system of measurement provides several (dis)advantages when compared (contrasted) with the English system.

B. Should banks be allowed to compete with insurance companies?

Thesis Statement: Banks should (should not) be allowed to compete with insurance companies (except) under certain circumstances.

C. What can this country do to reduce oil consumption?

Thesis Statement: This country can reduce oil consumption by taking several steps.

D. Does watching television make children more violent?

Thesis Statement: Watching television (does not) make(s) children more violent for the following reasons.

E. This country needs a universal system of health insurance. Agree or disagree.

Thesis Statement: This country definitely (does not) need(s) a universal system of health insurance because . . .

F. Is marriage a stronger institution at the present time than it was a decade ago?

Thesis Statement: Marriage definitely is (is not) a stronger institution at the present time than it was a decade ago because . . .

G. Assume that you are going to start a business selling toys to children. What steps would you take to make this business a success?

Thesis Statement: If I were starting a business to sell toys to children, I would do three things to make this business a success.

Section Six: Prewriting Your Timed Essay

Use a few mintues of your writing time to prewrite your answers to exams. On a piece of scratch paper, jot down topic sentences and plan ways to develop them. Brainstorming or a scratch outline will test your topic sentences. This will also help you strengthen them when you write your essays. Suppose an exam question in a history course asked you to sum up the causes of World War I. You could construct the following brief outline:

Militarism

    By 1870s 5 of 6 European powers introduced compulsory military training

    Great powers had nearly 4.5 million men under arms first decade of twentieth century

    At beginning of WWI, Central Powers mobilized 21 million men

    Allies called 40 million men to arms

Rival Alliances

    27 powers became belligerents

    Nations with similar interests joined to muster power

    Alliances provoked by competitors (Triple Alliance, Triple Entente)

Racism, Nationalism

    Leaders appealed to racial, national superiority to gain power

    Appeals especially powerful in Eastern Europe and the Balkans

---

EXERCISE 17.7

A. What paragraph or essay pattern would best develop an answer to the preceding essay question?

Description or explanation

B. How many parts should the answer include?

The answer should include three parts: (a) militarism, (b) political and economic competition, and (c) appeals to racism and nationalism.

C. How should the topic sentence be written?

The underlying causes of the First World War included militarism, political and economic competition, and appeals to racism and nationalism.

EXERCISE 17.8

Answers will vary.

Choose one of the following topics. Then take five minutes to prewrite by (a) deciding on an approach, (b) writing a topic sentence, and (c) jotting down a scratch outline.

A. Why have some animals become extinct in recent times?

B. How can businesses prevent employees from becoming bored with routine?

C. Why do children run away from home?

D. How does a university degree improve the quality of life for college graduates?

E. Why do friends in politics sometimes cause more trouble than enemies?

Section Seven: Writing Your Timed Essay

Once you have chosen an approach, written a topic sentence, and created a scratch outline, write your essay(s). Keep these principles in mind:

- Give special attention to the first parts of short and long essays, both in writing and rewriting. Your instructor will quickly estimate the quality of your writing from the first paragraph or two. He or she is then likely to read the rest of your material very quickly, mostly to confirm that early impression.
- Leave a space between each line and leave wide margins to allow for later revision.
- Use the third person—*he, she, it*—at all times. This will keep you from putting in personal opinions.
- Don't cross out and write in before you have finished your essay(s). Your reader will be reading rapidly. He or she will not be looking for refinement of style and detail. You will be judged on your ability to write forcefully, organize logically, and cover the topic.
- Choose major evidence and support.

Section Eight: Proofreading Your Essay

Proofread your paper carefully, looking for the following problems:

1. Run-on sentences
2. Comma splices
3. Fragments
4. Subject–verb agreement
5. Shifts in person or tense
6. Pronoun forms
7. Nonparallel structures
8. Dangling modifiers
9. Spelling errors
10. Punctuation problems

Section Nine: Summing Up

For timed essays and exams, follow this process:

1. Choose the question you understand best, or for which you can generate the clearest thesis and most specific examples.
2. Allocate your time carefully to prewriting, writing, and proofreading the essay(s) or exam.
3. Plan each essay: decide what approach to take, how many parts should be included, what examples to use for support.
4. Prewrite your thesis and topic sentences in advance.
5. Take time to tighten, add support, and proofread.

I don't believe it! You used way too much eye of newt and you didn't preheat the oven.

The Timed
Exit Exam

In many schools and school systems, lower-level students must prove that they are proficient writers. They do so by passing a timed essay exam. Grades on these exams may determine students' grades in a writing course, excuse them from a remedial composition course, or allow them to transfer or graduate. Such an exam often has these characteristics:

- A limited choice of topics (two or three)
- Previously unknown, generalized topics (though some may be quite specific)
- A time limit (often 50 or 60 minutes)

To do well in such an exam, use this specifically designed process approach:

During the First Ten Minutes

- Choose a familiar topic, one for which you can generate the most supporting examples. Avoid the more abstract questions.
- Respond to the topic with a brief statement stressing your own personal feelings if the topic calls for your opinion.
- List several possible *because* responses.
- Choose the best *because* response, and list eight to ten supporting examples.
- Place the examples in three groups.

During Most of the Exam Period (30–40 minutes)

- Write an introduction that includes a three-point thesis statement.
- Write three body paragraphs that:
  a. Begin with a transition
  b. Develop the aspects of the thesis in 1–2–3 order, and
  b. Support each aspect with at least two examples.
- Write a conclusion that restates your thesis.

276

- Proofread your paper carefully for grammatical, mechanical, and spelling problems.

Section One: Choosing a Topic

You will usually have a choice among two or three topics. Depending on the test, these will either be very explicit or rather general. These topics generally take the form of a statement or question; for example:

- Discuss changes which would make the public less hesitant to report crimes.
- How are you different from your parents?
- Discuss something in nature that should be preserved because of its beauty, rarity, or usefulness.
- Discuss a person in sports or entertainment who serves as a role model for children or adolescents.
- What are the most effective ways to find friends in college?

If possible, choose a topic with which you are familiar. If all topics seem easy to write about, pick the one for which you can generate the most examples. Generally, it's easier to write about specific, concrete topics like AIDS or the death penalty than about general topics like "happiness" or "honor."

Section Two: Generating Ideas

First, underline key words in the question. To generate ideas quickly and easily, list all the possible *because* responses. For the topic, "Which individual has most influenced your life?" one student jotted down the following reasons *why:*

My grandmother most influenced my life because:

1. She was kind
2. She set a good example
3. She listened to my problems and helped me solve them
4. She was very religious
5. She was a good cook
6. She worked very hard
7. She was always honest
8. She loved me
9. She encouraged me to read
10. She was always learning something new
11. She learned to water-ski when she was sixty

Once you have completed your list, narrow it down to two or three subtopics. For example, the student described above decided to use his grandmother's kindness, good example, and love for learning as major topic headings. Then he quickly scribbled down several subtopics: kindness, good example, and learning.

Next, he generated specific examples to support his ideas.

Kindness	**Good Example**	**Learning**
listened to problems	was religious	encouraged me
really loved me	worked hard	water-ski
	honest	

Let's look at each topic. For *kindness*, he would tell briefly about a time he talked to his grandmother about a problem. "For example, when I failed my first history exam in college, she listened to me talk about my fear of failure. Then she told me that sometimes it takes a little while before you know which way the wind is blowing. Then you can trim your sails just right and win the race." He'd also want to show how he knew she *loved* him. "When I was younger and fell off my bike, she'd always be there to hug away my tears." In the actual planning, the student would use only a few words, just to keep his ideas in order.

Then he decided which of the three possible areas of "good example" he'd like to explore. This student chose "religious" and "worked hard." His specific examples included "went to church twice a week and taught Sunday school," and "raised six children all by herself while working full time." For "learning something new," he decided to describe his grandmother's love of reading about different places and the way she learned to water-ski when she was sixty.

EXERCISE 18.1

Underline the key words in the following topics. Then suggest a way to narrow the topic down.

1. Who is the person in public life whom you least admire?

   To Narrow Down: Students must focus on *one* person who is familiar to the public whom they do not admire.

2. What is your favorite holiday? Why?

   To Narrow Down: Students must focus on *their* favorite day (Christmas, Thanksgiving, Flag Day) and why they like it. [*Note:* Some students might want to include their birthdays; however, many graders of such exams would not consider this a "holiday."]

3. Which advertisements do you consider most appealing or offensive? Why?

To Narrow Down: First, students must decide whether they have more material for appealing or for offensive ads. Then, they must explain why they consider the ads appealing or offensive.

4. "The best things in life are free." Discuss why you agree or disagree with this statement.

To Narrow Down: First, students must decide whether the best things for them are indeed free or if they cost a bundle. Then the student can begin a thesis with "I agree [disagree] that the best things in life are (are not) free because . . . ."

5. What problem in this contemporary world do you find most disturbing? Why?

To Narrow Down: The student should first decide what *one* contemporary problem he or she finds *most* disturbing and then explain *why* it is disturbing. For example, the thesis could begin: "I find the destruction of the ozone layer most disturbing because . . . ."

6. Is it beneficial for a high school graduate to work full-time for a year before entering college? Why or why not?

To Narrow Down: This is a complicated topic requiring several decisions by the student. First, students must decide whether it is beneficial to work before entering college or not. Then they must decide whether full-time work for a year is a good idea. Finally, they must be able to begin the thesis roughly as follows: "A high school graduate should [should not] work full time for a year before entering college because . . . ."

7. Should college students be required to attend classes? Discuss.

To Narrow Down: First-year students will be tempted to write about attending high school classes. However, this is not the topic. A typical thesis might read: "College students should [should not] be required to attend classes because. . . ."

8. Should an introduction to art, music, and drama be part of every college student's education? Explain why or why not.

To Narrow Down: Note here that *all three* areas are considered to be part of the question. The student cannot single out, say, art and ignore music and drama. A thesis might read: "Art, music, and drama should [should not] be part of a college student's education because . . . ." The question does *not* state that these courses should be required, only that they "be part of every college student's education."

9. Is there any job that you would absolutely refuse to take? Explain.

To Narrow Down: Students must first identify the sort of job they would

279

dislike the most [garbage person, latrine cleaner, secretary] and then explain *why they*, personally, would dislike that job. A sample thesis might read: "I would dislike being a file clerk because . . . ."

10. Is it better to have brothers <u>and</u> sisters than to be an <u>only</u> <u>child</u>? <u>Explain</u>.
To Narrow Down: The student needs to explain why it is or why it is not better to have *both* brothers and sisters than to be an only child. Basically, this is a comparison paper. A sample thesis might read: "It is better to be an only child because . . . ." or "It is better to have brothers and sisters than to be an only child because . . . ."

EXERCISE 18.2

Chapter 16, "Designing the Essay," lists and describes several approaches to writing essays. Review this section. Then identify the type of essay you would write for the following topics.

1. What characteristics do you think the president of the United States should have? Division

2. Discuss one cause for which you would be willing to risk your life. Analysis

3. Name someone you consider to be a modern hero or heroine, and explain why you consider the person heroic. Define

4. Do college students benefit from participation in extracurricular activities? Explain. Persuade

5. Discuss the influence that advertising has had on your life. Cause and effect

6. How has your attitude toward your home, town or family changed between the time you entered college and now? Discuss. Compare and contrast

7. What do you believe are the chief reasons for students' academic failure in college? Explain. Cause and effect

8. Should the 55 m.p.h. speed limit be retained? Discuss. Persuasion

9. What are the essential characteristics of an effective leader? Discuss. Definition

10. Each year, many teenagers run away from home. What do you think are the chief causes? Cause but **not** effect. The effect is mentioned in the question.

Section Four: Writing a Thesis Sentence

For your thesis sentence, write a brief sentence or two that *answers* the exam question. For example, "My grandmother was the most influential person in my life because of her kindness, good example, and love of learning." Another one might read, "I always vote because I consider it my duty, my responsibility, and my reward for being an American."

Be sure to make your thesis personal. The key word in both responses above is *I* or *me*. Don't wander off and discuss "a person who . . ." or "someone. . . ." This paper is about *your* reasons.

You'll often use the word *because*. For the topic, "Do you think it was smart, dumb, or comforting to belong to a group in high school?" one student wrote the following: "Being part of a group in high school was comforting *because* my group helped me solve problems, gave me something to do, and helped me set and complete goals."

EXERCISE 18.3

Taking ten minutes for each topic, generate ideas and write a sample thesis sentence.

1. What would cause you to end a friendship?

   The student needs to focus on which of a close friend's actions would destroy the friendship. The more specific he or she can be, the better the thesis sentence will be. A sample thesis might read: "If my best friend lied, stole from me, or gossiped about me, I would end the friendship."

2. Is it harmful for children to be in day-care centers all day? Explain why or why not.

   This is a tough topic because it assumes that all children and all day-care centers are alike. The student will have to go for the overall view. A sample thesis might read: "Children who are in day-care centers all day lack sufficient loving, attention, and personal instruction."

3. What are the chief causes of shoplifting? Discuss.

   Most students will decide that the causes are poverty, greed, amusement, or challenge.

4. If you could pass one law, what would it be? Why?

   First, students have to choose a law. They should take no more than two or three minutes to do this. Next, they must decide why that law should be enacted. For example, one student wrote: "Congress should pass a law that encourages and supports home schooling because home schoolers do better on standardized tests, receive better educations, and are not exposed to violence and drugs in the schools."

5. Why are many people afraid of growing old? Discuss.

This is fairly straightforward. Students typically decide that people are afraid of growing old because of disease, poverty, loneliness, pain, and/or fear of mental incompetence.

EXERCISE 18.4   *Generate ideas, a thesis sentence, and topic sentences for the following topics.*

1. What are the characteristics of a good college student?

This is a definition paper. A thesis sentence might read: "A good college student pays attention, asks questions, and has good study habits." One student wrote these topic sentences for body paragraphs: "First, one can be a successful student by paying attention in class." "Second, a good college student asks questions, if he or she doesn't understand what is being taught." "Finally, a good college sutdent has good study habits."

2. What causes a person to be superstitious?

The most frequently mentioned causes tend to be coincidence, bad luck, and ignorance. Topic sentences for body paragraphs might read: "First, many people become superstitious because of coincidence." "Second, bad luck might cause someone to become superstitious." "Third, most superstition is caused by ignorance."

3. Why do people play practical jokes?

A typical thesis might read: "People play practical jokes for pleasure, attention, or revenge." Topic sentences might read: "First, some people play practical jokes for fun." "Second, some play practical jokes to get attention." "Finally, a few people play practical jokes to get revenge."

EXERCISE 18.5   *List two specific examples for each topic sentence you wrote in Exercise 18.4.*

Answers will vary.

1. What are the characteristics of a good college student?

"First, one can be a successful student by paying attention in class." Examples might include listening to lectures, taking notes, reading the syllabus.

"Second, a good college student asks questions if he or she doesn't understand what is being taught." Examples might include asking an English professor to define "dependent clause" or "sentence fragment," asking a math professor to explain the assignment in Calculus, asking an accounting professor to explain "depreciation."

"Finally, a good college student has good study habits." Examples might include underlining specific terms in the text, allowing plenty of time to review before a test, writing out definitions of difficult terms.

2. What causes a person to be superstitious?

"First, many people become superstitious because of coincidence." Examples might include having a blue Christmas tree the year Uncle John died, having a black cat cross your path before you fell down, finding a penny the day you won the lottery.

"Second, bad luck might cause someone to become superstitious." Examples might include getting mugged, getting lost, wrecking a car.

"Third, most superstition is caused by ignorance." The student might focus on personal responsibility as opposed to "the fates." For example, he or she might suggest that you can't blame a broken mirror for that "F" in history if you didn't study. Another example might be seeing a trademark like that of Procter and Gamble as an occult sign.

3. Why do people play practical jokes?

"First, some people play practical jokes for fun." Examples might include getting people to laugh by putting a whoopee cushion on their chairs or putting disappearing ink on their clothes.

"Second, some play practical jokes to get attention." Many students will give examples of shy or ignored students who put tacks on the teacher's chair or give a popular student a can of peanuts containing a spring snake.

"Finally, a few people play practical jokes to get revenge." Examples might include putting a potato in a car's tail pipe, putting sugar or water in a car's gas tank, putting someone's name on a pornographic mailing list.

EXERCISE 18.6
Answers will vary.

Write a sample introduction for each of the following topics.

1. Many people believe that daydreaming is a waste of time. Agree or disagree.
   Daydreaming can be defined as thinking idly about many topics. Many Ameri-

cans condemn daydreaming as a waste of time. However, there are benefits from it, including building a lively imagination, setting goals, and uplifting one's spirits.

2. Should college students be required to take communications courses? Why or why not?

Only 50 percent of classes taken by college students have any effect on their lives. However, communications courses should be required for a college degree because they will help students in the working world. Graduates will be able to present themselves better to clients and deal more successfully with fellow workers. Finally, college graduates will be better able to understand and respond to both their clients and their bosses.

3. What are the characteristics of a "fully alive person"?

A fully alive person always lives for the moment, is constantly on the go, and is optimistic. People who are fully alive enjoy every minute of life and are prepared to take the bad with the good. These people also brighten the lives of their friends and family.

Section Five: Writing Your Essay

Now you are ready to write the essay. It should include an *introduction*, several *body* paragraphs, and a *conclusion*. Each of these parts of an essay is discussed in Chapter 16, "Designing the Essay."

THE INTRODUCTORY PARAGRAPH

Paragraph 1, the introductory paragraph, should begin with one of the following:

1. An unusual fact or detail,
2. A general statement,
3. A question,
4. An appropriate quotation, or
5. An illustration, anecdote, or joke.

In the second sentence, you should elaborate on, narrow down, answer, or explain sentence one. Your opening paragraph should answer the questions *who*, *what*, *how*, and/or *why*. Consider introducing several sentences to further explain, define, or narrow down the topic. To conclude your introduction, state your thesis.

As an *alternative* to this approach, begin with the central idea. Then discuss each separate point in a separate sentence.

THE BODY PARAGRAPHS

In the body of your essay, remember to answer the questions *what, why, how, when,* or *where*. Generally, a good paragraph will answer *at least* two of those questions. Expect paragraphs in the body of your essay to contain about five to eight sentences each.

Design your body paragraphs this way:

Paragraph 2 begins your topic sentence with a transition such as *First, To begin with,* or a similar phrase. Your topic sentence then discusses your first major point. The second sentence elaborates on, narrows down, or explains more about your topic sentence. In the next two or three sentences, bring in *specific examples*.

In *Paragraph 3*, begin your topic sentence with a transition such as *Second, Next, Then,* or some similar phrase. Your topic sentence discusses your second major point. The next sentence elaborates on, narrows down, or explains more about your topic sentence. In the next two or three sentences, support the topic sentence with *specific examples*.

In *Paragraph 4*, begin your topic sentence with a transition such as *Third, Most importantly, In addition, Finally, Lastly,* or some similar phrase. Your topic sentence discusses your third major point. The next sentence elaborates on, narrows down, or explains more about your topic sentence. In the next two or three sentences, support the topic sentence with *specific examples*.

THE CONCLUSION

Paragraph 5 is your conclusion. Restate your thesis in slightly different words. Then do one of the following:

1. Suggest that the reader look at larger issues, or
2. Suggest that the reader change his or her attitude toward the topic, or
3. Use a quote, a question, or an unusual fact.

Section Six: Analyzing the Timed Exit Exam

We have used the principles described above to analyze the following timed student exit exam.

The Most Influential Person in My Life: My Grandmother

Unusual fact or detail	My grandmother lived to be 96 years old. Her last words were "Not yet, Lord, I haven't cleaned the oven!" My grandmother was the most influential person in my life because of her kindness, good example, and love of learning.
Second sentence elaborates on first sentence	
Three-point thesis	

285

Transition "First" introduces topic sentence based on first point in thesis. Explains topic sentence Transition "For example" introduces first supporting detail	First, my grandmother influenced my life with her kindness. Whenever I had a problem, I knew I could talk to her. She never yelled at me or got angry. For example, when I failed my first history exam in college, she listened to me talk about my fear of failure. Then she told me that sometimes it takes a little bit before you know which way the wind is blowing. But then, you can trim your sails just right and win the race.
Second supporting detail linked by transition "too"	I remember, too, when I was younger and fell off my bike, she'd always be there to hug away my tears.
Transition "Second" introduces topic sentence based on second point of thesis. Explains topic sentence Transition "For example" introduces first supporting detail Transition "Then too" introduces second supporting detail	Second, my grandmother was a great example for any young person. Her values were admirable, and her energy was amazing. For example, she went to church twice a week, no matter what the weather or how tired she was. She even taught Sunday school. Then too, after her husband died, my grandmother raised her six children alone. She did a good job, even though she had to work full time.
Transition "Finally" introduces topic sentence based on third point of thesis Explains topic sentence Transition "For example" introduces first supporting detail Transition "Also" introduces second supporting detail	Finally, my grandmother had a deep love of learning. She always told me, "John, you're never too old to learn something new." For example, she loved reading because she learned about different places she'd never visited. Also, when she was 60, my grandmother learned to water-ski.
Transition "In conclusion" signals beginning of paper conclusion, which restates the thesis	In conclusion, my grandmother was a fine, admirable woman who was respected by everyone who knew her. We all loved her for her kindness, energetic morality, and love of knowledge.

EXERCISE 18.7   *Analyze the timed student essay below by finding and labeling the following elements:*

Thesis
Topic sentence
Introductory sentence
Explanatory sentence (for thesis or topic sentence)
Specific example
Transition

High School Groups Offered Comfort

Introductory sentence involving personal observation

As a person walks down the halls of a high school, he or she will notice different groups of people.

Explanatory sentence

Each group probably consists of friends who share the same interests and goals.

Three-point thesis indicating plan for essay

I think being a part of a group in high school was comforting because my group helped me solve problems, gave me something to do, and helped me set and complete goals.

Transition "First" introduces topic sentence basd on first point in thesis
Explains topic sentence

First, my group of friends were always willing to listen when I had problems. In high school many small problems seemed life-destroying.

Transition "However" introduces further explanation

However, my group always had advice and solutions to offer.

Transition "For instance" introduces first supporting detail

For instance, many times I would not have a date for a dance. My friends would always help me out, whether that meant finding me a date or changing their plans. This would always make me feel better and realize someone cared.

Gives specific example

My friends would also listen when I had problems with my parents.

Transition "also" introduces second supporting detail
Transition "For instance" leads into specific example

For instance, if I could not stay out as late as they could, they would make sure I got home in time or let me spend the night with them.

Transition "Second" introduces topic sentence based on second point of thesis
Explains topic sentence

Second, my group was always involved in different activities. These activities made the time pass faster and high school more fun.

Transition "For instance" introduces first specific example	For instance, if we went to the library, we would have fun because there were always new stories and events to be discussed.
Transition "Another example" introduces second specific detail	Another example is the Fridays and Saturdays when there were not any ball games being played. On these nights we would get together and think of something to do. Sometimes we would go to the show or ride around.
Transitional phrase "Another good quality of a group" introduces topic sentence based on third point of thesis Explains topic sentence	Another good quality of a group is the need for setting and reaching goals. I was in a group that made good grades and planned on going to college. Having friends like this helped me get more out of high school.
Transition "For instance" introduces first supporting detail	For instance, I wanted to be in the same classes as my friends. However, this meant taking college prep courses instead of easier classes. I decided to try a little harder and take the same classes my friends took.
Explains topic sentence	
Transition "Another example" introduces second detail	Another example of reaching my goals is going to college. All of my friends were going to college. Therefore, I went to college with them.
Transition "In conclusion" introduces conclusion restating thesis	In conclusion, I am glad I was part of a group. I think they comforted me and made high school more fun. Without my group of friends I might not have gone to college or cared about good grades.

Section Seven: Proofreading Your Essay

Proofread your paper carefully, looking for the following problems:

1. Run-on sentences
2. Comma splices
3. Fragments
4. Subject—verb agreement
5. Shifts in person or tense
6. Pronoun forms
7. Nonparallel structures

8. Dangling modifiers
9. Spelling errors
10. Punctuation problems

Usually, a timed essay must meet the following requirements:

1. It must have a clearly stated thesis, or central idea, which is *directly* related to the topic.
2. It should be well organized. Each topic sentence should be based on a point mentioned in the thesis. The topic sentences should follow the same order stated in the thesis. For example, the thesis might read: "My choice for governor of Georgia was Zell Miller because of his support for a state lottery, boot camps for drug offenders, and his claim to be the education governor." The first topic sentence in paragraph 2 would discuss Miller's support of the lottery. Paragraph 3 would deal with boot camps for drug offenders, and Paragraph 4 would discuss Miller's role as the education governor.
3. Paragraphs should be linked by appropriate transitions.
4. The essay should be mechanically correct: there should be no sentence errors, for example. Words should be used accurately, sentences should be as clear as possible, grammar should be correct. Careless errors should be avoided.

Fenton ponders: "Is it 'a flock of vultures is . . .' or 'a flock of vultures are' . . . ?"

The Simple
Sentence

SECTION ONE: Subjects
SECTION TWO: Prepositions
SECTION THREE: Verbs

Section One: Subjects

Writers use **subjects** and **verbs** to put sentences together. A subject is the *who* or *what* word that carries out the action; something is said about this word:

Few *people* ride bicycles to work.

In this sentence, *people* is the *who* word that acts.

The *government* should reserve traffic lanes for bicycles.

This sentence tells the reader something—"should reserve traffic lanes"—about the subject, *government*.
Some sentences have compound subjects linked by *and:*

Actresses and *businessmen* ate at the Automat.

In this sentence, *actresses* and *businessmen* are the two *who* words that carry out the action: "ate at the Automat."
Sometimes, an *-ing* word will carry out the action:

Running increases joggers' pulse rates.

Here, *running* is the *what* word that carries out the action—"increases joggers' pulse rates."

EXERCISE 19.1

In the following sentences, find the subjects. Ask whether they tell who *or* what *is doing something. Then underline the subjects.*

1. <u>St. Nicholas</u> was a genuine historical figure, the bishop of Myra.

2. <u>He</u> was born in the now-vanished Turkish town of Patara.

3. <u>Santa Claus</u> might well speak Turkish and ride a camel but for the twists of history.

292

4. Turkish <u>scholars</u> date his killing around A.D. 245.
5. <u>Tales</u> of his good deeds lived on.
6. <u>People</u> thought he performed miracles.
7. The <u>church</u> eventually made him a saint.
8. Greek <u>scholars</u> place the time of his life still later than that.
9. <u>Thieves</u> stole most of Nicholas's bones from the church tomb in Turkey.
10. <u>They</u> took them to Bari, a town in southern Italy.

Section Two: Prepositions

A preposition is a linking word like *at* or *with*. Many prepositions point out relationships in space or time. The following words may all be used as prepositions:

about	behind	from	since
above	below	in	through
across	beneath	inside	to
after	beside	into	toward
against	between	like	under
along	beyond	near	until
among	by	of	up
around	despite	off	upon
as	during	on	with
before	for	over	without

A preposition is always followed by a noun, a pronoun, or a verbal ending with *-ed* or *-ing*, its *object*. Together, they form a *prepositional phrase:*

Preposition	Object
off	(the) diving board
into	(the) river
around	(the) bend
for	them
(fond) of	running
after	being punished
before	walking the plank
above	blackened roofs
despite	knowing nothing
inside	lots of boxes

You cannot use the *object* of a preposition as the *subject* of a sentence. Canceling the prepositional phrases will make it easier for you to identify the subject:

> In St. Louis, Peter and Arthur Ressel are beer can collectors with a very large collection.

> ~~In St. Louis~~, Peter and Arthur Ressel are beer can collectors ~~with a very large collection~~.

Canceling the prepositional phrase—*In St. Louis*—helps you spot the *subject* of the sentence: *Peter and Arthur Ressel.*

> A collection ~~of 5,000 beer cans, with no duplicates~~, belongs to Peter Ressel and his son, Arthur.

In this sentence, the subject of the sentence, *collection*, is followed by *two* prepositional phrases, *of 5,000 beer cans* and *with no duplicates*.

EXERCISE 19.2

Cross out the prepositional phrases in the sentences below. Then underline the subjects.

1. ~~With great care,~~ they've collected cans ~~from the U.S. and Europe.~~
2. These cans ~~from many countries~~ vary ~~in size from 7 ounces to 5 liters, or approximately 5.28 quarts~~.
3. ~~In our measurements~~ a five-liter beer can would hold ~~over a gallon and a quarter~~.
4. The Ressels ~~of St. Louis~~ enjoy collecting cans ~~from all over the world~~.
5. One ~~of their favorite cans~~ was made ~~in 1934~~.
6. ~~In a marketing move,~~ the Krueger Beer Company decided to promote the idea ~~of canned beer~~.
7. Their director ~~of promotions~~ sent an unnamed beer ~~to breweries~~.
8. ~~Despite the curiosity of many beer can collectors,~~ the "Brewer Test Can" remains unopened.
9. ~~In 1968, for the first time,~~ canned beer outsold bottled beer ~~in yearly sales~~.
10. Collectors ~~of odd items~~ advise us to keep unusual beer cans ~~for future generations of beer can collectors~~.

EXERCISE 19.3

Responses will vary.

In the following sentences, fill in the objects of suggested prepositions. The sentences describe a college experience: starting back to school.

> **EXAMPLE:** Signing up _____ is not easy
>   for what?

_____ at _____
                                    where?

_____ .
    for what or whom?

Possible Response: Signing up <u>for classes</u> is not easy at <u>Middle State University</u> <u>for new students</u>.

1. <u>During the morning</u> I found myself standing
       during when?

   <u>in long lines</u> .
       in what

2. <u>Outside the Records Office</u>, I thought <u>of my wasted time</u> .
       where?   of what?

3. However, I ran <u>into my friend George</u> <u>inside the building</u> .
                      into whom?   inside where?

4. <u>Between noon and 3:00 P.M.</u> , I was finally able to register.
       when?

Section Three: Verbs

A complete sentence includes a verb as well as a subject. An action verb tells what the subject is doing.

> The huge diamond *glittered*.

The action verb *glittered* tells what the diamond did.

> Private owners often *operate* companies more profitably than governments *do*.

The verbs *operate* and *do* are action verbs.

A linking verb links or joins the subject to words that do one of the following:

> Identify,
> Rename, or
> Describe the subject.

> The horse *is* incredibly stupid.

The linking verb *is* joins *horse* with the adjective *stupid*.

> My arm *feels* numb.

295

The linking verb *feels* answers the question, "feels how?" Therefore, it joins *arm* with the adjective *numb*.

Linking verbs include all forms of the verb *to be*, as well as a few others:

is, are, was, were, am
have been, has been, might be,
appear, seem, feel, act, grow,
look, smell, taste, sound,
become, remain, prove

Remember: linking verbs must be followed by a noun, pronoun, or adjective. If followed by a verb, they are helping or auxiliary verbs.

AUXILIARY (HELPING) VERBS

Many verbs consist of only one word—*worked, play, are, prove.* However, other verbs consist of more than one word. The extra word is called an auxiliary or helping verb. These include the following:

have	be	will	may
has	am	shall	might
had	are	can	must, ought to
	is		
do	was	would	has to
does	were	should	have to
	been		used to

Auxiliary or helping verbs come before the main verb.

Motorcycle buyers *should look* for mechanical problems.

Should is the helping verb for the main verb, *look.*

I *had waited* for over six hours.

Had is the helping verb for the main verb *waited.*

Finally, they *are calling* my name.

Are is the helping verb for the main verb, *calling.*

EXERCISE 19.4

Underline the verbs in these sentences. If the sentence includes helping and main verbs, underline both of them.

1. Louis Braille was the son of a harness maker.
2. He lived in a small village outside of Paris.
3. At age six, he had driven an awl into one eye.
4. He completely lost his sight over a period of several weeks.

5. In those days, a blind child was given no chance.

6. He either begged or shoveled coal in a factory.

7. Simon René Braille, Louis's father, refused to accept such a fate for his son.

8. Until age ten, Louis was attending the village school.

9. Then his father enrolled him in a school for blind children in Paris.

10. The institution had only three books.

11. By then, Braille had developed a reading system of his own.

12. The French government ignored Braille's reading system for many years.

REVIEW
EXERCISE 19.5

Cross out the prepositional phrases in the sentences below. Then underline the subjects once and the verbs twice.

EXAMPLE: A two-faced approach is keeping tigers off people's backs in West Bengal.

1. The 17th century French Huguenots were skilled in metal crafting.

2. Their skills took them to Rhode Island.

3. Today, seventy wealthy makers of jewelry and metal are housed in Rhode Island.

4. Many houses in Rhode Island reflect the wealth of their owners.

5. One jewelry company for that matter, pays a flat hourly wage.

6. Pay for workers before taxes now amounts to $6.50 an hour.

7. After losses in income, one company, American Jewelry, trimmed its payroll significantly.

8. The trims in its work force rose.

9. For greater efficiency, the plants have also changed their layouts.

10. As supplements to their incomes, many retired workers plant vegetables and fruits in their gardens.

REVIEW
EXERCISE 19.6
Answers will vary.

Develop your sentence sense by using our clues to write complete sentences. Be sure to include a subject, a verb, and one or more prepositional phrases.

EXAMPLE: He was a _____
                                    how tall?
_____ man with a _____ face.
how thick?   what color?

Possible completion: He was <u>tall</u>, <u>thin</u> man with a <u>pale</u> face.

1. The _____elderly_____ , _____feeble_____ man wore
         how old?   how strong?

   his _____scarf_____ _____wrapped_____ around
       what?   done what with?

   his _____neck_____ .
   what part of body or article of clothing?

2. He often _____stumbled_____ and _____shuffled_____ .
         did what?   did what else?

3. He usually wore a _____baffled_____ look on
           what kind of?

   _____his face_____ .
       where?

4. Nevertheless, he aroused a _____curious_____ feeling
           what kind of?

   in _____other people_____ .
      whom?

5. She was a _____small_____ , _____friendly_____ girl
         what size?   what kind?

   with _____bright_____ eyes.
      what kind or color?

6. She had _____good_____ health and a
        how good?

   _____strong_____ appetite.
      what kind?

7. Men liked the _____color_____ of her
         what?

   _____rosy_____ cheeks.
      what kind?

ANSWER KEY

The answers to alternate questions in each exercise are included below.

EXERCISE 19.1

  2. <u>He</u> was born in the now-vanished Turkish town of Patara.

  4. Turkish <u>scholars</u> date his killing around A.D. 245.

  6. <u>People</u> thought he performed miracles.

  8. Greek <u>scholars</u> place the time of his life still later than that.

10. <u>They</u> took them to Bari, a town in southern Italy.

EXERCISE 19.2

2. These <u>cans</u> ~~from many countries~~ vary ~~in size from 7 ounces to 5 liters, or approximately 5.28 quarts~~.

4. The <u>Ressels</u> ~~of St. Louis~~ enjoy collecting cans ~~from all over the world~~.

6. ~~In a marketing move~~, the <u>Krueger Beer Company</u> decided to promote the idea ~~of canned beer~~.

8. ~~Despite the curiosity of many beer can collectors~~, the "<u>Brewer Test Can</u>" remains unopened.

10. <u>Collectors</u> ~~of odd items~~ advise us to keep unusual beer cans ~~for future generations of beer can collectors~~.

EXERCISE 19.3

2. Outside the Records office, I thought of my wasted time.

4. Between noon and 3 p.m., I was finally able to register.

EXERCISE 19.4

2. He <u>lived</u> in a small village outside of Paris.

4. He completely <u>lost</u> his sight over a period of several weeks.

6. He either <u>begged</u> or <u>shoveled</u> coal in a factory.

8. Until the age of ten, Louis <u>was</u> <u>attending</u> the village school.

10. The institution <u>had</u> only three books.

12. The French government <u>ignored</u> Braille's reading system for many years.

REVIEW EXERCISE 19.5

2. Their <u>skills</u> <u>took</u> them ~~to Rhode Island~~.

4. Many <u>houses</u> ~~in Rhode Island~~ <u>reflect</u> the wealth ~~of their owners~~.

6. <u>Pay</u> ~~for workers before taxes~~ now <u>amounts</u> to $6.50 an hour.

8. The <u>trims</u> ~~in its work force~~ <u>rose</u>.

10. ~~As supplements to their incomes~~, many retired <u>workers</u> <u>plant</u> vegetables and fruit ~~in their gardens~~.

REVIEW EXERCISE 19.6

2. He often <u>stumbled</u> and <u>shuffled</u>.

4. Nevertheless, he aroused a <u>curious</u> feeling in <u>other</u> <u>people</u>.

6. She had <u>good</u> health and a <u>strong</u> appetite.

CHAPTER

20

Fragments

SECTION ONE: Missing Subject Fragments
SECTION TWO: Fragments Beginning with an *-ing* or *to* Word
SECTION THREE: Fragments Beginning with Connecting Words
SECTION FOUR: Fragments Beginning with Subordinating Words

Complete sentences include both a subject and a verb. The *subject* tells us *who* or *what* is doing or being. The *verb* describes the action or state of being. A word group is a *fragment* if it

- Lacks *either* a subject or a verb, or
- Fails to express a complete thought.

People most frequently write the following kinds of fragments:

- Missing subject or verb fragment
- *-ing* or *to* fragment
- Connecting word fragment
- Subordinating word fragment

Section One: Missing Subject Fragments

A sentence fragment may be missing a subject. Some writers think the subject from one group will carry over to the next word group:

> An ice skating guard hands out skates to children. And deals with the tension they bring on.

The second word group is a fragment. It lacks a subject. The writer can correct it in one of two ways:

1. Connect the fragment to the sentence that comes before it:

   > An ice skating guard hands out skates to the children *and* deals with the tension they bring on.

2. Drop the connecting word (*and* in this case). Then add a pronoun referring back to the subject of the preceding word group (a transition may help your reader, *also* in this case):

   > *He* **also** deals with the tension they bring on.

302

EXERCISE 20.1

In each entry below, put an "F" in front of the fragment that lacks a subject. Then correct the problem in one of the two ways indicated above. If necessary, check the list of transitions in Chapter 2, "Designing the Paragraph."

EXAMPLE: Equipping people with masks has helped reduce the casualty rate from tigers. ___F___ And lessened the friction between people and tigers.

> **Rewrite 1:** Equipping people with masks has helped reduce the casualty rate from tigers *and* lessened the friction between people and tigers.
>
> OR
>
> **Rewrite 2:** Equipping people with masks has helped reduce the casualty rate from tigers. *It* has (also) lessened the friction between people and tigers. (In this version, *It* refers back to the *-ing* word, *equipping*.)

1. _____ The children start promptly at 8:00 in the morning. ___F___ But arrive at the rink at 7:30 a.m.

   Rewrite: The children start promptly at 8:00 in the morning, but (*they*) arrive at the rink at 7:30 a.m.

2. _____ They cluster like a mass of squealing rats. ___F___ And whine for their skates.

   Rewrite: They cluster like a mass of squealing rats and whine for their skates. OR: They cluster like a mass of screaming rats. Then they whine for their skates.

3. _____ The children resemble ocean waves, hundreds and hundreds of them. ___F___ And appear out of nowhere, wave after wave.

   Rewrite: The children resemble ocean waves, hundreds and hundreds of them, and appear out of nowhere, wave after wave. OR: The children resemble ocean waves, hundreds and hundreds of them. (They) appear out of nowhere, wave after wave.

4. _____ This event lasts no more than half an hour. ___F___ But feels like it will never end.

   Rewrite: This event lasts no more than half an hour, but it feels like it will never end. OR: This event lasts no more than half an hour but feels like it will never end.

5. _____ Finally, the guard has a moment of peace. ___F___ And enjoys ten minutes of silence.

   Rewrite: Finally, the guard has a moment of peace, and he enjoys ten minutes of silence. OR: Finally, the guard has a moment of peace and enjoys ten minutes of silence.

Section Two: Fragments Beginning with an *-ing* or *to* Word

Fragments often begin with an *-ing* word. This word group may lack a subject and part of the verb, the helping part: *may*, *should*, or *was*, for example. One of these word groups is a fragment:

Living in a rural area. I must drive a long distance to anyplace else.

The first word group, beginning with *living*, is a fragment. It is missing a subject and part of the verb. It can be fixed in one of two ways:

1. *Add a subject and helping verb to the fragment: I am* living (or *live*) in a rural area.
2. *Combine the word group with the sentence before or after it:* Living in a rural area, I must drive a long distance to anyplace else.

Remember: If the fragment comes first, put a coma after its last word. If the fragment comes last, however, do not separate it from the first clause by a comma.

A fragment may also begin with a *to* word:

To get the most out of my car. I must keep up expensive maintenance.

The first word group is missing both its subject and verb. The writer is probably looking ahead to the doer of its action, "I." You can fix this problem in one of two ways:

1. *Add a subject and a verb to the word group: I want* to get the most out of my car.
2. *Combine the word group with the sentence before or after it:* To get the most out of my car, I must keep up expensive maintenance.

EXERCISE 20.2   *Check the fragment in each of the groups below. Then rewrite it by using one of the ideas above.*

1. __X__ Hating to be stranded on the side of the road. _____ I often put my car in the shop.

   Rewrite: Hating to be stranded on the side of the road, I often put my car in the shop.

2. _____ I make regular appointments for my car. __X__ To get the oil and filter changed every 3,000 miles.

   Rewrite: I make regular appointments for my car to get the oil and filter changed every 3,000 miles.

3. __X__ While having its tires balanced and rotated. _____ The car also gets a tuneup.

   Rewrite: While having its tires balanced and rotated, the car also gets a tuneup.

4. _____ I do everything the car manual suggests. __X__ Knowing I can't afford a new car.

   Rewrite: I do everything the car manual suggests, knowing I can't afford a new car.

5. __X__ Feeling that Amoco has cleaner gas. _____ I always buy that brand. __X__ To keep my engine running smoothly.

   Rewrite: Feeling that Amoco has cleaner gas, I always buy that brand to keep my engine running smoothly.

6. __X__ Hearing some kind of weird noise. _____ I immediately take my car in for repairs.

   Rewrite: Hearing some kind of weird noise, I immediately take my car in for repairs.

7. _____ As a result, I avoid serious repair problems. __X__ To keep my car dependable until the end of my five-year payment plan.

   Rewrite: As a result, I avoid serious repair problems. This keeps my car dependable until the end of my five-year payment plan.

Section Three: Fragments Beginning with Connecting Words

Writers sometimes begin fragments with connecting words. The resulting word groups may lack subjects or verbs, or both. The following words often begin fragments:

just, especially, also, mainly, for instance, like, such as, for example

The following paragraph includes a fragment. See if you can find it.

The American Civil Liberties Union opposes a new University of Pittsburgh regulation. Mainly prohibits fraternities from staging female mud-wrestling matches. It also outlaws pornographic films.

The second word group, beginning with *mainly*, lacks a subject. The writer may have thought it carried over *regulation* as its subject. However, each word group must have its own subject and verb.

This fragment can be corrected in one of two ways:

1. Drop the connecting word, and join the fragment to the sentence before or after it:

   The American Civil Liberties Union opposes a new University of Pittsburgh regulation prohibit*ing* fraternities from staging female mud-wrestling matches. It also outlaws pornographic films.

   This change makes *prohibit* an *-ing* word.

2. Add the missing subject or verb to complete the sentence:

   Mainly, *it* prohibits fraternities from staging female mud-wrestling matches.

   This change adds the pronoun *it* as a new subject referring to the word *regulation* in the previous sentence.

It pays to test word groups for completeness. Do they sound complete when read aloud? Do they have subjects and verbs?

EXERCISE 20.3

Check the word groups below for fragments. Look for transitions like mainly *or* for example. *Correct the fragment by using one of the ideas above. Make sure your combination makes sense. If the fragment comes first in your new sentence, separate it from the rest of the sentence with a comma.*

1. _____ In a letter to the school, the ACLU argues that the regulation is stated too vaguely. __X__ Mainly infringing on the students' rights of privacy and freedom of speech.

   Rewrite: In a letter to the school, the ACLU argues that the regulation is stated too vaguely, infringing on the students' rights of privacy and freedom of speech.

2. _____ Marion Damick, executive secretary of Pittsburgh's ACLU chapter, says that the issue goes beyond mud-wrestling. __X__ Especially addresses an individual's freedom of expression.

   Rewrite: It addresses an individual's freedom of expression.

3. __X__ Indeed, confesses she has never seen a mud-wrestling match. _____ "I don't know that I would go out of my way to see one, either," she adds.

   Rewrite: Indeed, she confesses she has never seen a mud-wrestling match.

4. __X__ To some students, the university a double standard. _____ Last spring, Pitt's student-housing office had chocolate-pudding wrestling matches. __X__ Among others, a student newspaper editorial the ruling.

Rewrite: To some students, the university had a double standard. Among others, a student newspaper editorial attacked the ruling.

5. _____ They didn't see why the fraternity couldn't stage its event. __X__ Especially the university held pudding matches.

Rewrite: They didn't see why the fraternity couldn't stage its event when the university held pudding matches.

6. _____ The director of Pitt's student activities commented. __X__ In regard to the Greek system's image.

Rewrite: The director of Pitt's student activities commented in regard to the Greek system's image.

7. __X__ Five years ago the university itself to bring in a troupe. _____ They were female mud-wrestlers.

Rewrite: Five years ago the university committed itself to bring (OR brought) in a troupe of female mud-wrestlers.

8. _____ No students objected. __X__ However, at that time. __X__ Mud-wrestling seen as nothing but silliness.

Rewrite: However, at that time, mud-wrestling was seen as nothing but silliness.

Section Four: Fragments Beginning with Subordinating Words

Fragments often begin with subordinating words. Check for missing subjects or verbs after one of these examples:

after, although, so, so that, before, even though, until, as, as if, if, how, whenever, wherever, through, when, while, that, because, through, where, which

Whenever you begin a sentence with one of the words above, avoid writing a fragment. In the example below, a fragment begins with the word *because*:

My boyfriend doesn't like me to dance with other fellows. Because he gets really jealous.

A depencent clause beginning with a word like *because* cannot stand alone. It is not a complete thought. By itself, it is a fragment. A sentence beginning with one of these words leads the reader to expect more information. To correct the fragment above, combine it with the sentence that comes before it:

Rewrite: My boyfriend doesn't like me to dance with other fellows because he gets really jealous.

Sometimes, you can change the word order without changing the meaning. However, if the fragment *comes first* in the new combination, set it off from the next clause with a comma:

Rewrite: Because he gets really jealous, my boyfriend doesn't like me to dance with other fellows.

Here are other examples of fragments beginning with dependent words:

I got into real trouble at Frankie's wedding last week.
After I had a few glasses of champagne.

The second word group is a fragment beginning with *after.* It can't stand alone. The writer must change it by either taking out *after* or connecting the fragment to another sentence. It could read simply, "I had a few glasses of champagne." Or the writer could connect it with the sentence that comes before:

I got into real trouble at Frankie's wedding last week *after* I had a few glasses of champagne.

Note: If a fragment comes last in a new sentence, *no comma* separates it from the main clause it follows, as in this example:

I broke down and danced with some boys [new clause, no comma] I'd never met before.

To fix a dependent word fragment, connect it to either the sentence before or the one that follows:

I looked at some cars. That I had not seen before.
Rewrite: I looked at some cars *that* I had not seen before. (This fragment is attached to the sentence that comes before it.)

I know when my car is running badly. *Because I drive it day in and day out.*
Rewrite: I know when my car is running badly because I drive it day in and day out. (This fragment is attached to the sentence that comes before it.)

You can also fix the fragment by leaving out the dependent word.

~~Although~~ m(M)ost of my friends have finished college.
~~Since~~ m(M)y supportive parents encouraged me to do well in life.
~~After~~ I moved to Savannah two years ago.

Use this method sparingly, however. You may create a series of short, choppy sentences.

EXERCISE 20.4   *Check the fragment in each of the following word groups. Then correct the problem by combining it with either the sentence before or the one after. Change the order of the word groups if you wish. If you begin a new sentence with a fragment, set it off with a comma.*

1. _____ Anna Pavlova was one of the great geniuses of dance. __X__ Since she had incredible strength, stamina, and grace.

   Rewrite: Anna Pavlova was one of the great geniuses of dance since she had incredible strength, stamina, and grace.

2. __X__ Although she was a weak and frail child. _____ She showed amazing strength and endurance as an adult.

   Rewrite: Although she was a weak and frail child, she showed amazing strength and endurance as an adult.

3. __X__ When she was eight years old. _____ Her mother took her to see the Royal Imperial Ballet.

   Rewrite: When she was eight years old, her mother took her to see the Royal Imperial Ballet.

4. __X__ Because the ballerina was beautiful. _____ Pavlova decided to dedicate herself to the dance.

   Rewrite: Because the ballerina was beautiful, Pavlova decided to dedicate herself to the dance.

5. _____ She was admitted to the Imperial Theater School. __X__ Even though she had to wait two years.

   Rewrite: She was admitted to the Imperial Theater School even though she had to wait two years.

6. __X__ After she had seven years of difficult training. _____ She joined the ballet.

   Rewrite: After she had seven years of difficult training, she joined the ballet.

7. _____ She was both an excellent dancer and a good actress. __X__ Although many dancers lack acting talent.

   Rewrite: Although many dancers lack acting talent, she was both an excellent dancer and a good actress.

8. __X__ Even though it was an amazing feat. _____ She became prima ballerina within seven years.

   Rewrite: Even though it was an amazing feat, she became prima ballerina within seven years.

9. _____ She did a solo dance. __X__ That was called "The Dying Swan."

   Rewrite: She did a solo dance that was called "The Dying Swan."

10. __X__ Even after she bought a permanent home in London. _____ Pavlova traveled widely.

Rewrite: <u>Even after she bought a permanent home in London, Pavlova traveled widely.</u>

11. __X__ Although she was plagued by a painful knee injury. _____ She still continued her difficult schedule.

Rewrite: <u>Although she was plagued by a painful knee injury, she still continued her difficult schedule.</u>

12. __X__ When she began another tour in Holland in January, 1931. _____ She collapsed and soon died.

Rewrite: <u>When she began another tour in Holland in January, 1931, she collapsed and soon died.</u>

Wrap-up: Checking for Fragments

1. Read over your paper slowly, holding your finger under each word. Then read it aloud or ask a friend to do so. Check whether each group looks and sounds complete.

2. Look or listen for possible signals of fragments:
   - Missing subject or verb
   - A *to* or *-ing* word fragment (beginning with *to* or a word like walk*ing*, sing*ing*, or hav*ing*)
   - A connecting word fragment (often signaled by a transition such as *mainly, meanwhile,* or *for instance*)
   - A subordinating word fragment (begins with a word like *although, since,* or *after*

3. Query yourself:
   - Does the word group include *both* a subject (or **doer**) and verb (description of an action or state of being)?
   - Does the word group sound complete?

4. Correct the problem in one of three ways:
   - Add the missing word, or
   - Delete a subordinating or transitional word, or
   - Combine the fragment with a complete sentence before or after it.

Cautions:

1. Avoid short, choppy sentences.
2. If you begin a new sentence with a fragment, set it off from the complete word group by a comma.

REVIEW EXERCISE 20.5

Write complete sentences that use each of the following word groups.

Answers will vary.

Example: When my mother cooks.
Rewrite: When my mother cooks, *she uses fresh vegetables.*
Example: For lazy people.
Rewrite: For lazy people, *weekends are the best time.*

1. In order to pay the bills
   Rewrite: In order to pay the bills, John works part time.

2. Lying in the sun
   Rewrite: She got a superb tan lying in the sun.

3. In here with that big sack of groceries
   Rewrite: Come on in here with that big sack of groceries.

4. Then ran back into the sun
   Rewrite: He jumped in the pool and then ran back into the sun.

5. During our trip out to the Grand Canyon.
   Rewrite: We drove our recreational vehicle during our trip out to the Grand Canyon.

6. Honking his horn at people
   Rewrite: He screeched down the street, honking his horn at people.

7. After driving down the street
   Rewrite: After driving down the street, he jumped out in front of the quick shop.

8. Keeps everything organized
   Rewrite: I admire the way she keeps everything organized.

9. If you went to her house
   Rewrite: If you went to her house, you probably wouldn't find her.

10. My roommate who dresses neatly
    Rewrite: My roommate, who dresses neatly, is quite attractive.

REVIEW EXERCISE 20.6

Each of the following word groups contains a fragment. Check the fragment. Then make a complete sentence. If a fragment begins a new sentence, use a comma.

EXAMPLE: ___F___ Having noticed shortness of breath.

_____ I realized that I had to stop smoking

Rewrite: Having noticed shortness of breath, I realized that I had to stop smoking.

1. ___F___ While working for the college newspaper.

   _____ We were often censored.

   Rewrite: While working for the college newspaper, we were often censored.

2. ___F___ When we finished taking pictures.

   _____ We often wrote humorously about obscenity.

   Rewrite: When we finished taking pictures, we often wrote humorously about obscenity.

3. _____ A young man greeted everyone with a balloon.

   ___F___ After dressing as a clown.

   Rewrite: A young man greeted everyone with a balloon after dressing as a clown.

4. _____ The editor ran a story on him.

   ___F___ To liven up the newspaper with humor.

   Rewrite: The editor ran a story on him to liven up the newspaper with humor.

5. ___F___ Since they thought students should act more dignified.

   _____ The administration refused to let us print the story.

   Rewrite: Since they thought students should act more dignified, the administration refused to let us print the story.

6. ___F___ As spent more time on the college newspaper.

   _____ The censorship continued.

   Rewrite: As I spent more time on the college newspaper, the censorship continued.

7. _____ The editor told us to omit obscenity from our articles.

   ___F___ Just to avoid censorship.

   Rewrite: The editor told us to omit obscenity from our articles, just to avoid censorship.

8. _____ We argued that this violated our rights.

   ___F___ Protected by the constitution.

   ___F___ Especially by the Bill of Rights.

   Rewrite: We argued that this violated our rights protected by the constitution, especially by the Bill of Rights.

312

9. __F__ Saying these articles were in bad taste.

_____ The administration claimed they would give the school a bad name.

Rewrite: Saying these articles were in bad taste, the administration claimed they would give the school a bad name.

10. _____ We had to stay within the college guidelines.

__F__ For the pictures we printed.

Rewrite: We had to stay within the college guidelines for the pictures we printed.

11. __F__ To protect the reputation of the college.

_____ We couldn't show too much skin in our pictures.

Rewrite: To protect the reputation of the college, we couldn't show too much skin in our pictures.

12. _____ The administration censored us.

__F__ If we printed the picture of a woman.

__F__ Wearing a short dress.

Rewrite: The administration censored us if we printed a picture of a woman wearing a short dress.

13. _____ Once we wanted to photograph a man with no shirt on.

__F__ Just getting a tan on the patio.

__F__ With a soft drink in his hand.

Rewrite: Once we wanted to photograph a man with no shirt on just getting a tan on the patio with a soft drink in his hand.

14. _____ No one has the right to censor a newspaper.

__F__ By imposing his or her values on the staff.

Rewrite: No one has the right to censor a newspaper by imposing his or her values on the staff.

15. _____ A college newspaper functions best.

__F__ Mainly by appealing to the entire college community.

Rewrite: A college newspaper functions best mainly by appealing to the entire college community.

16. _____ Editors should be able to publish anything.

__F__ Whether humorous, obscene, or distasteful to someone.

Rewrite: Editors should be able to publish anything, whether humorous, obscene, or distasteful to someone.

17. __F__ To avoid suits for libel or slander.

_____ However, there have to be limits.

Rewrite: To avoid suits for libel or slander, however, there have to be limits.

18. _____ Special rules need to be written.

   __F__ For a newspaper on a college campus.

   Rewrite: Special rules need to be written for a newspaper on a college campus.

19. __F__ Speaking for myself and other reporters.

   _____ I believe that censorship should not interfere with freedom of the press.

   Rewrite: Speaking for myself and other reporters, I believe that censorship should not interfere with freedom of the press.

REVIEW EXERCISE 20.7

Identify the missing parts of the following fragments. Then add these parts to the fragments to make them complete sentences.

EXAMPLE:

1. Could hardly breathe.

   Missing Subject?__I__ Missing Verb? (Part)?_____

   Rewrite: I could hardly breathe.

2. In particular, not cure my bad headache.

   Missing Subject?__I__ Missing Verb? (Part)? could

   Rewrite: In particular, I could not cure my bad headache.

3. Earlier, my friend Lisa and I visiting my sister in Savannah, Georgia.

   Missing Subject?_____ Missing Verb? (Part)? were

   Rewrite: Earlier, my friend Lisa and I were visiting (OR visited) my sister in Savannah, Georgia.

4. The night before, all gone out.

   Missing Subject?__we__ Missing Verb? (Part)? had

   Rewrite: The night before, we had all gone out.

5. Just consumed too many drinks and cigarettes.

   Missing Subject?__I__ Missing Verb (Part) had

   Rewrite: I had just consumed too many drinks and cigarettes.

6. The following day, really to pay for it.

   Missing Subject?__I__ Missing Verb (Part) had

   Rewrite: The following day, I really (had) to pay for it.

7. About twelve noon left Rhonda's house.

   Missing Subject? we, I Missing Verb (Part)_____

   Rewrite: About twelve noon we (I) left Rhonda's house.

8. A two and a half hour trip ahead of us.

   Missing Subject? __we__   Missing Verb (Part) __had__

   Rewrite: __We had a two and a half hour trip ahead of us.__

9. After taking a couple of aspirins.

   Missing Subject? __we__   Missing Verb (Part) __took__

   Rewrite: __I (We) took a couple of aspirins.__

10. For instance, my headache a lot better.

    Missing Subject? _____   Missing Verb (Part) __got__

    Rewrite: __My headache got a lot better.__

11. However, still shortness of breath.

    Missing Subject? __I__   Missing Verb (Part) __felt__

    Rewrite: __However, I still felt shortness of breath.__

12. For example, Lisa a lot of cigarettes.

    Missing Subject? _____   Missing Verb (Part) __smokes__

    Rewrite: __For example, Lisa smokes a lot of cigarettes.__

13. I bet smoking two packs daily.

    Missing Subject? __she__   Missing Verb (Part) __is__

    Rewrite: __I bet she is smoking two packs daily.__

14. Whereas, I only several cigarettes daily.

    Missing Subject? _____   Missing Verb (Part) __smoke__

    Rewrite: __I only smoke several cigarettes daily.__

Answer Key

Answers to alternate questions in this chapter's exercises are provided below.

EXERCISE 20.1

2. They cluster like a mass of screaming rats and whine for their skates. OR: They cluster like a mass of screaming rats. Then they whine for their skates.

4. This event lasts no more than half an hour, but it feels like it will never end. OR: This event lasts no more than half an hour but feels like it will never end.

EXERCISE 20.2

2. I make regular appointments for my car to get the oil and filter changed every 3,000 miles.

4. I do everything the car manual suggests, knowing I can't afford a new car.

6. Hearing some kind of weird noise, I immediately take my car in for repairs.

EXERCISE 20.3

2. It addresses an individual's freedom of expression.

4. To some students, the university had a double standard. Among others, a student newspaper editorial attacked the ruling.

6. The director of Pitt's student activities commented in regard to the Greek system's image.

8. However, at that time, mud-wrestling was seen as nothing but silliness.

EXERCISE 20.4

2. Although she was a weak and frail child, she showed amazing strength and endurance as an adult.

4. Because the ballerina was beautiful, Pavlova decided to dedicate herself to the dance.

6. After she had seven years of difficult training, she joined the ballet.

8. Even though it was an amazing feat, she became prima ballerina within seven years.

10. Even after she bought a permanent home in London, Pavlova traveled widely.

12. When she began another tour in Holland in January, 1931, she collapsed and soon died.

REVIEW EXERCISE 20.5

2. She got a superb tan lying in the sun.

4. He jumped in the pool and then ran back into the sun.

6. He screeched down the street, honking his horn at people.

8. I admire the way she keeps everything organized.

10. My roommate, who dresses neatly, is quite attractive.

REVIEW EXERCISE 20.6

2. When we finished taking pictures, we often wrote humorously about obscenity.

4. The editor ran a story on him to liven up the newspaper with humor.

6. As I spent more time on the college newspaper, the censorship continued.

8. We argued that this violated our rights protected by the constitution, especially by the Bill of Rights.

10. We had to stay within the college guidelines for the pictures we printed.

12. The administration censored us if we printed a picture of a woman wearing a short dress.

14. No one has the right to censor a newspaper by imposing his or her values on the staff.

16. Editors should be able to publish anything, whether humorous, obscene, or distasteful to someone.

18. Special rules need to be written for a newspaper on a college campus.

REVIEW EXERCISE 20.7

2. In particular, I could not cure my bad headache.

4. The night before, we had all gone out.

6. The following day, I really had to pay for it.

8. We had a two and a half hour trip ahead of us.

10. My headache got a lot better.

12. For example, Lisa smokes a lot of cigarettes.

14. I only smoke several cigarettes daily.

Correcting Run-Ons and Comma Splices

Run-on Sentences

A sentence run-on connects two simple sentences (or *independent clauses*) without separating them by a mark of punctuation. The writer may have run them together thinking they were only one complete thought:

> Our team went to the playoffs they lost the championship by 57 points.

The first complete thought ends after the word *playoffs.* The writer should mark it with a period or semicolon; a capital letter should follow a period.

> I have never been hang gliding it is something I have always wanted to do.

The first complete thought ends after the word *gliding.* The writer should mark it with a period or semicolon; a capital letter should follow a period.

Comma Splices

Writers may combine two independent clauses by inserting a comma but no connecting word. However, a comma *without* a coordinator only interrupts. It is too weak to connect independent clauses. When used this way it *splices* two complete thoughts.

> The color black absorbs heat, white reflects it.

The comma after *heat* is a weak break. It should be replaced by a semicolon or period.

> I bought a racing cart for $400, then I cleaned and painted it.

The comma after *$400* is a weak break. It should be replaced by a semicolon or period.
Commas are not strong enough to mark off one complete thought from another.

Use these tips to find run-on sentences and comma splices:

1. Read your sentences aloud, or ask someone else to do so. When your (or their) voice drops or pauses, you need some punctuation: a period, semicolon, or comma.
2. Test each one of your sentences to see if it *both* has a subject and tells your reader something about the subject.
3. Count your sentences: if you don't have very many in your paragraph or essay, you may have written run-ons or used comma splices.

Correct a comma splice or a run-on in one of four ways:

1. Create two separate sentences. End the first one with a period, and capitalize the first letter of the next one:

   Aunt Virginia has been married to Uncle Mike for 49 years. He is a cement contractor.

2. Add a coordinator (*and, or, but, yet,* or *so*) after the comma:

   Leakproof tents had been invented by then, but ours was not one of them.

3. Replace the comma with a semicolon:

   Aunt Virginia has been married to Uncle Mike for 49 years; he is a cement contractor.

4. Connect the clauses with a subordinator:

   When our team went to the playoffs, they lost the championship by 57 points.
   OR
   Our team lost the championship by 57 points when they went to the playoffs.

Note: When a subordinator begins a sentence, its clause is set off by a comma. However, when a subordinate clause follows an independent clause, as in the example above, it is seldom set off by a comma.

Section One: Correcting by Creating Two Sentences

To correct a run-on, end the first independent clause with a period. Then begin the next independent clause with a capital letter. This works well if you want short sentences, or if the ideas are not very closely linked.

EXERCISE 21.1 *Find the boundary between the independent clauses in the run-ons below. These clauses are joined or "run on" with no punctuation between them. Correct the run-ons by inserting a period after the first independent clause. Then begin the next one with a capital letter.*

EXAMPLE: I needed a motor for the cart we spent countless hours looking through want ads.

> **Rewrite:** I needed a motor for the cart. We spent countless hours looking through want ads.

1. I have thought of joining the Secret Service the adventure and danger appeal to me.

   Rewrite: _I have thought of joining the Secret Service. The adventure and danger appeal to me._

2. I entered this university as a transfer student they didn't accept many of my credits.

   Rewrite: _I entered this university as a transfer student. They didn't accept many of my credits._

3. I tried to get the credits accepted by going through channels this did not work.

   Rewrite: _I tried to get the credits accepted by going through channels. This did not work._

4. A course in the principles of management should transfer anywhere in the country the university should accept it even if the numbers are different.

   Rewrite: _A course in the principles of management should transfer anywhere in the country. The university should accept it even if the numbers are different._

5. All teachers have different teaching philosophies students respond in different ways.

   Rewrite: _All teachers have different teaching philosophies. Students respond in different ways._

6. My fight for these credits will never end it is a challenge to me to get the rules changed.

   Rewrite: _My fight for these credits will never end. It is a challenge to me to get the rules changed._

7. There is a chance I can beat the system I would consider this an adventure in my life.

   Rewrite: _There is a chance I can beat the system. I would consider this an adventure in my life._

8. I would enjoy sky diving this sounds like an awesome adventure.

   Rewrite: _I would enjoy sky diving. This sounds like an awesome adventure._

9. I once drove my friend's Ferrari GTO at 155 miles an hour moving that fast was exhilarating.

   Rewrite: _I once drove my friend's Ferrari GTO at 155 miles an hour. Moving that fast was exhilarating._

10. In Colorado I skied down slopes at 50 miles an hour that gave me a feeling of high spirits.

Rewrite: _In Colorado I skied down slopes at 50 miles an hour. That gave me a feeling of high spirits._

EXERCISE 21.2

Find the boundaries between complete thoughts in the following word groups. Some of them are run-ons with no punctuation between thoughts. Others interrupt complete thoughts with comma splices. Make corrections by inserting a period between complete thoughts. Then begin the next complete thought with a capital letter.

1. It is 2:30 in the morning Bangkok's body collectors are on the prowl.

Rewrite: _It is 2:30 in the morning. Bangkok's body collectors are on the prowl._

2. A van glides quietly through deserted city streets then a voice squawks over the radio: "Crash on Lang Suan Lane."

Rewrite: _A van glides quietly through deserted city streets. Then a voice squawks over the radio: "Crash on Lang Suan Lane."_

3. The van makes a hasty U-turn it then speeds through back alleys.

Rewrite: _The van makes a hasty U-turn. It then speeds through back alleys._

4. The police hang back squeamishly the men in the van scurry over to the corpse.

Rewrite: _The police hang back squeamishly. The men in the van scurry over to the corpse._

5. They poke around for the fatal wound, afterwards, co-workers photograph and videotape the scene.

Rewrite: _They poke around for the fatal wound. Afterwards, co-workers photograph and videotape the scene._

6. Finally, they trundle the body off to the hospital for an autopsy one man stays behind to mop up the pavement.

Rewrite: _Finally, they trundle the body off to a hospital for an autopsy. One man stays behind to mop up the pavement._

7. In this city people shun corpses for fear of ghosts, the charity picks up after unnatural deaths.

Rewrite: _In this city people shun corpses for fear of ghosts. The charity picks up after unnatural deaths._

8. This charity has done this for many years it has had the streets to itself.

Rewrite: _This charity has done this for many years. It has had the streets to itself._

9. Another charity installed two-way radios, they did this to eavesdrop on police calls.

   Rewrite: Another charity installed two-way radios. They did this to eavesdrop on police calls.

10. Field workers dash to the scene of accidents first this brought competition for corpses.

    Rewrite: Field workers dash to the scene of accidents first. This brought competition for corpses.

Certain words cause writers to run or splice their sentences together. These words include connectives and pronouns:

then	now	however	I
finally	suddenly	you	he, she, it
there	we	they	who
consequently		moreover	therefore

In your own writing, look for these words. They are danger signals. The word group that follows one of them may be a fragment. Check each word group following a word in this list for both a *subject* and a *verb*.

EXERCISE 21.3

Answers will vary.

Add another sentence of your own to follow the sentences below. Begin your sentence with the word we suggest. Remember: *Follow a connective like* moreover *or* consequently *with a comma.*

EXAMPLE: I am at a major turning point in my life right now. **It**

It is exciting and enjoyable.

1. I am willing to work hard. **Now**
   Now I am working and going to school at the same time.

2. My family is very supportive. **They**
   They have helped me with my finances.

3. Graduating from high school showed me that I could attend college. **Suddenly**
   Suddenly, I must prove myself.

4. The main requirement for doing well in college is effort. **Therefore**
   Therefore, I must study hard.

5. I am a strong and dedicated person. **Moreover**

Moreover, I want to prepare for a successful career.

Section Two: Correcting by Adding a Coordinator

Run-ons and comma splices can be corrected by inserting a comma and a coordinator like *and, but, or, for, yet,* and *so*. Doing so creates a *compound* sentence with two independent clauses. Each clause has a subject and a verb. A comma comes *before* each one of these coordinators. Use the coordinator that best expresses the linkage between the two ideas.

I own an expensive car, <u>and</u> I like to repair it.

The *and* means that he likes to repair his car *in addition to* or *along with* owning it.

I own an expensive car, <u>but</u> I like to repair it.

The *but* means that he likes to repair his car *even though* or *in spite of the fact that* it is expensive.

I like to repair my car <u>for</u> it is an expensive one.

The *for* means that he repairs his car *because* the car cost so much.

I buy a car that needs repairs, <u>or</u> I buy an expensive one.

The *or* means that he makes a choice: he buys *either* one *or* the other kind of car.

I own an expensive car, <u>so</u> I like to repair it.

The *so* acts like *for:* it means *because* or *the reason why.*

EXERCISE 21.4

Read over the following sentences. Then fill in the conjunction that best expresses the relationship between them. Insert a comma in the right place.

EXAMPLE:

Both charities arrived at the same time to claim a body, <u>so</u> police had to fire shots in the air to stop the brawl.

1. The police arrested three corpse collectors from each side

_____, and _____ they wounded several others.

2. Each charity says the other pays collectors commissions _____, but_____ each denies doing so itself.

3. Both charities say they want to help the public _____, so, for_____ they earn "merit" in the Chinese religion.

4. Their form of public service is highly visible _____, and, so, for_____ it attracts public donations.

5. One charity was founded by an eleventh-century Chinese monk who nursed plague victims _____, and_____ he buried the dead.

6. It is the richest of Thailand's foundations _____, for, so_____ donations come to about $3.5 million a year.

7. This charity fields a fleet of 30 collection vehicles _____, and_____ uniformed crews man them.

8. They maintain four retrieval boats _____, and, but_____ they plan to buy two helicopters.

9. Their crews bring in 400 cadavers a month around Bangkok _____, and, so, for_____ business is booming.

EXERCISE 21.5

Add another sentence to each of those we have listed below. Use the connective we suggest, and insert a comma in the correct place. Be sure that the sentences make sense.

EXAMPLE:

I often drive to work too fast, for I get ready at the last minute.

1. I love to sleep late (and) _, and I am often late to work._

2. Everyone takes medicine at some time in his or her life (but) _, but I have never learned to like it._

3. Speaking before a group makes me nervous (so) _, so I always over-prepare._

4. We are required to speak from notes (or) _, (including,) or we must memorize our speeches._

5. Being well-prepared to speak helps me very much (yet) _, yet I always have butterflies in my stomach._

Section Three: Correcting by Replacing the Comma with a Semicolon

Another way to correct run-on sentences is to insert a semicolon at the boundary dividing independent clauses. A semicolon (;) is a period over a comma. It connects similar ideas. It interrupts the link between ideas more than a comma does. However, it separates less than a period does. The following word groups have two independent clauses; a semicolon by itself separates them.

Buying a home computer can be very difficult; hundreds of models and accessories are available.

Most of World War I was fought in France; this country suffered the most damage.

A thief stole my rims and tires; it cost me $200 to replace them.

EXERCISE 21.6

Insert a semicolon between the independent clauses in the following sentences. Make sure that the word groups on both sides of the semicolon are complete thoughts.

EXAMPLE: My friend is very impulsive; he often acts irresponsibly.

1. Chips was a sentry dog with the United States Army ; he was the first dog to be sent to Europe in World War II.
2. He landed in Sicily in 1943 ; Chips went with his division into combat.
3. His division fought its way into Germany ; Chips performed his most heroic deed there.
4. He attacked a German pilbox ; four enemy soldiers were forced to surrender.
5. The army awarded him the Purple Heart and Silver Star ; these awards were taken away later.
6. Army officials felt very awkward ; awarding medals to a dog was unusual.
7. Chip's company honored his heroics ; they presented him unofficially with battle ribbons.
8. Chips was discharged in 1945 ; his retirement was made official.

Section Four: Correcting by Using a Semicolon and a Connector

Independent clauses may sometimes be separated by semicolons followed by transitional words or phrases:

His mother works for the school district; <u>however</u>, his father is self-employed.

The semicolon separates independent clauses, while *however* signals a difference or contrast.

I need to become better organized; <u>therefore</u>, I need to buy a better alarm clock.

The transitional word *therefore* signals something added.

It is the time of year for a garage sale; <u>consequently</u>, I must clean out my closets and drawers.

The transitional word *consequently* shows a result.

Listed below are connectives that often follow a semicolon. A comma should mark off the independent clause that follows.

Type of Connective	Similar Connectives
furthermore	also, besides, in addition, likewise, moreover, similarly [**showing something added**]
however	despite this, instead, nonetheless, on the other hand, still [**showing something different**]
therefore	as a result, accordingly, because of this, consequently, hence, thus [**showing a result**]
for example	for instance, to illustrate, that is, namely [**pointing out**]
then	afterwards, eventually, later, meanwhile, presently, sometime, soon, subsequently, thereafter [**telling when something happens**]

EXERCISE 21.7

Answers will vary.

Insert a transitional word or phrase from the list above in the spaces below. Use a semicolon before the word or phrase and a comma after it.

EXAMPLE: Jumbo is a very common elephant name<u>; moreover,</u> it is the name of the largest elephant ever held in captivity.

1. Jumbo seemed mountainous in size _____ <u>; still,</u> _____ he lived in the London Zoological Gardens.

2. The English both loved and admired the large elephant _____ <u>; because of this,</u> many English children rode on Jumbo's back.

3. In 1882 Jumbo was sold to P. T. Barnum's circus _____ <u>; subsequently,</u> everyone, even Queen Victoria, protested.

4. It was too late to change their minds _____ <u>; therefore,</u> Jumbo was

sent to the United States __; consequently,__ he became famous there.

5. At age sixteen, he was the largest elephant in captivity __; moreover,__ he was larger than any elephant in the wild.

6. Jumbo died a bizarre death in 1885 __; afterwards,__ he was mourned by millions.

7. After a show, Jumbo and another elephant were led across a railroad track __; suddenly,__ a freight train roared by.

8. Jumbo became frightened and ran __; as a result,__ his head was crushed by the train.

Section Five: Correcting by Using Subordination

You can also correct run-ons and comma splices by using subordination. One of the independent clauses can be connected to the other by a word like *because, after,* or *when.* We discuss subordination more fully in Chapter 14, "Sentence Variety." The following subordinating words may be used to link a dependent thought to an independent one:

after	if, even if	when, whenever
although, though	in order that	where, wherever
as	since	whether
because	that, so that	which, whichever
before	unless	while
even though	until	who, whoever
how	what, whatever	whose

The following examples connect clauses with subordinating words:

Because Frisbee throwing is an art, you can't simply pick one up and throw it.

The first clause is connected to the second by the subordinating word *because.*

I love to throw Frisbees *because* I have done so all my life.

The first clause is connected to the second by the subordinating word *because.*

329

After you have thrown a frisbee for an hour, the snapping motion often begins to hurt your arm.

The first clause is connected to the second by the subordinating word *after*.

Remember: If the subordinate clause comes first, mark it off with a comma. If it comes last, use no punctuation. Do **not** use a semicolon (;) with a subordinating word.

EXERCISE 21.8

The sentences below include either run-ons or comma splices. Correct them by using one of the subordinating words listed above.

1. _____Although_____ Most home improvement people are honest, some are outright crooks.

2. Some exterminators promise to eliminate termites with a quick spritz of this or that _____even though_____ ridding a house of termites involves pumping in chemicals.

3. Always get a clear, detailed contract _____because_____ no contract can be too detailed.

4. _____After_____ A homeowner with a minor roof leak arranges to have broken shingles replaced, the contractor announces bad news.

5. _____Because_____ The decking is rotted out and has to be replaced, the job will cost thousands of dollars instead of hundreds.

6. Get another professional opinion before doing anything _____in order that_____ you aren't pushed into a hasty decision.

7. _____When_____ You add a room or finish an attic, you usually put dry wall on the interior walls.

8. _____If_____ The contractor installs dry wall, it is not as thick as the contract specifies.

9. _____Although_____ The thinner material looks the same and is cheaper, it provides less insulation.

10. _____While_____ Water-resistant dry wall is green, regular dry wall is gray.

Guarding Against Run-Ons and Comma Splices

1. Read your sentences aloud, or ask someone else to do so. When your (or their) voice drops or pauses, you need to add or replace some punctuation: a period, a semicolon, or a comma.

2. Count your sentences: if you don't have very many in your paragraph or essay, you may have written run-ons or used comma splices.

3. Look for words that signal run-ons. These include the following:

then	now	however	I
finally	suddenly	you	he, she
there	we	they	who
consequently		moreover	therefore

4. Correct your errors in the following ways:

- End the first clause with a *period;* begin the next one with a *capital letter.*

- Insert a *comma* followed by a coordinator like *and, but, or, for, yet,* or *so.*

- Insert a *semicolon* and a transitional word or phrase like *however* or *therefore.* Follow the word or phrase with a *comma.*

- Use a subordinating word like *after, because,* or *since. Remember:* If you begin the first clause in your word group with one of these words, mark the first clause off from the second clause with a comma.

REVIEW EXERCISE 21.9

Some of the following sentences are correct. Others are run-ons or contain comma splices. Correct the sentences with mistakes by (a) inserting a period and capital letter, (b) inserting a semicolon, or (c) adding a semicolon, transitional phrase, and comma.

1. Rome's leaders have been debating a serious problem.

2. They hope to close down their McDonald's.

3. It is located on the edge of the Piazza di Spagna, this is one of Rome's most beautiful squares.

4. The square becomes packed hundreds of hungry "sandwich fanatics" flock to McDonald's.

5. The noise and smell became overpowering, clothing designer Valentino complained to the mayor.

6. He claimed he could not work he could not design clothes.

331

7. City officials reacted, they made many attempts to close the restaurant.

                                     ; however,

8. They claimed that the company altered a historic building only the facade was historic.

9. Then they cited a fire law McDonald's had illegally converted a window to a fire escape.

                          ; therefore,

10. The window was originally a door, the charge was dropped.

                      ; therefore,

11. Other attempts also failed pro-McDonald's Romans want to replace the Communist mayor with Clint Eastwood.

REVIEW EXERCISE 21.10

Correct the sentences below that have mistakes by (a) inserting a period and capital letter, (b) inserting a semicolon, or (c) adding a semicolon, transitional phrase, and comma.

1. *, so*
   I'm an independent person I like doing things without outside interference.

2. *; moreover,*
   Independence is part of every person's ego, it is stronger in some people than in others.

3. *, for*
   I learned independence from my parents they learned to do everything on their own.

4. *; in addition,*
   Independence gives me self-confidence, a positive attitude backs it up.

5. *, for*
   I plan to get a college degree this will give me higher earning power.

6. *; as a result,*
   My positive attitude helps me get out of tangles, I am eager to expand my knowledge.

7. *; however,*
   Self-reliance varies with people's attitudes my outlook is always positive.

8. *;*
   Outside interference makes me unhappy, I like to decide on my own goals.

9. *; consequently*
   My father married at the age of twenty he found himself working in a retail job.

10. *, for*
    He lacked enough money to go to college there weren't many other jobs in the area.

Answers to every other question in this chapter's exercises are included below.

EXERCISE 21.1

2. I entered this university as a transfer student. They didn't accept many of my credits.
4. A course in the principles of management should transfer anywhere in the country. The university should accept it even if the numbers are different.
6. My fight for these credits will never end. It is a challenge to me to get the rules changed.
8. I would enjoy sky diving. This sounds like an awesome adventure.
10. In Colorado I skied down slopes at 50 miles an hour. That gave me a feeling of high spirits.

EXERCISE 21.2

2. A van glides quietly through deserted city streets. Then a voice squaks over the radio: "Crash on Lang Suan Lane."
4. The police hang back squeamishly. The men in the van scurry over to the corpse.
6. Finally, they trundle the body off to a hospital for an autopsy. One man stays behind to mop up the pavement.
8. This charity has done this for many years. It has had the streets to itself.
10. Field workers dash to the scene of accidents first. This brought competition for corpses.

EXERCISE 21.3

2. They have helped me with my finances.
4. Therefore, I must study hard.

EXERCISE 21.4

2. Each charity says the other pays collectors commissions, but each denies doing so itself.
4. Their form of public service is highly visible, and (so, for) it attracts public donations.
6. It is the richest of Thailand's foundations, for (so) donations come to about $3.5 million a year.
8. They maintain four retrieval boats, and (but) they plan to buy two helicopters.

EXERCISE 21.5

2. Everyone takes medicine at some time in his or her life, but I have never learned to like it.
4. We are required to speak from notes, or we must memorize our speeches.

EXERCISE 21.6

2. He landed in Sicily in 1943; Chips went with his division into combat.
4. He attacked a German pillbox; four enemy soldiers were forced to surrender.
6. Army officials felt very awkward; awarding medals to a dog was unusual.
8. Chips was discharged in 1945; his retirement was made official.

EXERCISE 21.7

2. The English both loved and admired the large elephant; because of this, many English children rode on Jumbo's back.
4. It was too late to change their minds; therefore, Jumbo was sent to the United States; consequently, he became famous there.
6. Jumbo died a bizarre death in 1885; afterwards, he was mourned by millions.
8. Jumbo became frightened and ran; as a result, his head was crushed by the train.

EXERCISE 21.8

2. Some exterminators promise to eliminate termites with a quick spritz of this or that even though ridding a house of termites involves pumping in chemicals.
4. After a homeowner with a minor roof leak arranges to have broken shingles replaced, the contractor announces bad news.
6. Get another professional opinion before doing anything in order that you aren't pushed into a hasty decision.
8. If the contractor installs dry wall, it is not as thick as the contract specifies.
10. While water-resistant dry wall is green, regular dry wall is gray.

REVIEW EXERCISE 21.9

2. Correct.
4. The square becomes packed, for hundreds of hungry "sandwich fanatics" flock to McDonald's.
6. He claimed he could not work; he could not design clothes.

8. They claimed that the company altered a historic building; however, only the facade was historic.

10. The window was originally a door; therefore, the charge was dropped.

REVIEW EXERCISE 21.10

2. Independence is part of every person's ego; moreover, it is stronger in some people than in others.

4. Independence gives me self-confidence; in addition, a positive attitude backs it up.

6. My positive attitude helps me get out of tangles; as a result, I am eager to expand my knowledge.

8. Outside interference makes me unhappy; I like to decide on my own goals.

10. He lacked enough money to go to college, for there weren't many other jobs in the area.

Verb Agreement, Present Tense

Section One: Defining Subject–Verb Agreement

In the present tense, the number of subjects and verbs must **agree.** Thus, if a subject is singular, it must take a verb with a singular ending. If a subject is plural, its verb must have a plural ending.

ENDINGS OF PRESENT-TENSE VERBS

Present-tense verbs must end in *-s* or *-es* with the following subjects: a singular *person* or *thing*, or *he, she,* or *it.* Here are some examples:

One person: The *boy* rips open the envelope.

The singular form of its subject, *boy,* takes the singular form of the verb, rip<u>s</u>.

One thing: The *sycamore* shimmers in the sunlight.

The singular form of the subject, *sycamore,* takes the singular form of the verb, shimmer<u>s</u>.

He: *He* laughs.

The singular form of the subject, *he,* takes the singular form of the verb, laugh<u>s</u>.

She: *She* dances gracefully.

The singular form of the subject, *she,* takes the singular form of the verb, dance<u>s</u>.

It: *It* intrigues me.

The singular form of the subject, *it,* takes the singular form of the verb, intrigue<u>s</u>.

338

EXERCISE 22.1   *Underline the subject once and the correct verb twice in each of the following sentences.*

EXAMPLE: At Bellevue Hospital in New York City an injured person sit/sits in the emergency room.

1. A New Yorker arrive/arrives at the restaurant straight from the office.

2. He eat/eats and run/runs to a show.

3. In Los Angeles, a diner get/gets a salad with something in it.

4. It look/looks fluffy and glitzy.

5. An Angeleno watch/watches calories.

6. Typical L.A. lunches feature/features the inevitable salad.

7. A New Yorker dine/dines with her best customers and make/makes deals.

8. Steve Martin catch/catches this yearning for the right table in the right spot in his movie *L.A. Story.*

9. Restaurant owners tell/tells him what main dish to order.

10. California cuisine include/includes light fare decorated with greens.

11. Californians check/checks out their dining strategies.

12. They relax/relaxes better than someone from Manhattan.

13. A New York waiter act/acts quieter, more professional than one in California.

14. It help/helps his tips.

15. Rock stars wake/wakes up between three and five in the afternoon.

Section Two: Irregular Verbs: Be, Do, Go, and Have

Some verbs like *be, do,* and *have* present special problems. They don't just add *-s* or *es* in the present tense. They actually change form. Look over the charts below:

To Do—Present Tense

Singular	Plural
I **do**	We **do**
You **do**	You **do**
He, she, it **does**	They **do**

To Be—Present Tense	
Singular	**Plural**
I **am**	We **are**
You **are**	You **are**
He, she, it **is**	They **are**

To Have—Present Tense	
Singular	**Plural**
I **have**	We **have**
You **have**	You **have**
He, she, it **has**	They **have**

EXERCISE 22.2

Add the correct present-tense verb to the blanks below.

EXAMPLE: Every artist (to have) <u>has</u> some source of inspiration.

1. Max Ernst (to have) _____ has _____ his hundredth birthday this year.

2. He (to be) _____ is _____ a brilliant maker of images.

3. His paintings (to have) _____ have _____ strength and ediginess.

4. He (to do) _____ does _____ his best work with collage, which means "gluing."

5. He (to have) _____ has _____ a knack for marrying things that (to do) _____ do _____ not belong together.

6. Collage (to be) _____ is _____ a static relative of film cutting.

7. His first collage, *Celebes,* (to be) _____ is _____ one of his funniest.

8. It (to have) _____ has _____ its beginnings in a photo of a corn bin.

9. We (to do) _____ do _____ not know who invented collage.

WE IS TEMPORARY

340

10. Ernst (to be) _____is_____ in love with images that count things.

11. They (to have) _____have_____ a factual neutrality.

12. In the '50s his works (to be) _____are_____ illustrations rather than true paintings.

13. They (to do) _____do_____ not affect us as deeply as his early work.

14. Ernst's work (to be) _____is_____ always open to chance.

15. You (to do) _____do_____ need to look at what Ernst (to do) _____does_____ with collage.

Section Three: Interruptions of Subject and Verb

Sometimes a prepositional phrase or clause comes between the subject and the verb. This may result in an agreement problem. To test for agreement, first, find the subject. See if the **signal** words below follow the subject:

- A preposition like *to*, *for*, *over*, or another similar word.
- The noun that follows a preposition. It is *never* the subject of a sentence.
- A word beginning a relative clause: *who*, *which*, *what*, *where*, *that*.

Then cross out prepositional phrases or relative clauses following the subject.
Finally, identify the verb. See if it agrees with the subject.

    subject   prepositional phrase   verb (plural)
The *men* on board, ~~still in their cabins~~, *pull* on orange life jackets.

The prepositional phrase, *in their cabins*, interrupts the plural subject *men* and the plural verb *pull*.

    subject   clause   verb (singular)
But the *water*, ~~which creeps over the engineer's knees~~, soon *reaches* the air-intake valves.

The relative **which** clause, *which creeps over the engineer's knees*, interrupts the singular subject *water* and the singular verb *reaches*.

EXERCISE 22.3   *Read over the sentences below. Cross out any prepositional phrases or relative clauses. Underline the subject once and the correct verb twice.*

1. Belize, ~~with its rain forests and jaguars,~~ is tiny.

2. Ruins, ~~which are still unrestored,~~ dot the lowland forests.

3. Belize, ~~for fishermen,~~ is a paradise.

4. Baron Bliss Day ~~on March 9~~ commemorates an eccentric English nobleman.

5. Belize ~~in its obscurity~~ gets only 1 percent of the tourist traffic to Central America.

6. Belize City, ~~which every guidebook dismisses as a noisy dump,~~ is full of intrusive hustlers.

7. The outer islands, ~~which include the Turnette Islands,~~ are geared up for sporting tourism.

8. The barrier reef, ~~which runs parallel to the coast,~~ lies less than a mile offshore.

9. Mangroves and shallow flats ~~to the west~~ stretch towards the sea.

10. Tourists ~~who go fishing~~ find it impossible not to catch something.

11. A handsome and well-run lodge ~~on Ambergris Cay~~ has all the best guides.

12. Their welcoming committee ~~of two ospreys~~ greets the arriving angler with shrill wheeps of alarm.

Section Four: Uncommon Structures

A singular verb must follow an indefinite pronoun subject like *either, neither, each, one,* or *every one.* Singular present-tense verbs end with *-s* or *-es.*

Either (one)   *Either* pecan pie or chocolate cake *is* available for dessert.

Either is a singular subject meaning "either one." It takes the singular verb *is.*

Neither (one)   *Neither* a cobra nor a rattlesnake *is* a satisfactory pet.

Neither is a singular subject meaning "neither one." It takes the singular verb *is.*

Each (one)   *Each* of the boys *plays* well.

Each is a singular subject meaning "each one." It takes the singular verb *plays.*

One (of)   *One* of them comes to the party.

One is a singular subject meaning "one, not both or more." It takes the singular verb *comes.*

Every one (of)   *Every one* of the mechanics picks up his tools.

Every one is a singular subject meaning "Every one of them." It takes the singular verb *picks.*

Every student shivers in the cold.

The word *every* is followed by a singular noun, *student* in this case, which takes the singular verb, *shivers.*
However, if one subject is singular and the other one is plural, the verb agrees with the noun closest to it:

Judy *or* her twin sisters always *bring their* favorite cookies to parties.

The second part of the subject, *twin sisters,* is plural. Since it is closest to the verb, it takes the plural verb *bring.* The pronoun *their* is also plural, referring back to its antecedent, *sisters.*

The surgeons *or* the nurse carefully *places* the scalpel on the table.

The second part of the subject, *nurse,* is singular. Since it is closest to the verb, it takes the singular verb *places.*

He is one of the students who study hard.

Because the word *who* refers to the plural word *students,* the verb *study* is also plural.

EXERCISE 22.4

Underline the subject once and the correct verb twice in each sentence.

1. Each of my friends Susie and Tracy is/are meeting me at the mall.

2. One of them, Susie, is/are a 5' 2" blonde.

3. Every one of us decide/decides to head down to Georgetown.

4. Either one of us is/are ready to drive.

5. One of the hottest bars in town, Neon's, is/are open all night.

6. Every one of us want/wants to dance to the band.

7. One of the girls, Tracy, has/have to leave for college the next morning.

8. Each of us decide/decides to head towards home.

9. Neither Tracy nor the others at the party feel/feels like driving.

10. Every one of us start/starts to go to sleep.

Section Five: Initial Use of *There* and *Here*

When a sentence begins with the word *there* or *here*, normal sentence order is reversed, and the verb comes *before* the subject rather than after it. Remember: the words *there* and *here* are never subjects themselves. When they start a sentence, look for the subject *after* the verb. The subject will be the first noun or pronoun you find that is *not* in a prepositional phrase.

There   *There* are flowers planted underneath it.

The true subject, *flowers*, takes the plural verb *are*.

Here   *Here* is a tree in the garden.

The true subject, *tree*, takes the singular verb *is*.
You can usually figure out the correct verb by reversing the word order:

```
        verb   subject
Here | is | a tree | in the garden.
```

EXERCISE 22.5   *Underline the subject once and the verb twice in the following sentences. Remember: cross out prepositional phrases that may confuse you.*

1. There is/are a few good techniques for failing college courses.

2. Here is/are the best way to begin—don't show up for class.

3. There is/are other ways of doing it.

4. There is/are disagreements among my friends about the next step.

5. Here is/are the set of directions I've been looking for.

6. There seem/seems to be a few responsible students in the class.

7. Here is/are the policies of the college on grading.

8. There is/are one particular policy regarding transfer credit.

9. Here is/are the computer and printer I've been looking for.

10. There seem/seems to be many survival techniques in a difficult course.

Section Six: Verb Agreement in Questions

In questions, the subject usually follows the verb, or comes between the helping and main verb:

How do you prepare for a garage sale?

The plural verb *do . . . prepare* agrees with the plural subject, *you.*

Why is this junk filling my closet?

The singular verb *is . . . filling* agrees with the singular subject, *junk.*
You can usually figure out the correct verb by reversing the word order:
"You *do prepare*" or "Junk *is filling.*"

EXERCISE 22.6

Underline the subject once and the correct verb twice in the following sentences.

1. What is/<u>are</u> the best <u>places</u> to start cleaning out?

2. Is/<u>are</u> my .32 <u>revolvers</u> on the top shelf?

3. Where is/<u>are</u> the best <u>places</u> to hide them?

4. When is/<u>are</u> <u>John and Robert</u> bringing their truck over?

5. Why <u>is</u>/are my <u>daughter</u> trying to climb up here?

6. How do/<u>does</u> my <u>sister</u> <u>feel</u>/feels about getting a used toy for Christmas?

7. Why <u>do</u>/does <u>I</u> keep <u>forgetting</u> I have them?

8. <u>What</u> make/<u>makes</u> this so exciting?

9. Where is/<u>are</u> the best <u>places</u> to sell my pocket books?

10. Who is/<u>are</u> those <u>people</u> in my front yard?

A rare case in which the interrogative word is the subject.

Section Seven: Verb Agreement in Relative Clauses

Dependent clauses beginning with *who, which,* or *that* are called **relative clauses.** The verb in these clauses must agree with the word referred to by *who, which,* or *that.*

Let me describe a strange person *who works with me.*

Who refers to the singular word *person.* It takes the singular verb "work<u>s</u>."

He is the only one of the students *who wears* a coat and tie.

Since *who* refers to the singular *one,* the singular verb *wears* agrees with it.

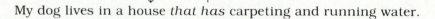

My dog lives in a house *that has* carpeting and running water.

That refers to the singular word *house*. It takes the singular verb *has*.

EXERCISE 22.7

In the following sentences, underline the word referred to by a wh- or th- word once. Underline the correct verb twice.

EXAMPLE: By official estimate, there are thousands of phobias that bother/bothers people.

1. Some people who do/does not like to wear clothes are called vestiophobes.

2. Almost everyone has some form of zoophobia, which is/are the fear of animals.

3. Acrophobia affects many men and women who is/are afraid of heights.

4. There are four names for the fear of thunder, which is/are astraphobia, caraunophobia, keraunophobia, and tonitrophobia.

5. This is almost matched by the names which apply/applies to the fear of loneliness—autophobia, eremophobia, and monophobia.

6. Some point to the nuclear bomb, which is/are responsible for a large number of new phobias.

7. People have other fears that relate/relates to modern living.

8. One unusual phobia that affect/affects people is arachibutyrophobia, the fear of getting peanut butter stuck to the roof of your mouth.

9. Generally, a person who is/are bothered by phobias knows that they is/are unreasonable.

10. One phobia which involve/involves fear of flying is often cured by group therapy.

REVIEW EXERCISE 22.8

The following sentences contain errors in subject–verb agreement. Underline the subjects once and the correct verbs twice.

1. Tom and Susan, a couple nearing thirty, has/have two children.

2. The kids is/are in school, and Susan decide/decides to go back to work.

3. The money help/helps, but Tom is/are feeling stressed.

4. Suddenly, Susan have/has a promising career, and Tom's own career is/are slowing down.

5. <u>Researchers</u> is/<u>are finding</u> that when a working <u>wife</u> ease/<u>eases</u> the strain on the budget, <u>she may</u> also demoralizes/<u>demoralize</u> her husband.

6. Current economic <u>developments</u> makes/<u>make</u> the idea of a single family provider obsolete.

7. Why is/<u>are</u> the husband's <u>feelings</u> a problem?

8. In theory many <u>men</u> today accepts/<u>accept</u> the idea of a working wife.

9. In fact, not <u>everyone</u> are/<u>is</u> happy with the situation.

10. Both <u>men and women</u> has/<u>have</u> identity crises.

11. Furthermore, <u>men</u> is/<u>are</u> not helping with the housework.

12. Every <u>man</u> are/<u>is</u> not splitting the domestic load.

13. <u>Sociologists</u> believes/<u>believe</u> crisis <u>time</u> have/<u>has</u> come for two-earner families.

14. In fact, if the wife's <u>salary</u> are/<u>is</u> significantly more than her husband's, the marriage may be temporary.

**REVIEW
EXERCISE 22.9**

In the sentences below, underline the correct verb twice and the word it agrees with once.

1. Although <u>speech</u> are/<u>is</u> not one of my better subjects, <u>I</u> usually makes/<u>make</u> good grades in it.

2. Our <u>instructor</u>, who drive/<u>drives</u> a laundry truck on the side, ask/<u>asks</u> us to make up a commercial.

3. <u>One</u> of the class members, who are/<u>is</u> a football player, do/<u>does</u> his commercial on shaving cream.

4. <u>He</u> rolls up his trousers and shave/<u>shaves</u> his legs.

5. There is/<u>are</u> <u>hoots and chuckles</u> from the rest of the class.

6. <u>I</u> bases/<u>base</u> my commercial on selling a brand of soda <u>pop</u> which pep/<u>peps</u> you up.

7. <u>One</u> of my friends help/<u>helps</u> me out.

8. <u>One</u> of his jobs are/<u>is</u> to taste the soda and say, ''Wow!''

9. <u>I</u> uses/<u>use</u> an iced tea can which I wraps/<u>wrap</u> with colored paper.

10. When <u>he</u> take/<u>takes</u> a big drink of the fake soda, <u>he</u> spit/<u>spits</u> the tea out.

11. He says, ''<u>This</u> taste/<u>tastes</u> terrible!''

12. At this time, the <u>color</u> of my cheeks are/<u>is</u> beet red.

13. Neither I nor my helper feel/feels too happy about this experiment that go/goes wrong.

Answer Key

Answers to every other question in this chapter's exercises are included below.

EXERCISE 22.1

2. He eats, runs
4. It looks
6. lunches feature
8. Steve Martin catches
10. cuisine includes
12. They relax
14. It helps

EXERCISE 22.2

2. is
4. does
6. is
8. has
10. is
12. are
14. is

EXERCISE 22.3

2. Ruins, [which are still unrestored], dot the lowland forest.
4. Baron Bliss Day [on March 9] commemorates an eccentric English nobleman.
6. Belize City, [which every guidebook dismisses as a noisy dump], is full of intrusive hustlers.
8. The barrier reef, [which runs parallel to the coast], lies less than a mile offshore.
10. Tourists [who go fishing] find it impossible to catch something.
12. Their welcoming committee [of two ospreys] greets the arriving angler with shrill wheeps of alarm.

EXERCISE 22.4

2. <u>One</u> of them, Susie, <u>is</u>/are a 5′ 2″ blonde.
4. <u>Either</u> <u>one</u> of us <u>is</u>/are ready to drive.
6. <u>Every</u> <u>one</u> of us want/<u>wants</u> to dance to the band.
8. <u>Each</u> of us decide/<u>decides</u> to head towards home.
10. <u>Every</u> <u>one</u> of us start/<u>starts</u> to go to sleep.

EXERCISE 22.5

2. Here <u>is</u>/are the best <u>way</u> to begin—don't show up for class.
4. There is/<u>are</u> <u>disagreements</u> among my friends about the next step.
6. There <u>seem</u>/seems to be a few responsible <u>students</u> in the class.
8. There <u>is</u>/are one particular <u>policy</u> regarding transfer credit.
10. There <u>seem</u>/seems to be many survival <u>techniques</u> in a difficult course.

EXERCISE 22.6

2. My .32 <u>revolvers</u> <u>are</u>
4. <u>John</u> <u>and</u> <u>Robert</u> <u>are</u>
6. My <u>sister</u> (does) <u>feel</u>
8. <u>What</u> <u>makes</u>—a rare case in which the interrogative word is the subject
10. Those <u>people</u> <u>are</u>

EXERCISE 22.7

2. <u>zoophobia</u> <u>is</u>
4. <u>names</u> <u>are</u>
6. <u>bomb</u> <u>is</u>
8. <u>phobia</u> <u>affects</u>
10. <u>phobia</u> <u>involves</u>

REVIEW EXERCISE 22.8

2. <u>kids</u> <u>are</u>, <u>Susan</u> <u>decides</u>
4. <u>Susan</u> <u>has</u>, <u>career</u> <u>is</u>
6. <u>developments</u> <u>make</u>
8. <u>men</u> <u>accept</u>
10. <u>men</u> <u>and</u> <u>women</u> <u>have</u>
12. <u>man</u> <u>is</u>
14. <u>salary</u> <u>is</u>

REVIEW EXERCISE 22.9

2. <u>instructor</u> <u>drives</u>, <u>asks</u>
4. <u>he</u> <u>shaves</u>
6. <u>I</u> <u>base</u>, <u>pop</u> <u>peps</u>
8. <u>one</u> <u>is</u>
10. <u>he</u> <u>takes</u>, <u>he</u> <u>spits</u>
12. <u>color</u> <u>is</u>

The great explorer Fenton paused and then dove into the crystal waters of the Amazon.

Verb Agreement, Past Tense

SECTION ONE: Past Tense of Regular Verbs
SECTION TWO: Past Tense of Irregular Verbs
SECTION THREE: Handling the Verb *To Be* in the Past Tense
SECTION FOUR: Handling the Verbs *Can/Could*, *Will/Would* in the Past Tense

Section One: Past Tense of Regular Verbs

Regular verbs in the past tense end in *-d* or *-ed*:

> God creat*ed* man, but could do better.
> Yesterday, my heater burn*ed* out.
> She dream*ed* about her boyfriend last night.

Created, *burned* and *dreamed* are all regular verbs in the past tense. All of these verbs have *-ed* endings.

Remember: If the verb ends in *y*, change the *y* to *i* and then add *-ed*. In the past tense, marr*y* becomes marr*ied*, and bur*y* becomes bur*ied*.

EXERCISE 23.1   *Fill in the past-tense form of the regular verbs in brackets.*

EXAMPLE: An executive just (retire) <u>retired</u> from a job at age 52.

1. He had (work) _____ worked _____ there for thirty years.

2. With his savings, he (purchase) _____ purchased _____ a small chocolate company.

3. This company (serve) _____ served _____ the Chicago area.

4. The executive (believe) _____ believed _____ he (possess) _____ possessed _____ fine marketing skills.

5. However, he soon (neglect) _____ neglected _____ his business.

6. Instead of going to the office, he (dawdle) _____ dawdled _____ at home.

7. He (delay) _____ delayed _____ going to work every day.

8. In the meantime, his company (founder) _____ foundered _____ from lack of leadership.

9. In a survey, nearly half of the students (admit) _____ admitted _____ they (procrastinate) _____ procrastinated _____ on writing term papers.

10. Their reasons (vary) _____ varied _____ .

11. Most often, they (fear) _____ feared _____ failure.

12. The executive had never (operate) _____ operated _____ a business by himself before.

13. The responsibility (terrify) _____ terrified _____ him.

14. As a result, he (exaggerate) _____ exaggerated _____ his fears.

15. When he (talk) _____ talked _____ through his fears, he (realize) _____ realized _____ how unrealistic they were.

Section Two: Past Tense of Irregular Verbs

A number of verbs called **irregular verbs** do not form their past tense by adding -*d* or -*ed*. Instead, they do so with internal changes.

> A burglar *broke* into a Chinese restaurant.
> He *fell* into a chip fryer.
> The fellow *found* no money.

In these sentences,

- *broke* is the past tense of *break*
- *fell* is the past tense of *fall*
- *found* is the past tense of *find*.

Here is a list of irregular verbs:

Simple Form	Past Tense
be, am, is	was, were
become	became
begin	began
bend	bent
bite	bit

Simple Form (cont.)	Past Tense (cont.)
blow	blew
break	broke
bring	brought
bought	bought
build	built
catch	caught
choose	chose
come	came
creep	crept
cut	cut
do	did
draw	drew
drink	drank
drive	drove
eat	ate
fall	fell
feed	fed
feel	felt
fight	fought
find	found
fly	flew
forget	forgot
forgive	forgave
freeze	froze
get	got
give	gave
go	went
grow	grew
have	had
hide	hid
hit	hit
hold	held
hurt	hurt
keep	kept
knew	knew
lay	laid
lead	led
let	let
lie	lay
lose	lost
make	made
meet	met
pay	paid
put	put
read	read

Simple Form (*cont.*)	Past Tense (*cont.*)
ride	rode
rise	rose
run	ran
see	saw
sell	sold
send	sent
set	set
shine	shone
shrink	shra[**u**]nk
sing	sang
sit	sat
sleep	slept
speak	spoke
speed	sped
spend	spent
stand	stood
steal	stole
stink	sta[**u**]nk
strike	struck
swim	swam
take	took
teach	taught
tear	tore
tell	told
think	thought
throw	threw
wake	waked, woke
wear	wore
win	won

EXERCISE 23.2

Locate the present-tense irregular verbs in the sentences below. Then fill in the past tense for each one. If you are unsure, check the list above. Do not guess.

EXAMPLE: A while ago, I (find) <u>found</u> my office in disarray.

1. I (know) _____<u>knew</u>_____ my filing system was inadequate.

2. To make matters worse, my secretary (get) _____<u>got</u>_____ pregnant and quit.

3. I (feel) _____<u>felt</u>_____ so anxious just thinking about the cleanup.

4. I (begin) _____<u>began</u>_____ to put it out of my mind.

5. Finally, I (tell) _____ told _____ myself to take action.

6. It (is) _____ was _____ a great relief when I (take) _____ took _____ that first step.

7. Working five minutes at a time (breaks) _____ broke _____ the tension.

8. I (know) _____ knew _____ I needed a publisher for my first book.

9. I (am) _____ was _____ an unknown author, and my book (is) _____ was _____ long-winded.

10. Ultimately, I (find) _____ found _____ a publishing house and an editor I liked, Maria.

11. She (tells) _____ told _____ me it would become a best-seller.

12. I (go) _____ went _____ home with Maria's advice ringing in my ears.

13. However, for ten days, I (sit) _____ sat _____ at my desk.

14. Finally, I (take) _____ took _____ a sheet of paper and (write) _____ wrote _____ down my negative thoughts.

15. The moment I (get) _____ got _____ the thoughts on paper, I (feel) _____ felt _____ a flood of relief.

Section Three: Handling the Verb *To Be* in the Past Tense

The verb *to be* changes in the past tense depending on person. The chart below lays out agreement between subjects and the forms of this verb:

To Be—Past Tense

	Singular		Plural	
Subject		**Verb**	**Subject**	**Verb**
First person:	**I**	**was**	**we**	**were**
Second person:	**you**	**were**	**you**	**were**
Third person:	**he**			
	she	**was**	**they**	**were**
	it			

Remember: Both first-person *I* and third-person *he, she,* and *it* take the same past-tense form: *was.*

EXERCISE 23.3

Choose the correct form of the past tense of the verb to be *in the sentences below. Check the chart above if you are uncertain.* Note: *Proper nouns take third person verbs.*

1. (Was/Were) _____ Was _____ Barbie's design lifted from a German doll named "Lilli"?

2. The real Barbie (was/were) _____ was _____ the daughter of Ruth and Eliot Handler.

3. Brigitte Bardot, with her perky good looks, (was/were) _____ was _____ one of the real-life Barbie models.

4. Grace Kelly's classy blondness (was/were) _____ was _____ also reflected in Barbie's design.

5. The first Barbie dolls (was/were) _____ were _____ sold for three dollars.

6. Barbie's features (was/were) _____ were _____ based on prevailing standards of beauty in 1959.

7. Why (wasn't/weren't) _____ weren't _____ the kissing Barbies a success?

8. Barbie's costumes (was/were) _____ were _____ definitely high fashion.

9. Wedding gowns (were/was) _____ were _____ the most popular Barbie outfits.

10. Whenever new costumes (was/were) _____ were _____ planned for the doll, Mattel designers (was/were) _____ were _____ sent to Europe to see Dior collections.

11. In the '70s, she (was/were) _____ was _____ an exercise nut in leotards, but by 1980, Barbie dolls (was/were) _____ disco singers wearing glitter togs.

12. How many fans (was/were) _____ were _____ in the Barbie Fan Club last year? (Wasn't/Weren't) _____ Weren't _____ there over 600,000 members worldwide?

13. A Barbie clothing line for real girls (was/were) _____was_____ introduced in 1986, but it (wasn't/weren't) _____wasn't_____ a success.

14. (Wasn't/Weren't) _____Wasn't_____ Barbie a college student once at State College?

15. My sister (was/were) _____was_____ a Barbie fan when she (was/were) _____was_____ only twelve; she (was/were _____was_____ always buying new clothes for her dolls.

Section Four: Handling the Verbs *Can/Could, Will/Would* in the Past Tense

The past tense of *can* is *could*.
Like many modern cities, Cahokia *can*not handle growth.
Their cornfields *could* not retain their fertility.

In the first sentence, the word *can* is present tense. In the second sentence, the word *could* is past tense.

EXERCISE 23.4   *Fill in either* can *or* could *in the sentences below.*

1. Warfare, disease and social unrest _____could_____ have added to the decline.

2. The first Americans were Asians, who _____could_____ have come over 12,000 years ago.

3. Modern Americans _____can_____ find great pleasure in diversity.

4. Columbus _____could_____ not explain why he enslaved the gentle Arawaks.

5. Women _____could_____ not attend councils in some tribes.

6. We _____can_____ now appreciate the genius of the Indian Mound Builders.

7. Pioneers _____can_____ not believe that Indians had built them.

8. Visitors _____can_____ stand atop a mound in the Ohio Valley.

9. At the time of the fall equinoxes, one _____can_____ still have a clear view of the sun.

10. This view _____could_____ also be found at Stonehenge.

11. Savages _____could_____ not have created these circles, squares, and octagons.

12. One of these earthworks _____can_____ cover four square miles.

13. Every explorer and settler _____could_____ smell smoke.

14. Visitors reported that sycamores _____could_____ grow seven feet in diameter.

15. New England trout that were nearly two feet long _____could_____ be found.

Would is often the past-tense form of *will*.

The president's wife *will* receive up to 10,000 pieces of mail next month. A largely volunteer staff *would* screen them and pass on a sampling of several hundred.

In the first sentence, the future is viewed from the present. In the second sentence, the past is seen from the present.

EXERCISE 23.5

Fill in either present-tense will *or past-tense* would *in the following sentences.*

1. A tableware company in Asia _____will_____ begin making plates and bowls of oatmeal.

2. After using them, diners _____would_____ either eat them or throw them away.

3. San Francisco Artisans _____will_____ scavenge junkyards for old inner tubes.

4. Then they _____<u>would</u>_____ make bags, belts, skirts, and vests out of them.

5. The average man _____<u>would</u>_____ rather shower than take a bath.

6. He _____<u>will</u>_____ also cry about once a month on the average.

7. The average American woman _____<u>would</u>_____ cry about four times as much.

8. The average man _____<u>will</u>_____ fall in love about six times during his life.

9. He _____<u>would</u>_____ not ask for directions when he's in the car.

10. He _____<u>will</u>_____ eat his corn on the cob in circles, not straight across.

REVIEW EXERCISE 23.6

Identify the verbs in the following sentences. Then write in the correct past-tense form above each verb.

             struck
1. Last year, vehicles strike deer over a half-million times.

             produced
2. However, collisions with all animals produce only 131 human fatalities in

    1989.

             resulted
3. However, the accidents result in thousands of serious injuries to people.

        thought   were
4. People think deer are creatures of the deep forests.

          adapted
5. However, deer adapt to suburbia.

     napped   got
6. They nap all afternoon and get up for dinner.

         would
7. In Maryland, deer will graze contentedly where tanks fire their guns.

             could
8. Deer can be one of nature's most adaptable species.

             gave
9. Suburbia gives the best protection for today's deer.

             became
10. From Chicago to Portland, Bambi becomes a "rat with antlers."

             tripled
11. During the 1980s, the number of deer virtually triple in Maryland.

             found
12. Homeowners and their children find deer ticks embedded in their skin.

             grew
13. In the past decade or so, the deer population grows to an estimated 25

million.

             caused
14. Increased use of fertilizer cause yields of corn to soar.

             led
15. This good eating leads to a higher deer population.

REVIEW EXERCISE 23.7

Check over the following paragraph for errors in forming the past tense. Cross out any incorrect verbs. Then write in the correct past-tense form above the line.

             chosen
Miss Moya Ann Church was ~~choosen~~ Miss National Smile Princess. Sixty seconds

        lost   *worn*
later, the 25-year-old beauty queen ~~losed~~ her crown. She had ~~weared~~ it very

       found   *thought*   *lost*
briefly. It was eventually ~~finded~~ in a pile of rubbish. She ~~thinked~~ it was ~~losed~~

       found,   *was*
forever. Once it was ~~founded,~~ she smiled with relief. This ~~were~~ the last time she

smiled   *broke*   *locked*
~~smile~~ all week. The next day her car ~~breaked~~ down, and she ~~lock~~ herself out of

       left   *got*
her house. When she ~~leaved~~ home to phone the garage, she ~~getted~~ a parking

       gone
ticket. "So many things have ~~went~~ wrong that you have to smile," she said.

       left
After her final photographic session, her train ~~leaved~~ without her.

Answer Key

The answers to alternate questions in this chapter's exercises are included below.

EXERCISE 23.1

2. purchased
4. believed, possessed
6. dawdled
8. foundered
10. varied
12. operated
14. exaggerated

EXERCISE 23.2

2. got
4. began
6. was, took
8. knew
10. found
12. went
14. took, wrote

EXERCISE 23.3

2. was
4. was
6. were
8. were
10. were, were
12. were, Weren't
14. Wasn't

EXERCISE 23.4

2. could
4. could
6. can
8. can
10. could
12. can
14. could

EXERCISE 23.5

2. would
4. would
6. will
8. will
10. will

REVIEW EXERCISE 23.6

2. produced
4. thought, were
6. napped, got
8. could
10. became
12. found
14. caused

REVIEW EXERCISE 23.7

Sixty seconds later, the 25-year-old beauty queen *lost* her crown. It was eventually *found* in a pile of rubbish. Once it was *found*, she smiled with relief. The next day her car *broke* down, and she *locked* herself out of her house. "So many things have *gone* wrong that you have to smile," she said.

Co-workers in the office soon noticed that although Louise's hair had an incredible body and luster from using the new experimental conditioner and mousse, her head had definitely shrunk.

Past-Participle Verbs

SECTION ONE: Regular Verb Past Participles
SECTION TWO: Irregular Verb Past Participles
SECTION THREE: Handling the Present Perfect Tense
SECTION FOUR: Handling the Past Perfect Tense
SECTION FIVE: Handling the Past Participle as an Adjective

Section One: Regular Verb Past Participles

The **past participle** of regular verbs may follow a helping verb like *have* or *has.* The resulting verb will contain more than one word.

Present Tense	Past Tense	Past Participle with Helping Verb
She walks	She walked	She has walked
They work	They worked	They have worked
Robin jumps	Robin jumped	Robin has jumped

Walks, work, and *jumps* are all regular verbs. Their past participles are *walked, worked,* and *jumped.*

The **past tense** and **past participle** of regular verbs like these end in *-d* or *-ed.*

Remember: The helping word *has* agrees with third-person nouns and pronouns like *he, she,* and *it.* The helping word *have* agrees with everything else.

EXERCISE 24.1

Each of the following sentences includes a past-tense regular verb. Add the helping verb have *or* has *to change these past-tense verbs to past participles.*

1. Our week's specials _____ have _____ appeared on Wednesday.

2. On Tuesdays, we _____ have _____ geared up by changing our displays.

3. He _____ has _____ walked a few steps to a five-foot stack of boxes.

4. They _____ have _____ placed unprofitable items such as flour and sugar down low.

5. People _____ have _____ looked for these staples anyway.

6. They _____have_____ priced a pound of whole carrots at 35 cents.

7. The store _____has_____ tagged precut carrot sticks at $1.89 per pound.

8. Intercom announcements _____have_____ interrupted the Muzak hundreds of times a day.

9. A woman _____has_____ waved a coupon.

10. A sign _____has_____ announced a two-for-the-price-of-one deal on popcorn.

11. The store's manager _____has_____ proposed a deal.

12. He _____has_____ substituted a store brand for a national brand.

Section Two: Irregular Verb Past Participles

When **irregular verbs** change tense from present to past, they change their form—*begin* changes to *began*, for example. When these verbs change tense from past to past participle, they often (though not always) change their form again, as with *began* to *begun*.

Present Tense	Past Tense	Past Participle with Helping Verb
She begins	She began	She has begun
They pay	They paid	They have paid
Robin teaches	Robin taught	Robin has taught

Irregular verbs change from present tense to past tense to past participle in unpredictable ways. You must memorize these changes. In the sentences above, *begun*, *paid*, and *taught* are all past-participle forms of irregular verbs. The past tense and past participle of *paid* and *taught* are the same.

Here is a list of the most common irregular verbs for your reference.

Irregular Verbs

Present Tense	Past Tense	Past Participle (often formed with *have* or *has*)
be	was, were	been
become	became	become
begin	began	begun

367

Present Tense (cont.)	Past Tense (cont.)	Past Participle (often formed with *have* or *has*) (cont.)
bend	bent	bent
bite	bit	bit
blow	blew	blown
break	broke	broken
bring	brought	brought
build	built	built
buy	bought	bought
catch	caught	caught
choose	chose	chosen
come	came	come
creep	crept	crept
cut	cut	cut
do	did	done
draw	drew	drawn
drink	drank	drunk
drive	drove	driven
eat	ate	eaten
fall	fell	fallen
feed	fed	fed
feel	felt	felt
fight	fought	fought
find	found	found
fly	flew	flown
forget	forgot	forgotten
forgive	forgave	forgiven
freeze	froze	frozen
get	got	gotten
give	gave	given
go	went	gone
grow	grew	grown
have	had	had
hide	hid	hidden
hit	hit	hit
hold	held	held
hurt	hurt	hurt
keep	kept	kept
know	knew	known
lay	laid	laid
lead	led	led
let	let	let
lie	lay	lain
lose	lost	lost
make	made	made

Present Tense *(cont.)*	Past Tense *(cont.)*	Past Participle (often formed with *have* or *has*) *(cont.)*
meet	met	met
pay	paid	paid
put	put	put
read	read	read
ride	rode	ridden
rise	rose	risen
run	ran	run
see	saw	seen
sell	sold	sold
send	sent	sent
set	set	set
shine	shone	shone
shrink	shrank or shrunk	shrunken or shrunk
sing	sang	sung
sit	sat	sat
sleep	slept	slept
speak	spoke	spoken
speed	sped	sped
spend	spent	spent
stand	stood	stood
steal	stole	stolen
stink	stank or stunk	stunk
strike	struck	struck
swim	swam	swum
take	took	taken
teach	taught	taught
tear	tore	torn
tell	told	told
think	thought	thought
throw	threw	thrown
wake	waked, woke	waked, woken
wear	wore	worn
win	won	won
write	wrote	written

EXERCISE 24.2

Each of the sentences below includes an irregular verb in the past tense. Change the verb to past participle by substituting have *or* has *and the past-participle form of the verb.*

1. Our chief financial officer (gave) _____has given_____ a tour of headquarters to a special group.

369

2. A particle of dust (made) _____<u>has made</u>_____ the core of the crystal.

3. It (drew) _____<u>has drawn</u>_____ water molecules to its surface.

4. The wind (blew) _____<u>has blown</u>_____ the flake through layers of temperature and humidity.

5. The flake repeatedly (struck) _____<u>has struck</u>_____ other flakes.

6. It finally (fell) _____<u>has fallen</u>_____ to earth.

7. The flake (wore) _____<u>has worn</u>_____ the scars of a turbulent life.

8. We (thought) _____<u>have thought</u>_____ of snowflakes as six-pointed stars.

9. The International Commission on Snow and Ice (thought) _____<u>has thought</u>_____ of several categories of flakes.

10. Different conditions (brought) _____<u>have brought</u>_____ each kind of flake into being.

11. Low, wet storms (gave) _____<u>have given</u>_____ birth to tree-shaped flakes.

12. Colder, drier clouds (began) _____<u>have begun</u>_____ the formation of needle-shaped flakes.

EXERCISE 24.3   *Each of the following sentences includes a past-tense verb in parentheses; it may be regular or irregular. Substitute* have *or* has *and the past-participle form of the verb.*

1. Every year, Michael Krasnow (gain) _____<u>has gained</u>_____ about seven pounds between Thanksgiving and New Year's.

2. He never (gets) _____<u>has gotten</u>_____ seriously obese.

3. However, he says, "My pants (start) _____<u>have started</u>_____ feeling tight."

4. "I (know) _____<u>have known</u>_____ it's time to take off weight."

5. For several weeks Krasnow (follows) _____<u>has followed</u>_____ his own program.

6. With it he (cuts) _____<u>has cut</u>_____ fat from his diet and (gets) _____<u>has gotten</u>_____ more exercise.

7. He (eats) _____ has eaten _____ more homemade low-fat soups, such as minestrone.

8. He (cuts) _____ has cut _____ his own firewood and (builds) _____ has built _____ houses with his friends.

9. He (hauls) _____ has hauled _____ and (chops) _____ has chopped _____ wood for his stove.

10. By mid-February his clothes (fit) _____ have fit _____ fine again.

Section Three: Handling the Present Perfect Tense

The **present perfect tense** is used to indicate that an action which began in the past is still going on in the present. The present perfect tense consists of the present tense of the verb *to have* along with the past participle.

1. Past tense: My teenage son *bagged* groceries at the supermarket.

2. Present perfect tense: My teenage son *has bagged* groceries at the supermarket.

In the first sentence, the boy once *bagged* groceries, but no longer does so. The verb *bagged* is past tense. In the second version, the boy *has bagged* groceries in the past and is still doing it. The use of *has bagged* suggests that the action is still going on.

EXERCISE 24.4

Read over the following sentences. Underline the verb that best expresses the meaning.

1. We (graduated/have graduated) from Marine boot camp a month ago.

2. They (sent/have sent) my buddy Jack to sick bay.

3. For the past several months, my sister (wrote/has written) to my brother, who is stationed in Germany.

4. In her last letter, she (asked/has asked) him how he liked the food.

5. The three of them (sat/were sitting) in silence for several minutes.

6. One lieutenant (looked/was looking) quickly at his watch.

7. He (shook/was shaking) his head once or twice.

8. My secretary (posted/has posted) unusual news articles on our bulletin board on a regular basis.

371

9. Ancient societies (rose/had risen) and (fell/fallen) here for centuries.

10. In 1492, 90 million people (lived/had lived) in the Western Hemisphere.

Section Four: Handling the Past Perfect Tense

The **past perfect tense** is used to indicate that one particular action occurred earlier in the past than another particular action. The past perfect tense consists of the past tense of the verb *to have* along with a past participle verb.

1. Past tense   He *went* all the way to the edge of the cliff.
2. Past perfect tense: He *had gone* all the way to the edge of the cliff before he *looked* over.

In the first sentence, *went* is past tense. No other past action followed it. In the second sentence, the past perfect *had gone* indicates that this action had been completed before another action in the past, *looked.*

EXERCISE 24.5

Read over the following sentences. Underline the form of the verb that best expresses the meaning: the past tense *or the* past perfect tense.

1. It all started one balmy day as I (sat/had sat) on the bench in our driveway.

2. Before I walked out, my son (perfected/had perfected) the art of skateboarding.

3. In my day we (kept/had kept) our feet firmly planted on the ground.

4. Before my son offered me his skateboard, I (gathered/had gathered) my courage.

5. As I stood upright on the board, he (offered/had offered) me encouragement.

6. I zoomed off after I (positioned/had positioned) my feet.

7. Our drive to the hospital seemed endless as my son (recounted/had recounted) every detail of my ride.

8. The doctor asked why I (rode/had ridden) a skateboard at my age.

9. I told him that I (spent/had spent) quality time with my son.

10. He responded that I (did/had done) a dumb thing.

Section Five: Handling the Past Participle as an Adjective

In its **past participle** form, a verb can follow a linking verb as an *adjective* (a word describing a noun):

The shaft is *bent*.

The adjective *bent* describes the subject, *shaft.*
Sometimes the past participle serves as an adjective before a noun or pronoun:

This *bent* shaft vibrates badly.

The adjective *bent* describes the subject, *shaft.*

EXERCISE 24.6

Change the verb in parentheses into a past participle adjective in the sentences below.

1. Cardiologists can see (thicken) _____thickened_____ arteries with a heart scanner.

2. The machine uses (focus) _____focused_____ sound waves.

3. A single crack of ultrasound results in (pulverize) _____pulverized_____ kidney stones.

4. Ultrasound has no (know) _____known_____ harmful effects.

5. The (scatter) _____scattered_____ sound waves reflect back to their source.

6. The resulting echoes can then be (collect) _____collected_____ and electronically (convert) _____converted_____ .

7. After the war, echo pictures were too (smudge) _____smudged_____ for reliable diagnoses.

8. The machine fires pulses and then listens for (reflect) _____reflected_____ echoes.

9. Ellie Morris is a (dedicate) _____dedicated_____ sonographer.

10. She was called to the hospital when a woman complained of a (smother) _____smothered_____ feeling.

11. Her heart was quickly (scan) _____scanned_____ .

12. With her problem (diagnose) _____diagnosed_____ , the woman quickly returned home.

13. Cardiologists can now see which muscles are (starve) _____starved_____ of blood.

14. Mothers of twins are no longer (surprise) _____surprised_____ .

15. X-rays have some (know) _____known_____ harmful effects.

EXERCISE 24.7   *Read over the following sentences for errors in the past participle. For uses that are incorrect, write in the correct verb form above the incorrect one.*

                                      outlived
1. Throughout the modern world, women have outlive men.

      fallen
2. At birth, the ratio has fell to about 105 boys to 100 girls.

      left
3. By age 30, there are only enough men leave to match the number of women.

      started
4. By then, women have start building a lead.

      looked
5. One researcher has look at the top ten or twelve causes of death.

      reported
6. She has report that every one kills more men than women.

      self-inflicted
7. Some of the reasons have been self-inflict.

      received
8. One group of farmers had receive $66 million from the Bureau of Reclamation.

      gotten
9. The same group had got $379 million from the Department of Agriculture.

      deserved
10. The money was well deserve, they believed.

      reported
11. Having report these facts, the government tried to explain.

      irrigated
12. The $66 million was paid for irrigate land.

Correct. 13. The $379 million had been paid to limit surplus crops.

restored
14. Somehow, sanity must be restore to government programs.

embarrassed
15. The Department of Interior seems embarrass by these disclosures.

REVIEW EXERCISE 24.8

All but one of the following sentences include errors in the use of the past participle. Correct them.

experienced
1. Bob Shannon, football coach, had experience a problem.

skipped
2. His unbelievably talented quarterback prospect had skip the off-season workouts.

seemed
3. He had seem to feel that his raw talent would prevail.

Correct. 4. The boy had a bazooka for an arm and could run.

expected
5. Shannon had always expect his quarterbacks to set an example of self-discipline.

demoted
6. When the player was demote to wide receiver, he angrily transferred to another school.

won
7. After Shannon's team had met its rival, they had win 61 to 7.

surrounded
8. Shannon's teams have been surround by crime and violence.

erupted
9. On several occasions, gun battles have erupt on adjacent streets.

depressed
10. The economy in East St. Louis is depress.

recruited
11. Despite handicaps, the coach has recruit a small band of warriors.

responded
12. His players have respond to his tough demands.

trampled
13. Their opponents have been trample.

disciplined
14. Before they enter his program, his players have been poorly discipline.

15. The coach's father was disable. *disabled*

16. Education had became his passion. *become*

Answer Key

The answers to alternate questions in this chapter's exercises are included below.

EXERCISE 24.1

2. have
4. have
6. have
8. have
10. has
12. has

EXERCISE 24.2

2. had made
4. have blown
6. has fallen
8. have thought
10. have brought
12. have begun

EXERCISE 24.3

2. has gotten
4. have known
6. has cut, has gotten
8. has cut, has built
10. have fit

EXERCISE 24.4

2. sent
4. asked
6. looked
8. has posted
10. lived

EXERCISE 24.5

2. had perfected
4. had gathered
6. had positioned
8. had ridden
10. had done

EXERCISE 24.6

2. focused
4. known
6. collected, converted
8. reflected
10. smothered
12. diagnosed
14. surprised

REVIEW EXERCISE 24.7

2. fallen
4. started
6. reported
8. received
10. deserved
12. irrigated
14. restored

REVIEW EXERCISE 24.8

2. skipped
4. Correct
6. demoted
8. surrounded
10. depressed
12. responded
14. disciplined
16. become

Did you say "rat" or "rats," dear?

Nouns

Section One: Singular and Plural

A noun is a word that points to a person, place, thing, or quality. A noun that points to just one of these is *singular*. A noun that points to more than one is *plural*. Many nouns form their plurals by adding -*s* or -*es*.

Singular	Plural
a girl	the girls
a monkey	the monkeys
the class	the classes

The nouns *girl* and *monkey* both form their plurals by adding -*s*. The noun *class* becomes plural by adding -*es*.

If a noun ends in *y*, change the *y* to *i* and then add -*es*.

Singular	Plural
boysenberry	boysenberries
eighty	eighties
fly	flies
sky	skies

If a noun ends in *ay*, *ey*, or *oy*, simply add *s* for the plural.

Singular	Plural
day	days
key	keys
boy	boys

Some nouns form their plurals in unusual ways:

Singular	Plural
appendix	appendices
child	children
criterion	criteria
foot	feet
goose	geese
man	men
mouse	mice

380

Singular (cont.)	Plural (cont.)
tooth	teeth
woman	women

Nouns ending in *f* or *fe* form their plurals in several ways:

Singular	Plural
belief	beliefs
hoof	hoofs OR hooves
knife	knives
life	lives
proof	proofs
self	selves
scarf	scarfs OR scarves
wife	wives

Nouns formed from two or more words base their plurals on the last word, unless they are hyphenated:

Singular	Plural
fisherman	fishermen
misstep	missteps
mother-in-law	mothers-in-law
passer-by	passers-by

A few words are the same in both the singular and the plural:

Singular	Plural
apparatus	apparatus (OR apparatuses)
deer	deer
fish	fish (OR fishes)
moose	moose
sheep	sheep
species	species

If you are unclear about forming the plural of a word, look it up in your dictionary or use the "Spell" utility of your word-processing program.

EXERCISE 25.1

Form the plural of these singular nouns.

1. crisis _____ crises _____
2. man _____ men _____
3. seventy _____ seventies _____
4. apparatus _____ apparatus (OR apparatuses) _____
5. appendix _____ appendices _____
6. deer _____ deer _____
7. sister-in-law _____ sisters-in-law _____
8. woman _____ women _____
9. mouse _____ mice _____

10. knife	knives	16. mother-in-law	mothers-in-law
11. toy	toys	17. proof	proofs
12. goose	geese	18. key	keys
13. self	selves	19. life	lives
14. tooth	teeth	20. misstep	missteps
15. hoof	hoofs, hooves		

Section Two: Specifier Words: Singular and Plural

A specifier word indicates whether the following noun will be singular or plural. Some of these specifier words indicate that a singular noun will follow:

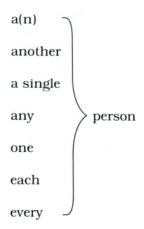

a(n)
another
a single
any
one
each
every
⎫ person

Other specifier words indicate that a plural noun will follow:

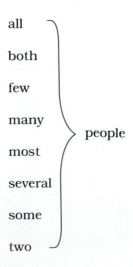

all
both
few
many
most
several
some
two
⎫ people

EXERCISE 25.2 *Some of the singulars and plurals used in the sentences below are incorrect. Find the errors and write in the correct forms above the incorrect ones.*

woman
1. Why can't every women be more like a man, the lament goes.
   scientists
2. Many scientist are searching for an answer.
   researchers
3. Some researcher have presented intriguing possibilities.
                                             researcher
4. Men and women are different, a researchers theorizes.
        differences   brains
5. There are some slight difference in the way their brain are constructed.
   men
6. Most man do better than women in tests of spatial ability.
                                                    concepts
7. Similarly, boys outperform girls in picturing most abstract concept.
                                          words
8. On the other hand, girls usually say a few word earlier than boys.
   studies   women
9. Several study have found that many woman speak longer sentences
        men
   than most man.
                                                            tests
10. Differences in the brains of men and women were shown by two test on

    brains obtained after autopsy.
                              sides
11. This might allow the two side of the brain to exchange more information.
    man
12. Every men may use the right side of his brain on abstract problems.

Section Three: Specifier Words with *Of*

Many specifier words are followed by a prepositional phrase beginning with *of* and *the.* The preposition usually takes a plural or grouping noun as its object. The writer uses this word group to separate one or more from a larger group.

one of the
each of the   } clocks *is*

most of the
several of the   } clocks *are*
some of the

Remember: the object of a preposition can never be the subject of a sentence. Thus, even though many words following *of* are plural, the verb is singular. The specifier word is the subject of the sentence:

1. *One* of the boys *is* smart.
2. *Each* of the clocks *strikes* twice.

EXERCISE 25.3

Some of the objects of the preposition of *are incorrect in the sentences below. Underline the correct word.*

1. One of the child's (tooth/<u>teeth</u>) had been loose for weeks.

2. However, neither of her (parent/<u>parents</u>) could figure the Tooth Fairy's going rate.

3. Each of her (parent/<u>parents</u>) felt confused.

4. Both of the (adult/<u>adults</u>) had received a quarter for baby teeth.

5. However, some of her (classmate/<u>classmates</u>) were getting a dollar for each of their (tooth/<u>teeth</u>).

6. Her parents relied on tradition for these kinds of (decision/<u>decisions</u>).

7. Knowing every one of their (choice/<u>choices</u>) could not be right, the parents settled on a quarter.

8. The mother substituted a quarter for the tooth under one of the girl's (pillow/<u>pillows</u>).

9. "She came!" the girl shouted the next morning, waving both of her (hand/<u>hands</u>).

10. "She was more beautiful than any of the (fairy/<u>fairies</u>) on TV!"

EXERCISE 25.4

Some of the singular and plural words in the sentences below are incorrect. Underline the correct word.

1. Americans have regarded each of their (birthday/<u>birthdays</u>) after 30 as a loss.

2. 30- to 39-year-olds are now the largest of the age (group/<u>groups</u>) in this country.

3. Getting older is one of those (thing/<u>things</u>) that are getting better.

4. We do lose some of our brain (cell/<u>cells</u>) with age.

5. My two (brother/<u>brothers</u>)-in-law seem to have lost more cells than most people.

6. However, connecting branches between each of our brain cells increase with (ages/<u>age</u>).

7. One of the (<u>criteria</u>/criterion) for a long, happy life is a sense of humor.

8. In most research (study/<u>studies</u>), people get healthier as they get older, particularly (woman/<u>women</u>).

9. Many (child/<u>children</u>) protect themselves with impulsive acting-out.

10. Creativity is one of those apparatus/<u>apparatuses</u>) which people use to survive.

REVIEW EXERCISE 25.5

Find the errors in the sentences below. Then write in the correct word above the incorrect one.

(1) Sometimes the best way to tackle something is to stop doing it. **(2)** Norman

<u>men   women</u>

Vincent Peale counsels busy man and woman to drop everything. **(3)** Simply

<u>criterion   chores</u>

walking for half an hour meets his criteria for relaxation. **(4)** Peale finds chore

<u>mysteries   solutions</u>

to do or just reads mystery as he waits for solution to his problems. **(5)** Some

<u>hours   periods</u>

of the best hour we spend can appear useless at first. **(6)** Spending long period

<u>beliefs</u>

of time idling about violates many of our deeply held believes. **(7)** We can't

<u>delays   songs</u>

control most of life's nagging delay. **(8)** One of Larry Gatlin's best country song

was composed during a Los Angeles traffic jam. **(9)** One sect, the Pennsylvania

<u>conveniences</u>

Amish, severely limits the use of modern convenience. **(10)** The perception of

<u>devices</u>

rushing seems to increase directly with the number of "time-saving" device.

<u>crises</u>

(11) Finally, a good vacation must allow one to ignore crisis by engaging in

thoroughly engrossing activities.

Answer Key

Answers to alternate questions for this chapter's exercises are included below.

EXERCISE 25.1

2. men
4. apparatus
6. deer
8. women

10. knives
12. geese
14. teeth
16. mothers-in-law
18. keys
20. missteps

EXERCISE 25.2

2. scientists
4. researcher
6. men
8. words
10. tests
12. man

EXERCISE 25.3

2. parents
4. adults
6. decisions
8. pillows
10. fairies

REVIEW EXERCISES 25.4

2. groups
4. cells
6. age
8. studies, women
10. apparatuses

REVIEW EXERCISES 25.5

2. men, women
4. chores, mysteries, solutions
6. periods, beliefs
8. songs
10. devices

Oscar and I are having a great time even though it is the end of our vacation.

Pronouns

SECTION ONE: Pronoun Agreement with Antecedents
SECTION TWO: Clear Pronoun Reference
SECTION THREE: Consistent Pronoun Point of View

Pronouns are words that take the place of nouns—names for persons, places, or things. Pronouns keep us from repeating nouns unnecessarily:

> Carla opened Carla's closet door and took out Carla's new hat to give to Carla's mother.

Personal pronouns improve this sentence considerably:

> Carla opened *her* closet door and took out *her* new hat to give to *her* mother.

Here are other examples of pronoun use:

> Frank and Jennifer started *their* new business.

The word *their* replaces *Frank and Jennifer*('s).

> George painted *his* car fuschia because *it* was *his* favorite color.

The word *it* stands for *fuschia*, and *his* takes the place of *George*.

> Making fireworks in a factory can be hazardous because *they* can ignite.

The word *they* refers back to *fireworks*.

Several agreement rules apply to pronouns:

- Pronouns must agree in number with the words they refer to—nouns, other pronouns, or phrases.
- Pronoun reference must be clear to avoid confusing the reader.
- Pronouns must keep a consistent point of view.

Section One: Pronoun Agreement with Antecedents

Pronouns replace or refer to other words like nouns, other pronouns, or phrases. The words to which they refer are called **antecedents.** If you remember that an antecedent is "what goes before," you will find this rule easy to follow.

1. The Prime Minister's wife painted *her* room pink because *it* was *her* favorite color.

388

2. When the team members saw the score *they* cheered.
3. The country believed *it* had a new hero because *he* had led a victorious army.

In the first sentence, *her* refers to *wife*, and *it* refers to *pink*. These words are all **singular**, referring to **one**. In the second sentence, *they* refers to *members*. These words are both **plural**, referring to **more than one**. In the third sentence, *it* refers to *country*, and *he* refers to *hero*. These words are all singular.

EXERCISE 26.1

For the sentences below, write the pronouns and their antecedents in the blanks at right.

	Pronoun	Antecedent
EXAMPLE: Bill Coleman stumbled upon a remote valley that *he* had never before seen.	he	Coleman
1. This remote valley had no telephone lines in it.	it	valley
2. In an article, Coleman described his time there.	his	Coleman
3. The valley people had created harmony between themselves and their land.	themselves / their	people / people('s)
4. Most of the 700 residents of this valley who lived there were Old Order Amish.	who	residents
5. Descendants of a strict religious sect, they avoid most strangers.	they	descendants
6. Although the Amish greeted Coleman with suspicion, they came to tolerate him.	they / him	Amish / Coleman
7. Coleman tried to document their daily lives without exploiting them.	their / them	(Amish's) / Amish
8. "I liked finding out about their little surprises; it helped me understand them."	I / their / it / me / them	(Coleman) / (Amish's) / finding out / (Coleman) / (Amish)

INDEFINITE PRONOUNS

Any word ending in *-one*, *-body*, or *-thing* is singular:

anybody	nobody
anyone	no one

389

everybody   one
everyone   somebody
someone   something

Everybody **wants** Sybil for *her* best friend.

Something **is** definitely wrong with my car.

Indefinite pronouns such as *everybody* and *something* require singular pronouns.

Each + a noun and *every* + a noun are also considered singular.

Each horse **is** circling the paddock.

OR

Every horse **is** circling the paddock.

Other indefinite pronouns are singular when used as subjects:

another   either
neither   much

Another man **wants** to revise the calendar.

Either idea **is** a good one.

Since both *another* and *either* are singular, they take singular verbs, *wants* and *is*.

EXERCISE 26.2

Underline the correct pronoun and verb.

EXAMPLE: On the Fourth of July, a special celebration took place in Chapel Hill, North Carolina; (it/he) (was/were) called Harry's reunion.

1. Harry's Bar and Grill opened in 1926, and many of the students visited (it/him) while (he/they) (was/were) attending the University of North Carolina.

2. Harry's sister-in-law and her husband took over the grill in 1940; (they/she/he) ran (it/them) until 1967 when their son took (him/her/it) over.

3. In the 1960s, (he/it) (was/were) the place to be.

4. Anybody could spend all day at Harry's, where (he or she/they) could eat, sit, or drink beer.

5. Former members of the *Daily Tar Heel Newspaper* and PlayMakers Repertoire, retired hippies and beatniks returned; (they/it) (was/were) the people who made Harry's the place (it/they) (was/were).

6. The group admitted (it/they) (were/was) hard to teach in those days.

7. Some agreed that (he or she/they) had made mistakes and used psychedelic drugs when (it/they) (were/was) in school.

8. Nonetheless, many of Harry's former customers (tell/tells) present-day students (he or she/they) should get involved.

9. A person should worry more about what (they/he or she) (doesn't/don't) say than about what (they/he or she) (do/does) say.

10. Some of Harry's people (is/are) now involved in advertising, real estate, writing, editing, reporting, and acting; (he or she/they) stayed involved, trying to make the world a better place for (his or her/their) children.

SINGULAR AND PLURAL ANTECEDENTS

Some indefinite pronouns are plural when used with the words *of, any, both, few,* or *many.* Unfortunately, some indefinite pronouns can be *either* singular or plural, depending on their usage. You must find which **noun** is being referred to by pronouns like *all, most, none, any, more,* or *some.* This will help you decide which verb form to use.

> *All* of the *pie* is left.

Since *pie* is singular, it takes a singular verb, *is.*

> *All* of the *cupcakes* are sold.

The word *cupcakes* is plural; it takes a plural verb, *are.*
In a clause following *who, which,* or *that,* the verb should agree with the noun to which it refers.

> Margaret is one of the students *who irritate* me.

The verb *irritate* refers to *students* and is plural.

> Margaret is the one who *irritates* me.

The verb *irritates* refers to *one* and is singular.

EXERCISE 26.3

Underline the correct form of the verb in the following sentences.

EXAMPLE: Some people (choose/chooses) unusual ways to make a living.

1. Some people who (have/has) always wanted to be clowns (go/goes) to clown training school in Venice, Florida.

2. Few of today's teenagers (considers/consider) becoming chimney sweeps.

3. Those who (put/puts) on the black suit and top hat and (learns/learn) their trade (makes/make) a very good living.

4. On the other hand, anyone who (prefer/<u>prefers</u>) peace and quiet (have/<u>has</u>) a slightly wider choice of jobs.

5. Someone who (like/<u>likes</u>) solitude can (<u>choose</u>/chooses) to become either a shepherd or a forest fire lookout.

6. Unfortunately, most of these jobs (doesn't/<u>don't</u>) pay very well, and the work is very lonely.

7. Most individuals (<u>forget</u>/forgets) the profession of farming Christmas trees, which (are/<u>is</u>) lonely but can be lucrative.

8. Not everybody (are/<u>is</u>) happy with solitude; some people (<u>like</u>/likes) to be where the action is.

9. Anybody who (enjoy/<u>enjoys</u>) crowds (have/<u>has</u>) a wider choice; some jobs that (<u>involve</u>/involves) people (<u>are</u>/is) street vending and belly dancing.

10. Someone who (like/<u>likes</u>) to move a lot and (<u>doesn't</u>/don't) mind long hours can be a carnival barker.

Section Two: Clear Pronoun Reference

A pronoun should refer to *some* specific word, and to *only* one word. Sometimes the word is not stated:

> "Dog days" begin in July, when *it* is hot and sultry.

The word *it* does not refer to some specific word earlier in the sentence.
The sentence should be revised to clear up the pronoun reference as follows:

> "Dog days" begin in July, when *the weather* is hot and sultry.

The pronoun reference is cleared up by substituting *the weather* for the vague *it.*
At other times, the pronoun reference is confusing:

> Frances told Mary that *she* wrote excellent letters.

The reader cannot tell whether the word *she* refers to *Frances* or *Mary.*
As revised, the sentence would read like this:

> Frances told Mary, "I write excellent letters." OR: Frances wrote excellent letters, she told Mary.

EXERCISE 26.4

Answers will vary.

Revise the following sentences, taking out vague or unclear pronoun references. Make your versions clear and specific.

1. I'll be typing weather forecasts into a computer when it gets cloudy.

    Revised: I'll be typing weather forecasts into a computer when the sky gets cloudy.

2. Sandie told her friend that she shouldn't have sent the flowers.

    Revised: Sandie told her friend, "You shouldn't have sent the flowers."

3. It is the best oil to protect your engine because it contains detergent.

    Revised: Oil that contains detergent protects your engine best. OR: To best protect your engine, use oil that contains detergent.

4. Campfires twinkled near the waves as they roared loudly.

    Revised: Campfires twinkled and roared loudly near the waves. OR: Campfires twinkled near the loudly roaring waves.

5. The launch was so dangerous that they ordered the viewing area evacuated.

    Revised: The launch was so dangerous that the officials ordered the viewing area evacuated. OR: The launch was so dangerous that the viewing area was ordered evacuated.

6. As Bill ate breakfast with Frank, he was friendly and talkative.

    Revised: Bill was in a friendly and talkative mood as he ate breakfast with Frank.

7. Joe Schmitt laid out our equipment in the suiting room, and it sparkled.

    Revised: Joe Schmitt laid out our sparkling equipment in the suiting room. OR: Joe Schmitt laid out our equipment in the sparkling suiting room.

8. At this base, they assign everyone a seat for liftoff.

    Revised: This base assigns everyone a seat for liftoff.

9. The mission commander told the astronaut that he would not be flying today.

    Revised: The mission commander said to the astronaut, "You will not be flying today." OR: The mission commander said that the astronaut would not be flying today.

10. In the command module they were ready for me.

    Revised: The command module was ready for me.

Section Three: Consistent Pronoun Point of View

Pronouns must agree with each other and with the main subject of the sentence. These pronouns should agree with the words they refer to:

Type of Person	Singular	Plural
First person	I (my, mine, me)	we (our, us)
Second person	you (your)	you (your)
Third person	he (his, him)	they (their, them)
	she (her)	they (their, them)
	it (its)	

Any person, place, or thing is a third-person word. Keep the same person and number you begin with.

Incorrect: I like blue skies that soothe and comfort *you.*

The first-person subject *I* shifts to the second-person *you.*

Revised: I like blue skies that soothe and comfort *me.*

Incorrect: If *you* eat bad mushrooms, the fungus can make *people* sick.

The second-person *you* shifts to the third-person *people.*

Revised: If *you* eat bad mushrooms, the fungus can make *you* sick.

EXERCISE 26.5   *Look over the sentences below for pronoun mistakes. Cross out errors and write in the correct form above the incorrect one.*

1. If financial problems plague you, ~~we~~ ^{us} often have to get a job.

2. Whenever we go into business for ourselves, ~~you~~ ^{we} need to put in long hours.

3. In the business world today, we usually need capital before ~~you~~ ^{we} start ~~your~~ ^{our} own business.

4. An independent business manager can usually take a vacation only when a relative or friend takes ~~your~~ ^{his or her} place.

5. When a person went to high school, ~~you~~ ^{he or she} needed to be an honor student.

REVIEW EXERCISE 26.6

Underline the correct pronoun or verb in the following sentences. Revise the sentence if necessary.

1. Few of Maria's children (stays/<u>stay</u>) at home.

2. Some people who want an education (goes/<u>go</u>) away to a university.

3. Anyone who (wear/<u>wears</u>) bright clothing (attract/<u>attracts</u>) a lot of attention.

4. She looks sharply at Ernesto and me, who (hides/<u>hide</u>) our eyes.

5. A person should read about politics if (they/<u>he or she</u>) (plan/<u>plans</u>) to vote.

6. Anybody could attend that school, and (they/<u>he or she</u>) could spend all day in the library if (they/<u>he or she</u>) wanted.

7. Every one of the workers (benefit/<u>benefits</u>) from the profits the company made.

8. Each of the drivers drove (their/<u>his or her</u>) favorite color car.

9. He went home to lunch, the main meal of (their/<u>his</u>) day.

10. He wonders about his children, who (wants/<u>want</u>) many things.

11. Each member of the family ate (their/<u>his or her</u>) favorite meal.

12. One of the engines had a sharp squeal in (their/<u>its</u>) gears.

Frank told Henry to apologize.

13. Frank told Henry that he should apologize.

Twenty-five people said that the car manufacturer had a faulty sedan.

14. Twenty-five people told the car manufacturer that they had a faulty sedan.

Henrietta's mother is an archeologist, but Henrietta does not want to become one.

15. Henrietta's mother is an archeologist, but Henrietta does not want to study it.

Answer Key

Answer to alternate questions in this chapter's exercises are included below.

EXERCISE 26.1

2. his, Coleman
4. who, residents
6. they, Amish; him, Coleman
8. I, Coleman; their, Amish('s); it, finding out; me, Coleman; them, Amish

EXERCISE 26.2

2. Harry's sister-in-law and her husband took over the grill in 1940; <u>they</u> ran <u>it</u> until 1967 when their son took <u>it</u> over.

4. Anybody could spend all day at Harry's, where <u>he</u> <u>or</u> <u>she</u> could eat, sit, or drink beer.

6. The group admitted <u>they</u> <u>were</u> hard to teach in those days.

8. Nonetheless, many of Harry's former customers <u>tell</u> present-day students <u>they</u> should get involved.

10. Some of Harry's people <u>are</u> now involved in advertising, real estate, writing, editing, reporting, and acting; <u>they</u> stayed involved, trying to make the world a better place for <u>their</u> children.

EXERCISE 26.3

2. Few of today's teenagers <u>consider</u> becoming chimney sweeps.

4. On the other hand, anyone who <u>prefers</u> peace and quiet <u>has</u> a slightly wider choice of jobs.

6. Unfortunately, most of these jobs <u>don't</u> pay very well, and the work is very lonely.

8. Not everybody <u>is</u> happy with solitude; some people <u>like</u> to be where the action is.

10. Someone who <u>likes</u> to move a lot and <u>doesn't</u> mind long hours can be a carnival barker.

EXERCISE 26.4

2. Sandie told her friend, "You shouldn't have sent the flowers."

4. Campfires twinkled and roared loudly near the waves. OR: Campfires twinkled near the loudly roaring waves.

6. Bill was in a friendly and talkative mood as he ate breakfast with Frank.

8. This base assigns everyone a seat for liftoff.

10. The command module was ready for me.

EXERCISE 26.5

2. Whenever we go into business for ourselves, <u>we</u> need to put in long hours.

4. An independent business manager can usually take a vacation only when a relative or friend takes <u>his</u> <u>or</u> <u>her</u> place.

REVIEW EXERCISE 26.6

2. Some people who want an education <u>go</u> away to a university.

4. She looks sharply at Ernesto and me, who <u>hide</u> our eyes.

6. Anybody could attend that school, and <u>he</u> <u>or</u> <u>she</u> could spend all day in the library if <u>he</u> <u>or</u> <u>she</u> wanted.

8. Each of the drivers drove <u>his</u> <u>or</u> <u>her</u> favorite color car.

10. He wonders about his children, who <u>want</u> many things.

12. One of the engines had a sharp squeal in <u>its</u> gears.

14. Twenty-five people said that the car manufacturer had a faulty sedan.

CHAPTER

27

*Confused and nearly exhausted, the great explorer Fenton slowly climbed
the rocky gorge to the sacred nose of Thantor (a primitive tribe of Elvis
impersonators).*

Using Modifiers

Section One: Distinguishing Between Adjectives and Adverbs

English uses two kinds of words to modify or describe other words: *adjectives* and *adverbs*. **Adjectives** describe, limit, or qualify nouns and pronouns:

> Coffee tastes better in *thick* mugs.
>
> It is hard to open an *ordinary milk* carton.

In the first sentence, the adjective *thick* modifies the noun *mugs*. In the second sentence, the adjectives *ordinary* and *milk* describe the noun *carton*. In most cases, adjectives come directly before the nouns or pronouns they modify.

Adverbs describe or modify the action of verbs, adjectives, other adverbs, even phrases, clauses, or sentences:

> On Larry King's TV show, callers phone in *nightly*.
>
> They claim they *really* love his show.

In the first sentence, the adverb *nightly* modifies the verb *phone* (*in*). In the second sentence, the adverb *really* describes the verb *love*.

Adverbs answer questions such as "How?" "Why?" "Where?" or "When?" They are located close to the words they modify. Most adverbs are derived from adjectives. Adverbs are usually spelled the same as adjectives, with the addition of *-ly*. The adjective *regular* becomes the adverb *regularly*, *even* becomes *evenly*, and *quick* changes to *quickly*. The forms are easily confused in a number of pairs:

bad	badly
sure	surely
good	well
real	really
slow	slowly
loud	loudly
quiet	quietly
quick	quickly
sharp	sharply
wrong	wrongly

He made a *wrong* turn.

The boy *wrongly* directed the motorist.

In the first sentence, the adjective *wrong* modifies the noun *turn.* In the second sentence, the adverb *wrongly* modifies the verb *directed.*

EXERCISE 27.1

Underline the correct adjective or adverb in the following sentences. Keep in mind that adjectives modify nouns or pronouns; adverbs describe verbs, adjectives, or other adverbs.

1. Larry King is (virtual/<u>virtually</u>) inescapable.

2. He trained himself by announcing the names of cars in a (<u>loud</u>/loudly) voice from the stoop of his family's apartment.

3. He earns more than $2 million (annual/<u>annually</u>) for his mouth.

4. A lady from Forth Worth calls to argue (sharp/<u>sharply</u>) about religion.

5. A guy in Pittsburgh is (real/<u>really</u>) interested in hockey.

6. Callers phone in (quick/<u>quickly</u>) from places like London, Tokyo, and Jidda, Saudi Arabia.

7. When asked about his (incredible/<u>incredibly</u>) popularity, King answers (slow/<u>slowly</u>).

8. He (simple/<u>simply</u>) isn't like anyone else who has earned such stature.

9. At 23, he (eager/<u>eagerly</u>) took a train to Miami, where he worked his way up (careful/<u>carefully</u>) at a small radio station.

10. When the morning disc jockey quit (sudden/<u>suddenly</u>), Larry filled the slot (competent/<u>competently</u>).

11. King poses as a regular guy who likes to ask (<u>unusual</u>/unusually) questions.

12. When his guests talk, he listens (quiet/<u>quietly</u>) and (intent/<u>intently</u>), unlike many talk show hosts.

13. He asked Richard Nixon if he felt (<u>weird</u>/weirdly) when he drove by the Watergate.

14. Reagan was asked if he got (real/<u>really</u>) frustrated by not being able to remember something.

15. He always asks authors why they (actual/<u>actually</u>) wrote a book.

Section Two: Distinguishing Between Comparative and Superlative

Many comparative adjectives and adverbs change their form or add a word to indicate a comparison of two people or objects:

Letter writing is *harder* than making a phone call.

George Bush is a *more famous* letter writer than Horace Piepkorn.

In the first sentence, letter writing is being compared with phoning. The comparative word, *harder*, adds the ending, *-er*. In the second sentence, George Bush is compared with Horace Piepkorn. The word *more* before *famous* indicates the comparison.

In the superlative degree, one person or thing is compared with two or more people or things:

One young reporter got a letter from the *closest* big-city paper, the *Toledo Blade*.

It was the *most exhilarating* letter he had ever received.

In the first sentence, one big-city paper is being compared with several others. In the second sentence, one letter is being compared with all others.

Short adjectives and adverbs form the **comparative** by adding *-er*. They form the **superlative** by adding *-est*.

Adjective	Comparative	Superlative
near	near*er*	near*est*
sturdy	sturdi*er*	sturdi*est*
slow	slow*er*	slow*est*

Adjectives and adverbs with two or more syllables usually form the **comparative** by using *more*. They form the **superlative** with the word *most*.

Adjective	Comparative	Superlative
fortunate	*more* (or *less*) fortunate	*most* (or *least*) fortunate
inactive	*more* (or *less*) inactive	*most* (or *least*) inactive
challenging	*more* (or *less*) challenging	*most* (or *least*) challenging

A number of two-syllable adjectives that end in a vowel sound (words like *dirty, shallow,* or *crazy*) change the *-y* to *i* and ad *-er* or *-est*.

Adjective	Comparative	Superlative
dirty	dirt*ier*	dirt*iest*
shallow	shallow*er*	shallow*est*
crazy	craz*ier*	craz*iest*

Be careful, however, not to use both *more* and *-er* to form the comparative degree, or both *most* and *-est* to form the superlative degree.

Not: The laundry could hardly have been *more* dirt*ier*.

Rather: The laundry could hardly have been dirt*ier*.

The adjective *good* is often used mistakenly in place of the adverb *well*. The adjective *good* describes a noun or pronoun, while the adverb *well* modifies verbs. The word *well* can also be used as an adjective describing good health.

Archie was a *good* quarterback.

He often played *well* under pressure.

Adjective	Comparative	Superlative
good	better	best
bad	worse	worst

Adverb	Comparative	Superlative
well	better	best
badly	worse	worst

EXERCISE 27.2

Underline the correct comparative or superlative form of the words indicated in the sentences below.

1. "When I make others feel (good/well) about themselves," he told me, "I feel (good/well) too."

2. Even though letter writing may take (longer/longest) than phoning, some busy people do it.

3. Later on, I got to know him (good/well).

4. I've tried to emulate writers who are (busier/busiest) than I am. The president may be the (busier/busiest) letter writer I know of.

5. A letter attaches a ~~more~~ (greater/greatest) importance to well-wishing than a phone call.

6. He keeps track of people more (careful/carefully) than most politicians.

7. Abraham Lincoln was perhaps our (most gifted/giftedest) note writer.

8. One of his (most famous/famousest) letters was a condolence to Mrs. Lydia Bixby, who had lost two sons in battle.

9. His wartime letter of loss recalls a (more recent/recenter) conflict.

10. As one woman wrote to a Gulf War soldier, they gradually became (warmer/warmest) friends.

11. Top corporate managers are usually (more tough/tougher) than other leaders.

12. Human beings find praise (more/most) enjoyable than criticism.

13. Giving people positive reinforcement was one of the (more/most) valuable contributions made by Donald Petersen, chairman of Ford.

14. Petersen turned the company around in the 1980s (more quickly/quicklier) than anyone would have believed.

15. Writing something sincere is (better/best) than filling someone's sails with smoke.

16. The thought is (more valuable/valuabler) than fancy stationery.

17. The use of superlatives like "(greater/greatest)," "(smarter/smartest)," or "(prettier/prettiest)" makes everyone feel good.

403

18. Norman Vincent Peale is the (better/best) three-sentence letter writer I have ever known.

19. He pens his letters (more carefully/carefuller) than I do.

20. His recent note made it (easier/easiest) for me to write some overdue notes.

Section Three: Avoiding Misplaced Modifiers

As the previous sections indicate, adjectives and adverbs are modifiers. Although many of them are single words, phrases or clauses may also describe other words.

WORDS

It looks like a *movie* stunt.

Someone dives *steeply* off a bridge.

In the first sentence, the word *movie* modifies the word *stunt*. (Note that a noun like *movie* can sometimes serve as an adjective.) In the second sentence, the adverb *steeply* modifies the word *dives*.

PHRASES

The bridge is 230 feet *above a river*.

He wears a long rubber cord tied *to his ankles*.

In the first sentence, the prepositional phrase *above a river* modifies the noun *feet*. In the second sentence, the prepositional phrase *to his ankles* modifies the predicate adjective *tied*.

CLAUSES

It's a sport called "bungy jumping" *that has become a tourist attraction* in Queenstown, in South Island.

Bungy jumping isn't the only daredevil activity *that has helped turn New Zealand into the Temple of Thrill*.

In the first sentence, the clause *that has become a tourist attraction* modifies the noun *jumping*. In the second sentence, the clause *that has helped turn New Zealand into the Temple of Thrill* modifies the noun *activity*.

If modifiers are not placed close to the words they modify, they may confuse or amuse the reader. Here are some examples:

Misplaced Modifiers	Corrected
The city of Osage, Iowa, *which its police department operates*, pays for the system.	The city of Osage, Iowa, pays for the system, which its police department operates. (*which its police department operates* modifies *system*)
Harvey dates only girls with red hair that like the outdoors.	Harvey dates only red-headed girls *that like the outdoors.*

A number of modifiers are commonly misplaced: *almost, only, just, even, hardly, nearly,* and *merely.* These words must be placed immediately before the words they modify.

    I *almost* counted 100 people at the party.

The sentence should read, "I counted *almost* 100 people at the party." This means that the speaker counted all the people at the party, but found fewer than 100.

    He nearly painted his room until eight o'clock.

The sentence should read, "He painted his room until *nearly* eight o'clock." This means that the *he* in the sentence stopped work before eight o'clock.

EXERCISE 27.3

Underline the words that are misplaced in the following sentences. Then rewrite the sentences to place the previously misplaced words nearer the words they modify.

1. Several philosophers in Holland are opening private practices tired of working in the mines of academe.

   Rewrite: In Holland, several philosophers, <u>tired of working in the mines of academe</u>, are opening private practices.

   Note: The phrase in Holland is moved to the beginning of the sentence to avoid confusion.

2. You can talk about anything you wish, like the meaning of life, at $50 an hour.

   Rewrite: You can talk about anything you wish, <u>at $50 an hour</u>, like the meaning of life.

3. In Papua, New Guinea, by the groom's family, the bride's clan must be paid a price.

   Rewrite: In Papua, New Guinea, the bride's clan must be paid a price <u>by the groom's family</u>.

4. A bride price, from investment bankers to farmers, is still paid by almost every groom.

   Rewrite: A bride price is still paid by almost every groom, <u>from investment bankers to farmers</u>.

405

5. In the Southern Highlands, worth about $6,200, the going rate is 20 pigs.

   Rewrite: In the Southern Highlands, the going rate is 20 pigs, worth about $6,200.

6. I once had a car that created a clearly lit path with a delay cutoff switch for the headlights.

   Rewrite: I once had a car with a delay cutoff switch for the headlights that created a clearly lit path.

7. Ants are among the dominant forces acting together of our terrestrial environment.

   Rewrite: Acting together, ants are among the dominant forces of our terrestrial environment.

8. The 880 known species except for the polar regions cover most of the land surfaces of the world.

   Rewrite: The 880 known species cover most of the land surfaces of the world except for the polar regions.

9. Ants turn most of the world's soil together with termites.

   Rewrite: Together with termites, ants turn most of the world's soil.

10. These tiny creatures colonized the earth including soldiers, nurses, farmers and hunters.

    Rewrite: Including soldiers, nurses, farmers, and hunters, these tiny creatures colonized the earth.

11. Desert ants in food for the rest of the colony carry home 15 to 20 times their own weight.

    Rewrite: Desert ants carry home 15 to 20 times their own weight in food for the rest of the colony.

12. The fire ant has burning compounds in its venom which has spread widely through the southern United States.

    Rewrite: The fire ant, which has spread widely through the southern United States, has burning compounds in its venom.

13. Large leaf cutters cut away fragments of leaves and flowers with powerful jaws.

Rewrite: <u>Large leaf cutters with powerful jaws cut away fragments of leaves</u> <u>and flowers.</u>

14. Among the ants I studied as a boy in Alabama, which is the largest genus of ants in the world, was a species of Pheidole.

    Rewrite: <u>Among the ants I studied as a boy in Alabama was a species of</u> <u>Pheidole, which is the largest genus of ants in the world.</u>

15. Now I, a huge and difficult undertaking, am studying the whole genus.

    Rewrite: <u>Now I am studying the whole genus, a huge and difficult under-</u> <u>taking.</u>

Section Four: Avoiding Dangling Modifiers

A modifier that begins a sentence must be followed immediately by the word it modifies. If it is not, it is called a **dangling modifier.** The word it modifies may not appear in the sentence at all. As a result, the reader must guess what word it modifies. The following sentence begins with a dangling modifier:

Working as a job counselor, my students needed my help.

At first glance, it appears that the phrase *working as a job counselor* describes *students.* The writer means that *he* was the job counselor. He could correct this problem in one of two ways.

1. Make the modifier a clause by adding a subordinating word such as *when, while, after,* or a similar word. Then add a subject and/or verb as needed. "While *I was* working as a job counselor. . . ."

2. Follow the modifier with the word it modifies: "While working as a job counselor, *I* found that my students needed my help."

Here are some more examples:

Dangling Modifier	Correction
Asking one correspondent her age, she became a little confused.	When I asked one correspondent her age, she became a little confused. (The phrase *asking one correspondent her age* should be rewritten to identify the person asking the question, not the person answering.)
Handing my boss a printout, he had to struggle to read the material.	When *I handed* my boss a printout, he had to struggle to read the material. (A rewritten version of the phrase *handing my boss a printout* should describe the person doing the handing, not the reader.)

407

Each of the sentences below includes a dangling modifier. Rewrite the sentence, correcting the problem.

1. Opening the door, his head was stuck inside.

   Rewrite: Opening the door, he put his head inside.

2. Running the four-mile course in full uniform, everyone was surprised by one of the conservation officers.

   Rewrite: Running the four-mile course in full uniform, one of the conservation officers surprised everyone.

3. Questioned about his attire, his reply amused me.

   Rewrite: Questioned about his attire, he amused me with his reply.

4. Standing knee deep in the water, three generations of dolphins played near me in the shallows.

   Rewrite: As I stood knee deep in the water, three generations of dolphins played near me in the shallows.

5. Rolling onto its back, a dolphin's pale belly is exposed.

   Rewrite: Rolling onto its back, a dolphin exposes a pale belly.

6. Whirling among us, their tails were flourished.

   Rewrite: Whirling among us, they flourished their tails.

7. Naming the dolphin Charlie, it became a mascot to Watts.

   Rewrite: When Watts named the dolphin Charlie, it became his mascot.

8. Waiting for him more than a mile offshore, Ernie's boat was met by Charlie.

   Rewrite: Waiting for him more than a mile offshore, Charlie met Ernie's boat.

9. Watching Nipper's antics, the male dolphin swam up and nudged me.

   Rewrite: As I watched Nipper's antics, the male dolphin swam up and nudged me.

10. Lifting his head completely out of the water, a single strand of brown seaweed was offered me.

    Rewrite: Lifting his head completely out of the water, he offered me a single strand of brown seaweed.

11. Clenching the strand between his teeth, another visitor was offered it.

    Rewrite: Clenching the strand between his teeth, he offered it to another visitor.

12. Part of a core group of about sixty, we can study their actions in detail.

    Rewrite: Since they are part of a core group of about sixty, we can study their actions in detail.

13. Persisting in tugging a dolphin's fin, it punished a woman with two sharp bites on the finger.

Rewrite: Persisting in tugging a dolphin's fin, a woman was punished with two sharp bites on the finger.

14. I awaited the dolphins sitting on the beach at dawn for a final encounter.

Rewrite: Sitting on the beach at dawn, I awaited the dolphins for a final encounter.

15. Sounding the horn again and again, we were summoned by the bus driver.

Rewrite: Sounding the horn again and again, the bus driver summoned us.

REVIEW EXERCISE 27.5

Underline the correct form of the adjective or adverb below.

1. (Real/Really) tired from waiting for their (incredible/incredibly) overdue baby, Margaret and Dave broke the monotony.
2. They (quick/quickly) went to the (better/best) movie they could find.
3. Margaret went inside to get seats (nearer/nearest) the door, while Dave (slow/slowly) joined her after getting popcorn.
4. Paying for the refreshments, Dave (sudden/suddenly) knocked over the refreshments.
5. The clerk (quiet/quietly) mopped up the mess and refilled his cup.
6. (Awful/Awfully) rattled, Dave then rejoined his wife.
7. However, that was not the (most awkward/awkwardest) thing he did that evening.
8. Talking (loud/loudly) over the background music, he (graphic/graphically) described the embarrassing incident.
9. One of his expressive gestures (sudden/suddenly) upset the bucket of popcorn.
10. Dave (sheepish/sheepishly) headed back to the lobby.

REVIEW EXERCISE 27.6

The following sentences all have misplaced or dangling modifiers. Rewrite them, correcting the mistake.

1. In twenty years as a nutrition counselor, a lot of people feel miserable about their weight.

Rewrite: In my twenty years as a nutrition counselor, I have seen a lot of people who feel miserable about their weight.

2. If eaten slowly, your child will find his food more enjoyable.

Rewrite: If eaten slowly, your child's food will be more enjoyable.

3. Coming into our store, a large hammock was bought by a customer.

   Rewrite: Coming into our store, a customer bought a large hammock.

4. Sitting in a pub, a mouse was pulled out of a man's pocket.

   Rewrite: Sitting in a pub, a man pulled a mouse out of his pocket.

5. A police officer called the station sent to patrol a nudist colony.

   Rewrite: Sent to patrol a nudist colony, a police officer called the station.

6. A gambler drove off a cliff named Biff.

   Rewrite: A gambler named Biff drove off a cliff.

7. During 14 years of pounding along California highways, an accident had never happened to the truck driver.

   Rewrite: During 14 years of pounding along California highways, the truck driver had never had an accident.

8. She had taken the world by storm, already a grandmother.

   Rewrite: Already a grandmother, she had taken the world by storm.

9. Spreading outward in concentric circles, nearby towns and cities were swept by the earthquake's power.

   Rewrite: Spreading outward in concentric circles, the earthquake's power swept nearby towns and cities.

10. Emilio Lopez was at his mother's house, an upholsterer.

    Rewrite: Emilio Lopez, an upholsterer, was at his mother's house.

Answer Key

Answers to alternate questions in this chapter's exercises are included below.

EXERCISE 27.1

  2. loud
  4. sharply
  6. quickly
  8. simply
  10. suddenly, competently
  12. quietly, intently
  14. really

EXERCISE 27.2

  2. longer
  4. busier, busiest

6. carefully

8. most famous

10. warmer

12. more

14. more quickly

16. more valuable

18. best

20. easier

EXERCISE 27.3

2. You can talk about anything you wish, <u>at $50 an hour</u>, like the meaning of life.

4. A bride price is still paid by almost every groom, <u>from investment bankers to farmers</u>.

6. I once had a car <u>with a delay cutoff switch for the headlights</u> that created a clearly lit path.

8. The 880 known species cover most of the land surfaces of the world <u>except for the polar regions</u>.

10. <u>Including soldiers, nurses, farmers, and hunters</u>, these tiny creatures colonized the earth.

12. The fire ant, <u>which has spread widely through the southern United States</u>, has burning compounds in its venom.

14. Among the ants I studied as a boy in Alabama was a species of Pheidole <u>which is the largest genus of ants in the world</u>.

EXERCISE 27.4

2. Running the four-mile course in full uniform, one of the conservation officers surprised everyone.

4. As I stood knee deep in the water, three generations of dolphins played in the shallows.

6. Whirling among us, they flourished their tails.

8. Waiting for him more than a mile offshore, Charlie met Ernie's boat.

10. Lifting his head completely out of the water, he offered me a single strand of brown seaweed.

12. Since they are part of a core group of about sixty, we can study their actions in detail.

14. Sitting on the beach at dawn, I awaited the dolphins for a final encounter.

REVIEW EXERCISE 27.5

2. quickly, best

4. suddenly

6. awfully

8. loudly, graphically
10. sheepishly

REVIEW EXERCISE 27.6

2. If eaten slowly, your child's food will be more enjoyable.
4. Sitting in a pub, a man pulled a mouse out of his pocket.
6. A gambler named Biff drove off a cliff.
8. Already a grandmother, she had taken the world by storm.
10. Emilio Lopez, an upholsterer, was at his mother's house.

I think the capitalization of the United States is right here.

Mechanics

Section One: Capitalization

Use capital letters with the following:

- The first word of a sentence, as in "It is easy to propose impossible remedies."
- The first person pronoun *I*, as in "I love you."

Also capitalize the following:

- The names of nationalities, races, or languages like Spanish, English, or Hungarian, as in "The Hungarian preferred American jeans."
- Deities, religions, and holy books: God, Ishtar, Roman Catholic, Hinduism, Koran, Talmud
- Names of buildings, cities, states, countries, and geographical regions: Sproul Hall, Chapel Hill, North Carolina, Bangladesh, the Mideast, the South
- Names of persons: Irving L. Beansprout
- Days, months, and special holidays: Friday, May, Columbus Day
- Recognized groups and organizations: the Democratic Party
- Documents and ages: the Declaration of Independence, the Victorian Age
- Specific events: World War II
- Specific course names, committees, and semesters: Psychology 100, Honors and Awards Committee, Fall Semester (or Quarter)
- Proper nouns referring to specific things, animals, products, and so on: The Busted Flush (a boat), Cannonade (a horse), Tag (a dog), Rice Krispies

Capitalize the following *only* when they refer to a noun that names something: *buildings, directions, family relationships, historical events, organizations, streets,* and *titles:*

Dr. Rodriguez entered the Odd Fellows Hall on South Eamons Street to discuss Uncle Sam's role in the Gulf War.

Do not capitalize common nouns. They are often preceded by definite

articles such as *a* and *an* or by limiting modifiers such as *every* or *several.*
Common nouns may refer to the following:

- professions, such as nursing, (the practice of) medicine
- levels of school, such as freshman, high school, college
- family relationships, such as *my* mother, *your* aunt

The doctor entered the hall on the south side of town with his uncle to discuss the effects of warfare.

EXERCISE 28.1

Rewrite the following sentences, correcting the capitalization.

EXAMPLE: doug hodge from honolulu, hawaii, has an unusual collection.

Correction: Doug Hodge from Honolulu, Hawaii, has an unusual collection.

1. doug hodge said, "i like to make english and american history come alive."

   Correction: Doug Hodge said, "I like to make English and American history come alive."

2. he has collected over 20,000 american radio broadcasts made during world war ii.

   Correction: He has collected over 20,000 American radio broadcasts made during World War II.

3. the english-language broadcasts include documentaries, newscasts, and commercials related to the war in europe and asia.

   Correction: The English-language broadcasts include documentaries, newscasts, and commercials related to the war in Europe and Asia.

4. television made vietnam a reality to the american people; radio made world war ii a reality to millions.

   Correction: Television made Vietnam a reality to the American people; radio made World War II a reality to millions.

5. hodge's favorite cbs radio broadcast was made in may 1942.

   Correction: Hodge's favorite CBS radio broadcast was made in May 1942.

6. the mauna loa volcano had erupted on the island of hawaii.

   Correction: The Mauna Loa volcano had erupted on the island of Hawaii.

7. american military personnel, still jittery over pearl harbor six months before, were much concerned.

   Correction: American military personnel, still jittery over Pearl Harbor six months before, were much concerned.

415

8. they feared that the spectacular lava flow would serve as a beacon to japanese planes.

   Correction: <u>They feared that the spectacular lava flow would serve as a beacon to Japanese planes.</u>

9. as a result, cbs ordered its correspondent, webley edwards, to keep this news item secret for nearly a month until mauna loa subsided.

   Correction: <u>As a result, CBS ordered its correspondent, Webley Edwards, to keep this news item secret for nearly a month until Mauna Loa subsided.</u>

10. cbs then gave edwards several minutes to give his startling eyewitness account of the incredible hawaiian eruption.

    Correction: <u>CBS then gave Edwards several minutes to give his startling eyewitness account of the incredible Hawaiian eruption.</u>

11. the johns hopkins sleep disorders center in baltimore, maryland, helps insomniacs like uncle frank cure themselves.

    Correction: <u>The Johns Hopkins Sleep Disorders Center in Baltimore, Maryland, helps insomniacs like Uncle Frank cure themselves.</u>

12. psychologist richard allen, co-director of the johns hopkins center, considers insomnia a 24-hour disorder.

    Correction: <u>Psychologist Richard Allen, co-director of the Johns Hopkins Center, considers insomnia a twenty-four-hour disorder.</u>

13. allen draws on research done by dr. arthur spielman of the sleep disorders center of the city college of new york.

    Correction: <u>Allen draws on research done by Dr. Arthur Spielman of the Sleep Disorders Center of the City College of New York.</u>

14. pete mcknight described the street scenes at the 4100 block of north kenmore in chicago.

    Correction: <u>Pete McKnight described the street scenes at the 4100 block of North Kenmore in Chicago.</u>

15. one evening in april, 1984, frederick miller shot a man during a street robbery in brooklyn, new york.

    Correction: <u>One evening in April, 1984, Frederick Miller shot a man during a street robbery in Brooklyn, New York.</u>

Section Two: Titles

Capitalize all words in the titles of works of art, literary works, or movies, *except* the articles *a*, *an*, and *the*, prepositions, and conjunctions. However, always capitalize the first and last words of a title, regardless of what parts of speech they are.

He decided to see the movie *Home Alone* rather than *What about Bob?*

Italics or <u>underlining</u> are used with the following:

- Titles of books, as in *The Booklover's Birthday Book.*
- Titles of magazines, as in *The Atlantic.*
- Newspapers, as in *The New York Times.*
- Movie and play titles, as in *Hamlet.*
- Longer musical works such as operas, as in *Figaro.*
- Book-length poems, as in *The Rime of the Ancient Mariner.*
- Books of art, as in the *Mona Lisa.*
- Foreign words and phrases, as in "*Haus* is German for house."

Put quotation marks around shorter works or parts of long ones: articles, chapters from books, poems, short stories, one-act plays, and songs:

We read Anton Chekhov's "The Druggist's Wife" in *Studies in Fiction.*

"The Druggist's Wife" is a short story. *Studies in Fiction* is a collection of short stories.

EXERCISE 28.2

Capitalize the following titles correctly. Do not use quotation marks or italics.

1. old mortality <u>Old Mortality</u>

2. the country wife <u>The Country Wife</u>

3. the limits of religious thought <u>The Limits of Religious Thought</u>

4. songs of innocence <u>Songs of Innocence</u>

5. how to win friends and influence people <u>How to Win Friends and Influence People</u>

6. the dynamics of literary response <u>The Dynamics of Literary Response</u>

7. el dorado <u>El Dorado</u>

8. the atlanta constitution <u>The Atlanta Constitution</u>

9. this morning, this evening, so soon <u>This Morning, This Evening, So Soon</u>

10. the great hoggarty diamond <u>The Great Hoggarty Diamond</u>

11. how to make a million in the stock market <u>How to Make a Million in the Stock Market</u>

12. the latchkey kids <u>The Latchkey Kids</u>

13. a child's garden of verses <u>A Child's Garden of Verses</u>

14. lady or the tiger _____

15. paradise and the peri _____

EXERCISE 28.3

Underline or place within quotation marks the following titles. Note: Be sure to enclose end punctuation like periods or question marks within quotation marks (.'').

1. The Reader's Digest pays $400 for contributions to Life in These United States.

   Correction: The Reader's Digest pays $400 for contributions to "Life in These United States."

2. Allan Bloom wrote a book called The Closing of the American Mind.

   Correction: Allan Bloom wrote a book called The Closing of the American Mind.

3. Hemingway's novel, For Whom the Bell Tolls, was written later than Crane's novel, The Red Badge of Courage.

   Correction: Hemmingway's novel, For Whom the Bell Tolls, was written later than Crane's novel, The Red Badge of Courage.

4. Stories such as Going to Meet the Man and The Sky Is Gray appear in the anthology Studies in Fiction.

   Correction: Stories such as "Going to Meet the Man" and "The Sky Is Gray" appear in the anthology Studies in Fiction.

5. The album by Elvis Podsnuffle includes endearing favorites such as I Ate My Dog Hot at the Picnic and My Sweetie Lies about the Z.

   Correction: The album by Elvis Podsnuffle includes endearing favorites such as "I Ate My Dog Hot at the Picnic" and "My Sweetie Lies about the Z."

6. The article entitled A Neighborly Sort of Way was printed in The Burlington Free Press.

   Correction: The article entitled "A Neighborly Sort of Way" was printed in The Burlington Free Press.

7. The school drama department is presenting Rosencrantz and Guildenstern Are Dead next week.

   Correction: The school drama department is presenting Rosencrantz and Guildenstern Are Dead next week.

8. Last Sunday at the movies, we saw Back to Kindergarten and Die Hard Two.

   Correction: Last Sunday at the movies, we saw Back to Kindergarten and Die Hard Two.

9. The compact disk version of the Encyclopedia Britannica costs $795.

Correction: The compact disk version of the *Encyclopedia Britannica* costs $795.

10. Frank Dooley is the lead actor in the new sitcom The Frenchy House.

Correction: Frank Dooley is the lead actor in the new sitcom *The Frenchy House*.

Section Three: Quotation Marks

Quotation marks are used to enclose direct quotations.

> Edgar insisted unhappily, "Marriage is not a word but a sentence."

A comma or colon comes *before* the quotation marks.

Capitalize the first letter of a direct quotation, as with "Marriage. . . ."

Place end punctuation *inside* the quotation marks, as in "sentence." However, notice whether the complete statement *or* the quotation is being punctuated, as in the following:

> John D. MacDonald said, "Isn't a news story like a hot-air balloon?"

However, the following example asks a question about a quotation:

> Didn't John D. MacDonald say, "Isn't a news story like a hot-air balloon"?

> Ralph shouted, "Love is a mental disease!"

Question marks and exclamation points go inside quotation marks.

> "If you haven't got anything nice to say about someone," said Alice, "come sit next to me."

In this sentence, the words *said Alice* interrupt a single direct quotation. As a result, a comma comes after the last interrupting word, *Alice*, and no capital is used with *come*.

> "In winter, sea offers me a spectacle," said M. K. Wren. "It parades huge breakers."

In this sentence, the quotation consists of two *separate* sentences. This is indicated by the period that follows the name of the speaker. Thus, a capital begins the first word, *It*, of the second sentence of the quotation.

419

Insert the correct punctuation in the following.

1. Can I help you? I asked, smiling.

   Correction: <u>"Can I help you?" I asked, smiling.</u>

2. Are you Mrs. Keelock? he asked, tapping his pipe on his Gucci loafers.

   Correction: <u>"Are you Mrs. Keelock?" he asked, tapping his pipe on his Gucci</u>
   <u>loafers.</u>

3. Yes, and you are? . . .

   Correction: <u>"Yes, and you are? . . ."</u>

4. He held out a smooth, perfectly groomed hand. Edward Leone. You can call me Ed. I work for Vince Vendutto, Miss Vendutto's uncle.

   Correction: <u>He held out a smooth, perfectly groomed hand. "Edward</u>
   <u>Leone. You can call me Ed. I work for Vince Vendutto, Miss Vendutto's</u>
   <u>uncle."</u>

5. I shook hands carefully, not wanting to ruin his manicure. Is she all right? Did you see her?

   Correction: <u>I shook hands carefully, not wanting to ruin his manicure. "Is</u>
   <u>she all right? Did you see her?"</u>

6. Suddenly, I heard a crash of china from the cottage, and Isolde's voice raised in a shriek. I don't give a canary's patootie if it was stupid! Get the bleep out of my life, you half-witted son of a toad!

   Correction: <u>"I don't give a canary's patootie if it was stupid! Get the bleep</u>
   <u>out of my life, you half-witted son of a toad!"</u>

7. Ed shook his head resignedly. Ah, he murmured. Miss Vendutto does have a temper, doesn't she?

   Correction: <u>Ed shook his head resignedly. "Ah," he murmured. "Miss</u>
   <u>Vendutto does have a temper, doesn't she?"</u>

8. Celebration is more than a happy feeling, Douglas Stuva said. Celebration is an experience.

   Correction: <u>"Celebration is more than a happy feeling," Douglas Stuva said.</u>
   <u>"Celebration is an experience."</u>

9. Commented Pete Hamill, I don't ask for the meaning of the song of a bird.

   Correction: <u>Commented Pete Hamill, "I don't ask for the meaning of the</u>
   <u>song of a bird."</u>

10. Reputation is character minus what you've been caught doing, according to Michael Iapoce.

    Correction: <u>"Reputation is character minus what you've been caught do-</u>
    <u>ing," according to Michael Iapoce.</u>

Section Four: Abbreviations

Generally, avoid abbreviations in your writing. When in doubt, write it out. However, the following abbreviations are usually acceptable:

- Titles when they are part of a name: Mr., Mrs., Ms., Sr., Jr., Dr.

  Mr. Johnson Ms. Smith Dr. Jones

- Academic degrees: B.A., M.A., D.D.S. Do not attach *both* titles and degrees to the same name: *not* Dr. William Ransom, Ph.D.
- Organizations whose names are long or that are primarily known by their initials: NASA, IBM, FBI. Note that the periods are omitted from *acronyms*, words formed from the first letters of a group of words.
- Certain foreign expressions: etc., ad lib
- Some abbreviations that have become common in usage: C.O.D.
- A dollar sign ($) when the sums are very large: $400,000, $5 billion.
- Time references: A.M. or a.m., P.M. or p.m., B.C. or A.D.

Do not use abbreviations in the following cases:

- The terms used to describe businesses—*company, corporation, incorporated,* etc. should be spelled out unless the abbreviation is part of the legally authorized name: Southwestern Heating Company, Prentice Hall, Inc.
- Percent or cents: twenty percent, fifty-five cents.
- Weights and measures: fifty-five pounds, twenty-six inches.
- Days, months, streets, avenues, boulevards in formal writing: Monday, June, South Street, Francis Avenue
- The names of states or countries
- The United States, unless it precedes the name of a ship or government agency: U.S. Accounting Office.

EXERCISE 28.5

Draw a line through words that should not be abbreviated. Write them out in the space provided.

1. On ~~Sat.~~, Nov. 7th, the delivery man dropped off the 75-~~lb~~ barbecue grill at 75 Elm ~~St.~~, Omaha, ~~Neb.~~

   Correction: On Saturday, November 7th, the delivery man dropped off the 75-pound barbecue grill at 75 Elm Street, Omaha, Nebraska.

2. I took six ~~hrs.~~ to reach the Hialeah Barber ~~Coll.~~ on the corner of Franklin ~~Blvd.~~ and Rich ~~St.~~ in ~~L.A., Calif.~~

   Correction: I took six hours to reach the Hialeah Barber College on the corner of Franklin Boulevard and Rich Street in Los Angeles, California.

3. After her ~~sci.~~ and ~~psych.~~ classes, Georgine mailed a check for $45.00 to her dent., Doc. Frank Jones, D.D.S.

After her science and psychology classes, Georgine mailed a check for forty-five dollars to her dentist, Dr. Frank Jones.

Section Five: Numerals

Generally, it is wise to write out numerals:

- Write out all numbers that can be stated in one or two words: ten, twenty-eight.

  The Seeing Eye, Inc., was founded seventy-two years ago.

  Sixteen of us have assembled for the first session.

  The dog extended my body by thirty-six inches.

- On the other hand, use numbers for numerals with three words or more: 325, 696.

  More than 422 people crowded into the room.

  George spent $625 to repave his driveway.

  Frank has 5,263 books in his attic.

- Use figures for exact times, sums, dates: 1:30 p.m., $2.95, 1776. However, spell out numbers before the word *o'clock:*

  At 2:00 a.m., Mrs. Culkin heard a prowler in her living room.

  However, she waited until three o'clock to call the police.

  Her dining room table cost $295.50 in 1982.

- A numeral at the beginning of a sentence is usually spelled out:

  Thirteen cats stood on the fence.

- All numbers from twenty-one to ninety-nine are hyphenated.

  The harbor yachts extended from thirty-six to eighty-four feet in length.

- Figures are used in dates, pages, statistical data, decimals, dimensions, exact amounts of money, exact times, and addresses: June 4, 1976, p. 66, 1″ × 2″, $2.95, 7:25 a.m., 311 Creek's Edge Road.

  On November 8, 1991, Henry paid $6.42 for a piece of 2″ × 4″ lumber to repair the porch at his home, 516 Oak Drive.

EXERCISE 28.6

Draw a line through mistakes in numbers. Write out the correct version in the spaces provided.

1. The couple arrived in Las Vegas on February ~~fourteenth, nineteen ninety-one~~.

   Corrected: The couple arrived in Las Vegas on February 14, 1991.

2. After 4-days, they had just ~~two dollars and fourteen cents~~ left.

    Corrected: <u>After four days, they had just $2.14 left.</u>

3. At 8-o'clock the next morning, they found themselves in a boat 80 yards from shore.

    Corrected: <u>At eight o'clock the next morning, they found themselves in a boat eighty yards from shore.</u>

REVIEW EXERCISE 28.7

Correct the problems in the following sentences with capitalization, titles, quotations, abbreviations, and numbers.

1. Looking through his son's record collection, a father noticed albums by the beatles, the animals, and the who.

    Corrected: <u>Looking through his son's record collection, a father noticed albums by the Beatles, the Animals, and the Who.</u>

2. The famous italian movie star antonio castello was inducted into the twentieth century movie hall of fame.

    Corrected: <u>The famous Italian movie star Antonia Castello was inducted into the Twentieth Century Movie Hall of Fame.</u>

3. On june sixth, nineteen forty-six, dr. david sellings stepped gingerly into his 30-foot sailboat to start the carlsberg single-handed transatlantic race.

    Corrected: <u>On June 6th, 1946, Dr. David Sellings stepped gingerly into his thirty-foot sailboat to start the Carlsberg Single-handed Transatlantic Race.</u>

4. He was later to say that his trip more closely resembled the movie jaws than it did the rime of the ancient mariner.

    Corrected: <u>He was later to say that his trip more closely resembled the movie Jaws than it did The Rime of the Ancient Mariner.</u>

5. In an article entitled doc sellings' marvelous voyage, the new york times of june fourteenth, nineteen forty-seven chronicled his exploits.

    Corrected: <u>In an article entitled ''Dr. Sellings' Marvelous Voyage,'' The New York Times of June 14, 1947, chronicled his exploits.</u>

6. Sensing an odd presence, he said, there's something out there!

    Corrected: <u>Sensing an odd presence, he said, ''There's something out there!''</u>

7. As of nineteen-eighty, reports the national center for health statistics, the average american male had gotten about 6 pounds plumper, the female about 4 pounds plumper, compared with the nineteen-sixties.

    Corrected: <u>As of 1980, reports the National Center for Health Statistics, the average American male had gotten about six pounds plumper, the female about four pounds plumper, compared with the 1960s.</u>

8. In his new book, the l.a. diet, james kenney, a nutrition researcher at the pritikin longevity center in santa monica, calif, touts his low-fat eating program.

Corrected: In his new book, The L.A. Diet, James Kenney, a nutrition researcher at the Pritikin Longevity Center in Santa Monica, California, touts his low-fat eating program.

9. He says, i tell people they can eat all the broccoli, fruit, beans and hot cereals they want.

Corrected: He says, "I tell people they can eat all the broccoli, fruit, beans and hot cereals they want."

10. it's much easier to rebuild fat than muscle, explains doc peter d vash, assistant clinical professor of medicine at u.c.l.a.

Corrected: "It's much easier to rebuild fat than muscle," explains Dr. Peter D. Vash, Assistant Clinical Professor of Medicine at U.C.L.A.

Answer Key

The answers to alternate questions in this chapter's exercises are included below.

EXERCISE 28.1

2. He has collected over 20,000 American radio broadcasts made during World War II.
4. Television made Vietnam a reality to the American people; radio made World War II a reality to millions.
6. The Mauna Loa volcano had erupted on the island of Hawaii.
8. They feared that the spectacular lava flow would serve as a beacon to Japanese planes.
10. CBS then gave Edwards several minutes to give his startling eyewitness account of the incredible Hawaiian eruption.
12. Psychologist Richard Allen, co-director of the Johns Hopkins Center, considers insomnia a twenty-four-hour disorder.
14. Pete McKnight described the street scenes at the 4100 block of North Kenmore in Chicago.

EXERCISE 28.2

2. The Country Wife
4. Songs of Innocence
6. The Dynamics of Literary Response

8. The Atlanta Constitution
10. The Great Hoggarty Diamond
12. The Latchkey Kids
14. Lady or the Tiger

EXERCISE 28.3

2. Allan Bloom wrote a book called <u>The Closing of the American Mind</u>.
4. Stories such as "Going to Meet the Man" and "The Sky Is Gray" appear in the anthology <u>Studies in Fiction</u>.
6. The article entitled "A Neighborly Sort of Way" was printed in <u>The Burlington Free Press</u>.
8. Last Sunday at the movies, we saw <u>Back to Kindergarten</u> and <u>Die Hard Two</u>.
10. Frank Dooley is the lead actor in the new sitcom <u>The Frenchy House</u>.

EXERCISE 28.4

2. "Are you Mrs. Keelock?" he asked, tapping his pipe on his Gucci loafers.
4. He held out a smooth, perfectly groomed hand. "Edward Leone. You can call me Ed. I work for Vince Vendutto, Miss Vendutto's uncle."
6. "I don't give a canary's patootie if it was stupid! Get the bleep out of my life, you half-witted son of a toad!"
8. "Celebration is more than a happy feeling," Douglas Stuva said. "Celebration is an experience."
10. "Reputation is character minus what you've been caught doing," according to Michael Iapoce.

EXERCISE 28.5

2. I took six hours to reach the Hialeah Barber College on the corner of Franklin Boulevard and Rich Street in Los Angeles, California.

EXERCISE 28.6

2. After four days, they had just $2.14 left.

REVIEW EXERCISE 28.7

2. The famous Italian movie star Antonia Castello was inducted into the Twentieth Century Movie Hall of Fame.
4. He was later to say that his trip more closely resembled the movie <u>Jaws</u> than it did <u>The Rime of the Ancient Mariner</u>.
6. Sensing an odd presence, he said, "There's something out there!"

8. In his new book, the <u>L.A. Diet</u>, James Kenney, a nutrition researcher at the Pritikin Longevity Center in Santa Monica, California, touts his low-fat eating program.

10. "It's much easier to rebuild fat than muscle," explains Dr. Peter D. Vash, Assistant Clinical Professor of Medicine at U.C.L.A.

Confused between the escape hatch and the door to the men's room, Fenton, the great explorer turned astronaut, found himself alone, weightless, and uncomfortable.

The Comma

Section One: Separating the Parts of a Series

Use commas to separate the parts of a series:

> Frank always ate bagels, lox, and cream cheese.
>
> Oxygen blocks the sun's rays, nourishes animals, and helps new species evolve.
>
> People should fill what's empty, empty what's full, and scratch where it itches.

Note: The comma is optional before the final item of a series. However, be consistent from one sentence to another.

> The local minister will baptize, marry, and bury you.
>
> OR
>
> The local minister will baptize, marry and bury you.

At times, two or more coordinate adjectives will modify (or describe) the same word or word group. These adjectives should be separated by a comma unless a conjunction joins them:

> A number of ordinary people wear *strange, garish* clothes.
>
> For him, studying statistics was *difficult, demanding, frustrating* work.

In these sentences, the adjectives are not joined by a conjunction. Thus, they are separated by commas.

Sometimes a word will appear to be modified by several adjectives which, in fact, describe different word groups. Here is an example:

> The ship unloaded forty new, blue cars.

In this sentence, only the words *new* and *blue* describe the word *cars.* The word *forty* modifies the entire word group *new, blue cars,* so it is not followed by a comma.

428

Do not use a comma, however, if all three parts are joined by *and* or *or:*

You are what you eat and eat and eat.

EXERCISE 29.1   *Insert commas where they are needed in the following sentences.*

1. Club mosses, giant horsetails, and ferns were the first plants to overshadow other plants.

2. The apes branched off from monkeys, developed larger brains, and began walking upright.

3. Plants attract insects with flowers, insects fertilize other plants, and both plants and insects thrive.

4. Crocodiles, lizards, and turtles evolved from amphibians.

5. Lemurs and other primates once thrived in Madagascar, Europe, and North America.

6. The largest land mammal roamed Asia and Europe, stood eighteen feet high, and weighed thirty-three tons.

7. Early sheep sported huge horns, baboons were as big as gorillas, and mammoths were incredibly huge.

8. Cro-Magnon man invented the harpoon, the lamp, and art.

9. The earliest man weighed less than eighty pounds, stood just fifty-seven inches high, and probably outran four-footed animals.

10. Cro-Magnons died from deficiency diseases, intense cold, and predator attacks.

11. To study their paintings, one must enter highly inaccessible, deep caves.

12. These early painters used various colored clays as well as brushes of ancient, carefully selected animal hair.

Section Two: Setting Off Introductory Material

Use a comma after an introductory phrase that is longer than two words:

> In the end, that which does not kill me makes me stronger.
> In literature as in love, we are astonished at what others choose.

Use a comma after transitions:

> In fact, the group always makes jokes.
> During the 1960s, the band traveled across the country.

Use a comma after introductory clauses:

> While we were in architecture school, we thought of building.
> If you've got an itch, scratch it.

EXERCISE 29.2   *Insert a comma after introductory word groups in the following sentences.*

1. On one wall, an autographed picture hangs.
2. As they understand it, the change happened around the end of the last century.
3. To their clients, the house is more than just another box.
4. Besides the twelve-room house, the complex includes a guesthouse.
5. But right now, there's even a gift-wrapping room.
6. Until the client vetoed it, the pool was shaped like a heart.
7. With the Hoagie house in order, the architects are dreaming of new challenges.
8. If they have a dream commission, it is to design the new Rock and Roll Hall of Fame.

Section Three: Setting Off Word Groups That Interrupt the Flow of a Sentence

Use commas to set off word groups that interrupt the flow of a sentence. Some of these interrupting words are parenthetical expressions like *by the way* or *at long last:*

> The Gulf Coast of Texas, *by the way,* was never very radical.
> Voters in Crystal Beach, *at long last,* decided to get rid of city hall.

Other interrupting words are appositives—words that substitute for or describe other words:

> Bill Stirling, *defrocked mayor,* lost his job.
> *An unincorporated area,* Crystal Beach still has local government.
> It cannot provide a crucial local service, *garbage collection.*

Phrases such as *defrocked mayor, an unincorporated area,* and *garbage collection* stand for or rename nouns or pronouns—*Bill Stirling, Crystal Beach,* or *service,* respectively.
Single-word appositives are usually not separated by commas:

Texan Craig Dejean saw waves loosen two anchor buoys.

The word *Texan* is an appositive for the proper name, Craig Dejean.

If you can leave out a word group that interrupts a sentence without affecting a reader's understanding of the sentence, set it off by commas. In the following sentence, the *who* clause is not essential to its meaning:

Benny Goodman was a rather ordinary-looking man, *who wore a business suit.*

The clause "*who wore a business suit*" adds information rather than identifying the word *man*. It can be omitted without confusing the reader about *who* is meant.

At times, however, a word group that interrupts a sentence is essential to its meaning. These word groups are often clauses beginning with *wh-* or *th-* words such as *who, which, where,* or *that*. These essential word groups should *not* be set off by commas. In the example below, the *who* clause is essential to the meaning of the sentence:

People saw a human being who could play the clarinet like no one before or since.

In this sentence, the clause "*who could play the clarinet like no one before or since*" helps tell the reader **which** *human being*. It cannot be omitted because it is essential to the meaning of the sentence.

Here is another example:

Joe DiMaggio, Ernest Hemingway, and Jonas Salk, who were outstanding Americans, have stood out from the flock.

In this sentence, the three people are already identified by name. The clause *who were outstanding Americans* provides additional information about these famous people. It is not essential. Thus, it should be set off by commas.

On the other hand, a *who* clause is essential in this sentence:

Other Americans who have stood out from the flock include Joe DiMaggio, Ernest Hemingway, and Jonas Salk.

The *Americans* who are described by the clause *who have stood out from the flock* are not named until late in the sentence. Therefore, the *who* clause helps identify the subject of the sentence.

EXERCISE 29.3

Insert commas where they are needed to punctuate interrupting words and word groups in the sentences below. Some are correct as they stand.

1. Howard Fields, a Sausalito entrepreneur, plunged into pool design.

2. He is now a leading creator, by the way, of aquatic fantasies.

3. He has built about 200 projects, an outlandish splash in business.

4. One of them, a pool masquerading as a river, flows for six blocks.

5. He likes to work, as a rule, only on zany challenges.

6. Fields' latest project, a 3000-square-foot lake, will feature hundreds of live koi fish.

Correct. 7. To sum up, all that sloshing around pays off.

8. Fields' fourteen-member firm, Howard Fields & Associates, exceeded $1 million in revenues last year.

9. To tell the truth, he likes being called a water swami.

10. Fields prefers, in fact, being considered all wet.

Correct. 11. There are several ways to get you moving, whether you always put things off or are stuck in a temporary rut.

Correct. 12. Those who procrastinate often assume that successful people achieve their goals easily.

13. One couple's daughter, Signe, put off studying science, which frustrated her.

14. Another student had to straighten out his priorities, which were badly confused.

15. He had put off nearly everything, which included getting out of bed in the morning.

Section Four: Separating Two Independent Word Groups Linked by *And, But, For, Or, Nor, So,* or *Yet*

Use a comma to separate complete thoughts linked by *and, but, for, or, nor, so,* or *yet. Remember:* when one of these conjunctions joins complete thoughts, it follows a comma; no comma follows it.

Friends may come and go, *but* enemies accumulate.

Beverly Hills restaurants banned smoking, *and* tempers are flaring.

H. L. Mencken said he was in favor of common sense, *so* that made him ineligible for public office.

Do not use a comma to separate brief complete thoughts:

Bob pleased everyone and Frank pleased no one.

The joke failed for it insulted them.

The meeting was canceled so they stayed home.

In a sentence with only one subject, do not separate a double verb with a comma:

You can't steal second base and keep one foot on first.

He overflowed with learning and stood in the slop.

Men should stop fighting among themselves and start fighting insects.

EXERCISE 29.4

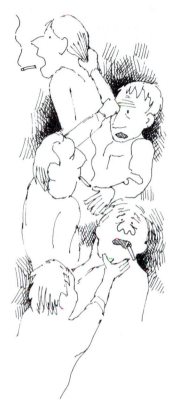

Add commas where they are needed in the following sentences. All but one join independent word groups with and, but, or, nor, for, yet, *or* so.

1. A woman refused to put out her cigarette, so an annoyed patron yanked her hair.

2. A woman told her companion he must snuff his cigar, and he punched her out.

3. Cigar-smoking George Burns doesn't like the no-smoking rule, but he's willing to conform.

4. The Beverly Hills police have made no arrests and have answered only two calls.

5. Two years ago, Aspen, Colorado, passed the first no-smoking law, and New York State recently joined the trend.

6. The law is directed at residents, so hotel dining rooms are exempt.

7. Explained the city attorney, "We're not out to reform human nature, for French movie moguls can't do business without smoking."

8. A local restaurant owner said, "You can just walk from here to another city, so what chance do they have in Beverly Hills?"

9. The Beverly Hills Restaurant Association threatens a lawsuit, but it is unlikely the law will be repealed.

10. Patrick Reynolds saw his father die of emphysema, and he supports the ban.

Section Five: Separating a Direct Quotation from the Rest of the Sentence

Use a comma to separate a direct quotation from the rest of the sentence.

If the comma comes at the *beginning* of a quote, it goes *outside* the quotation marks:

Ralph said, "Love is a mental disease."

If the comma comes at the *end* of a quote, it goes *inside* the quotation marks:

"You have to learn to forget not the bad reviews, but the good ones," Lawrence Olivier said.

Here is an example of both uses of the comma to separate direct quotations:

> "Someday, when I become a general," young Norman said, "I want people to know that I'm serious."

EXERCISE 29.5   *Insert commas where they are needed in the following sentences.*

1. "It's very original," I commented.

2. I thought to myself, "What else could I say?"

3. "Yes," she agreed, "before I married, I considered being a decorator."

4. "I have the talent," she simpered proudly, "but Robert never allowed me to work."

5. "I should have left him years ago," she muttered, "but it's not too late."

6. "I know that now," she whispered again.

7. As if reassuring herself, she remarked, "I have plans, many carefully laid plans."

8. Shivering suddenly, she carefully replied, "My friends will help me when I need it."

9. Tripping back down the hall, she called over her shoulder, "Which newspaper are you with?"

10. I answered carefully, but vaguely, "The biggest one in town."

Section Six: Minor Uses

Use a comma to separate the name of a person who is addressed directly:

> Beam me up, Scotty; there's no intelligent life down here.
> John, be careful.

Use commas to separate days of a month from the year:

> July 4, 1776.

Use commas to separate parts of an address:

> 101 Rosemary Street, Chapel Hill, North Carolina 27514

Note that no comma separates the state name from the zip code.
Use a comma to introduce an informal letter or close *any* letter:

Dear Mom,
Sincerely yours,

Use a comma to separate a title following a name:

I. M. Boring, Ph.D.

Use a comma in numbers with four digits or more:

After thirteen minutes, Mariner I's booster engine would speed up to 25,820 miles; after forty-four minutes, 9,800 solar cells would unfold.

EXERCISE 29.6   *Insert commas where they are needed in the following sentences.*

1. The *Commonwealth Sentinel* opened on February 6,1965,and closed on the seventh.

2. The paper was founded by Mr. Lionel Burleigh,M.A.

3. Needing capital, he had addressed a letter to his banker beginning, "Dear Franklin, Please send me some cash," and closed it simply, "Sincerely,Lionel."

4. On the following day, Tuesday, February 7, Burleigh got a frantic phone call.

5. "Lionel,come get your papers," said the caller.

6. There are 50,000 of them outside Brown's Hotel,Fleet Street, London.

7. On Tuesday,March 14,1973,a fire broke out at 2 Crisp Road,Henley, London.

8. The owners had been visiting 14 Elm Street,Portland, Maine, since November 24,1972,however.

9. A computer installed for the Aiken School District,15 Messup Road, Aiken,went wild and paid a janitor $2,600 for a week's work on June 4,1975.

10. Fortunately,the janitor had moved from 16 Whiskey Road,Aiken,South Carolina,to 46 Easy Street,Augusta,Georgia.

REVIEW EXERCISE 29.7   *Punctuate the following sentences correctly.*

1. On February 25,1859,Congressman Daniel Sickles discovered that his wife had been having an affair.

2. Her lover,the son of a very famous man,was named Philip Key.

3. Philip's father was,of course,Francis Scott Key.

4. The senior Key, it is well known, wrote the famous anthem, "The Star-Spangled Banner."

5. On February 27, 1859, two days later, Sickles confronted Key, and shot him twice.

6. Shouting, "Dan, I'll never forget this!" Key died almost immediately.

7. During the trial, James T. Brady, Sickles' attorney, defended his client with, by the way, a previously unknown defense.

8. Standing dramatically before the jury, Brady entered a plea of "temporary insanity."

9. Sickles was acquitted, for his lawyer convinced the jury.

10. Later, during the Civil War, Sickles became a distinguished general.

REVIEW
EXERCISE 29.8

Punctuate the following sentences correctly.

1. Between 1953, when it was built, and 1976, when it sank, the *Argo Merchant* suffered every known form of disaster.

2. In 1967 the ship collided with a Japanese ship, caught fire three times, and had to stop for repairs five times.

3. In 1967 there was a mutiny, and in 1969 she went aground off Borneo for thirty-four hours.

4. In the next five years, she was laid up in Curaçao, grounded off Sicily, and towed to New York.

5. In 1976 her boilers broke down six times, and she once had to travel with two red lights displayed.

6. This indicated, we can assume, that the crew could no longer control the ship, for its steering and engine had failed.

7. The ship was banned from Philadelphia, Boston, and the Panama Canal.

8. To round off a perfect year, she ran aground and sank off Cape Cod.

9. On March 16, 1976, she deposited the country's largest oil slick near Boston, Massachusetts.

10. At the time of the final grounding, the ship had been "lost" for fifteen hours.

11. The day before, the ship's equipment had broken down, the ship was eighteen miles off course, and the crew was navigating by the stars.

12. What is more, the course to be steered was in Greek, so the West Indian helmsman could not read it.

13. At a hearing later, held at Old Helmsley Street, Providence, Rhode Island, on August 15, 1977, a court official assessed the owners $15,000 for negligence.

14. To cap things off, a naval expert afterwards said, "The ship was a disaster looking for somewhere to happen."

15. The New England Shipping Line, next owners of the ill-fated boat, were happy to scrap it.

Answer Key

Answers to alternate questions in this chapter's exercises are included below.

EXERCISE 29.1

2. The apes branched off from monkeys, developed larger brains, and began walking upright.

4. Crocodiles, lizards, and turtles evolved from amphibians.

6. The largest land mammal roamed Asia and Europe, stood eighteen feet high, and weighed thirty-three tons.

8. Cro-Magnon man invented the harpoon, the lamp, and art.

10. Cro-Magnons died from deficiency diseases, intense cold, and predator attacks.

12. These early painters used various colored clays and brushes of ancient, carefully selected animal hairs.

EXERCISE 29.2

2. As they understand it, the change happened around the end of the last century.

4. Besides the twelve-room house, the complex includes a guesthouse.

6. Until the client vetoed it, the pool was shaped like a heart.

8. If they have a dream commission, it is to design the new Rock and Roll Hall of Fame.

EXERCISE 29.3

2. He is now a leading creator, by the way, of aquatic fantasies.

4. One of them, a pool masquerading as a river, flows for six blocks.

6. Fields' latest project, a 3000-square-foot lake, will feature hundreds of live koi fish.

8. Fields' fourteen-member firm, Howard Fields & Associates, exceeded $1 million in revenues last year.

10. Fields prefers, in fact, being considered all wet.

12. Those who procrastinate often assume that successful people achieve their goals easily. Correct.

14. Another student had to straighten out his priorities, which were badly confused.

EXERCISE 29.4

2. A woman told her companion he must snuff his cigar, and he punched her out.

4. The Beverly Hills police have made no arrests and have answered only two calls.

6. The law is directed at residents, so hotel dining rooms are exempt.

8. A local restaurant owner said, "You can just walk from here to another city, so what chance do they have in Beverly Hills?"

10. Patrick Reynolds saw his father die of emphysema, and he supports the ban.

EXERCISE 29.5

2. I thought to myself, "What else could I say?"

4. "I have the talent," she simpered proudly, "but Robert never allowed me to work."

6. "I know that now," she whispered again.

8. Shivering suddenly, she carefully replied, "My friends will help me when I need it."

10. I answered carefully, but vaguely, "The biggest one in town."

EXERCISE 29.6

2. The paper was founded by Mr. Lionel Burleigh, M.A.

4. On the following day, Tuesday, February 7, Burleigh got a frantic phone call.

6. There are 50,000 of them outside Brown's Hotel, Fleet Street, London.

8. The owners had been visiting 14 Elm Street, Portland, Maine, since November 24, 1972, however.

10. Fortunately, the janitor had moved from 16 Whiskey Road, Aiken, South Carolina, to 46 Easy Street, Augusta, Georgia.

REVIEW EXERCISE 29.7

2. Her lover, the son of a very famous man, was named Philip Key.

4. The senior Key, it is well known, wrote the famous anthem, "The Star-Spangled Banner."

6. Shouting, "Dan, I'll never forget this!" Key died almost immediately.

8. Standing dramatically before the jury, Brady entered a plea of "temporary insanity."

10. Later, during the Civil War, Sickles became a distinguished general.

REVIEW EXERCISE 29.8

2. In 1967 the ship collided with a Japanese ship, caught fire three times, and had to stop for repairs five times.

4. In the next five years, she was laid up in Curaçao, grounded off Sicily, and towed to New York.

6. This indicated, we can assume, that the crew could no longer control the ship, for its steering and engine had failed.

8. To round off a perfect year, she ran aground and sank off Cape Cod.

10. At the time of the final grounding, the ship had been "lost" for fifteen hours.

12. What is more, the course to be steered was in Greek, so the West Indian helmsman could not read it.

14. To cap things off, a naval expert afterwards said, "The ship was a disaster looking for somewhere to happen."

Minor
Punctuation Marks

Section One: The Apostrophe

SINGULAR AND PLURAL OWNERS

When someone or something is an owner, an apostrophe is added to the noun to show ownership. If the noun does *not* end in *s*, add an apostrophe and *s* ('s).

> Lucille's dog
> month's end

Lucille and *month* are **singular** nouns that do not end in *s*. They show ownership by adding 's.

If the noun does end in *s* or *es*, it adds an apostrophe (s').

> students' lockers
> cars' headlights
> houses' paint

The words *students*, *cars*, and *houses* are **plural** nouns that end in *s*. They show ownership by adding '.

COMPOUND OWNERS

With compound nouns, an apostrophe and *-s* are added to the last noun if *both* own what is being discussed:

> John's and Carla's jogging shoes

John and Carla own the car *together*.
    With compound nouns, an apostrophe and *-s* are added to *both* nouns if each noun possesses something:

> John's and Carla's jogging shoes

Each owns his and her own pair of jogging shoes.

442

POSSESSIVE PRONOUNS

Do *not* use an apostrophe with possessive pronouns (*my, mine, your, his, hers, its, ours, yours, theirs, whose*).

> The contractor replaced *my* wooden doors.
> That spindle-legged dog is *yours*.

The pronouns *my* and *yours* add no apostrophes.
Remember: When *its* means "belongs to it," it is possessive. This *its* requires *no* apostrophe.

> *Its* wheels were out of alignment.
> *Its* paint had begun to flake badly.

In these two sentences, *wheels* and *paint* belong to *it*.

USE OF AN APOSTROPHE TO INDICATE A MISSING LETTER

When *it's* means "it is," it requires an apostrophe to show that the *i* is left out of the verb, *is*.

> *It's* a shame she dumped him.
> *It's* an old story.

In these two sentences, *It's* is a contraction for *It is*.
An apostrophe is also used to show that something has been left out of a word or date:

> Don't

The *o* is left out of the word *not*.

> The winter of '56

The *19* is left out of the date 1956.

USE OF AN APOSTROPHE TO INDICATE PLURALS

An apostrophe is used to indicate the plural of a letter, number, or name of a word:

> Three M's
> Fourteen 10's
> Twenty-nine and's

In these sentences, *M*, *10*, and *and* are used as words.
With the exception of names of words, the apostrophe never forms the plural. Avoid mistakes like the following:

He earned three paycheck's

The dealer sells Honda's and Hyundai's.

The plural words in these sentences should include no apostrophes: pay-checks, Hondas, and Hyundais.

EXERCISE 30.1

Use the apostrophe correctly to indicate possession or contraction in the following phrases, changing word order if necessary.

EXAMPLE:

The tail of the dog—*the dog's tail*
I will—*I'll*

1. The tennis rackets of John and Sue
   John's and Sue's tennis rackets

2. The house of Charlie and Alice
   Charlie and Alice's house

3. I do not
   I don't

4. The computers of the offices
   The offices' computers

5. Where is
   Where's

Note: Since the word *women* is already plural, the word forms its possessive with *'s.*

6. The hats of the women
   The women's hats

7. It is
   It's

8. The ignorance of Charlie
   Charlie's ignorance

9. The books of Ed and Al
   Ed and Al's books

10. The cat of Donna and Charlie
    Donna and Charlie's cat

EXERCISE 30.2

Correct errors in apostrophe use above the line in the sentences below.

           couldn't   pounds   Linda's
(1) My daughter couldnt lose unwanted pound's. **(2)** She lamented, "Lindas so
        makes   don't
skinny that it make's me sick." **(3)** I replied, "Why dont you do something about
               can't   your problems
it?" **(4)** "Just talking about it cant possibly solve your' problem's." **(5)** I had
        Sherry's   books   That's
been reading Frank and Sherrys diet book's. **(6)** "Thats a good idea," she
                George's   Charlie's
responded. **(7)** "Hey, Linda," she shouted, "have some of Georges and Charlies
                 It's   haven't   your
chocolate bars." **(8)** I muttered to her, "Its a good thing you havent lost your'
        isn't
sense of humor, isnt it?"

Section Two: The Colon

The colon is used to introduce a formal list:

A good recipe for chili requires the following ingredients: chili, beans, and a good steak to eat instead of the chili.

The three nouns following the colon are *chili*, *beans*, and *steak*.
The colon is used to introduce an important piece of information:

My spouse is interested in only one thing: money.

The colon is used to introduce a formal quotation. It *always* comes before the quotation marks.

John F. Kennedy said: "Forgive your enemies, but never forget their names."

The colon is used after the salutation of a formal letter. Such letters are written to someone you may not know, often about a business matter.

Dear Senator Ledbetter:

Colons are used to separate hours from minutes and chapter from verse:

12:02 p.m.
Luke 2:4

I think this is where my colon is.

Insert the colon where needed in the sentences below.

1. Since I live near a lake, I decided to sell a high-demand item: night-crawlers.
2. I put up a sign that read: "Self-service—put money in container."
3. Seeing my sign, someone wrote me a letter that began, "Dear Dummy:".
4. A man with three boys drove up about 1:20 p.m.
5. I directed a comment to him: "How nice it is that there is so much honesty in the world."
6. He made this response: "Fishermen aren't thieves—just liars!"

Section Three: The Semicolon

The semicolon is used to separate two or more independent clauses which are *not* joined by a coordinating conjunction such as *and, but, for, or, yet,* or *so.* The word that follows a semicolon *never* begins with a capital letter, unless it is the pronoun "I" or a proper noun such as Nebraska.

It doesn't matter whether you win or lose; what matters is whether I win or lose.

Like the colon, the semicolon appears *outside* any quotation marks.

I read Poe's "The Telltale Heart"; however, I should have read "The Fall of the House of Usher."

A semicolon is used when two sentences are joined by an adverbial connective such as those in the following lists:

therefore, however, nevertheless, consequently, hence, accordingly, moreover, furthermore, besides, indeed, in fact

Be sure to follow the connective with a comma. Do not use *only* commas, as you may be creating a comma splice:

I've been on a diet for three weeks; *however,* all I've lost is three weeks.

The semicolon comes *before* the adverbial connective; therefore, a comma comes *after* it.

Warning: Be certain there is an independent clause on *both* sides of the adverbial connective.

A semicolon is used in place of a comma to avoid confusion when sentences joined by a coordinating conjunction contain a lot of internal punctuation.

First, we drove north, then south, then east, then west; but finally, we had to admit that we were lost.

EXERCISE 30.4   *Combine the following sentences using semicolons and, where appropriate, adverbial connectives.*

1. Asa Dunbar was Henry David Thoreau's grandfather. He was also one of the first student protesters.

   Asa Dunbar was Henry David Thoreau's grandfather; he was also one of the first student protesters.

2. Dunbar set the pattern for student rebellions over 200 years ago. Students have followed his example ever since.

   Dunbar set the pattern for student rebellions over 200 years ago; students have followed his example ever since.

3. In 1766, he protested against the quality of food at Harvard. His slogan was, "Behold, our butter stinketh."

   In 1766, he protested against the quality of food at Harvard; his slogan was, "Behold, our butter stinketh."

4. The faculty condemned him for "insubordination." His rebellion continued.

   The faculty condemned him for "insubordination"; however, his rebellion continued.

5. Dunbar and his followers organized an "eat out." They all had breakfast off campus.

   Dunbar and his followers organized an "eat out"; they all had breakfast off campus.

Section Four: The Dash

The dash is used to indicate an abrupt change in thought:

Tomorrow—if it ever comes—will be better.

The dash is also used to add emphasis:

I'll go to his party—if he invites me.

Section Five: The Hyphen

The hyphen is used between parts of compound words such as "brother-in-law" and "heavy-handed."

> His dim-witted sister-in-law tried to assemble the Japanese bicycle.

In this sentence, *dim-witted* and *sister-in-law* are hyphenated because they are compound words.

The hyphen is used to break a word into syllables at the end of a written line. If you aren't sure how to break a word into syllables, check your dictionary, which separates a word like *spontaneous* in this way: spon-ta-ne-ous. One-syllable words cannot be separated. Also, don't separate one-letter syllables or prefixes at the beginnings of words, or three-letter syllables or suffixes at the ends of words.

The hyphen is also used to form one-time-only, special phrases or words.

> He had an I-couldn't-find-my-way-out-of-a-wet-paper-bag expression.
>
> I heard the computer go beep-beep-beep.

The hyphen is used to form fractions, numbers, and compounds with numbers, as in *two-thirds*, *twenty-eight*, and *seven-day wonder*.

The hyphen is used to avoid having identical vowels next to one another, as in *re-enter*.

The hyphen is used to form certain words like *ex-wife* or *President-elect*.

The hyphen is also used between compound modifiers that come *before* a noun.

> Craig Claiborne is a *well-known* expert on food.
>
> The starving poet lived a *hand-to-mouth* existence.

When a compound modifier comes *after* a noun, it is *not* hyphenated.

> Craig Claiborne's food expertise is well known.

EXERCISE 30.5

Insert the dash and hyphen correctly where needed in the following sentences.

(1) Remember the so called [so-called] futurists who claimed we would run out of ninetenths [nine-tenths] of our oil in the 1990s? **(2)** They told us to keep our eyes on time shaping [time-shaping] people. **(3)** However, they never mentioned — I clearly recall — an anticommunist [anti-communist] former movie actor, Ronald Reagan. **(4)** Some foolish stuff has been written — it seems obvious to me — under the flag of futurism. **(5)** However,

near-term   seven-day

we do know something about the near term future, despite what the seven

day wonders say. **(6)** The United States it has been said is in relative decline and
re-energized
will never be reenergized. **(7)** By the end of the 1990s, our major competitors

Japan and the nations of Western Europe will have stagnant populations.

(8) Because the United States takes in a substantial number of immigrants, we

will grow even of our birthrate stays low.

Section Six: Parentheses and Brackets

Parentheses are used to enclose information which, while important, disrupts the thoughts of a sentence:

> William Blake (1757–1827) insisted that it is easier to forgive an enemy than to forgive a friend.

Parentheses are used when numbering a series:

> A recipe in the *Eskimo Cookbook* tells us to prepare boiled owl as follows: (1) Take feathers off, (2) Clean owl, (3) Put in pot with boiling water, and (4) Add salt to taste.

Brackets are used to set off your own additions to quoted materials:

> "Our [Stoic] motto, as you know, is to live according to Nature." Seneca.

EXERCISE 30.6   *Insert parentheses and brackets correctly in the following sentences.*

1. Young women (16 to 24 years old) now have earnings close to those of men of comparable age.
2. There are four compelling reasons to cut the capital-gains tax: (1) The tax hurts everyone, (2) The tax takes away money that could be producing wealth, (3) The tax increases the cost of doing business, and (4) The tax actually decreases federal revenues.
3. Some people spend precious time searching (always successfully) for evidence of aliens from outer space.
4. All kinds of growth (aspen, fir, and maple trees) flourished.
5. Everything he had planted over the past months (trees, grasses, bushes) had vanished.

Rewrite the sentences below, using the following marks of punctuation correctly: apostrophes, colons, semicolons, dashes, hyphens, parentheses, and brackets.

1. Joe Theismann enjoyed an illustrious 12 year career if memory serves as the Washington Redskins quarterback.

   Joe Theismann enjoyed an illustrious 12-year career—if memory serves—as the Washington Redskins' quarterback.

2. He led a first rate team to two Super Bowl appearances winning in 1983 before losing the following year.

   He led a first-rate team to two Super Bowl appearances—winning in 1983 before losing the following year.

3. He was forced out of football in the mid 80s by physical damage a leg injury.

   He was forced out of football in the mid-'80s by physical damage: a leg injury.

4. At that time you could look it up he was entrenched in the record books as Washingtons all time leading passer.

   At that time—you could look it up—he was entrenched in the record books as Washington's all-time leading passer.

In this example, the parentheses could be replaced by dashes.

5. The tail end of Theismann's career taught him he now realizes a bitter lesson ''I got stagnant.''

   The tail end of Theismann's career taught him (he now realizes) a bitter lesson: ''I got stagnant.''

6. ''I thought the team revolved around me however I should have known it was time to go.''

   ''I thought the team revolved around me; however, I should have known it was time to go.''

7. ''I should have known it was time to go I didnt care whether a pass hit Art Monks 8 or the 1 on his uniform.''

   ''I should have known it was time to go; I didn't care whether a pass hit Art Monk's 8 or the 1 on his uniform.''

8. ''Today, I wear my two rings the winners ring from Super Bowl XVII and the losers ring from Super Bowl XVIII.''

   ''Today, I wear my two rings—the winner's ring from Super Bowl XVII and the loser's ring from Super Bowl XVIII.''

9. Waiting in line at the tellers window, my sister in law lamented to the middle aged man behind her.

   Waiting in line at the teller's window, my sister-in-law lamented to the middle-aged man behind her.

10. "My children are in their 20s however Im still giving them money."
    "My children are in their 20's; however, I'm still giving them money."

11. Early on race day, I drove my four wheel drive truck onto the disorienting tundra.
    Early on race day, I drove my four-wheel-drive truck onto the disorienting tundra.

12. My husband and I attended a murder mystery dinner during the meal, several performers disguised as fellow diners acted out a murder.
    My husband and I attended a murder-mystery dinner; during the meal, several performers disguised as fellow diners acted out a murder.

13. Make sure your roof is made of fire resistant material asphalt, concrete shingle, or sheet metal.
    Make sure your roof is made of fire-resistant material: asphalt, concrete shingle, or sheet metal.

14. Heres another precaution trim overhanging tree limbs in addition clear debris out of gutters regularly.
    Here's another precaution: trim overhanging tree limbs; in addition, clear debris out of gutters regularly.

Answer Key

Alternate answers for the questions in this chapter's exercises are included below.

EXERCISE 30.1

2. Charlie and Alice's house
4. The offices' computers
6. The women's hats. *Note:* Since the word *women* is already plural, the word forms its possessive with *'s.*
8. Charlie's ignorance
10. Donna and Charlie's cat

EXERCISE 30.2

2. Linda's, makes
4. can't, your, problems
6. That's
8. It's, haven't, your, isn't

EXERCISE 30.3

2. I put up a sign that read: "Self-service—put money in container."

4. A man with three boys drove up about 1:20 p.m.

6. He made this response: "Fishermen aren't thieves—just liars!"

EXERCISE 30.4

2. Dunbar set the pattern for student rebellion over 200 years ago; students have followed his example ever since.

4. The faculty condemned him for "insubordination"; however, his rebellion continued.

EXERCISE 30.5

2. time-shaping

4. Some foolish stuff has been written—it seems obvious to me—under the flag of futurism.

6. The United States—it has been said—is in relative decline and will never be re-energized.

8. Because the United States takes in a substantial number of immigrants, we will grow—even if our birthrate stays low.

EXERCISE 30.6

2. There are four compelling reasons to cut the capital-gains tax: (1) The tax hurts everyone, (2) The tax takes away money that could be producing wealth, (3) The tax increases the cost of doing business, and (4) The tax actually decreases federal revenues.

4. All kinds of growth (aspen, fir, and maple trees) flourished.

EXERCISE 30.7

2. He led a first-rate team to two Super Bowl appearances—winning in 1983 before losing the following year.

4. At that time—you could look it up—he was entrenched in the record books as Washington's all-time leading passer.

6. "I thought the team revolved around me; however, I should have known it was time to go."

8. "Today, I wear my two rings—the winner's ring from Super Bowl XVII and the loser's ring from Super Bowl XVIII."

10. "My children are in their 20's; however, I'm still giving them money."

12. My husband and I attended a murder-mystery dinner; during the meal, several performers disguised as fellow diners acted out a murder.

14. Here's another precaution: trim overhanging tree limbs; in addition, clear debris out of gutters regularly.

CHAPTER

31

Improving Spelling

Correct spelling helps a reader follow your thoughts. If you don't misspell words, readers will have confidence in the rest of your writing. Readers distrust writers who misspell words. Following are a number of ways you can improve your spelling.

Section One: Ways to Improve Your Spelling

Look up words in the dictionary. Check the pronunciation, too. Develop tricks to help you spell. For example, there is "a rat" in "sep*arat*e." If you like two desserts, remember that dessert has two -*s's.*

Keep a list of spelling demons. Set aside a page in your journal for frequently misspelled words. When your instructor marks such words, copy them down as you misspelled them. Circle the part that gave you a problem. Then write down the correct spelling. Look over your list from time to time. Use the form below:

My Misspelling

Correct Spelling

1. _____proly_____   _____prob__ab__ly_____

2. _____   _____

3. _____   _____

4. _____   _____

5. _____   _____

Look at words closely, sound them out phonetically, and write them out. For example, the word *government* is easily misspelled as *govment* if you leave out the middle syllable. Your pronunciation may be influencing your spelling—*tole* for *told, ax* for *ask, use* for *used.* Listen to the national news on television to hear newscasters use standard English. Develop the habit of using the "Spell" utility included with your word-processing program.

Divide words into syllables.

Words that sound alike, such as *to/two/too* and *weather/whether,* often create considerable confusion. Memorize the spelling differences. Later in this chapter, we deal with like-sounding words.

Memorize certain spelling tricks like the ei/ie rule:

I before E

except after C

or when sounding like a

as in neighbor or weigh.

454

Section Two: A List of Commonly Misspelled Words

Here is a list of frequently misspelled words. You will often use these words in your speaking and writing.

1. accept	40. caught	79. government
2. ache	41. chief	80. grammar
3. again	42. children	81. guard
4. all right	43. choose	82. guess
5. almost	44. chose	83. guide
6. already	45. color	84. half
7. almost	46. conscience	85. haven't
8. always	47. cough	86. hear
9. angel	48. cousin	87. heard
10. angle	49. crowded	88. heavy
11. answer	50. decide	89. height
12. argument	51. definite	90. here
13. asked	52. describe	91. hers
14. aunt	53. desperate	92. hole
15. author	54. different	93. hoping
16. awful	55. disappoint	94. hour
17. beginning	56. disapprove	95. illegal
18. behavior	57. divide	96. immediately
19. believe	58. doesn't	97. important
20. bother	59. don't	98. integration
21. bought	60. early	99. intelligent
22. break	61. eighth	100. interest
23. breakfast	62. embarrass	101. interfere
24. breathe	63. enough	102. its
25. broken	64. environment	103. it's
26. brother	65. every	104. January
27. brought	66. exact	105. let's
28. bruise	67. exaggeration	106. listen
29. build	68. except	107. loose
30. business	69. excite	108. lose
31. busy	70. expect	109. jewelry
32. buy	71. familiar	110. judgment
33. by	72. finally	111. knowledge
34. calendar	73. forty	112. maintain
35. cannot	74. fourth	113. mathematics
36. can't	75. Friday	114. meant
37. career	76. friend	115. minute
38. careful	77. goes	116. muscle
39. catch	78. going	117. necessary

118. neighbor	147. really	176. tried
119. nervous	148. receive	177. tries
120. nickel	149. reference	178. truly
121. ninety	150. rhythm	179. two
122. ninety-nine	151. ridiculous	180. tying
123. ninth	152. right	181. unknown
124. occasion	153. Saturday	182. until
125. often	154. separate	183. unusual
126. once	155. similar	184. wasn't
127. opinion	156. since	185. wear
128. optimist	157. speech	186. weather
129. other	158. strength	187. Wednesday
130. particular	159. stretch	188. weight
131. people	160. success	189. weird
132. perform	161. surely	190. we'll
133. perhaps	162. surprise	191. we're
134. personnel	163. taught	192. weren't
135. possess	164. temperature	193. we've
136. possible	165. their	194. where
137. prefer	166. theirs	195. which
138. prejudice	167. they're	196. whole
139. principal	168. they've	197. witch
140. privilege	169. thorough	198. won't
141. probably	170. those	199. wouldn't
142. psychology	171. though	200. write
143. pursue	172. thought	201. writing
144. quite	173. through	202. written
145. quit	174. tied	203. you're
146. quite	175. tired	204. yours

Section Three: Helpful Spelling Rules

RULE A:

When a word ends in a **consonant** plus *y*, change *y* to *i* when adding an ending.

To form the **plural**, change *y* to *ies*.

EXAMPLES:

ready + ness = readiness

ready + es = read<u>ies</u>

EXERCISE 31.1   *Follow the rule above to combine endings with the words below:*

1. army + ies   = armies
2. copy + ied   = copied
3. worry + ies   = worries
4. marry + ied   = married
5. carry + ies   = carries
6. terrify + ied   = terrified
7. duty + ies   = duties
8. occupy + ied   = occupied
9. try + ies   = tries
10. mutiny + ies   = mutinies

RULE B:

When a word ends in a **vowel** plus *y*, keep the final *y* when adding an ending.

EXAMPLES:

buy + er = buyer
coy + ness = coyness

EXERCISE 31.2   *Follow the rule above to combine endings with the words below.*

1. key + ed   = keyed
2. buoy + s   = buoys
3. toy + ed   = toyed
4. donkey + s   = donkeys
5. day + s   = days
6. annoy + ed   = annoyed
7. destroy + s   = destroys

457

8. ploy + s   = ploys

9. play + ed   = played

10. ray + s   = rays

RULE C:

Drop the final -*e* when adding an ending beginning with a vowel.

EXAMPLES:

come + ing = coming
fame + ous = famous

EXERCISE 31.3   *Follow the rule above to combine endings with the words below.*

1. guide + ed   = guided

2. ridicule + ous   = ridiculous

3. write + ing   = writing

4. ache + ed   = ached

5. angle + ing   = angling

6. believe + able   = believable

7. decide + ed   = decided

8. excite + able   = excitable

9. lose + ing   = losing

10. receive + able = receivable

RULE D:

Keep the final -*e* when adding an ending that begins with a consonant (any letter *but a, e, i, o,* or *u*).

EXAMPLES:

hope + less = hopeless
care + ful = careful

EXERCISE 31.4   *Follow the rule above to combine endings with the words below.*

1. desperate + ly   = <u>desperately</u>

2. conscience + less   = <u>conscienceless</u>

3. definite + ly   = <u>definitely</u>

4. here + by   = <u>hereby</u>

5. hope + ful   = <u>hopeful</u>

6. immediate + ly   = <u>immediately</u>

7. loose + ly   = <u>loosely</u>

8. minute + ly   = <u>minutely</u>

9. nine + ty   = <u>ninety</u>

10. arrangement + ment   = <u>arrangement</u>

RULE E:

Double the final consonant if the following are true:

- the word has only one syllable *or* the last syllable is accented, as in stop + ing = stopping
- The word ends in a single consonant with a single vowel before it, as in beg<u>in</u> + ing = beginning
- The ending begins with a vowel, as in contr<u>ol</u> + ing = controlling

EXERCISE 31.5   *Follow the rule above to combine endings with the words below.*

1. swim + ing   = <u>swimming</u>

2. run + ing   = <u>running</u>

3. repel + ing   = <u>repelling</u>

4. commit + ed   = <u>committed</u>

5. clog + ing   = <u>clogging</u>

6. allot + ing   = <u>allotting</u>

7. omit + ing = _omitting_

8. prefer + ed = _preferred_

9. admit + ing = _admitting_

10. forget + able = _forgettable_

RULE F:

Nouns form the plural by adding -s or -es.

- Add an *s* or *es* ending to verbs following the third-person singular (he, she, it).
- Add -es instead of -s if a word ends in *ch, sh, ss, x,* or *z*. The -es is sounded out.

EXAMPLES:

attorney + s = attorneys
work + s = works
box + s = box<u>es</u>
church + s = church<u>es</u>

EXERCISE 31.6

Follow the rule above to combine endings with the words below.

1. turkey + s = _turkeys_

2. manage + s = _manages_

3. itch + s = _itches_

4. whiz + s = _whizzes_

5. business + s = _businesses_

6. guess + s = _guesses_

7. match + s = _matches_

8. swing + s = _swings_

9. quiz + s = _quizzes_

10. teach + s = _teaches_

Section Four: Words That Sound Alike

A number of words in English sound alike but have different spellings. They are called **homonyms.** Other words are near-homonyms, but must be used differently. Some of these words are included below.

an, a, and

Both *a* and *an* mean **one.** Use *an* before words beginning with a vowel (*a, e, i, o, u*):

> *an aspirin, an egg, an instance, an oboe, an umbrella*

Use *a* before words beginning with everything else (consonants):

> *a ball, a horse, a journey*

Use *and* to connect two words or word groups together:

> Willy *and* Joseph; I walked *and* he ran

EXERCISE 31.7

Use a, an, *or* and *correctly in these sentences.*

1. Jim Day was _____an_____ unemployed manager with two kids in college _____and_____ a third about to start.

2. Dismissed in _____a_____ major cutback, Day had talked with _____an_____ enormous number of people—over 200.

3. Arriving for _____an_____ interview with a large glass company, he was smiling _____and_____ confident.

---

accept, except

Accept is a verb meaning to take or receive.

> He was willing to *accept* a lower-paying job.

Except is a preposition meaning to keep out or exclude.

> He would take anything *except* a job in Turkestan.

EXERCISE 31.8   *Use* accept *and* except *correctly in these sentences.*

1. He _____accepted_____ questions in front of a home video camera.

2. His boss was so touchy that he wouldn't _____accept_____ any comments _____except_____ flattering ones.

3. A new game called S&L Monopoly is like the original _____except_____ you buy houses and hotels with other people's money.

---

affect, effect

Affect is a verb meaning to influence or change.

> Drinking and gambling may *affect* the length of your life.

Effect is a noun meaning a result or outcome.

> The *effect* of his drinking and gambling was a shortened life.

EXERCISE 31.9   *Use* affect *and* effect *correctly in these sentences.*

1. Self-confidence will strongly _____affect_____ your interviewing techniques.

2. One _____effect_____ of today's tight job market is middle-class joblessness.

3. Arriving on time for an interview will _____affect_____ your interviewer favorably.

---

been, being

Been is the past participle of *be*, pronounced "ben." It usually follows auxiliary verbs like *have, has,* or *had.*

> You should tell where you have *been* working.

Being is the *-ing* form of *to be*. It often (but not always) follows auxiliaries like *is, are, am, was,* or *were*. It is pronounced "bee-ing."

I was *being* put in a job I wasn't hired for.

EXERCISE 31.10

Use been *and* being *correctly in these sentences.*

1. He thought that _____being_____ taken for 52, instead of 57, would help him get a job, but he had _____been_____ mistaken.

2. However, his interviewer was _____being_____ very careful.

3. The interviewer wondered why the applicant had _____been_____ on the job market two years.

---

fewer, less

Fewer means a smaller number of countable items.

One person became vice president in *fewer* than ten years.

Less means a smaller quantity of something not easily measured.

Try to answer tough questions in *less* than a minute.

EXERCISE 31.11

Use fewer *and* less *correctly in these sentences.*

1. Try not to give _____less_____ than an honest answer.

2. One placement director surveyed _____fewer_____ than 320 company recruiters.

3. There used to be much _____less_____ tolerance of job hopping since _____fewer_____ companies promise lifetime job security.

463

know, knew, no, new

Know means to understand some idea or recognize some person.

> An interviewer wants to *know* what an applicant can do for the company.

Knew is the past-tense form of the verb *know*.

> Applicants who *knew* little about the company seldom got jobs.

No is a negative word meaning *zero* or an absence of any quantity.

> An unprepared applicant reveals *no* interest in the job.

New means recently made, unused, or encountered for the first time.

> It's easy to research a *new* employer.

EXERCISE 31.12   *Use the words* know, knew, no, *and* new *correctly in these sentences.*

1. You should _____ know _____ that enthusiasm is
   _____ no _____ drawback in an interview.

2. One recruiter _____ knew _____ that _____ new _____
   graduates should not be narrow specialists.

3. Applicants may include _____ no _____ professors on a list
   of references because they _____ knew _____ none of their
   professors well enough.

---

loose, lose

Loose is a descriptive word meaning unfastened or flexible.

> Interviewers want a new hire to be *loose* and adaptable, not a narrow specialist.

Lose is a verb meaning to misplace.

> An employer may *lose* interest in an applicant without discipline.

EXERCISE 31.13   *Use the words* loose *and* lose *correctly in these sentences.*

1. When an interviewer tries to identify your skills, don't be too
   _____ loose _____ or too narrow.

2. You could easily _____ lose _____ a job offer by seeming too
   cocky or arrogant.

3. Although you want to appear _____ loose _____ and relaxed, try
   not to _____ lose _____ eye contact, even for an instant.

pass, passed, past

Pass means to move ahead of or to earn an acceptable grade.

> He applied tenacity to *pass* his courses.

Passed is the past tense form of *pass*. It sometimes follows an auxiliary verb
like *was*, *has*, or *had*.

> He was *passed* over for promotion.

Past is a descriptive word meaning to be over or gone by. The word may be
used with an auxiliary like *is* or *was* or as an adjective. It is often confused
with *passed*.

> The time is *past* when genes were thought to totally determine perfor-
> mance.

EXERCISE 31.14   *Use the words* pass *and* passed *correctly in these sentences.*

1. The report card showed that the child failed to
   _____ pass _____ two important courses.

2. The time had _____ passed _____ when extra study would help
   her _____ pass _____ her algebra course.

3. In the _____ past _____ , teachers would often
   _____ pass _____ students with social promotions.

quiet, quite

Quiet means still or without speaking.

> Parents sometimes criticize their children when they should be *quiet*.

Quite means entirely or completely.

> She was *quite* happy with her two-year-old's success.

EXERCISE 31.15 *Use the words* quiet *and* quite *correctly in these sentences.*

1. Teach your child to be _____ quiet _____ until he or she
   is _____ quite _____ relaxed.

2. Your child's list of achievements should be _____ quite _____
   simple.

3. If you remain _____ quiet _____ instead of criticizing your child,
   you will be _____ quite _____ happy with the results.

---

suppose, supposed

Suppose is a present-tense verb meaning to assume or conclude. It is often used mistakenly instead of its past-tense form, *supposed*.

> Many parents *suppose* their children should be just like them.

Supposed is a past-tense verb. It may mean one of the following:

- to have assumed or concluded, or
- to have been expected or ordered.

It often follows an auxiliary verb like *am*, *was*, or *were*. If it means "to be expected or ordered," the preposition *to* will follow it: *supposed to*.

> We *supposed* that the child was frightened. (means "assumed")
> She *was supposed to* play a trumpet solo before the whole school. (means "was expected to")

EXERCISE 31.16   *Use the words* suppose *and* supposed *correctly in the following sentences. Add the preposition* to *if necessary.*

1. You are _____*supposed to*_____ talk positively to yourself about yourself.

2. Experts _____*suppose*_____ that a positive self-image improves performance.

3. Tell yourself, "I'm really _____*supposed to*_____ play well today."

---

though, thought, taught

Though is a subordinating word which means "despite the fact that," "but," or "while." It usually links a dependent clause to an independent one.

Heredity affects performance *though* it's not everything.

Thought is either a noun meaning "an idea" or a past-tense verb meaning "to have used one's mind."

A *thought* occurred to her.
They *thought* about their early careers.

Taught is a past-tense verb meaning "instructed."

Their parents *taught* them at home.

EXERCISE 31.17   *Use the words* though, thought, *and* taught *correctly in these sentences.*

1. She _____*taught*_____ her child what she wanted her to do, _____*though*_____ she usually followed up carefully.

2. Find a single _____*thought*_____ that puts your child in a relaxed mood.

3. She _____*thought*_____ she would assemble the instrument the way she had been _____*taught*_____ to do it.

use, used

Use is a noun meaning a "function," or a verb meaning "to employ."

> He had a *use* for that hammer.
> They *use* that hammer to pound nails.

Used has the following meanings:

- As a past-tense verb meaning "employed":

  The children *used* their crayons vigorously.

- As an adjective meaning "secondhand":

  He bought a *used* car.

- As an auxiliary verb with *to* meaning "accustomed to" or "familiar with":

  They *used to* wander alongside the river.

EXERCISE 31.18

Use the words use *and* used *correctly in these sentences.*

1. _____Use_____ your imagination to "see" a task in your mind.

2. She wasn't _____used_____ to driving a
   _____used_____ car.

3. What _____use_____ is a broken screwdriver?

4. He _____used_____ a good report card to remind his daughter
   that she could do well.

REVIEW EXERCISE 31.19

Correct the spelling errors in the following paragraph. Write the correct spelling in the space above the misspelled word. Use a dictionary if necessary.

called
Napoleon's son, Napoleon IV, was caled the Prince Imperial. On a holiday in
                    Prince
Biarritz, when the Pince Imperial was still a young child, an odd happening
occurred   seemed   attendants
occured. The child seemd afraid to enter the sea. One of his attendents, pick-
                    bodily   threw
ing him up bodyly, through the Prince Imperial into the sea. The little boy,
struggling   mightily   completely
struggleing mightyly, crawled out of the water and, completely hysterical, ran

        terrified   Finally   calmed

away, terrifyed and weeping. Finaly, he was caught and clamed, and then

            to   attendants tried discuss irrational

spoken too. The atendants tryed to discus his irational fear. Why, they asked

                  panicked   courageous unafraid

the prince, had he paniced in the sea when he had been couragous and unafriad

              cannons   fired

when canons were fried? The young prince considered for a minute before

        replied   conceded   command   soldiers   I'm

he replyed. "Because," he conceeded, "I'm in comand of the soliders, but Im

      command   sea

not in comand of the see."

REVIEW
EXERCISE 31.20

Correct the spelling errors in the following paragraph. Write the correct spelling in the space above. Use a dictionary if necessary.

        building construction   apprentice

I work in the bilding constuction industry as an apprentise electrician. I am

        journeyman   professionally

supervised by a journyman electrician who is experienced and prophesionaly

licensed   field   wiring   digging

lisenced in the feild. My tasks range from wireing control panels to diging

ditches basically   journeyman   want

ditchs, basicaly anything the journyman does not wat to do. The journeyman

controls   extension

controlls the situation. I am an extention of his control. In other words, I do

everything   understanding   situation

everthing he tells me without unnerstanding why. This situaton gives me a

feeling   esteem   task

feling of low self-estem. When a taks is completed, the journeyman feels a

sense   accomplishment   knows

sence of accomplisment. He nos that a task was done well. I have no sense of

                 just   menial

accomplishment for I jsut do little meneal tasks as demanded by the jour-

neyman.

REVIEW
EXERCISE 31.21

The following sentences include errors in the use of words that look or sound alike. Find these errors, and write in your correction in the space above.

           been affected   a

(1) My husband and I had always being effected with an dream of raising our

                    thought

own food. **(2)** Before purchasing our farm, I taught we would pass platters of

home-raised vegetables across our table. **(3)** But today, accept for a occasional
[except] [an]
[a]
vacation, we lug 50-pound sacks of chow to an crowd of animals. **(4)** These
[quite] [affecting] [Being]
constant chores are quiet tiring, effecting us with deep fatigue. **(5)** Been a
[thought] [Though] [knew]
farm person is harder work than I though it would be. **(6)** Thought we new

nothing about farming, we began our own garden, which was a disaster.

Answer Key

Answers to alternate questions from this chapter's exercises are included below.

EXERCISE 31.1

2. copied
4. married
6. terrified
8. occupied
10. mutinies

EXERCISE 31.2

2. buoys
4. donkeys
6. annoyed
8. ploys
10. rays

EXERCISE 31.3

2. ridiculous
4. ached
6. believable
8. excitable
10. receivable

EXERCISE 31.4

2. conscienceless
4. hereby

6. immediately
8. minutely
10. arrangement

EXERCISE 31.5

2. running
4. committed
6. allotting
8. preferred
10. forgettable

EXERCISE 31.6

2. manages
4. whizzes
6. guesses
8. swings
10. teaches

EXERCISE 31.7

2. Dismissed in *a* major cutback, Day had talked with *an* enormous number of people—over 200.

EXERCISE 31.8

2. His boss was so touchy that he wouldn't *accept* any comments except flattering ones.

EXERCISE 31.9

2. One *effect* of today's tight job market is middle-class joblessness.

EXERCISE 31.10

2. However, his interviewer was *being* very careful.

EXERCISE 31.11

2. One placement director surveyed *fewer* than 320 company recruiters.

EXERCISE 31.12

2. One recruiter *knew* that *new* graduates should not be narrow specialists.

EXERCISE 31.13

2. You could easily *lose* a job offer by seeming too cocky or arrogant.

EXERCISE 31.14

2. The time had *passed* when extra study would help her *pass* her algebra course.

EXERCISE 31.15

2. Your child's list of achievements should be *quite* simple.

EXERCISE 31.16

2. Experts *suppose* that a positive self-image improves performance.

EXERCISE 31.17

2. Find a single *thought* that puts your child in a relaxed mood.

EXERCISE 31.18

2. She wasn't *used* to driving a *used* car.
4. He *used* a good report card to remind his daughter that she could do well.

REVIEW EXERCISE 31.19

On a holiday in Biarritz, when the *(Pince)* Prince Imperial was still a young child, an odd happening *(occured)* occurred. One of his *(attendents)* attendants, picking him up *(bodyly)* bodily, *(through)* threw the Prince Imperial into the sea. *(Finaly)* Finally he was caught and *(clamed)* calmed, and then spoken *(too)* to. Why, they asked the prince, had he *(paniced)* panicked in the sea when he had been *(couragous)* courageous and *(unafriad)* unafraid when *(canons)* cannons were *(fried)* fired? "Because," he *(conceeded)* conceded, "I'm in *(comand)* command of the *(soliders)* soldiers, but *(Im)* I'm not in *(comand)* command of the *(see)* sea."

REVIEW EXERCISE 31.20

I am supervised by a *(journyman) journeyman* electrician who is experienced and *(prophesionaly) professionally (lisenced) licensed* in the *(feild) field*. The journeyman *(controlls) controls* the situation. In other words, I do *(everthing) everything* he tells me without *(unnerstanding) understanding* why. When a *(taks) task* is completed, the journeyman feels a *(sence) sense* of *(accomplisment) accomplishment*. I have no sense of accomplishment for I *(jsut) just* do little *(meneal) menial* tasks as demanded by the journeyman.

REVIEW EXERCISE 31.21

(2) Before purchasing our farm, I *(taught) thought* we would pass platters of home-raised vegetables across our table. (4) These constant chores are *(quiet) quite* tiring, *(effecting) affecting* us with deep fatigue. (6) *(Thought) Though* we *(new) knew* nothing about farming, we began our own garden, which was a disaster.

Index

479

ERROR TRACKING REPORT

Assign. No.	Rhetorical Problems							Mechanical Problems												
	awk	ex	pass	tr	w	ww	??	agr	coord sub	cs	dm mm	frag	gr	r-o	punc	ref	shift	sp	vt	vf
1																				
2																				
3																				
4																				
5																				
6																				
7																				
8																				
9																				
10																				
11																				
12																				
13																				
14																				
15																				
16																				
17																				
18																				
19																				
20																				